Rethinking Dance History

Issues and Methodologies

Geraldine Morris and Larraine Nicholas

LONDON AND NEW YORK

Second edition published 2018
by Routledge
2 Park Square, Milton Park, Abingdon, Oxon, OX14 4RN

and by Routledge
711 Third Avenue, New York, NY 10017

Routledge is an imprint of the Taylor & Francis Group, an informa business

© 2018 selection and editorial matter, Geraldine Morris and Larraine Nicholas; individual chapters, the contributors

The right of Geraldine Morris and Larraine Nicholas to be identified as the authors of the editorial material, and of the authors for their individual chapters, has been asserted in accordance with sections 77 and 78 of the Copyright, Designs and Patents Act 1988.

All rights reserved. No part of this book may be reprinted or reproduced or utilised in any form or by any electronic, mechanical, or other means, now known or hereafter invented, including photocopying and recording, or in any information storage or retrieval system, without permission in writing from the publishers.

Trademark notice: Product or corporate names may be trademarks or registered trademarks, and are used only for identification and explanation without intent to infringe.

First edition published by Routledge 2004

British Library Cataloguing-in-Publication Data
A catalogue record for this book is available from the British Library

Library of Congress Cataloging-in-Publication Data
Names: Morris, Geraldine, author, compiler, editor. | Nicholas, Larraine, author, compiler, editor.
Title: Rethinking dance history : issues and methodologies / [compiled and edited by] Geraldine Morris and Larraine Nicholas.
Description: Second edition. | Abingdon, Oxon ; New York, NY : Routledge, 2017. | Revised edition of: Rethinking dance history : a reader / edited by Alexandra Carter. 2004. | Includes bibliographical references.
Identifiers: LCCN 2016057909 | ISBN 9781138682900 (Hardback) | ISBN 9781138682917 (Paperback) | ISBN 9781315544854 (eBook)
Subjects: LCSH: Dance—History.
Classification: LCC GV1781 .R48 2017 | DDC 792.809—dc23
LC record available at https://lccn.loc.gov/2016057909

ISBN: 978-1-138-68290-0 (hbk)
ISBN: 978-1-138-68291-7 (pbk)
ISBN: 978-1-315-54485-4 (ebk)

Typeset in Bell Gothic and Perpetua
by Apex CoVantage, LLC

Rethinking Dance History

The need to 'rethink' and question the nature of dance history has not diminished since the first edition of *Rethinking Dance History* (2004). This revised second edition addresses the needs of an ever-evolving field, with new contributions including, for example: new archival practices; the subtleties of gender and ethnic inclusivity in creating historical narratives; and the increasing importance of performing dances from the past as a route to historical knowledge.

A two-part structure divides the book's contributions into:

- Why Dance History? – the ideas, issues and key conversations that underpin the study of dance history.
- Researching and Writing – discussions of the methodologies and approaches behind successful research in this area.

Everyone involved with dance creates and carries with them a history, and this volume explores the ways in which these histories inform a sense of the past – from memories which establish identity to re-invention or preservation through shared and personal heritages. Considering the potential significance of studying dance history for scholars, philosophers, choreographers, dancers and students alike, *Rethinking Dance History* is an essential starting point for anyone intrigued by the rich history of dance.

Geraldine Morris is Reader in Dance Studies in the Department of Dance at the University of Roehampton.

Larraine Nicholas is Honorary Research Fellow in the Dance Department at the University of Roehampton.

This volume is dedicated to the memory of Dr. Giannandrea Poesio (1959–2017), historian and teacher, colleague and friend.

Contents

Notes on contributors x
Preface to the second edition xiii

PART 1
Why dance history? 1

    Introduction to Part 1: why dance history? 3
    GERALDINE MORRIS AND LARRAINE NICHOLAS

1 Memory, history and the sensory body: dance, time, identity 8
    LARRAINE NICHOLAS

2 Cara tranders's reveries: the Autobiography of Cara Tranders, Ballet Girl at the Empire Palace of Varieties, 1892–99 21
    CARA TRANDERS

3 Beyond fixity: Akram Khan on the politics of dancing heritages 32
    ROYONA MITRA

4 African-American dance revisited: undoing master narratives in the studying and teaching of dance history 44
    TAKIYAH NUR AMIN

5 Dance works, concepts and historiography 56
    ANNA PAKES

viii CONTENTS

6 Reconstruction and dance as embodied
   textual practice   69
   HELEN THOMAS

7 Preserving the repertory and extending
   the heritage of Merce Cunningham   82
   KAREN ELIOT

8 Making dance history live – performing the past   94
   HENRIETTA BANNERMAN

PART 2
Researching and writing   107

Introduction to Part 2: researching and writing   109
GERALDINE MORRIS AND LARRAINE NICHOLAS

9 Destabilising the discipline: critical debates
   about history and their impact on the study
   of dance   114
   ALEXANDRA CARTER

10 Decolonising dance history   123
   PRARTHANA PURKAYASTHA

11 Many sources, many voices   136
   LENA HAMMERGREN

12 'Dream no small dreams!': impossible archival
   imaginaries in dance community archiving in
   a digital age   148
   ASTRID VON ROSEN

13 When place matters: provincializing the 'global'   160
   EMILY E. WILCOX

14 Considering causation and conditions of possibility:
   practitioners and patrons of new dance in
   progressive-era America   173
   LINDA J. TOMKO

15 'Dancin' in the street': street dancing on film
   and video from Fred Astaire to Michael Jackson   186
   BETH GENNÉ

16 Judson: redux and remix   197
   MARCIA B. SIEGEL

17 **Ruth page, feminine subjectivity, and generic subversion** 210
JOELLEN A. MEGLIN

18 **Extensions: Alonzo King and Ballet's LINES** 223
JILL NUNES JENSEN

19 *Giselle* and the Gothic: contesting the Romantic idealisation of the woman 235
GERALDINE MORRIS

Index 248

Notes on contributors

Takiyah Nur Amin is a critical dance studies scholar. Her research and teaching interests include Black performance and aesthetics, twentieth-century American concert dance and pedagogical issues in dance studies. Dr Amin is currently working on a book project that explores the work of Black women choreographers during the height of the US-based Black Power and Black Arts movements.

Henrietta Bannerman is Head of Research at London Contemporary Dance School, specialising in dance history, aesthetics and critical studies, with a particular interest in the works of Martha Graham, on whom she has published widely. Publications include 'Ancient Myths and Modern Moves: The Greek-Inspired Dance Theatre of Martha Graham', in *The Ancient Dancer in the Modern World: Responses to Greek and Roman Dance* (Fiona Macintosh, ed., 2012).

Alexandra Carter holds a Professor Emerita post from Middlesex University. She edited the first edition of *Rethinking Dance History* (2004), two editions of *The Routledge Dance Studies Reader* (1998, 2010) and *Dancing Naturally* (2011) and sole-authored a book on the music hall ballet (2005). Since formal retirement she has been working in the field of performance for the mature dancer.

Karen Eliot, formerly a dancer with the Merce Cunningham Dance Company, is a Professor in the Department of Dance at Ohio State University. She is co-editor, with Melanie Bales, of *Dance on Its Own Terms: Histories and Methodologies* (2013) and author of *Dancing Lives: Five Female Dancers from the Ballet d'Action to Merce Cunningham* (2007) and of *Albion's Dance: British Ballet during the Second World War* (2016).

Beth Genné, Professor of Dance History at the University of Michigan, has published a book on Ninette de Valois and contributed articles to a variety of books and journals. Her next book, *Dance Me a Song: Astaire, Balanchine, Kelly, and Style, Genre and Culture in the American Film Musical*, will be published by Oxford University Press.

Lena Hammergren is Professor at Stockholm University (Performance Studies) and Stockholm University of the Arts (Dance Studies). Her most recent publications in English include chapters in *Choreography and Corporeality* (2016), T. DeFrantz & P. Rothfield, eds, and *Nordic Dance Spaces* (2014), K. Vedel & P. Hoppu, eds. She has been a board member of the Society of Dance History Scholars.

Jill Nunes Jensen is on the faculty at Loyola Marymount University and El Camino College. Her research on Alonzo King LINES Ballet of San Francisco has been published widely. With Kathrina Farrugia-Kriel she organised the Society of Dance History Scholars Special Topics Conference, 'Contemporary Ballet: Exchanges, Connections and Directions' (2016). They are currently developing an anthology on contemporary ballet.

Joellen A. Meglin is Professor Emeritus, Dance, at Temple University, Philadelphia. Areas of expertise range from twentieth-century Chicago choreographer Ruth Page to the eighteenth- and nineteenth-century French ballet, to dance modernism and jazz. She is co-editor of the peer-reviewed journal *Dance Chronicle*. Writings include a chapter in *Women's Work: Making Dance in Europe before 1800* (Lynn Matluck Brooks, ed., 2008). She is author of a forthcoming book on the choreographer Ruth Page.

Royona Mitra is Senior Lecturer in Theatre at Brunel University, London. She performed with the intercultural theatre company, Kinaetma Theatre. She is the author of a new monograph, *Akram Khan: Dancing New Interculturalism* (2015).

Geraldine Morris is a Reader in Dance Studies in the Department of Dance at the University of Roehampton. She was a dancer with the Royal Ballet and worked with Frederick Ashton, among others. She specialises in aesthetics, dance history, and dance analysis and has published widely. Morris is author of the monograph *Frederick Ashton's Ballets: Style, Performance, Choreography* (2012) and of chapters in several books

Larraine Nicholas, author of monographs *Dancing in Utopia: Dartington Hall and Its Dancers* (2007) and *Walking and Dancing: Three Years of Dance in London, 1951–53* (2013), is Honorary Research Fellow in the Dance Department at the University of Roehampton. She currently investigates the professional lives of dancers at the Windmill Theatre, London, 1932–64, including an oral history project.

xii NOTES ON CONTRIBUTORS

Anna Pakes is a Reader in Dance Studies in the Department of Dance at the University of Roehampton. As a philosopher she has a particular interest in the nature of dance works. She is the editor (with Bunker and Rowell) of *Thinking through Dance: The Philosophy of Dance Performance and Practices* (2013), which includes her authored chapter, 'The Plausibility of a Platonist Ontology of Dance'.

Prarthana Purkayastha is a Senior Lecturer in Dance in the Department of Drama and Theatre, Royal Holloway, University of London. Her book *Indian Modern Dance, Feminism and Transnationalism* (2014) won the prestigious De La Torre Bueno prize of the Society of Dance History Scholars, 2015.

Astrid von Rosen is a senior lecturer in Art History and Visual Studies at the University of Gothenburg, Sweden and a research coordinator for the Archives cluster at the Centre for Critical Heritage Studies. Her research interests include historiographical and participatory approaches to independent dance community archives and archiving, and border crossing methodological development.

Marcia B. Siegel is an internationally known dance critic, historian and teacher. Her writing has appeared in major US publications, including the *Boston Phoenix*, *Hudson Review* and, currently, *ArtsFuse.org*. She was a faculty member of the Department of Performance Studies, Tisch School of the Arts, New York University. Collections of her own critical writing include *Mirrors & Scrims: The Life and Afterlife of Ballet* (2010). She has also written dance biographies of the choreographers Doris Humphrey and Twyla Tharp.

Helen Thomas is Professor of Dance Studies at Trinity Laban Conservatoire of Music and Dance and Professor Emerita of the University of the Arts, London. Widely published, her most recent book is *The Body and Everyday Life* (2013)

Linda J. Tomko is Associate Professor of Dance at the University of California, Riverside, and author of *Dancing Class: Gender, Ethnicity and Social Divides in American Dance, 1890–1920*. She is editor of the Wendy Hilton Dance & Music book series, a past president of the Society of Dance History Scholars and a founding member of Les Menus Plaisirs, a Baroque Dance troupe.

Cara Tranders was a dancer at the Empire Palace of Varieties between 1892 and 1899. Soon after writing her reveries in her diary she was moved to the front row of the *corps de ballet* but her lack of consistent training prevented further promotion. And what did she do after she left the ballet? Dear readers, it is up to your imagination.

Emily E. Wilcox is Assistant Professor in the Department of Asian Languages and Cultures at the University of Michigan, Ann Arbor. She is the recipient of a humanities fellowship from the American Council of Learned Societies for her book project *National Movements: Socialist Postcoloniality and the Making of Chinese Dance*.

Preface to the second edition

THIS SECOND EDITION of *Rethinking Dance History* builds on the scholarship of the earlier volume (2004). Edited by Alexandra Carter, it set a benchmark for the study of dance history in the twenty-first century.

In considering the structure and contents of the new edition we have taken into account new research in the dance history field over the intervening decade, as well as the needs of students and scholars as we perceive them now. As with the first edition, this is a volume dedicated to the discipline of dance history and not a history of dance with what that implies in terms of 'landmarks' in the development of the art form. In revising, we have had in mind how new approaches to thinking about the past have influenced the way we investigate dance history and its continuing importance to the field of dance studies. That said, we acknowledge that theory from other disciplines is also a significant factor in historical investigation and to issues of time, continuity and change, which we consider to be the essence of dance history. As Carter remarked in the first edition, 'Almost everything we do carries an historical dimension. . . . History is, therefore, woven into all our studies' (2004: 1).

Our aim is to provide as broad a scope as possible in dance history's issues and methodologies. Newly commissioned essays have been added to ones retained from the first edition to display some of the rich innovative material that has developed since the publication of the first edition some twelve years ago, but we are adamant that all of those essays from the first edition retain their validity and should be sought out on library shelves. However, this is not a complete guide to the field; rather it is indicative of *some* of the 'rethinkings' that continue to enliven dance history and which must do so into the future. It would never be possible in such a volume as this to encompass historical issues in every dance genre, historical period or geographical area. All of our contributors have something stimulating to contribute, which should lead the reader into thinking afresh about the histories of dance forms, times and locations in which they are most interested.

The original structure, which was arranged in one roughly chronological sequence, has been revised, so that this new edition has two sections: Part 1: *Why Dance History?* and Part 2: *Researching and Writing*. A new subtitle for the book indicates this focus: *Rethinking Dance History: Issues and Methodologies*. We have pedagogical reasons for this structure in encouraging students to read consecutive essays around linking historical issues, but we recognise how these categories are not hermetically sealed. For this reason, our editorial introductions to each part range over the whole volume, pulling together related ideas.

We thank Routledge for deciding to produce this second edition and acknowledge the guidance of Ben Piggott and Kate Edwards there, who have been helpful, considerate and efficient at responding to our queries. Managing our copyediting and typesetting, Autumn Spalding of Apex CoVantage has given us consistent and much appreciated support through the final complexities of getting into print. Our special thanks to our contributors, who have provided us with material that is both stimulating and controversial. Above all, we need to thank Alexandra Carter, who by declining Routledge's original call to re-edit the volume which so much bore her imprint has allowed us this very exciting opportunity. It has been difficult to follow in her footsteps and we do so aware of how far we need to go in emulating her vision.

Geraldine Morris
Larraine Nicholas

Part 1

Why dance history?

Introduction to Part 1
Why dance history?

GERALDINE MORRIS AND LARRAINE NICHOLAS

WHY DANCE HISTORY? Our title for Part 1 was chosen in the knowledge it has two possible readings. Clipped of some words, it sounds like a challenge for us to show why we consider dance history to be an essential study. Read in another way, it asks why we still perform dances and techniques from earlier times, and how that might work as an embodiment of the past, supplementing the reading, writing and discussion. When there are so many stimulating methodologies and theories to engage with in the field of dance studies – anthropology, critical theory, neuroscience, philosophy, postcolonial theory, practice as research, sociology (just some examples) – why is it still important to locate dances and their contexts historically? While our authors also engage with a variety of theoretical areas, the essays in Part 1 are indicative of a range of answers to these questions, which remain relevant to the wider community involved in dance as well as to the dance student. Whereas we have not attempted to answer the question 'What is dance history?', some answers are implicit in the way our writers (in both parts) have engaged with their historical fields. We invite readers to consider and discuss.

Part 1 is also concerned with routes into history, whether through notions of personal identity, social identity or embodiment through dancing. How do we find that spark of connection that makes sense of a past moment? Our primary access to the past of dance is always through sources, whether written, pictorial or embodied. More methodological issues in relation to sources are considered in Part 2. Here in Part 1 there are some particular questions raised about the identity or authenticity of what we are studying as dance works from the past as well as the pleasures encountered in embodying them. The essays in Part 1 demonstrate the radical nature of historical inquiry, challenging received notions, such as time, heritage/tradition and the concept of the dance work.

Why dance history? Whose history?

Larraine Nicholas (Chapter 1) makes a case for everyone having a stake in history through consciousness of their own lived pasts. That being so, we must become aware of how many voices from the past have been historically inhibited by social and political power. Oral history projects documenting the participation of the many whose names are not 'writ large' by conventional histories are important, both to provide sources for future histories and to affirm the worth of individual lives in dance. Cara Tranders (Chapter 2) is one of those subaltern characters whose voices have been ignored, distorted or suppressed by history as written. As a *corps de ballet* dancer at the Empire, a variety theatre in Victorian and Edwardian London, she did not have a voice because of her insignificance as a lower-class dancer, and her perceived low moral standing, at least not until a historian spoke for her.

Other voices are commonly obscured by racist and colonial ideologies. Takiyah Nur Amin (Chapter 4) argues passionately that the dance history syllabus regularly reinforces the meta-narrative of American modern and postmodern dance as belonging to White women, whereas African American dance forms have been foundational in what is understood as American dance history. It is not so much about bringing African American dancers in from the margins of history as expanding what is seen as the central focus of the field. Amin's argument can be applied to other geographic locations – for example in the UK, where ethnic diasporas, particularly from the Caribbean and Indian subcontinent, currently question how they are represented in dance history texts. Histories ignored or suppressed are the results of specific ideologies that conceive of dance history from a Euro-American viewpoint. Some of this unease is expressed by Royona Mitra (Chapter 3) as she reflects on perceptions that non-western dance forms are seen as fixed in the past, and not 'contemporary'. Prarthana Purkayastha (Chapter 10) highlights how dance of the Indian subcontinent has been constructed as part of a binary notion of East and West, invented by western scholars, and therefore not integrated into the historical narrative. As Alexandra Carter discusses (Chapter 9; see also Nicholas, Chapter 1) we always need to be aware of how bias works in what is included and excluded from an historical narrative.

Memory, time and heritage

How do we find our way into thinking historically? Several of our essays deal directly or indirectly with the connection, linguistic and conceptual, between memory and history. Nicholas (Chapter 1) suggests that the connection to the past through personal memory is analogous to the 'time travelling' of historical study. We can also see our own past experience in dance, great or small, as the raw material of dance history, giving 'meaning to individual experience as part of wider historical forces'. The autobiographical memories of Cara Tranders are a case in point. Akram Khan (Chapter 3) illuminates how the fluidity and emotional triggers that come with autobiographical memory provide fuel for his work.

If memory and history are 'partners in time' (Nicholas, Chapter 1) they suggest ways to bridge the divide between past and present. Given that histories are written about the past and that the past must be as elusive as memory, it is unsurprising that notions of time underlie a number of essays in this volume and it goes without saying that the past as experienced is a quite different thing to the 'stories about the past' (Carter, Chapter 9) that constitute history. Helen Thomas (Chapter 6) reflects that the perceived temporal impermanence of dance as an art form is one reason for the rush to reconstruct 'lost' works. Lena Hammergren (Chapter 11) discusses the tropes of time, such as 'rise and fall', that structure many historical narratives. However, we must remember that these tropes are culture-specific and not universal. Royona Mitra's interview with the choreographer Akram Khan brings into focus how western notions of temporality consign dance forms like *kathak* to an unchanging past, whereas they evolve along with their best exponents. Khan's works consciously embody notions of time. He weaves his embodied knowledge of the past into his ever-changing present, so that past, present and future coexist. As Mitra claims, there is thus a need to reconsider dance history, as living and dialogic across temporalities. Emily Wilcox (Chapter 13) shows how temporal values can be seen as 'placist', in assuming that western ideas of what is considered 'modern dance' should be applied to China. Further challenging our tendency to project concepts from our own time onto the past, Anna Pakes (Chapter 5) argues that we should not impose a twentieth-century concept of a dance work onto dances made in earlier centuries. Dance historians have tended to see the history of ballet and its dances as a continuous thread, each new 'product' building on a previous one. While accepting that continuities through time cannot be dismissed, she challenges our tendency to project our own aesthetics backwards through time: '[W]e should guard against a form of present-oriented conceptual anachronism which unreflexively subsumes earlier dances under modern categories' (p. 66).

The notion of 'collective memory' has been theorised as a received understanding about the past that provides a group identity and cohesion, ensuring a collective connection to the past, commonly understood as 'heritage' or 'tradition'. Maintaining a connection to the past of dance through its heritage works as embodied history is the subject of three essays in Part 1. Are these dances to be seen as fixed in an 'authentic' past or is there room for variation that accommodates change through time? Is the heritage of dance a closed book or, as Akram Khan insists, is heritage 'like a museum, but one that keeps collecting, because its doors are always open' (Chapter 3: 34)?

Sources and tradition

Our routes into dance history are through the sources, multifarious and complex. Written accounts, notation, film and oral history are all important but outside of those are the culturally codified constructed bodies of dancers and, as Susan Foster argues, also of historians (1995: 3). Older dancers' bodies are living archives of past training and artistic practice, perhaps the only record of choreographed dances, and stylistic nuances that might have been lost through altered training styles. Foster (1995) contends that the objective and partisan historians treat the past in different ways. The objective voice, despite striving not to sully the evidence, treats the 'historical subject as a body of facts', while the partisan voice approaches the past as 'a fixed set of elements whose relative visibility needs only an adjustment'. If, as she points out, 'the past becomes embodied, then it can move in dialogue with historians, who likewise transit to an identity that makes such dialogue possible' (1995: 10). She is arguing for the merging of the dancing body with the writing body of the historian.

Issues of reconstruction, reimagining and restaging are currently highly relevant as companies remount or reconstruct past works. But this is an area that is greatly disputed and it is not clear what exactly it is that we try to restage. Helen Thomas (Chapter 6) interrogates some of these issues, examining notions of revival, reconstruction, re-creation, co-authorship, reinvention and more. Scholars use these terms in a variety of ways and she reasons that each is dealing with a different approach to returning a past dance to the stage. Behind each discussion is the issue of authenticity. Even when a multitude of sources remain along with links to the choreographer, an authentic version of a dance as well-known as Mikhail Fokine's *The Dying Swan* (1905) is challenged. The choreographer's granddaughter, Isabelle Fokine, is adamant that hers is the 'correct' version, while the Mariinsky Ballet is equally convinced that its different and popular version is also authentic. Thomas concludes that the identity of the iconic dance must leave room for competing interpretations. 'The construct of tradition with which I would want to work is one that lives and breathes through embodied textual practice' (Chapter 6: 79).

Two essays outline approaches to re-embodying dances from the past that chime with the quotations of both Thomas and Khan. Karen Eliot (Chapter 7) asks how the work of Merce Cunningham can be historicised, since his ethos depended on experimentation. Because Cunningham had made plans for his material before his death, it is clear that he intended something to be preserved. In creating Dance Capsules, containing films of performances and rehearsals, his choreographic notes and details of design and music, he left a usable legacy. According to Eliot, he aimed not for exact replicas of his works but for their fluidity and protean qualities to continue. In this way his ideas and philosophy could be disseminated. This is another approach to the contested area of reconstruction and preservation and Eliot's essay gives us access to these ideas. Henrietta Bannerman (Chapter 8) asks,

'Can we dance history?' In other words, 'Can we dance the past?' Her essay travels a similar path to that of Eliot but in different institutional contexts, specifically with vocational dance students in the UK. She reports on students developing a psychophysical understanding of dance history through learning repertoire from knowledgeable practitioners, a more profound knowledge than from reading and watching videos. Her essay is supported by testimonies of students who experienced such practical history. Both Eliot and Bannerman emphasise that there is more to understanding a dance from the past than learning steps. Each dance work needs to be understood in terms of its own cultural ethos. At the same time, as Marcia Siegel shows so eloquently (Chapter 16), historical time is 'porous', allowing dance from the past to speak to us in the present.

The essays of Part 1 invite our readers to consider their own experienced pasts in dance (and these pasts could be as recent as yesterday) as an entry to the nature of time and the narratives of history. Seeing ourselves as participants in history and not just passive consumers, we should approach historical studies in dance – viewing, reading, discussing and dancing – as pleasurable encounters with people who are somewhat like ourselves but nevertheless fascinatingly different.

Bibliography

Foster, Susan (1995) 'An Introduction to Moving Bodies', in Susan Foster, ed. *Choreographing History*, Bloomington: Indiana University Press, 3–24.

Chapter 1

Memory, history and the sensory body
Dance, time, identity

LARRAINE NICHOLAS

I REMEMBER MYSELF WALKING in bare feet (horrid tactile memory) from London's Covent Garden underground station to the Dance Centre in Floral Street in 1968. For me, the Dance Centre was the epitome of 'cool': it had a wood-lined coffee bar[1] backed by a huge aquarium and there was constant music and rhythm from studios in the background. Coming from work or college, you could cross over with professionals leaving their daytime classes and feel pride by association. As I walked, my long, straight hair, my thigh-length tunic, bare legs and discarded rubber flip-flops (that had become unbearable) signified my own desire for that 'cool' aesthetic. My 'hippy' persona was naïve and short-lived, but my class is still vivid in my body, with Molly Molloy, an inspiring American jazz dancer, and her assistant, Arlene Phillips.[2] How I remember trying to embody Molly's characteristic double step (a syncopated ball-change) on the upbeat, body coolly relaxed inwards before exploding into a sequence to *The Son of Hickory Holler's Tramp*.[3]

Note that this little vignette has visual, tactile, auditory and kinaesthetic components. Memories from events that we have personally experienced can come with such associated multi-sensory imagery that they are convincingly real, despite all that is currently understood of memory distortions (Cubitt 2007: 82–89). This is further illustrated by my two perspectives. I feel the dirt on my feet; enjoy the jazz dance phrases with my own body; see Molly from my own eyes (field memory), but I can also see myself walking from a third-person perspective, in the less emotionally involved observer memory (Schacter 1996: 21–22). Memories result from and often express themselves vividly as sensory experience. As is common with autobiographical memory this is a rehearsed anecdote which I have narrated to myself many times (perhaps less often to other people) as I have constructed a meaningful sense of my own past in dance. Over time, as a sense of my identity has developed, I have added historical context, with later consolidated knowledge of the cultural past I lived through but the significance of which I could hardly understand at the time. Memories are malleable and permeable, not just belonging to one point in the past but subject to the needs of a present moment.

Each of us carries a personal history of our pasts in dance. In my own case, I soon rejected the 'cool' of jazz dance for the drama of Graham technique, to which I remained devoted while its influence faded around me in the late twentieth century. Even those of us perpetually pushing forwards to the next new thing cannot escape from what we have experienced, embodied in dance knowledge and answerable to recall through memory. The first class, a charismatic teacher, a memorable performance, the change of bodily feeling encountering a newly experienced dance genre – all of these are significant personal events that inform individual identity.

Remembering is something we do in the present moment, and so is our most solid evidence that there really was a past because we believe that we participated in it. This access to the past is a kind of time travel, as psychologist Endel Tulving originally stated, perhaps the only kind of time travel that we will ever experience (Schacter 1996: 17). Short- and medium-term memory allows access to the immediate past (that thing you just did) while consolidation of experience into long-term memory (that thing that happened hours/weeks/years ago) is accruing all the time so that, consciously or not, a sense of the past is always running in the background of what we do.

I have let you share a moment from my past that brings to light some characteristics of the personal (autobiographical) memory. We are all expert users of our own pasts. How that personal expertise might translate in relation to dance history is the essence of this essay. Paying attention to our personal memories, especially in dance, makes us notice with what complexity they integrate: (1) bodily experience; (2) time; (3) identity. I am going to suggest that these three form a foundation for the mindset with which we can approach historical studies. First, this will necessitate an examination of the terminology of memory and history, which have a complex relationship to each other. The final section will return to the three foundational concepts listed earlier to outline an approach to dance history that develops from memory as an experience that is paradoxically distinctly individualistic while offering a platform for the understanding of historical others.

From memory to history

The study of memory ('memory studies') is now an established interdisciplinary field across biological sciences, social sciences and humanities. The diverse nature of these fields calls into question whether the concept of memory can mean the same in all circumstances (Cubitt 2007: 6). The study of memory in neuroscience and psychology focusses on processing and anatomy within different experimental paradigms. The processes of memory and recall encompass not only memories of the autobiographical kind as introduced earlier but also memory as learning for skills or facts – for example knowing how to dance as well as knowing facts about dance. In the humanities, there has been a 'turn to memory', particularly in history (Cubitt 2007: 2). In history and sociology memory has acquired multiple meanings, as for example a social practice of memorialising specific national events, or the methodology of oral history, in which memories are gathered as evidence of the past. The conflation of terms, where 'memory' is sometimes made to stand in for history, is a controversial concomitant of this vibrant multi-disciplined area (Cubitt 2007: 5–6). Dance research further opens up questions about how danced memory remains in the body as a special kind of knowledge, as a bodily consciousness of past experience, as kinaesthetic or body memory (Koch et al. 2012).

As I have initiated this discussion on the level of personal memory, I begin with some highly simplified points about the science of memory, in which psychologists and neuroscientists study the workings of memory formation and memory retrieval. Memory is a fundamental human capacity, essential to normal functions of consciousness, including learning and movement. Nerve cells (neurons) form connections, axons passing signals to other neurons via the many branching dendrites. The billions of neurons form complex neuronal networks through electrical charges facilitated by chemical transmitters.[4] This is a whole-body system connecting peripheral sensory organs through the spinal cord to the brain and back again but it is also a dynamic system, always in the process of reordering itself behind the scenes. 'Learning and creating memory are simply the process of chiseling, modeling, shaping, doing, and redoing our individual brain wiring diagrams' (Damasio 2010: 300). So what we know and what we remember are subject to a constant turnover, where knowledge and memories are being kept freshly in mind or buried deeper beneath more recent concerns, but which may re-emerge with a different set of neuronal connections.

It is no longer possible to think of memories like little packages of impressions stored neatly in a corner of the brain. The analogy with a computer's memory, where a file should sit in its original form, either unchanged by what goes on around (or totally corrupted) until called up again, is even less appropriate. In the forest of dendrites in the billions of neurons, connections switch as a reaction to current body states (Damasio 2010: 111). Perhaps my biochemical excitation at recalling my horrid, grimy feet stirs up some other connections, reactivating the less travelled memory trace of the purple dress. It is currently understood that different components – linguistic, sensory, conceptual, interpretative – are stored differently. In all likelihood, 'grimy feet', 'purple dress', *Hickory Holler* and 'upbeat ball-change' are distributed across my brain's anatomy.[5] Memory recall is thus a matter of construction, pulling together the different features to meet present circumstances, so that the process has the potentiality to be a contemporary variation on the original event (Schacter and Addis 2007: para. 2).[6]

Within long-term memory, two broad types are generally accepted based upon the experience of recall. Explicit memory, such as my autobiographical memory, is a conscious association with a past event, often accompanied by vivid sensory imagery, whereas implicit memory is typically for learned skills (typing, riding a bike) or facts, which can be reproduced in a seemingly automatic response, without searching back in memory for an originary episode. Another way of defining these differences is between declarative memory and non-declarative memory. Declarative memory includes those memories about which we commonly verbalise when we recall them, including the semantic (or cognitive) memory for learned facts and the episodic (or autobiographical) memory, where we mentally re-experience past events. Non-declarative memory includes the procedural memory for a physical or mental skill, as well as habits and conditioned responses.[7]

Phenomenologist Maxine Sheets-Johnstone warns that typologies like these too easily divide into the now rejected 'oppositional pair . . . the mind/body dichotomy or the mental/physical dichotomy . . . the conscious/unconscious dichotomy, the verbal/nonverbal dichotomy, and so on' (2012: 44) that imply the inferiority of what the body implicitly knows. (Note that when I use the term 'body' in this essay, it implies the totality of mind-body experience.) Kinaesthetic memory, as in dancing for example, could be both a well-known movement pattern that seems to roll out from the body without conscious effort and one which can be brought into consciousness at will (Sheets-Johnstone 2012: 45). Experimental psychologists who study dancers in rehearsal and creation have also confirmed that contemporary dance practices include both non-declarative and declarative memory. Not only are dancers able to articulate memories of movement experience and use memories from personal experience to inform dance creation and performance, but also in its intention to communicate affective information, dance can be seen as a form of declarative memory, albeit non-verbal, 'thought made visible' (Stevens and McKechnie 2005).

Scientific and interdisciplinary research into dance and consciousness brings into view special dance memories that give a personal and physical access to the past. In a small but indicative study into the memory retention of technique exercises taught by the choreographer Margaret Barr (1904–1991) it appeared that those memories could remain in the bodies of former students for decades and that they are multi-modal: accompanied by kinaesthetic, visual, auditory (especially musical), environmental, olfactory and emotional imagery (Stevens, Ginsbourg and Lester 2010). This just serves to expand upon the other kinds of memory that have a bearing on dance history: from factual knowledge accrued (e.g. Nijinsky's *Sacre du printemps* was premiered in 1913); to events personally experienced (e.g. specific classes or performances); to social knowledge (e.g. how a dancer should behave in rehearsal); to habitual 'knowing how to' that is the product of training (e.g. how to stand at the *barre*; how to locate precisely in space); to complex strings of movement that have been assigned to memory as specific movements or dances. The body-mind of the professional, student or amateur dancer includes past and present experience (cognitive, autobiographical sensory and kinaesthetic; explicit and implicit) that can be recalled, danced and spoken. Because the contents of our minds are highly individualised through the unique nature of each person's experience, it is worth remembering that what we bring to our research and study in dance history is a mind-body that is deeply invested in its own past and memory of practising and thinking about dancing. I will later discuss how we can utilise this personal resource.

Historical usages of the term 'memory' take us beyond personal memory to the notion that 'memory' in humanities research can stretch to encompass kinds of knowledge about the past that are essentially social or communal. The work of French sociologist Maurice Halbwachs from the 1920s is foundational towards conceiving of memory in this expanded form. He showed that social frameworks both enable and construct individual memories. The archetype of this is social remembering in the family, and the way that members of the group share and reinforce certain memories (Marcel and Muccielli 2010). Not only this but also families and other social groups (we might here include college year groups or dance company members) develop ideas about what is important to remember, so that memory is a matter not just of an individual's personal processing but also of minds constructed by social and environmental factors.

More controversially, Halbwachs coined the term 'collective memory' (*mémoire collective*) as a kind of memory that accrues in institutions or nations even after those who experienced the events no longer exist. This is where we start to encounter the conflation of memory and history. Concepts of heritage, legacy or tradition are indicative of a national or group relationship to the past, but we are aware now they do not even need to result from a continuously transmitted memory but, more often than not, are constructed, as in the now famous book *The Invention of Tradition* (Hobsbawm and Ranger 1983). In the late twentieth century, Pierre Nora in France argued that organic communal remembering in national life had given way to the cultural imposition of this symbolic function onto places, commemorations, rituals and artefacts (*lieux de mémoire*) 'where memory crystallizes and secretes itself' (Nora 1989: 7).[8] As conceptualised by Halbwachs and Nora, 'memory' has become a broader category of communal rather than personal identities.

There is now a bountiful literature that pairs 'memory' in its various formulations with history. Astrid Erll (2011: 39–45) summarises the complexity of the history/memory debate in her term 'history **and/or/as** memory'. In other words, we can consider history **and** memory as ontologically different yet intersecting; **or** we can take that ontological difference to be so much indicative of fundamental dissimilarities that we must oppose them, even to the extent of history **versus** memory; or we can flatten the memory/history differences to highlight the commonalities that make it possible to see history **as** memory.

A generally accepted point of view would be that history **and** memory go hand in hand along parallel but intersecting paths. Philosopher Paul Ricoeur emphasised the historical centrality of witness statements, consigned to memory and communicated in some form. He proposed 'the witness's triple declaration: (1) I was there; (2) believe me; (3) if you don't believe me, ask someone else' (2004: 278).[9] This may seem a simplistic formula, but widened out as it should be from personal memory to include the unwitting testimony of other artefacts it highlights the centrality of primary source material in historical research. And even when the 'memory' of a particular witness or artefact is to be believed, the search for a historically valid interpretation needs corroboration. Even though autobiographical memory is prone to distortion, many traditional historical sources (e.g. documents; images) also bear the traces of inaccuracies or biases resulting from the perspective of the originator. The historian's task is to evaluate sources of all kinds judiciously. As Ricoeur adds, 'we have nothing better than testimony and *criticism of testimony* to accredit the historian's representation of the past' (2004: 278 [italic emphasis added]). So memory (testimony and sources) **and** history (critical representation of testimony and sources) are not the same. While they are mutually dependent, only history has the advantage of the skills of comparison and evaluation coming from critical/historical method.

This difference between memory and history can also be seen as the antagonism between the two: history **or** memory; memory **versus** history. While the traditional view outlined earlier elevates the special discipline needed to hone an historical narrative, questions are still raised as to whether history as written adequately serves the memories of subordinate groups. Whose memory is important enough to recruit into historical testimony? Whose memory is important enough to preserve? These haunting questions give impetus to oral history research among those who were not in control of events. Ricoeur's 'triple declaration' quoted earlier affirms the ownership that participants in events are entitled to feel even though their perspectives on events might be limited by their own viewpoint. In dance history there is still more to be done in giving a voice to the 'ordinary' dancer in the chorus line, troupe or *corps de ballet* (see Tranders, this volume), and the 'ordinary' dance student whose career may or may not flourish.[10] What is now understood as the uniqueness of oral testimony is that it reveals how people evaluate their lives and ascribe meaning to their experiences, and shows how the past infiltrates the present through personal recollection. Autobiographical memory as oral history is now an important subdivision of historical research (Perks and Thomson 2006).

The memory **versus** history coupling could also be seen as wayward, often deluded, memory versus the objectivity of the historian. For different reasons both Halbwachs and Nora denied that their conceptualisations of memory could be equated to history. Halbwachs believed in an organic thread of memory connecting the past to the present through the collective, but distinct from his belief in the historian's objectivity. Nora saw the rupture between past and present through the decline of memory being replaced by manufactured *lieux de mémoire* and constructed histories (Erll 2011: 22–25). More currently, critical accounts of the historian's work are more likely to see it as subject to biases and selectivity in the same way as memory (Burke 1997). So the idea of history **as** memory draws on a greater value given to the particularised remembering of specific social groups and a more humble attitude of historians towards their own biases. Both are constructive and present-minded explorations of the past. 'It is important to ask the question, who wants whom to remember what, and why? Whose version of the past is recorded and preserved?' (Burke 1997: 56)

Consciousness and memory are exclusively a potential of individual minds, so that 'memory' used in a term such as 'collective memory' is best seen as metaphorical (Erll 2011: 96). This means that we can do things in history **as** memory in a way analogous to the way we do things in personal memory, including the natural ability we have to time-travel and feel the past through all our senses. While bemoaning the lack of clarity in the usages of the term 'memory', Geoffrey Cubitt writes that memory (in both its neuronal and figurative meanings) and history have this important similarity: that they are 'relationships to the past that are grounded in human consciousness' (2007: 9). Memories occur in a present moment, time-travelling to a past moment just as historical thinking requires thinking back in time, but in this case a time not centred upon ourselves. Is there a way to harness the intensely personal experience of autobiographical memory to serve the scholarly balance, the critical judgements, needed to practise dance history?

Sensory body, time, identity

It is evident that the individual consciousness we bring to the study of dance history includes a complex of experience in life and dance that resides in memory as factual and skill knowledge as well as autobiographical events (history **and** memory). This final essay section returns to the three foundational aspects of personal memory that I originally identified – bodily experience (sensory and kinaesthetic), time and identity – to make connections with the interpreted pasts that are the subject of history.

I propose the first way into this issue is through the experience of dance practice and through the memories in our own bodies. As Susan Leigh Foster reminds us, our personal experiences of the continuity of the body over time are also a changing body to which we should feel attuned from the practice of dance (Foster 1995: 4). I would add that bodies of flesh, muscle and bone are animated by their neuronal networks. Almost ceaselessly throughout life cells die and are replaced; neurons make new connections; memories accrue; we learn new things. The passing of time within social life leaves its imprint on the body. For Thomas Fuchs, the body with its memory is 'the ensemble of organically developed predispositions and capacities to perceive and to act, but also to desire and to communicate. . . . to actualize our past and, with this, to make ourselves feel at home in situations' (2012: 11).

With this knowledge of our own bodies in our own time we can consider how biological similarity is worked upon by environmental and social difference when we attempt to understand our historical subjects.

This attempt at understanding across time raises the controversial and contested issue of empathy. If empathy is to mean a direct access to the minds of others from the past then it is impossible and has been strenuously disputed (Jenkins 1991: 39–47). But discoveries in neuroscience have more recently identified neural activity (mirror neurons) that suggests humans are strongly attuned to interpreting affect in others through attention to their bodily behaviour (Gallese 2008). So the notion of kinaesthetic empathy is now very much on the agenda, especially in audience reception of dance in performance (Foster 2011; Reynolds and Reason 2012).

The biographical memory-body can also participate in historical research. Lena Hammergren proposes that the historian's own body is a tool in a kinaesthetic historical discourse, prioritising the non-visual in favour of other embodied sensory faculties she knows from her own sensory memory. She asks 'how "source material" can operate kinesthetically on the writer', and as she notionally 'walks through' an event from long ago she is researching, 'What bodily sensations do I get?' (Hammergren 1995: 56) In this spirit we can ask of our historical subjects questions arising from our own sensory experience. What were the sounds and smells of the spaces in which they moved? How did they experience their bodies as shaped by training, nutrition and societal constraints? Memory may well be at the heart of empathic feeling for others both of our own time and the past. Neurobiologist Antonio Damasio writes, 'Memory, tempered by personal feeling, is what allows humans to imagine both individual well-being and the compounded well-being of a whole society, and to invent the ways and means of achieving and magnifying that well-being' (2010: 296).

Both history and memory require mental time travel for which our own ability to move backwards in time through a normal act of everyday consciousness is the model. Not only do we move back in memory but also we move forwards to the present time in an act of comparison: that was 'then'; this is 'now'. I have clearly shared a narrative about my young self 'with the feeling that those things happened in another epoch', as Ricoeur states. He attributes this to a fundamental understanding of the 'otherness' of a past historical time compared to the present one (2004: 97). However, the time travel of memory is not only towards the past. In the science of memory, autobiographical memory is now seen not just as an end in itself but also as a skill in understanding 'the lived past and the anticipated future' (Damasio 2000: 196). What evolutionary benefits have our superior memory abilities given us as a species? Being able to remember past events is key to projecting thoughts into the future and into hypothetical situations. In our own lives we can compare events from the past and make plans for the future based on probable outcomes (Schacter and Addis 2007). Current thinking in the science of memory endorses long-standing phenomenological enquiry that time-consciousness involves thinking both backwards and forwards in time through the collaboration of remembering and imagining (Casey 1977: 199–205). This has the potential for empathic engagement when considering the distant lives of the others we study in dance history. This faculty, if harnessed by the proper historical consciousness, is equivalent to what I have previously argued as 'the historical imagination' (Nicholas 2013), a form of mental 'time travel' which is nevertheless constrained by the strict methodological parameters of critical evaluation.

Memory provides us with the somatosensory body we can use imaginatively in the time travel that is both history and memory. However, there is a tension between the profoundly personal identity inscribed through an individual's own memory and the wider picture of historical forces in societies, collectives, groups or nations. Nevertheless, broad historical narratives are made up of the micro-histories of individual people such as ourselves with personal memories and identities. Contrary to an atomised notion of identity, we can also look to the cohesive social function of memory as evidenced in collective or social memory. Memory-sharing in groups reinforces personal memory and group understanding and passes on ideas about the past that have important implications for the present. The educational and artistic institutions of dance are prime examples of how the metaphorical collective memory secures collective identity. Institutions such as dance companies take care to transmit the memory **as** history of their institutions through education and commemorative events, such as archiving, galas and repertory revivals. Established dancers pass on their traditions to younger ones, including memories in the body. The distinction drawn by Diana Taylor between the archive and the repertoire is significant here. Archival 'memory' holds objects in abeyance, awaiting interpretation, sequestered from the bodies they referred to, but the repertoire (not necessarily in the sense we understand dance company repertory) is the passing on of memory or knowledge in a bodily enactment (2003: 19–24).[11]

At the same time the identity markers of individual memory remain strong. Recent decades have been marked by increased respect for the personal testimony of ordinary participants, even within the major narratives of national history. Increasingly, oral testimony shapes theatrical performance and especially in 'verbatim theatre' scripting directly from oral testimony (Little and High 2015: 240–256). Choreographers may also approach history through individual memory. For example San Francisco–based choreographer Joanna Haigood has developed a number of site-specific projects using oral sources, including *Invisible Wings* (1998) about the 'underground railroad' for escaping slaves, and *Sailing Away* (2010), which further examined the nineteenth-century African American experience in San Francisco (Prickett 2013: 108–113). The centenary of the First World War has motivated a number of projects exploring the rich first-hand source material. In the 'Lest We Forget' programme by English National Ballet in 2014, recorded voices of combatants are heard in the scores of both *Second Breath* (Russell Maliphant) and *Dust* (Akram Khan). Such examples emphasise that personal pasts are evidence not only of a private life but also of a life lived within the temporality that will become increasingly in the passing of time the raw material of history not yet written.

Memory and history might be called 'partners in time'. Certainly there is a strong academic tradition that brings them into collusion – history **and/or/as** memory. Recalling my walk in Covent Garden brought back the vivid sensory images of autobiographical memory, including kinaesthetic ones, and I was made to consider anew the pleasures of 'mental time travel'. Cultivating somatosensory knowledge, remembering how senses are awakened in different situations, gives clues to asking questions about how dancers in the past sensed their worlds. Memories are a major part of personal identity formation, too, and although history is always aware of larger forces at work in society, the larger forces comprise individuals with their own memories and identities, sometimes merging with the collective and sometimes not. Individual memories not only are a source for history but also validate the significance of individual lives. To have memories is already to be a historical subject and already to be equipped with the first skill of the historian. German philosopher Wilhelm Dilthey proposed the connection between personal memory, the past and history: 'The power and breadth of our own lives and the energy with which we reflect on them are the foundation of the historical vision. It alone enables us to give life back to the bloodless shadows of the past' (quoted in Cubitt 2007: 34). So as dance artists, dance scholars, enthusiastic lay dancers and followers of dance in performance we should look to our own memories of a past in dance to find a prototype for a useable dance history that gives meaning to individual experience as part of wider historical forces.

Notes

1   The Beatles song 'Norwegian Wood' (1965) made reference to the trend for interior pine cladding.
2   Molly Molloy (1940–2016) trained at the High School of Performing Arts in New York and studied jazz dance with the celebrated teacher Luigi. She taught and choreographed in New York, London and Paris, including the stage musical *Chess* (1986), Michael Flatley's *Celtic Tiger* (2005) and shows at Le Crazy Horse, Paris. Arlene Phillips continued to choreograph and teach. Her breakthrough was in creating 'Hot Gossip', a popular female dance team on television in the 1970s. From 2004 she became a familiar figure as a judge on the UK television show *Strictly Come Dancing*.
3   Recording artist: O.C. Smith. Words and music: Dallas Frazier. Released in 1968, it reached no. 2 in the UK charts in the summer.
4   For an accessible account of neurons and brain structure see Damasio (2010: 299–312).

5   See Damasio (2000: 220–221), where he illustrates this with differently processed aspects of the concept 'hammer'. See Damasio (2010: 132–133) for the nature of memory records.
6   See also Mitra, this volume, where Akram Khan speaks about his experience of memory recall and how it informs his dance work.
7   For more on the forms of memory, see Markowitsch (2012: 275–283).
8   Nora's examples of French *lieux de mémoire* include broad categories of 'anything pertaining to the cult of the dead, anything relating to the patrimony, anything administering the presence of the past within the present' (1989: 20). In the British context I would suggest as *lieux de mémoire* the image of Big Ben; wearing red poppies on Remembrance Day; and singing 'Jerusalem', particularly on the last night of the Promenade Concerts. These are all currently ritualised and performed through media and illustrate that *lieux* do not need to be material places for their performative nature to be effective.
9   Ricoeur's insistence on the guiding force of witness testimony can be seen in large part because of his attention to traumatic memory, as for example in holocaust survivors.
10 The author's current oral history project, 'The Professional Lives of Dances at the Windmill Theatre, 1932–1964', is one such example.
11 See also Bannerman and Eliot, this volume.

Bibliography

Burke, Peter (1997) 'History as Social Memory', in *Varieties of Cultural History*, Ithaca, NY: Cornell University Press, 43–59.
Casey, Edward (1977) 'Imagining and remembering', *The Review of Metaphysics*, 31:2, December, 187–209.
Connerton, Paul (1989) *How Societies Remember*, Cambridge: Cambridge University Press.
Cubitt, Geoffrey (2007) *History and Memory*, Manchester: Manchester University Press.
Damasio, Antonio (2000) *The Feeling of What Happens: Body, Emotion and the Making of Consciousness*, London: Random House, Vintage Books.
Damasio, Antonio (2010) *Self Comes to Mind: Constructing the Conscious Brain*, London: Heinemann, Kindle Edition.
Dean, David, Yana Meerzon and Kathryn Prince, eds. (2015) *History, Memory, Performance*, Basingstoke: Palgrave Macmillan.
Erll, Astrid (2011) *Memory in Culture*, trans. Sara B. Young, Basingstoke: Palgrave Macmillan Memory Studies.
Foster, Susan Leigh (1995) 'An Introduction to Moving Bodies', in Susan Leigh Foster ed., *Choreographing History*, Bloomington: University of Indiana Press, 3–21.

Foster, Susan Leigh (2011) *Choreographing Empathy: Kinesthesia in Performance*, London: Routledge.
Fuchs, Thomas (2012) 'The Phenomenology of Body Memory', in Sabine Koch, Thomas Fuchs, Michela Summa and Cornelia Muller eds., *Body Memory, Metaphor and Movement*, Amsterdam: John Benjamin, 10–22.
Gallese, Vittorio (2008) 'Empathy, embodied simulation, and the brain: Commentary on Aragno and Zepf/Hartmann', *Journal of the American Psychoanalytic Association*, 56:3, September, 769–781.
Hammergren, Lena (1995) 'The Return of the Flâneuse', in Susan Leigh Foster ed., *Corporealities: Dancing, Knowledge, Culture, and Power*, London: Routledge, 54–71.
Hobsbawm, Eric and Terence Ranger (1983) *The Invention of Tradition*, Cambridge: Cambridge University Press.
Jenkins, Keith (1991) *Re-Thinking History*, London: Routledge.
Koch, Sabine, Thomas Fuchs, Michela Summa and Cornelia Muller, eds. (2012) *Body Memory, Metaphor and Movement*, Amsterdam: John Benjamin.
Little, Edward and Steven High (2015) 'Partners in Conversation: Ethics and the Emergent Practice of Oral History Performance', in David Dean, Yana Meerzon and Kathryn Prince eds., *History, Memory, Performance*, Basingstoke: Palgrave Macmillan, 240–256.
Marcel, Jean-Christophe and Laurent Muccielli (2010) 'Maurice Halbwachs's *Mémoire Collective*', in Astrid Erll and Ansgar Nünning eds., *A Companion to Cultural Memory Studies*, Berlin: De Gruyter, 141–149.
Markowitsch, Hans (2010) 'Cultural Memory and the Neurosciences', in Astrid Erll and Ansgar Nünning eds., *A Companion to Cultural Memory Studies*, Berlin: De Gruyter, 274–283.
Nicholas, Larraine (2013) 'Dance and the Historical Imagination', in Jenny Bunker, Anna Pakes and Bonnie Rowell eds., *Thinking through Dance: The Philosophy of Dance Performance and Practices*, Alton: Dance Books, 242–255.
Nora, Pierre (1989) 'Between memory and history: Les Lieux de Mémoire', *Representations, No. 26, Special Issue: Memory and Counter-Memory*, Spring, 7–24.
Perks, Robert and Alistair Thomson (2006) 'Critical Developments: Introduction', in Robert Perks and Alistair Thomson eds., *The Oral History Reader*, 2nd edition, London: Routledge, 1–13.
Prickett, Stacey (2013) *Embodied Politics: Dance, Protest and Identities*, Binsted: Dance Books.
Reynolds, Dee and Matthew Reason (2012) *Kinesthetic Empathy in Creative and Cultural Practices*, Bristol: Intellect.
Ricoeur, Paul (2004) *Memory, History, Forgetting*, trans. Kathleen Blamey and David Pellauer, Chicago: University of Chicago Press.
Schacter, Daniel (1987) 'Implicit memory: History and current status', *Journal of Experimental Psychology: Learning, Memory, and Cognition*, 13:3, July, 501–518.

Schacter, Daniel (1996) *Searching for Memory: The Brain, the Mind and the Past*, New York: Basic Books.

Schacter, Daniel and Donna Rose Addis (2007) 'The cognitive neuroscience of constructive memory: Remembering the past and imagining the future', *Philosophical Transactions of the Royal Society B*, 362: 1480, May [online].

Sheets-Johnstone, Maxine (2012) 'Kinesthetic Memory: Further Critical Reflections and Constructive Analysis', in Sabine Koch, Thomas Fuchs, Michela Summa and Cornelia Muller eds., *Body Memory, Metaphor and Movement*, Amsterdam: John Benjamin, 43–72.

Stevens, Catherine, Jane Ginsbourg and Garry Lester (2010) 'Backwards and forwards in space and time: Recalling dance movement from long-term memory', *Memory Studies*, 4:2, 234–250.

Stevens, Catherine and Shirley McKechnie (2005) 'Thinking in action: Thought made visible in contemporary dance', *Cognitive Processing*, 6, 243–252 [online].

Taylor, Diana (2003) *The Archive and the Repertoire: Performing Cultural Memory in the Americas*, Durham: Duke University Press.

Chapter 2

Cara Tranders's reveries
The Autobiography of Cara Tranders, Ballet Girl at the Empire Palace of Varieties, 1892–99 (Interspersed with the Voices of Poets, Novelists, Lyricists, Critics and Historians)

CARA TRANDERS

A history teacher addresses his class:

And did I not bid you to remember that for each protagonist who once stepped on the stage of so-called historical events, there were thousands, millions, who never entered the theatre – who never knew that the show was running – who got on with the donkey work of coping with reality? True, true. But it doesn't stop there. Because each one of those numberless non-participants was doubtless concerned with raising in the flatness of his own unsung existence his own personal stage, his own props and scenery – for there are very few of us who can be, for any length of time, merely realistic ... even if we miss the grand repertoire of history, we yet imitate it in miniature and endorse, in miniature, its longing for presence, for feature, for purpose, for content.

(Swift 1984: 40–1)

It looms up, a large greyish shape with ill-defined edges. I like to think of it as a friendly whale in murky sea waters. Out of the dusky green of the fog, the bus that will take me to the Palace crawls to a stop. Like Jonah, I climb in. Its soft lights envelop me and the conductor greets me warmly, for he doesn't fear my travelling alone. He knows I am a dancer but he has seen my sharp eyes as I repel any potential threat to my reputation. Some people think, you know, that if you show your body to the public on stage you must be willing to show it to anyone in private. My aunt was horrified when mother told her I was hoping to be a dancer.

A ballet girl? Are you mad, Florence? Why, what a disgrace . . . an Actress? Better put her on the streets at once.

(Mackenzie [1912] 1929: 76)

The professional dancer is looked upon as one who has sadly misapplied talents which might have won reputation in some worthier path of life.

(Grove 1895: 1)

Aunt changed her attitude, though, when she came to see me in our new show. Escorted by Uncle (for she would never have gone on her own) she was quite dazzled by the spectacle of it all, even though Uncle himself said that he couldn't tell which one was me, being so far from the stage and us all looking alike with our wigs and red and gold costumes and all holding the same long batons in our hands.

Though all alike in their tinsel livery
And indistinguishable at a sweeping glance
   They muster, maybe
   As lives wide in irrelevance
A world of her own has each one underneath
   Detached as a sword from its sheath.

(Hardy 1917 in Gibson 1976: 492)

Uncle was a bit quiet when we left the theatre and stopped going on about it was all 'bally nonsense'. I wouldn't tell Aunty, not even to spite her, but I believe he's been back to the ballet on more than one occasion since.

I'm a very strong admirer of the ballet and the play
   But I haven't told the missus up to now!
And to watch the fairies dancing I pass may (sic) an hour away
   But I haven't told the missus up to now!
When I see their graceful attitudes with love I'm burning hot,
And when the angels flap their wings, they mash me on the spot,
And I feel as if I'd like to go at once and kiss the lot,
   But I haven't told the missus up to now!

(Cornell 1887)

I sink into my seat, relishing the ride from Kentish Town up to Leicester Square when, trapped by my transport, I can do nothing. My body is exhausted, for we were at the theatre at eleven this morning for rehearsal of the new production.

Finishing at two, I have time to get home to give mother her late lunch, for she's poorly now and since Dad ran off there's no one but me to look after her. What I will do when I meet that young chap of my dreams who'll want to whisk me away and look after me, I do not know. Perhaps my young man will take her in, too, because he'll be wealthy enough. Not too much out of our class, of course, because that would be unnatural, but he'll have just enough money for us to be 'comfortable', as they say. Till then, it seems I'm destined to be always tired, for I don't get the bus home after the show till gone eleven at night then it's up in the morning to tidy both mother and the rooms before I leave for the theatre.

Rehearsals were strenuous and frequent, and the girls appeared each morning with the regularity of factory workers. Their life seemed one incessant hurrying backwards and forwards from home to theatre.

(Willis in Green 1986: 180)

She must devote herself each day to practice. At night she must report herself sober and competent. Shortly after eleven you may see her at Charing Cross waiting for the Brixton bus . . . she is the sedate, painstaking artisan of the stage, with her sick clubs, and her boot clubs, and all the petty prudences of the working class.

(Hibbert 1916: 197–8)

Some girls are lucky; they don't have to come and go but can wait at the Rehearsal Club, started by that nice Lady Magenis for the likes of us to flop around during the afternoons when we've a few hours off. My wages aren't too bad, for I'm on twenty shillings a week now and if I can be promoted to the front row of the *corps* I can make thirty five, though by the time I've paid my Sick Club and other clubs that arise from time to time, my take-home's not special. Sometimes I get fined for being late which is a bit unfair because it's always such a rush and I can't help the traffic, especially in the pea-soupers. The scene painters earn three pounds, though. This doesn't seem fair either because they just slap on paint and no one cares about where the edges are because the audience can't see that close anyway.

At least I'm lucky to have a job. We had a scare at the Empire only last year. That Mrs Ormiston Chant nearly got us closed down for good, complaining as she did to the Council. She said the ballets were immoral and I said she was an interfering old busybody who should mind where she pokes her nose but some said she wasn't accusing us, just the management of promoting licentious shows. I don't know what licentious means, myself, but it doesn't sound like a compliment.

The works (The Girl I Left Behind Me, 1893 and La Frolique, 1894) 'seemed to be for the express purpose of displaying the bodies of women to the utmost extent. There is not the least attempt to disguise that which common sense and common decency requires should be hidden.'

(Chant in Donahue 1987: 58)

My friend Emily wrote to the Council appealing to them not to close the Empire, which was ever so brave of her. She's only in the middle row of dancers, like me, but she's become a bit of a star now.

Dear Sirs,
My engagement at the Empire theatre is of subordinate character but as my position is my livelihood I am emboldened to appeal to you, not only in my own name but also in that of my two sisters and other ladies.

Emily Banbury (Empire dancer)
(LCC 1894a)

Fortunately, they did renew the Empire's licence and our jobs were saved. People get mixed up, of course, and confuse those 'ladies' of the night who ply their trade in the promenade at the front of the theatre, and us ladies of the ballet. We don't want to be tarred with the same immoral brush as them, though I must say, I do envy their elegance. Some say the men just enjoy the company of these women, but quite a lot goes on at the front there. Not just women but men, too, exchange their company for money.

An anonymous letter to the LCC Licensing Committee revealed that the writer had been informed by a theatre attendant that more than half the audience in the shilling promenade were 'sodomites' and that 'he often gave them a good kicking'.

(LCC 1894b)

Sometimes I wonder if it's worth being on this side of the curtain rather than out there in the promenade. Not seriously, of course, but I daydream a little when I suffer the conditions in which we have to work. Our dressing rooms are so cramped, and with a hundred and fifty of us in the big ballets, backstage is worse than Piccadilly Circus on Boat Race night. We have to fly down the stairs after our scenes to get changed for the next one, knocking over anyone who gets in the way – especially that critic chap who lurks around. All you can think of is getting to your room. We just ignore men like him – we've got a job to do.

Every few minutes half a dozen pretty girls would rush to their dressing rooms to change, leaving me heart-broken, while another contingent would arrive in fresh costume, as though to console me.

('S.L.B.' 1896: 524)

It's off with one costume and on with another, then running back up the stairs to make my next entry, panting hard but smiling. Hard, that is, panting and smiling. But we get used to it. We don't always get used to the rats, though they scarper and we just see their tails disappear. They don't like all the activity and, as you can imagine, twelve of us all cramped together in one little dressing room can be a very active occasion — elbows and legs everywhere. You're never sure whose hose you're putting on. We're not allowed out of the room during the break between the two nightly ballets when the other acts are on. It's less frantic then; we might knit or catch up with our sewing, but it's the smell we don't like. We can't help the sweat and the greasy make-up, but there's no air and it's hot and sometimes you just hold your breath, so you're panting even more. But you have to keep smiling, because the management said so and we do what they say or we'll never make the front row. If I go to the back row before I go forward, I'll just die. The back row is for those who are beginners or those who are past it. Some of the girls' mothers are in the back row. Quite companionable, being on the same stage as your mum, but you can see your future in hers if you're not careful. Mme Lanner, our ballet mistress, danced professionally until she was nearly fifty, so it can be a long career for those who are lucky, those who work hard and keep out of trouble.

Most of us are really careful to keep out of trouble. And we do work hard, even though it can be boring at times, especially towards the end of a six-month run which is quite normal for each ballet. Although we all think we can do more, most us know secretly that we're not trained to be able to display our skills. I learned at Mme Lanner's National Training School of Dancing in Tottenham Court Road, from where she gets most of the Empire girls. Not the principals of course — they come from abroad where the training's much better. That's why they star. Isn't fair, really. We are pretty well a world apart, as they don't have much to do with us and we wouldn't dare speak to them. But we watch them secretly, when we're framing their performance, and we talk about them after. Some of the girls can be quite nasty. Jealousy, really, for that's all we are on the stage — a coloured frame around a pure white dancing image. The ballerinas can go up and stay on their toes. I've tried, time and time again, but my legs won't let me do it. But they've got the muscles for it. Men don't see the muscles, though. I don't really know what they see. The ballerinas are a bit out of their class, being skilled and foreign and all that, but I suppose the men can dream.

Elly (we call her Elly behind her back, just to bring her down a bit; her name's really Elena Cornalba) wears a lovely gauzy dress in our current ballet, *Faust*. She doesn't do much else, mind. Got no 'character' to play but she does the proper steps. There's rumours that she's leaving and they're looking to Moscow for another star. That will be interesting. Management can't seem to find a permanent ballerina from Italy. Mme Cavallazzi as Faust is as strong as ever; we know all her mime actions of course but could never do them as well as she can. I can imagine myself in that black Mephistopheles costume of Zanfretta's with those grand arm gestures which tell the story. So dramatic.

My reverie comes to a jolting halt. I like having reveries as they sound foreign and glamorous — but it's time to get off the bus. Mme Lanner will be furious if we're late; she's like a big black beetle in her bombazine. She is good at her arrangements of us *corps de ballet*. Should be by now, for she's been with the Empire since 1887 they say. Her and Mr Wilhelm work on most of the ballets together. For this *Faust* he's written the story (based on someone else's we think), so he worked more closely with her on each scene as well as designing the costumes as usual. We all know he's actually called William Pitcher and his dad is a shipbuilder, but he changed his name to sound more foreign because it helps in this business. You can't blame him. Sometimes when I'm standing there in yet another tableau I dream up names I'd choose for myself. I fancy Cara Taglioni so I could keep the same initials, but there's already been a Taglioni and I wouldn't want people to get mixed up.

Costumes – I must get into mine. I fly off the bus and walk ever so quickly to the side street entrance of the Empire where I meet up with my friend Maria. Maria used to be with the Salvation Army but there wasn't much life there and she kept banging her tambourine in the wrong place. So she came to us.

Sister 'Ria, Sister 'Ria of the Army soon began to tire
So she's sold her tambourine
Now she's nightly to be seen
Dancing in the ballet at the Empire.

(Mills and Lennard 1895)

For tonight's ballet I'm a soldier in the first scene. We play quite a lot of soldiers. There aren't any men dancers except for the occasional foreigner but they're not much liked even when they're good, like that Mr Cecchetti who was with us a couple of years ago. Went on to become a teacher of sorts, I think. 'They're all the same,' says my Uncle, 'one of those.' It took me a while to know who 'those' were and it isn't really fair because some of these gentlemen dancers were married. But you never know. The 'male' characters are nearly always played by women; 'en travestie', they call it. Nice to know a bit of French. We know that the audience like to look at our legs when we're dressed as soldiers and we have to keep our waists trim. Difficult if one of us girls gets pregnant and wants to hide it for as long as possible. But the men can look at what they like. It's all part of the show to us. We march off after the first scene in *Faust*, being careful to keep in time and not rush, for we have a brisk break of one scene before the third, in which I'm a will-o'-the-wisp. It's the last scene that's the worst. We play angels, with lovely golden wigs, but we have to climb these very steep ladders backstage and perch on the top, sticking our heads through a hole in the backdrop, so our faces appear like 'angels in the sky'. We're terrified, because we're so high up and the ladders wobble and it's freezing cold up there, but we have to keep smiling. I imagine it must look good from the audience's point of view but we don't feel much like angels when we're up there, I can tell you.

A crystal stair, and in the air
  the angels hover round . . .

No more those angels deck the sky —
those angels hail from Peckham Rye,
  From Bow or Kentish Town.

('J.M.B.' 1896: 524)

No wonder we get coughs and colds or worse, all this going from those damp and muggy dressing rooms up those cold stairs to the stage, then hot again under the lights. That's why the Sick Club is so important, to help us through those times when we're poorly.

The little painted angels flit
  See, down the narrow staircase, where
The pink legs flicker over it!

Blonde, and bewigged, and winged with gold,
  The shining creatures of the air
Troop sadly, shivering with cold.

(Symons 1895: 21)

Sometimes, as I said, the work does get a little boring, though we do two ballets a night. This *Faust* is quite different to the other recent one, *On Brighton Pier*, which has nice popular melodies and we had to learn to move a bicycle around on the stage to show how modern we were. Will Bishop used to make us laugh. He's not a 'real' dancer, of course, but he entertains us with his clog dancing and in *Brighton* he had a really clever masher dance – you know, showing off as a young man about town. The management like these different kinds of ballets – sometimes a really up-to-date work, or one celebrating Britain's Empire; sometimes one from fairy tale or legend. Keeps everyone happy. The Alhambra are doing *Titania*, based on a Shakespeare play, but they're not as good as us. They say we just hold up the scenery which is a typical thing to come from an Alhambra girl. Admittedly, the movements we're given in all of the ballets are pretty much the same, and are not that difficult in themselves – but it's just the same at the Alhambra. We march a lot, and strike poses, drawing attention to the ballerina. The management always ask Mme Lanner to get a vision scene in, a 'transformation', as the audience love these. There'll be tinkly water music and the flimsy curtain at the back of the stage will be drawn back to reveal another tableau, a 'transformed' picture within the picture of the stage. Clever, really. The best bits for us are when we waltz or galop as then you can really be carried away with the music and feel that you're really dancing. We're not on our toes but we are still an important part of the show. Often there are long periods when we do nothing at all, just stand in position. Sometimes I try to find faces in the audience but of course you can't see them individually in that great sea of half darkness. My mind wanders then. I think about mother at home and feel the pity for her, all day in that room. That's why I try to get home in the afternoons but it makes my day such a squash. I always seem to feel tired. Sometimes I use those tableaux when the ballerina is doing her thing to plan the next days' meals. A neighbour gave us some beef dripping, so we can have that with bread tomorrow. Nice and nutritious.

Suddenly I saw a beautiful girl whose face was strange to me. She was exotic, with passionate lips and eyes, magnetic. Then she . . . that is you . . . fixed her eyes on mine without surprise, without hesitation, as if drawn by some instinct, your eyes fixed on mine at every turn you made as you danced with the others.

(Symons in Beckson 1977: 160)

Yes, beef dripping would be lovely. Useful thinking time, these tableaux are, so long as I don't forget to move on the sixteenth beat after the big crash of the drums. (For *Faust* they've had an organ built and it's a lovely sound – sort of heavenly but majestic.) You don't often miss your cue, though. Even if your mind has wandered you sense it from the girls when it's time to move as their breath and their muscles prepare. We've been working together so long we almost dance as one, especially when Mr Wilhelm dresses different groups of us in different colours. We must look like an artist's paint palette. Green's my favourite as it goes with my eyes. Not that anyone could see my eyes.

. . . the members of the corps de ballet . . . become convenient units in the development of the (colour) scheme.

('T.H.L.' 1893: 344)

The important thing, though, is to keep looking at the audience as if you can really see them. We know we've got to 'communicate'. Not go over the top on our character, of course (it's a bit difficult going over the top on being a daisy, anyway), but just sharing our joy of dancing and trying to look attractive. That's important because many of the people in the audience really do love the ballet.

London audiences now began to regain an appreciation of the technical basis of the Dance and Ballet which they had lost . . . thus, they were enabled the better to understand the Russian ballet when it eventually arrived and achieved instant success.

(Perugini 1925: 1177)

Some of them just come for a night out, because the Empire means all that is 'home' to them, especially when they've been away in our colonies.

Something more than a mere music hall . . . it was . . . an Englishman's club, an Empire club, famous wherever Englishmen fought, worked, adventured. Britishers prospecting in the Klondyke, shooting in jungles, tea-planting in Ceylon, wherever they fore-gathered in cities of Africa, Asia and America would bid one another goodbye with a 'See you at the Empire one day when we're back in town.'

(Booth 1929: 142)

We know that some men also come to eye us up and some of the girls even walk out with men they've met at the stage door. I personally don't like to hang around with those johnnies – I'm in too much of a rush to catch the bus – but I don't blame those who do. Some of the dancers from the Alhambra used to go to the Crown public house, just off Leicester Square, where they'd meet the young men who claimed they were poets. The girls used to try and explain how the ballets worked and how the steps were performed and they'd get really angry because the men didn't seem to take them seriously. These men belonged to some club – the Rhymers Club, I think. Violet Piggot had an affair with one of them called Arthur. He seemed very keen at first but some of these men don't seem to realise that you can't go to the public house in all your stage finery and in your real clothes, and close-up, you look rather different. What do they expect, a dancing will-o'-the-wisp in a pub? Arthur turned quite nasty, apparently, and dropped Violet pretty quickly. We hear these stories all the time. At least this Arthur writes nicely about the ballet in the *Star* and the *Sketch* and stories come down to us girls about what he, and other writers, have said about the new ballets. They're nearly always complimentary, thank goodness. One critic said how much the dancing of the rank and file (that's us) had improved; that made us glow. Sometimes there are photographs and I was nearly in one of the *corps* photos once, but I didn't get chosen in the end. The girls have to pose for these in whatever position pleases the photographer, often with their arms bent up and their hands behind their heads. This doesn't appear anywhere in the ballet, of course, but the more worldly amongst us know that this position pushes up your bust, making you more attractive. The drawings on the covers of the Empire programmes don't look much like us in real life, either. You'd think we danced half naked, which is nonsense because we always have our fleshings over legs and arms, or that we all look the same when we're actually all shapes and sizes. But I suppose the management like to present an image of us that will draw in the crowds. And if we don't get the crowds, there won't be the money to pay our wages, so we don't complain.

We do try to look attractive, those who can, that is. It's all part of showing off our skills. One critic, a Mr Bensusan who is probably so ashamed that he has to write under the letters 'S.L.B.', said in a review of an Alhambra work that so long as us ballet girls have good looks talent goes for nothing. That made us cross but it is all part of the attraction of the ballets. For some girls, this is all they care about. Most of us, though, are proud of what we do. The ballet goes way back in to history, and we're part of that history. We get nearly two thousand people in on full nights (I shake a little when I think about it). Toffs; artists; soldiers on leave; men about town and ordinary people including, more and more, the women. No one knows what they think about the ballet. I imagine they get a different kind of pleasure in watching, perhaps imagining themselves as us, perhaps just enjoying all the colour and lights and movement and a night out. No one tells us what the women think.

What do I think? I think a lot. My body is nearly always exhausted, but I wouldn't do another job. It's wonderful, really, to be able to dance, to be part of such a long artistic tradition. I know I'll never be a real ballerina, but that's all right. My job is secure, more or less, and the work is varied compared to the factory or even the office, where so many young girls work nowadays. And it's a million times better than the domestic. The ballet can take me out of my own domestic, out of the worry about home. When I'm dancing, I can dream, and sometimes my mind is empty as my body just takes over. But I also think a lot. About my aching arms, holding this heavy pole at the exact right angle; about how late the bus will be in the fog; about how Cornalba can't get that crisp finish to her pirouettes; about what I would look like if I were out there in front like her and how that applause would be for me alone as I dazzled them with my spins and turns and jumps and balances. My legs would be strong as iron; my arms as light as muslin. My smile would be confident, my gaze at the audience assured as I returned theirs. I think about a man who will come along and look after me and mother. But he'll have to know the real me from the pretty picture he sees on stage. Yes, I think a lot. But nobody knows what I think. My thoughts won't go down in history. But the ballet will, and I'm proud to be a part of it.

The history teacher addresses his class:

Children you are right, there are times when we have to disentangle history from fairy-tale. There are times . . . when good dry textbook history takes a plunge into the old swamps of myth and has to be retrieved with empirical fishing lines. History, being an accredited sub-science, only wants to know the facts. History, if it is to keep on constructing its road into the future, must do so on solid ground . . . At all costs let us avoid mystery-making and speculation, secrets and idle gossip . . . and above all, let us not tell stories . . . let us get back to solid ground.

(Swift 1984: 86)

Bibliography

Beckson, K. (ed.) (1977) *The Memoirs of Arthur Symons: Life and Art in the 1890s*, University Park, PA: Pennsylvania State University Press.

Booth, J. B. (1929) *London Town*, London: T. Werner Laurie.

Cornell, C. (1887) *Music Score: 'I Haven't Told the Missus Up to Now'*, London: Francis Bros. & Day.
Donahue, J. (1987) 'The Empire Theatre of Varieties Licensing Controversy of 1894: Testimony of Laura Ormiston Chant before the Theatres and Music Halls Licensing Committee', *Nineteenth Century Theatre*, 15, Summer: 50–60.
Gibson, J. (ed.) (1976) *The Complete Poems of Thomas Hardy*, London: Macmillan.
Green, B. (ed.) (1986) *The Last Empires: A Music Hall Companion*, London: Pavilion.
Grove, L. (1895) *Badminton Library of Sports and Pastimes: Dancing*, London: Longmans, Green.
Hibbert, H. G. (1916) *Fifty Years of a Londoner's Life*, London: Grant Richards.
'J.M.B.' (1896) 'An Earthly Paradise', *Sketch*, 1 January: 524.
LCC (1894a) MIN/10,803, 13 October, London Metropolitan Archives, 40 Northampton Rd., LONDON EC1R 0HB.
LCC (1894b) MIN/10,803, 15 October, London Metropolitan Archives, Address as above.
Mackenzie, C. ([1912] 1929) *Carnival*, London: Martin Secker.
Mills, A. J. and Lennard, A. (1895) *Music Score: 'Sister Ria'*, London: Francis, Day & Hunter.
Perugini, M. E. (1925) 'Where Are We Going?', *Dancing Times*, August, 1171–7.
'S.L.B.' (1896) 'Behind the Scenes II: The Empire', *Sketch*, 1 January: 523–4.
Swift, G. (1984) *Waterland*, London: Picador.
Symons, A. (1895) *London Nights*, London: Leonard Smithers.
'T.H.L.' (1893) 'A Chat with a Costumier: Wilhelm at Home', *Sketch*, 8 March: 343–4.

Chapter 3

Beyond fixity
Akram Khan on the politics of dancing heritages

ROYONA MITRA

Introduction

THERE HAS BEEN a long-standing western tendency to view non-western performance traditions as fossilised and monolithic heritages that must be preserved. Furthermore, artists of colour who train in these non-western traditions are seen as bearers of these antiquated and 'authentic' pasts, incapable of speaking to and for the present.[1] The label 'contemporary *kathak*', which has often been applied by scholars and critics alike to the works of the influential British Bangladeshi dancer/choreographer Akram Khan, perpetuates such limited and limiting thinking.[2] Khan's unique aesthetic arises out of his embodied negotiations between his training in multiple movement vocabularies and his complex identity politics as a London-based, second-generation British Bangladeshi, and a father to children of mixed racial and cultural heritages with his Japanese partner. Yet, despite these obvious multilayered complexities that catalyse Khan's art-making, it is his training in the north Indian classical dance style of *kathak* that remains the primary lens through which his art is received and perceived within the British and global dance landscape.

Assuming that Khan's *kathak* becomes contemporary only when it comes into contact with his western dance training, the label 'contemporary *kathak*' equates contemporisation with westernisation, and reinforces that therefore, in and of itself, *kathak* belongs to a culturally monolithic past. This is of course far from the truth. My monograph *Akram Khan: Dancing New Interculturalism* (2015) launches from this critical position, dismantling the problematic nature of the label itself, and arguing instead, that while Khan's work is popularly believed to be contemporising *kathak*, it is in fact transforming the contemporary British and global dance landscape in fundamentally intercultural ways, through his dramaturgical interventions that derive from his *kathak* training. Consequently, Khan is also starting to transform the ways in which *kathak*'s characteristic components, such as *abhinaya*, the expressive, emotive and codified modalities through which its storytelling occurs, are reinvented and made pertinent to a twenty-first-century British diasporic context. Khan's approach to dance making is therefore characterised by a continuous and oscillatory relationship between and across temporalities, while he weaves his embodied knowledge of the past into his multidimensional and ever-changing present, signalling his futures as both unpredictable and therefore full of unknown possibilities, waiting to be discovered.

In this interview with Akram Khan I challenge western ideas that continue to perpetuate non-western performance traditions, such as *kathak*, as fixed, ancient and monolithic. I seek ways to question and extend our understanding of Khan's embodiment of multiple and intercultural dance heritages. I ask Khan to speak of his relationships to multilayered temporalities that simultaneously signal and embody intercultural pasts, presents and futures. In doing so I argue for the dancing body as an ongoing and unfolding living history that can claim a plurality of heritages with equal prowess, and that can dismantle western ideas of non-western cultural heritages as contained and unchanging.

My intellectual framework unfolds in and through a set of interview questions that I formulated while watching Khan in rehearsal with the English National Ballet for his interpretation of *Giselle* on 19 May 2016 in London. Witnessing Khan and three English National Ballet dancers working trans-historically through multiple dance heritages in order to give birth to new embodied manifestations of movement and gestures in and through these ballet-codified bodies seemed like a fortuitous framing context for this interview. In his introductory chat with the dancers at the start of the rehearsal, Khan candidly admitted that for him, the making of *Giselle* is an open-ended process, full of unanswered questions. He made it clear that he was not coming in with predetermined answers, and that their participation through embodied research was crucial to discovering answers together. He shared how he is still in search of a codified gestural language for his *Giselle* that is distinct to both ballet's and *kathak*'s codified conventions, but one that will speak to his twenty-first-century retelling of the classical narrative. He explained the highly sophisticated nature of *kathak*'s gestural codes, describing its nuanced distinctions, for example, between the gestures for greeting one's mother, one's lover and one's teacher. He demonstrated the codified use of the *palta*, the pure movement prelude that consists of a stylised turn performed by a solo *kathak* dancer to signal her shift from one character or theme to another, and then encouraged one of the dancers to discover his own embodiment of the *palta*, so as to use it as a signpost to audiences of his intention to shift between different characterisations. Khan's approach with the ballet dancers was to allow them to discover their own ways to embody a movement or even a principle, giving them the agency to transform his material, in order to own the gestures as their own. What was apparent from witnessing this corporeal translation process was Khan's emphasis on embracing errors, to foreground the spirit of experimentation before finding the gestures that felt most embodied, and exploiting the inevitable awkwardness that surfaced in the ballet bodies as part of these tricky processes of translations. It is in these very moments of exposing vulnerabilities and imperfections that a new aesthetic emerged, moving dance histories and heritages forward in dynamic and energising ways.

Interview

RM:
What does 'dancing heritages' mean to you in relation to your evolving artistic and aesthetic practices?

AK:
I think it is an embodied record of time, but it is not one-dimensional – instead it is the embodiment of past, present and future. It does not signal just the past and it does not belong just within one time frame. Heritage is like a museum, but one that keeps collecting, because its doors are always open. It is a living museum.

RM:
How would you distinguish between 'dance heritage' and 'dancing heritage'?

AK:
For me, 'dance heritage' is inheriting a body of information through training while 'dancing heritage' is knowledge. Knowledge that is inhabited, relived, transformed to become reflective of an artist's unique truth. Information is what we receive from the outside, we witness something, we experience it though our eyes and our five senses. This is data that we assimilate and then we absorb it. But knowledge is when we process this information from within and it becomes embedded within us.

RM:
You talked about truth – what do you mean by truth?

AK:
Yes, truth is a difficult concept to talk about because it is as ambiguous and slippery as spirituality. In Sufism the second you take God's name 'Allah', God disappears. It is in between the inhalation and the exhalation of the first syllable that God is believed to exist. It's the same with truth – it is never one thing, it is never concrete, you cannot pin it down, and the meaning of truth changes constantly even to oneself. So when I say truth, I suppose I refer to an artist's reality, which is constantly changing.

RM:
You have clearly described that you view 'dancing heritages' as a process of ongoing knowledge production. But as a dance artist of colour, how do you think other people view your relationship to 'dancing heritage'?

AK:
It depends on who is viewing me. If it is from a White perspective, I think they find my dancing of heritage fascinating and exotic. And if it is from a South Asian or a brown perspective, then they would feel that I have no heritage, until and unless I am doing pure classical work.

RM:
How do you feel about both these perceptions?

AK:
I feel nothing; it doesn't bother me. But it has taken me time to get to this mindset. It's only in recent times that I am all right with it, because I know my flaws and my strengths and I know what I am doing, because I am comfortable to not know what I am doing most of the time. And that means I know I am doing something right by not knowing what I am doing. And I know that I always turn to my classical heritages for inspiration in order to move forward.

RM:
I know your relationship to the label 'contemporary *kathak*' has changed over the years. Could you talk me through your journey vis-à-vis this label?

AK:
I was naïve. It is something Farooq termed with me . . . actually to be honest with you, people started to label my work as such and then we stuck with it.[3] *I don't know what it means actually – contemporary* kathak. *I haven't seen anybody do it yet. But then again, what Maharajji was doing thirty years back was moving* kathak *forward. Kumudini Lakhia moved* kathak *forward.*[4] *They added things to it; repertoire, ways of thinking that nobody had done before them. Maybe that in its time was a contemporary moment for* kathak. *But where the definition dies, where is the edge of that definition of contemporary, where is the edge of* kathak, *I don't know. But that is how I would now perceive the label. And I also think it is too limiting. It is limiting because we are living in a cultural moment determined by technology and global economics – and this is both a good and bad thing. People have access to YouTube. We are able to borrow from every culture because we have easy access and because we want to learn – this open access is as exciting as it is problematic of course. My own key interest, however, is in the body, so I don't want to simply replicate and mimic a form, but want to use new information gathered from these sources as stimulus within bodies, in order to see how these bodies are transformed by it.*

RM:
How do you feel when artists of colour who work between classical and contemporary languages, such as yourself, are viewed as fixed and antiquated bearers of particular traditions?

AK:
I think it's . . . erm . . . problematic. It's, erm, it's everything that I fight against. Erm, I, fought Pina Bausch on it. We had a huge debate, let's say. I have immense respect for her; she has been a huge influence in my life. She invited me to perform in a dance festival. And she wanted to programme me on the same evening with Malavika Sarukkai, the award-winning Indian bharatnatyam *exponent. And I asked why. She said because there is something very specific about the aesthetic that belongs to a particular cultural context and time, and yours belongs to the present time and hers is fixed. It's history. It was a very personal dialogue that we had, just her and me, and it wasn't an argument but a real debate, because I was really resisting performing alongside Malavika. Firstly, because I love her as a dancer, but more importantly I didn't want to be put into that bracket, because I didn't like the way people generally think of Indian classical dance. Which is it's a bit like a dinosaur, preserved in a museum. But at the same time, I do feel we have an issue right now. Because unless we get people like Pandit Durgalal, Maharajji, Nahidji, Kumudini Lakhia, artists of that calibre but of today's generation, nobody is going to take* kathak *forward. It will start to dilute and die away. I feel that there are some artists like Aditi Mangaldas, who are pushing from within, but it has to be of that calibre. People like Aditi who know the form to break it from within. But I strongly resisted being put on in the same evening as Malavika, but Pina being Pina, I gave in ultimately because I have so much respect for her. But the point was I did not want to represent the present and the future and Malavika the past; it isn't as simplistic and black and white as that.*

RM:
Do you think with hindsight, had she asked you now, would you have done it?

AK:
No, I wouldn't have.

RM:
You have already mentioned that your relationship to time in your art-making is complex and that you constantly negotiate past, present and future simultaneously in your works. That it is in this cross-temporal treatment of gestures that you invent new ones. Could you explain this further?

AK:
I would love to say I invent something. But I think the truth is I find them, I discover them by accident or by questioning and putting people into interesting situations. I believe that

everything is old, the present is already in the past, because the light that you and I see now and that enables us to see is already eight minutes old. So the present is the past. And for me the past is also connected to the future, because I think of everything cyclically. For example say with my daughter, the state I leave the earth in she will inherit. So her future is my present, but will also be my past. It is all interconnected. So personal histories and inheritances also form a crucial part of my work, because I play with memory a lot.

RM:
Could you talk about how memory and heritage interplay in your work?

AK:
Memory is something that is fascinating for me, because memory is a lie, a fabrication. And the older the memory, the more you have filled in the blanks. And I find that whole process fascinating. So, for example the story I say in the opening of Zero Degrees, *not entirely all of it is true, and the reason I say this is because my cousin has pointed this out to me, saying that is not how it happened.*[5] *But then even his memory of the event is not entirely true. Memory for me is a tremendous fuel and resource in my creative process, because it is stuff we have lived through and experienced and is highly charged with emotional triggers. So you see a woman wearing a yellow coat with brown shoes, and you suddenly connect with that. But what you are perhaps connecting with is the memory of maybe your mother, and she had a yellow bag and the brown shoes belonged to your father's sister who passed away, but the brain plays a trick and replaces details and fabricates a new association for you.*

RM:
And then this instance can become the fuel for further deconstruction of memory in your work . . .

AK:
Yes, absolutely. We have to find ways to deal with memory of course, because they often come with trauma or even beautiful joy. And the way we survive and deal with those memories is to fabricate them.

RM:
Watching you rehearse today in the ballet world with ballet bodies, it was wonderful to see the vulnerability in you as you undertake this journey of absorbing new knowledge through this process. It made me wonder what it is like for you to work with and between multiple heritages, particularly two classical heritages of ballet and *kathak*. How are you negotiating between these worlds?

AK:
Until this point, I have never really worked with multiple heritages, but I have worked with multiple cultures. But the dancers I work with, even though they are contemporary

technique–trained, sometimes come to the process with their own cultural art forms. For example someone from Vietnam might bring to our process training in Vietnamese dance, so their embodied knowledge of these heritages will always bleed into the process. And of course their personal inheritance of memories will always inform my performance-making processes. But here, with English National Ballet, lies a significant shift because when working with ballet, it is clearly a very distinct and codified heritage. Even at a physical level, ballet is ethereal and anti-gravity, trying to reach the sky. Kathak is grounded through weighted contact between the ground and the feet. One is trying to defy gravity and the other is using gravity. Kathak works on a horizontal plane, ballet works on a vertical plane. When I decided to work with ballet bodies in collaboration with English National Ballet I told myself that I should not look back one day on the work and think, my dancers could have done this better, because then there is no point doing this in the first place, because I would not have tapped into their technique, their language. I will have both betrayed their language and learnt nothing in the process. All I will have learnt is just how badly my aesthetic can be delivered. And vice versa. So I knew I had to meet them halfway. It's interesting because if you had asked me this question ten years ago, my ego would have been in the way, because then I was predominantly a performer. But now, since I have already started to psychologically let that status go and accepted that my interest now lies in choreography, that involves learning new things and putting myself into vulnerable situations. And I feel that because of this, my work is getting richer. Because it is no longer about me, it's about the work. And it is no longer about me carrying an entire performance – it's about the dancers carrying the work. And that had always been challenging when I was in the company pieces. So with this process, I am deeply invested in learning about their ballet vocabulary, which I didn't even do with Sylvie.[6] With the English National Ballet, I am working with so many of them that it has the danger of failing and looking like they are simply embodying somebody else's information if I don't tap into their own information. And I have worked with other bodies with other coded information. But what I am interested in here is I don't ask the question 'What do I do to them?', but I ask, 'What do they do to my language and where are they going to take my language?' And they are changing the language in unimaginable ways because my own body is not present, because my body is limited by flexibility. I have more legwork in ENB's work than ever before. I hardly jump in my performances – it is just not my strength. I can't point my feet, so I have never had a clear line, my upper half, yes, perhaps. But had my body been able to do these things, my own language would have been different. But because I couldn't, it is these ballet dancers that are taking my language elsewhere. And this is exciting.

RM:
How do you feel about the framing of your work as an evolving and living archive, instead of fixed and immovable?

AK:
It's interesting because talking about archives, we are archiving stuff, like say our costumes from previous performances at the Victoria & Albert Museum. So on the one hand, we are

starting to consider our legacy, so people can tap into it. But legacy is about the future. So it is a big contradiction for me because the pieces going into the museum belong to the past. The costumes I probably won't ever wear again; they have happened. But my perception of them is still changing and ongoing. So even though we decided to archive the items in agreement with me and the board of the company, I like to think of it in the same vein as Merce Cunningham did and I could be wrong, but I think he said that when he died his work should die with him . . .

RM:
And I believe the Indian choreographer Chandralekha said the same thing . . .

AK:
Ah, really? If someone were to ask me to hand over my past works to them as legacy, to be remade and reinterpreted in order for them to live as my repertoire after I die, I would have conflicting views on this issue of dance legacy. I think every moment is fleeting and the realities in which I make a certain work change, and so the contexts change. However, someone else fifty years from now, working with my material, will find their own reality in and through them. So my work could evolve in new ways through someone else's treatment of it. It's like Big Dance – it's not the choreography I have made, it's the pledge by the Bollywood group, the elderly group, the taxi drivers, the blind group – they have all made their own versions of this dance with the rules I have given them to the same music.[7] And this is, in effect, a microcosmic example of a living legacy, panning out in the moment. So I have conflicting feelings about it.

RM:
How do you think your work differs from your peers who are other artists of colour?

AK:
I have a feeling that there has been a generational shift in the attitude towards performance making. I don't want to say this, but perhaps, I am guessing, that Sidi Larbi and I embraced and brought about a change for our generation and the ones that follow, by embracing collaboration. I think for earlier generations the hierarchies between choreographers, composers, performers was strictly observed, and the choreographer had the final say where they did not collaborate, but rather commissioned partners. From Kaash *onwards, Nitin, Anish and myself were all equal and we all had opinions about the others' contributions and we each drove the creative process. So for example Nitin's perception of the set, Anish's perception of the dance and my perception of the music worked in a cyclical manner towards a holistic vision.[8] So what I am trying to say is, the person who makes a cup, their perception of the cup is not as interesting as the person who pours tea into the cup. It is the latter person's perception of the cup that I am interested in. So hearing Anish or Sylvie's relationship to my* kathak *made me relearn my art form in ways I had never imagined.*

I am interested, though, how would you as a scholar distinguish between the concepts of tradition and heritage?

RM:
From my scholarly perspective, a tradition doesn't just apply to an artistic practice; it is just a set of conventions or codes through which a particular act has been ritualised, which could be anything: the tradition of making tea, or the tradition of a Christian wedding, or any wedding ceremony.

AK:
It's a ritual. And heritage?

RM:
Erm, it's usually considered to stand for artistic practices handed down from the past, usually, though not exclusively, applied to non-western performance cultures/traditions. But actually to me heritage is embodied knowledge of the past. And that could be in terms of performance codes or it could be in terms of family histories.

AK:
The key word here is it's embodied.

RM:
Exactly.

As our interview draws to a close, I am left with several thoughts. In my capacity as a dance scholar who has been in close collaboration with Khan over the last decade, I have had the privilege to chart not only his artistic trajectory but also his growing allegiance to his art as fundamentally political. In an interview I conducted with him for the Indian *Seminar* magazine's special issue on the theme of 'Why Dance?', he had already started to recognise this shift in himself:

> The older I get, the more political I am becoming, yes. And while my dancing is not about politics, it always is and will be political. It will always try to explore a position that represents a resistance to the dominant stance.
>
> (Khan in Mitra 2015b: 4)

In this interview, though, he begins to articulate that what fuels the politics of his art is essentially his postcolonial response to being 'othered' as a British dance artist of colour. To this end he shows critical awareness that the racialisation of his identity, and in turn his art, varies, and is dependent upon the racialised identities of those encountering it. He reveals a deeply rooted frustration against the western tendency to consider non-western performance traditions and artists as fixed and incapable of evolution. In sharing his memory of debating with Bausch the inappropriateness of labelling Sarukkai's *Bharatanatyam* performance as a fixed tradition from the past, and his own aesthetic as belonging to the present, Khan admits that even if he failed in that instance, these imagined dichotomies between non-western tradition as unchanging pasts and western contemporisation as evolving presents need to be persistently challenged.

Khan's observations on his relationship to time as cyclical and the interconnectedness between pasts, presents and futures are useful insights with which to complicate western notions of time as linear, which situates history as belonging to the past. Instead, if the past, present and future are indeed interconnected, then we might reconsider histories as living and dialogic cross-temporalities. This dialogic nature of Khan's relationship to time is further revealed in his contested relationship with the terms 'contemporary' and 'legacy', as he resists his work being categorised by any sense of time-boundedness. His discomfort with both the present and the future is articulated poignantly in his response to the hypothetical idea of someone carrying on his dance legacy. To entertain this possibility, Khan emphasises the need to consider the unique, interconnected bodily realities that trigger artists' works in their specific temporalities, while simultaneously acknowledging that while these same realities cannot be re-embodied, there does exist the possibility that these works might find resonance in the new and different realities of those who interact with them in the future. By emphasising the importance of embodiment within an artist's creative process, Khan complicates western dance history's preoccupation with legacies and reconstructions, and questions whether bodies of work should die with the artists who birthed them. Finally, and most crucially for me, Khan's last contribution to this anthology that is dedicated to rethinking dance histories is the distinction he draws between 'dance heritage' as a collection of objective and sealed data that can be acquired and 'dancing heritage' as a proactive processing of such data which becomes inhabited and transformed into lived knowledge, to reflect the realities of the artist herself. This shift from heritage as fixed and acquired to heritage as processual and lived is a crucial intervention to reframing dance artists of colour as agents of change.

Notes

1   For similar critiques of western romanticisation of non-western performance traditions and artists as fixed, see Chakravorty (2008) and Coorlawala (1999). Further, for championing of parallel non-western modernities, defined on their own cultural and temporal terms, see Chatterjea (2004) and Purkayastha (2014).

2 See Annalisa Piccirillo (2008) and Lorna Sanders (2004, 2008) for scholarly references to Khan's aesthetic as 'contemporary *kathak*'.

3 Farooq Chaudhry co-founded Akram Khan Company with Khan in 2000 and is the company's producer. A British Pakistani man, Chaudhry left his own dancer career to complete an MA in arts management from City University in London in 1999. He has been lauded internationally for his vision of cultural entrepreneurship and in 2013 also became producer to English National Ballet. Chaudhry's contribution to the growth and success of Akram Khan Company has been key. In this interview, Khan refers here to discussions between himself and Chaudhry in the early days of the company, as they navigated their way conceptually around how to describe the unique aesthetic that Khan was generating in his performances, such as *Loose in Flight* (1999). This is when and how they initially endorsed the label 'contemporary *kathak*', which was being used by critics to describe Khan's emerging practice, but which they have then consequently gone on to problematise themselves.

4 Khan here refers to iconic and internationally renowned Indian *kathak* exponents and gurus Pandit Birju Maharaja and Sreemati Kumudini Lakhia.

5 *Zero Degrees* (2005) is a critically acclaimed collaboration between Khan, the Belgian Moroccan choreographer Sidi Larbi Cherkaoui, the British Asian musician Nitin Sawhney and the British sculptor Antony Gormley. The piece functions as a confessional about a traumatic train journey undertaken by Khan and his cousin through the border checkpoint between Bangladesh and India. On this journey Khan witnessed a dead man in the arms of his wailing wife, whom no one helped or consoled for fear of being held responsible for the death. Khan's cousin categorically told him to not get involved in the situation, resulting in him carrying this memory and guilt since. *Zero Degrees* became Khan's artistic reflection on not only this guilt but also the liminal points between life and death, belonging and non-belonging and community and isolation.

6 Khan here refers to his duet *Sacred Monsters* (2006) with former ballerina Sylvie Guillem.

7 The *Big Dance Pledge* (2016) provided anyone in the world an opportunity to learn an original choreography for free, to transform it and take ownership of the piece and then to perform it anywhere in the world as part of a worldwide performance event. Khan created this three-minute choreography and a set of resources responding to the themes of identity, journey and migration and human rituals, and an especially composed music track by the British Asian musician Nitin Sawhney. Khan's choreography took into consideration a diverse range of people and levels of movement experience, placing emphasis not on technical aspects of the dance but on the communal and powerful experience of diverse groups of people dancing together. More information on the *Big Dance Pledge* is available on www.bigdance.org.uk.

8   *Kaash* (2002) was Khan's first full-length ensemble production in which he performed, made in collaboration with British Asian visual artist Anish Kapoor and musician Nitin Sawhney, who provided the visual and aural environment in which Khan's movement experiments unfolded. Using the starting points of Hindu gods, black holes, Indian time cycles, tabla, creation and destruction, *Kaash* started to explore Khan's unique performance aesthetic in and through the bodies of the ensemble of dancers who accompanied Khan in his experimentations. In 2014, *Kaash* was revived by the company on a new international cast of performers.

Bibliography

Chakravorty, Pallabi (2008) *Bells of Change: Kathak Dance, Women and Modernity in India*, Calcutta: Seagull Books.

Chatterjea, Ananya (2004) *Butting Out: Reading Resistive Choreographies through Works by Jawole Willa Jo Zollar and Chandralekha*, Middletown, CT: Wesleyan University Press.

Coorlawala, Uttara (1999) 'Ananya and Chandralekha – A Response to "Chandralekha": Negotiating the Female Body and Movement in Cultural/Political Signification', *Dance Research Journal*, 31:1, 7–12.

Mitra, Royona (2015a) *Akram Khan: Dancing New Interculturalism*, Basingstoke: Palgrave Macmillan.

Mitra, Royona (2015b) 'Akram Khan: Dance as Resistance', *Seminar Magazine*, 676, 38–42.

Piccirillo, Annalisa (2008) 'Hybrid Bodies in Transit: The "Third Language" of Contemporary *Kathak*', *Anglistica*, 12:2, 27–41.

Purkayastha, Prarthana (2014) *Indian Modern Dance, Feminism and Transnationalism*, Basingstoke: Palgrave Macmillan.

Sanders, Lorna (2004) *Akram Khan's Rush: Creative Insights*, Alton: Dance Books.

Sanders, Lorna (2008) 'Akram Khan's *ma* (2004): An Essay in Hybridisation and Productive Ambiguity', in Janet Lansdale ed., *Decentring Dancing Texts: The Challenge of Interpreting Dance*, Basingstoke: Palgrave, 55–72.

Chapter 4

African American dance revisited
Undoing master narratives in the studying and teaching of dance history

TAKIYAH NUR AMIN

Introduction

TO UNDERTAKE THE STUDY and teaching of dance history is both a personal and political act. One must make choices about what is included or excluded from the exploration and in so doing, reveal a set of intellectual priorities that can either reinforce dominant narratives or choose to move in a direction that troubles or complicates such notions. While I am generally suspicious of dichotomies, the tension inherent in this choice-making has typified my experience as both a student and teacher of dance history; I have 'danced' along this intellectual tightrope, inevitably making choices along the way about which perspectives, narratives and aesthetics will sit at the centre of inquiry. The difficulty has been that academic success in the study of dance history has long since been predicated on being conversant in master narratives about the development of performance traditions that have largely marginalized the cultural and aesthetic contributions of people of colour in general and persons of African descent in particular. Routinely, I am struck by the ways in which the work of Black dance artists and Afro-descended performance traditions are often left out, diminished, misrecognized or rendered as a mere 'contribution' to a more dominant understanding of 'western dance history', which is often read as remarkably and persistently White. On more occasions than I care to admit, my own students have articulated upon beginning their focused study of twentieth-century US dance history that the creative and artistic domain of concert dance 'belonged' to White women. Encountering such perspectives in the classroom has meant that much of my work has become a recuperative effort, meant to ensure that my students are familiar with dominant narratives in dance history in order to interrogate those legacies and offer expanded, alternative readings that centre the work of non-dominant cultural groups. This is not a novel undertaking; rather, this effort to complicate dance history is imperative in ensuring that we move towards a more complete and thorough understanding of the performance traditions, movement vocabularies and theatrical practices that constitute dance history.

The history of African American dance has been especially rich, offering a potent area of inquiry that has aided me and my students in rethinking the development of US performance traditions. As such, I proceed in this chapter to briefly define the contours of African American dance, articulate several imperatives for studying this history and outline the ways in which African American dance can be read into mainstream narratives about American concert dance traditions. I end with a brief discussion on resources for further study. The ultimate goal is to encourage readers to expand the centre of their inquiry in dance history and to complicate dominant readings of that history by becoming familiar with and conversant in the work of African American dancers and choreographers.

A brief note on terminology

I have discussed the use of the term 'Black dance' elsewhere at length and interrogated the ways in which the definition of the term has shifted historically (Amin 2011). For the purposes of this chapter, it is critical to note that by African American dance I am referring to the embodied performance traditions that both emanate from and have been reshaped by persons of African descent living in the United States, via the growth and development of the early colonies and the trans-Atlantic slave trade, also known as the middle passage or maafa.[1] While my focus in this chapter will primarily consider theatrical traditions, it should be understood that Black dance encompasses concert performance traditions as well as social and vernacular practices that are present in both sacred and secular contexts.

I have written elsewhere about the problem of referring to Africanist aesthetics in American dance as a 'contributory' force, particularly in the development of jazz dance (Amin 2014). While the language of 'contribution' may be commonplace in thinking about the ways in which people of African descent have impacted US cultural institutions, I resist this framing. 'Contribution' suggests a pre-existing, often White, cultural scaffold upon which African American aesthetics came to rest. Rather, I am interested in exploring the ways in which African American dance itself is, in many instances, the scaffold upon which other aesthetic predilections are grafted.

Why study or teach African American dance history?

In a world where White supremacist capitalist patriarchy[2] persists, some might question the value of, or argue against, the necessity of studying African American dance history. I offer that there are at least four imperatives or essential considerations that support the study of African American dance history:

- African American dance history is foundational: It is impossible to meaningfully and honestly engage the development of American performance traditions and ignore the impact of African Americans. While some historians argue that there was a sustained presence of Africans in the Americas much earlier, it is a well-documented fact that persons of African descent have been present in what we know today as the United States since 1619, when approximately twenty such persons arrived to Jamestown, Virginia, on the ship known as Cape Comfort. Their presence and the subsequent presence of other persons of African descent in the new colonies shaped the social, cultural, political and artistic context of the emerging nation.
- African American dance history is global: African American dance traditions have been exported globally as a result of trade, travel and media. While the circulation of African American musical innovations and literary work has been arguably easier to track due to written documentation, the transmission and dissemination of African American dance are of no lesser impact; this is demonstrated by the ways in which the signature of American dance abroad is often intimately tied to African American movement aesthetics.[3]
- African American dance history is contemporary: There is no single period of US history where dance and other artistic and cultural practices have not emanated from African American communities. As such, those interested in understanding current modes of performance and social/vernacular dance practices in the United States have to account for and wrestle with how African American aesthetics shape the present.
- African American dance history is generative: Social and vernacular movement vocabularies continue to emanate from African American communities. Often, as with forms like hip-hop dance, as these dance forms garner mainstream interest and valuation, they are infused into a broad range of performance contexts and are amplified both on the stage and beyond.

A critical point: the execution or performance of African American dance does not depend necessarily on the presence of African American bodies. Such movement vocabularies have been danced by bodies that claim other sociocultural identities. While African American bodies might accurately be read as a spectre in spaces where they are not present but their dance forms are, the key here is that the absence of African American bodies in motion is not a reasonable justification for refusing to study or engage these vocabularies. Plainly, the foregoing imperatives and this critical point about African American dance history articulates a framework for why studying this topic is fundamental to any accurate understanding of global dance forms today and American dance in particular.

Lastly, while one might certainly propose an inquiry into African American dance history on its own and for its own merits, it is possible to infuse this history within the teaching and study of more dominant historical narratives in order to interrogate and deconstruct them. In so doing, the work of African American dancers and the movement vocabularies and traditions that emanate from African American communities are not so much 'moved from the margins' as it is the 'centre' itself which expands; our field of inquiry becomes elastic enough to embrace the multiple movement practices that constitute American dance.

Pathways and considerations

In my own study and teaching of American dance history, I have been especially interested in the ways in which the development of modern and postmodern performance traditions are discussed. While this is of no less importance than the histories of social and vernacular vocabularies, I choose here to focus in on considering the ways in which African American dance history can be infused into discussions of American modern and postmodern performance, to expand, complicate and arguably reshape our understanding of these genres. While my interest is primarily in the twentieth century, I will offer some points of departure for those interested in considering African American dance prior to 1901.

Notably, the African American presence had been firmly established in the new colonies that would become the United States by the eighteenth century (1701–1800). Those with a keen interest in African American dance during this period might best study how movement practices emanated from plantation contexts, given the pervasiveness of enslavement in the United States during this period. Katrina Hazzard-Donald's *Jookin': The Rise of Social Dance Formations in African-American Culture* (1992) traces such practices from 1619 onward and Jacqui Malone's *Steppin' on the Blues: The Visible Rhythms of African American Dance* (1996) explores the meaning and style of dances emblematic of this period. Lynn Fauley Emery's ever popular *Black Dance from 1619 to Today* (1989) provides useful thick descriptions of plantation-era dance practices. Interestingly, it is in this period where the practice of gathering on Sundays for music and dance in Congo Square in New Orleans, among enslaved Africans, free persons who had managed to purchase themselves, and traders of primarily French and Spanish descent was commonplace, a history explored in depth by Freddi Williams Evans (2011) and others.

While the legal slave trade technically ended in 1808 by order of the US Congress, the illegal practice of smuggling African bodies into the United States persisted well into the nineteenth century (1801–1900) up to and through the end of the Civil War in 1865. A fear of the mobility of African Americans if they were to be freed from slavery fuelled the rise of White minstrel performers from the 1820s onward, who regularly lampooned African American social dance traditions by trafficking in stereotypical depictions of Black Americans in their performances for White audiences. During the post-war era known as Reconstruction, Black Codes, laws meant to restrict the social and political mobility of newly freed African Americans, proliferated across the US south at the same time that African American-derived, plantation-era dances like the cakewalk were being assimilated into American performance. In 1889, an all-Black production with White producers, *The Creole Show*, was showcased in Boston and New York City; the production ended with a cakewalk, which solidified a popular interest in African American vernacular dance forms in the United States. By the mid-1890s, ragtime, America's first indigenous popular music form and precursor to jazz, was a national phenomenon, accompanied by the two-step, slow drag and the foxtrot, all African American-derived social dances. Given the shift from minstrel shows (which regularly featured songs, dances and skits) to vaudeville performances (which often included all of the former performance styles, plus acrobatics, comedy, magic acts, jugglers and trained animals) by the end of the era and into the early decades of the twentieth century, African American popular music and dance styles were firmly ensconced in American popular culture, as they blended with European aesthetics and cultural influences.

Dance scholars generally date the experimental roots of American modern dance to the early explorations of artists like Isadora Duncan, Loie Fuller and Ruth St Denis in the late 1890s and earliest years of the twentieth century. It is of some interest perhaps to consider that at the same time that these dancers were engaging both naturalist and orientalist modes of expression, African Americans were largely locked in a long freedom struggle for rights, protection and access, indicated by the establishment of the Niagara Movement, a Black civil rights organization, in 1905 and the founding of the National Association for the Advancement of Colored People (NAACP) in 1909. Those interested in dance history might do well to consider the implications of White women dancers exploring 'freedom of movement' during the same period when African Americans were fighting the instantiation of Jim Crow laws that restricted their mobility and political access from Reconstruction up to and through this period; Jim Crow laws did not effectively come to an end until some six decades later.

In 1914, the same year that World War I began, Ruth St Denis and Ted Shawn established Denishawn, their training school for modern dance. At the close of the war in 1918 and into the following year, African Americans were subject to lynching and increased racial terror in response to a greater demand for political access and equality after having served the United States during the war. The summer of 1919 is known historically as 'Red Summer' due to the more than eighty recorded lynchings of African Americans during the period. The violence and economic exploitation of African Americans in the United States spawned the 'Great Migration', a period when African Americans flocked to northern cities, looking for better living conditions and work. It is through this migration that dances like the black bottom, the charleston, jitterbug and other social dances, which had been popular in the south, found their way into Harlem and were propagated in various urban dance halls. White Americans in urban centres quickly learned these social dances, which became a hallmark of newly loosened social etiquette, a stark contrast to dances like the waltz and polka, which had been popular in previous years.

Generally, the period from 1917 to 1928 marked an increase in African Americans advocating for full political and social access, a refusal to submit to Jim Crow laws and a flourishing of African American art, known as the New Negro movement. This term, derived from Alain Leroy Locke's edited collection, *The New Negro: An Interpretation* (1925), was made popular during the Harlem Renaissance, a literary and artistic outgrowth of the period. While White modern dancer Helen Tamiris is heralded for her work choreographing and performing a suite of dances to Negro spirituals in the late 1920s and into the early 1940s, it is a lesser celebrated fact that Black dancers were experimenting with traditional African dances, non-narrative dances and works inspired by African American spirituals on the campuses of some historically Black colleges and universities, most notably Hampton Institute (now Hampton University), as early as 1920.[4] At the same time, African American-derived social dances were increasingly popularized through Broadway shows like *Shuffle Along* (1921) and *Runnin' Wild* (1923) and hyperstylized through theatrical revues like the Ziegfield and Greenwich Village Follies. One might consider how the shift away from dance as an entertainment form on the part of several modern dance 'pioneers' to a focus on dance as art was occasioned by a desire to distance oneself from the African American-tinged popular culture sweeping the United States at that time. Isadora Duncan's insistence that a truly 'American' dance would be absent of the 'sensual lilt of jazz', something she proclaimed as the expression of the 'primitive savage', and that the charleston, a Black vernacular dance, was akin to 'tottering ape-like convulsions' may provide a useful clue in this regard (1927: 306–307).

By 1926, when Martha Graham established her centre for contemporary dance after breaking with Denishawn, she was just one of many dancers working in New York pursuing new pathways and possibilities for movement. Recognized as the first African American modern dancer, Hemsley Winfield made his debut in the play *Wade in the Water* in 1927 and performed later that year in Oscar Wilde's *Salome*. By 1931, Winfield danced alongside former Denishawn student and fellow African American dancer Edna Guy in a concert titled *First Negro Dance Recital in America* in April of that year. The 1930s continued to be a prolific period for African American modern dancers. While dominant narratives of the period might prioritize the work of Doris Humphrey, Charles Weidman, Hanya Holm and other members of the famed New Dance Group, it is important to note that African American dancers, including Winfield, Katherine Dunham and others, were active during the era of interest, with Dunham establishing her short-lived company Ballet Negre in 1930 and Winfield choreographing for and performing in the Metropolitan Opera Company's *The Emperor Jones* (1931). The shape of American modern dance performance in this period was also prominently impacted by Asadata Dafora, an immigrant from Sierra Leone whose music and dance contributions included the 1934 work *Kykunkor*, a full-length music and dance drama based on African-derived material. During this period, known widely as the Great Depression, American unemployment was tempered by broad-based policies known as the New Deal, and while choreographers like Graham, Weidman and others were active in modern dance, their efforts existed alongside and in conversation with the work of African American dancers, including those mentioned earlier, as well as Herbie Harper, Marjorie Witt Johnson, Add Bates and countless others.

From 1939 to 1945 World War II gripped the global economy and cultural milieu. Katherine Dunham's career continued to flourish with her work on Broadway and in film and positioned her as an iconic and international star at the same time that other African American artists continued to explore concert dance. Notably, in 1943, Felicia Sorel and Wilson Williams created the Negro Dance Company, performing works by Anna Sokolow, a prolific American-born dancer/choreographer of Russian Jewish heritage. Against the backdrop of a prolonged and protracted war, Americans witnessed the failure of the passage of anti-lynching legislation (again) and increased police brutality and unemployment in urban areas. It is in this context that Trinidadian-born dancer and choreographer Pearl Primus debuted *Strange Fruit* (1943), an anti-lynching solo, alongside two other protest dances, *Rock, Daniel* and *Hard Time Blues*. By the close of the war in 1945, Katherine Dunham had established her school in New York City, and in 1946, African American dancers Talley Beatty, Joe Nash, Alma Sutton and Primus performed on Broadway in a revival production of *Showboat*, choreographed by Helen Tamiris. The collaboration between dancers of African descent and others is an oft-untold story in mainstream discussions of the development of American dance and performance traditions.

The post-war period leading up to 1950 saw a flurry of activity in American dance. In 1947, Talley Beatty choreographed his celebrated work, *Southern Landscape*, a five-part suite that explored American history during the reconstruction era. Notably, the plot of the work concerned a group of multiracial farmers who are living peacefully until the community is obliterated by the Ku Klux Klan. African American dancer Donald McKayle made his debut with the New Dance Group in 1948 before performing on Broadway and dancing as a guest artist with Anna Sokolow and Merce Cunningham some two years later. During the same year, Pearl Primus earned what would become the last Rosenwald Fellowship to study dances in Africa for eighteen months; these studies formed the basis for many of her subsequent choreographic explorations. While mainstream narratives of this period might prioritize the work of the 'second generation' of American modern dancers (i.e. students of Martha Graham, Doris Humphrey, Charles Weidman and Hanya Holm), African American dancers were prolific during this period and were sometimes collaborating with these more recognized dance pioneers.

The turbulent decade of the 1950s was rife with conflict, including the Korean War (1950–1953), the beginnings of the Vietnam War (which extended until

1975), McCarthyism (the practice of accusing others of subversion or treason without regard for evidence) and the end of legal school segregation on racial grounds in 1954. The persistence of Jim Crow laws and post-war racial violence encouraged many African American dancers to explore explicitly Black themes in their choreographic endeavours, including Katherine Dunham's controversial anti-lynching work, *Southland*, in 1951 and Donald McKayle's ode to abolitionist Harriet Tubman in *Her Name Is Harriet* in 1952. While McKayle performed with Anna Sokolow and Merce Cunningham during this period, newcomer Alvin Ailey took over the direction of the Lester Horton Dance Theater upon his death in 1953. Pearl Primus continued to explore dance vocabularies across the Black diaspora, extending her formal research into the West Indies. Concurrently, choreographers Merce Cunningham, Paul Taylor and Erick Hawkins were exploring abstraction in dance, free-flowing balletic movement and nature-inspired dance, respectively. Notably, the dance company established by Alvin Ailey in this period would become the premiere repertory company for American modern dance over the next three decades; the company's stunning debut at the 92nd Street Y in New York City in 1958 was only the beginning of a global love affair with Ailey's dance theatre work.

The simmering racial and cultural politics of the 1950s gave way to the height of the civil rights movement in the United States in the 1960s. Against the backdrop of this broad-based movement to end legal segregation and racial terrorism, African American dancers continued to expand and explore the boundaries of their creativity. While protestors demonstrated for access to services at lunch counters across the American south and civil rights workers risked their lives to register voters nationally, Thelma Hill and Alvin Ailey collaborated to found and develop the Clark Center for the Performing Arts (1960). Notably, the Clark Center became the creative home for the Alvin Ailey American Dance Theatre and for scores of other African American dancers, including Fred Benjamin, Lavinia Williams and Rod Rodgers. This decade posed concerns for many dance artists who considered whether narrative or topical work should typify modern dance as opposed to favouring more avant-garde approaches to performance. From 1962 to 1968, dancers including Trisha Brown, Steve Paxton, Lucinda Childs, Yvonne Rainer and others inaugurated what has become known in dance studies circles as the Judson period, named after the flexible arts space at Judson Church in New York City. These 'Judsonian' artists favoured minimalist approaches, pedestrian movement and a blurring of the lines between performer and audience. Notably, African American dancers were influenced by, and active in, this push towards a more cutting-edge approach to dance, including Gus Solomons, Jr., Joan Miller and Blondell Cummings. Conversely, many Black artists favoured an approach to dance that prioritized thematic material, theatrical approaches and connections with the community; this ethos encompassed the work of choreographers like Alvin Ailey, Eleo Pomare and Jeraldyne Blunden, founder of the Dayton Contemporary Dance Company. While mainstream dance histories tend to prioritize a focus on the Judson movement, the 1960s was an era that held many perspectives on dance, embodied in the work of several Black dancers emboldened by the US-based Black Power and Black Arts movements (1960–1975); choreographic examples include Eleo Pomare's *Blues for the Jungle* (1966) and *Narcissus Rising* (1968), Joan Miller's *Pass Fe White* (1970) and Alvin Ailey's *Cry* (1971), among other diverse works by Black dance-makers in this period.

Contextualized by the Nixon presidency, persistence of the Vietnam War and demand for Black power in urban communities across the United States, the 1970s saw dancers less concerned with fidelity to specific techniques or approaches to movement. Many artists sought to rethink what might count or qualify as dance (like Anna Halprin, Meredith Monk and Pilobolus) while others, like Twyla Tharp, favoured a return to virtuosic movements that were more akin to the pre-Judson period. In the 1970s, African American dancers, including Jawole Willa Jo Zollar and Dianne McIntyre, chose to use narrative and dance to explore untold and undertold stories from the Black experience, as did choreographers George Faison and Garth Fagan. From the advent of the 1980s to the close of the twentieth century, modern and postmodern dancers embraced the idea of dance as a site for autobiography, probing of one's identity, social histories and personal storytelling; choreographic examples include Bill T. Jones's *Still/Here* (1994) and *The Breathing Show* (2000), Bebe Miller's *Going to the Wall* (1998) and Cynthia Oliver's *SHEMAD* (2000). Contemporarily, American dancers have deepened their connection and collaborations with artists from all over the globe, with African American dancers especially developing projects over the last twenty-five years with artists from throughout the African diaspora. Plainly, the creative labour of Black dancers has been integral to the development of modern and postmodern dance history in the United States, from its earliest inklings up to and through the contemporary period. The ways in which African American dancers responded to the social, political and aesthetic contexts in which they found themselves is no less consequential than the work of other artists – in fact, the history of US concert dance traditions is, arguably, woefully incomplete without an understanding of their ongoing work in this regard. Moreover, one might consider that many of the African American dancers noted here established pick-up groups or companies that provided opportunities to explore dance, perform and be paid, allowing dancers across racial lines to benefit. As such, African American dancers are as much a part of the aesthetic history and entrepreneurial lineage of modern and postmodern dance as their counterparts from other cultural backgrounds.

A brief note on resources

While the foregoing narrative is by no means exhaustive, I have endeavoured to demonstrate that African American dance history is inextricably linked to explorations of American performance and concert dance traditions. I can recall during my years of undergraduate study feeling alienated and frustrated in my dance history courses. It was appalling to me, even at that young age, that one might endeavour to teach the history of American performance without critical attention to African American dance practices and artists. Often my frustration was met with the explanation that there were simply not enough resources available to teach African American dance history and that well-meaning faculty simply could not teach content without accessible resources for students. While this explanation raises serious questions about power and access – that is, whose work and contributions are preserved and written into the narrative for further study – scholars in the area of critical dance studies and other fields have worked diligently to change this absence for several decades. Academic dance publications like *Dance Chronicle* and *Dance Research Journal* (DRJ) have published articles on African American dance history that have passed through rigorous peer review. Journals in the field of Africana studies, including the *Journal of Pan African Studies* (JPAS) and *The Black Scholar* (TBS), have devoted special issues to contemporary considerations of Black dance, more broadly. Similarly, the *Journal of Dance Education* (JODE) has published scholarship on infusing African American dance history into the curriculum and how to structurally diversify course offerings. Dance departments in the United States have slowly, but increasingly, hired faculty members who specialize in movement vocabularies of the African diaspora, including African American dance forms like jazz and hip-hop. Organizations exist to promote, affirm and preserve Black dance traditions, including the following:

- IABD. The International Association of Blacks in Dance preserves and promotes dance by people of African ancestry or origin, and assists and increases opportunities for artists in advocacy, audience development, education, funding, networking, performance, philosophical dialogue, and touring. (www.iabdassociation.org)
- CADD. The Collegium for African Diaspora Dance is an egalitarian community of scholars and artists committed to exploring, promoting and engaging African diaspora dance as a resource and method of aesthetic identity. Through conferences, roundtables, publications and public events, CADD aims to facilitate interdisciplinary inquiry that captures the variety of topics, approaches and methods that might constitute Black dance studies. (www.cadd-online.org)

Additionally, African American dance scholars, including Kariamu Welsh, Thomas F. DeFrantz, John Perpener, Brenda Dixon-Gottschild and many others, have published book-length inquiries into the multifaceted legacies of African American dance. Digital resources, including the website for the three-part PBS documentary series *Free to Dance*, which 'chronicles the crucial role that African American choreographers and dancers have played in the development of modern dance as an American art form' (www.thirteen.org/freetodance/), are readily available. While there are areas of inquiry within the context of African diaspora dance that are worthy and ripe for deeper research and study, there are increasingly abundant resources for those interested in revisiting African American dance beyond dominant formulations of the western theatrical dance and performance tradition. There is no reasonable excuse to exclude this information from one's research or teaching.

Notes

1 The word 'maafa' (pronounced 'ma - ah-fah') comes from the Swahili language and refers to the atrocities inflicted upon African people, including the slave trade, colonialism, imperialism and contemporary modes of oppression. The translation of the word from Swahili to English is most akin to tragedy or disaster. For more information, see Ani (1994).
2 Black feminist scholar and author bell hooks began employing this term in 1999 to describe the interlocking and overlapping set of oppressions that define contemporary life, without prioritizing any singular point of identity (like race or gender) above the other. For more information, see hooks (1999).
3 In Part 2 of her book-length study of hip-hop Carla Stalling Huntington discusses at length the global circulation of hip-hop dance as an international commodity and ties it to historical circulations of other African American art forms. See Huntington (2007).
4 Historically Black colleges and universities, known colloquially as 'HBCUs', are institutions of higher education that exist in the United States which were established prior to 1964. While these schools have always welcomed students of other races, they were each founded with the primary purpose of serving the African American community given that Black students were legally disallowed to attend most other American colleges and universities. Most HBCUs were founded after the close of the US Civil War in 1865 and over 100 of these institutions still exist today.

Bibliography

Amin, Takiyah N. (2011) 'A Terminology of Difference: Making the Case for Black Dance in the 21st Century and Beyond', *Journal of Pan African Studies*, 4:6, 7–15.

——— (2014) 'The African Origins of an American Art Form', in Lindsay Guarino and Wendy Oliver eds., *Jazz Dance: A History of Its Roots and Branches*, Gainesville: University of Florida Press, 35–44.

Ani, Marimba (1994) *Let the Circle Be Unbroken: The Implications of African Spirituality in the Diaspora*, Trenton: Red Sea Press.

Brown, Jean M. and Naomi Mindlin (1989) *The Vision of Modern Dance: In the Words of Its Creators*, Hightstown: Princeton Book.

DeFrantz, Thomas (2004) *Dancing Revelations: Alvin Ailey's Embodiment of African American Culture*, New York: Oxford University Press.

Duncan, Isadora (1927) *My Life*, New York: Boni & Liveright.

Evans, Freddi Williams (2011) *Congo Square: African Roots in New Orleans*, Lafayette: University of Louisiana at Lafayette.

Fauley Emery, Lynn (1989) *Black Dance from 1619 to Today*, Hightstown: Princeton Book.

Foner, Eric (2011) *Give Me Liberty!: An American History*, New York: W.W. Norton.

Hazzard-Donald, Katrina (1992) *Jookin': The Rise of Social Dance Formations in African-American Culture*, Philadelphia: Temple University Press.

hooks, bell (2004) *The Will to Change: Men, Masculinity and Love*, New York: Washington Square Press.

Huntington, Carla Stalling (2007) *Hip-Hop: Meanings and Messages*, Jefferson: McFarland.

Locke, Alain Leroy, ed. (1925) *The New Negro: An Interpretation*, New York: Albert and Charles Boni.

Malone, Jacqui (1996) *Steppin' on the Blues: The Visible Rhythms of African American Dance*, Columbus: University of Illinois Press.

Perpener, John O. III (2001) *African-American Concert Dance: The Harlem Renaissance and Beyond*, Urbana: University of Illinois Press.

Reynolds, Nancy and Malcolm McCormick (2003) *No Fixed Points: Dance in the Twentieth Century*, New Haven: Yale University Press.

Chapter 5

Dance works, concepts and historiography

ANNA PAKES

LINCOLN KIRSTEIN'S (1984) *Four Centuries of Ballet: Fifty Masterworks* presents a history of theatrical dance from the sixteenth to the twentieth century. As the back cover proclaims, the story is told through Kirstein's 'penetrating interpretations of 50 seminal works of theatrical dance'. Kirstein begins his chronological 'conspect' of ballets with an account of the *Ballet des Polonais* (1573), ending roughly 200 pages later with Frederick Ashton's *Enigma Variations* (1968). The volume is erudite, impressive in scope, rich in historical detail and lavishly illustrated. Each of the fifty ballets is discussed under the same five headings: 'Priority', detailing the work's impact on the tradition; 'Precedent', recognizing continuities with earlier works; 'Politics', explaining power relations in the management and effects of dances; 'Plot or Pretext', describing the narrative or action; and 'Production', noting details of performances but 'with minimal reference to individual performers, except as they are specially used' (49). The book's focus is not performer personalities: rather, '[i]f there is a hero, it is choreography' (v). This is not a story of dancers, practices or institutions, but rather the history of ballet told as the history of its *choreographic works*.

In this essay, I question whether long-term dance history can appropriately be told as a history of choreographic works. My focus is not the inevitable selectivity of such a narrative, nor the political significance of the exclusions it operates. Rather, I want to show how the historical character of the dance work-concept itself compromises the viability of this historiographic approach. For all of its detailed attention to the diverse contexts of the ballets discussed, Kirstein's book implies an essential continuity in the way dances are conceived across four centuries. Very diverse phenomena are categorized as belonging to the same art kind, despite their different frameworks and values: they are all somehow still 'ballets' or 'works', which can be arrayed alongside one another, compared and contrasted, to reveal the evolution of the art form. Kirstein recognizes that dance has become an independent art only in the last fifty years, yet he still focuses his analysis, even of earlier ballets, on their choreography, defined as 'sequences in steps' (v) or 'a map of movement – patterns for action that ballet masters ordain by design' (4). I think that this imposes an essentially twentieth-century concept of the dance or choreographic work on earlier practice, and risks misleading the dance historian about what was at stake in such practice. This essay is not concerned so much with Kirstein's historical scholarship in relation to specific ballets, although it focuses the argument around two 'works' from his catalogue, *Le Ballet Comique de la Reine* (1581) and *Giselle* (1841). In fact, I focus less on Kirstein in particular, and more on a critical exploration of how the kind of historical story it is possible to tell – and the kind of historical understanding it is possible to develop – is affected by the way historians conceptualize the products of dance activity.

Historicizing the choreographic work-concept

Why suggest that the choreographic work is a distinctively twentieth-century concept? Clearly people danced and made dances in earlier centuries. They might even have used the word 'work' to describe what they created or performed. But did earlier practitioners understand what they made in the same (or a reasonably similar) way to twentieth-century choreographers and performers? Probably not – or, at least, it should not be assumed that they did. Although I cannot fully develop and justify this argument in a short essay, I aim to point to some reasons to question approaches that take conceptual continuity for granted.[1]

A number of other scholars agree that the modern concept of the dance or choreographic work was consolidated in the twentieth century. In Stephanie Jordan's discussion of relationships between ballet and music, for example, she discerns a shift towards conceptualizing dances as authored movement compositions, with structures set by their choreographers and composers whose artistic choices then guide performance interpretation. This 'stabilization of the dance work as an independent conceptual entity during our century, with a relatively fixed form, devised by one acknowledged choreographer and usually one composer' contrasts with 'earlier practice where ballets were highly flexible conceptions that could be edited, added to, or remoulded for different occasions and casts' (2000: 4). In other words, dances become more permanent and less provisional, moving from one context to another yet remaining relatively stable in terms of what was performed. Philosopher Renee Conroy suggests, meanwhile, that 'the idea of the dancework as a stable, enduring art object is a distinctly twentieth-century notion, one that is plausibly the product of analogizing dance to other art forms in an attempt to improve its artistic status' (Conroy 2012: 162). She too, then, emphasizes increased objective persistence and fixedness as characteristics of the (twentieth-century) dance work-concept: these were features that dance's products needed to acquire for the art form to vie with music, literature and the visual arts, where the production of scores, texts and physical objects more readily ensures the longevity of works.

Such views point to the dance work-concept as a configuration of subsidiary concepts: authorship, relative fixity, persistence and autonomy (at least to some degree) in combination. This aligns with the musical work-concept as analysed by Lydia Goehr, on whose writings my own historization of the dance work-concept draws (Pakes forthcoming). In her book *The Imaginary Museum of Musical Works* (2007), Goehr analyses ancient and modern music theory, composers' writings and the kinds of practices presupposed in both, showing how the idea(l) of the work assumes clear contours and normative force only around 1800. Prior to this, she claims, composition was an essentially pragmatic affair. Musicians were commissioned to write music, often for a specific occasion or context which shaped its artistic form. It was common for composers to borrow passages from others, and to recycle material they had developed earlier. It was also normal for performers to improvise around the composition, exercising their own musical artistry and varying elements to suit the particular circumstances of performance. But around 1800, composers began to conceive of themselves as creating original, autonomous compositions, notated in a score that set strict parameters by which performers should abide. Performance practice became governed by the ideal of *Werktreue*, that is, truth or fidelity to the work and, by implication, to the intentions of its composer. And the focus of audiences' appreciation became the authored work, implicitly arrayed alongside other objects of the same kind in a canon (or imaginary museum) of masterworks.

Goehr's book is provocative and her thesis contentious. I do not have the space here to examine in detail the extensive critical literature it has generated.[2] Rather my focus is on how her approach to historicizing the work-concept might be extended to the dance domain. Her notion of the 'imaginary museum' seems an apt description also of Kirstein's conspect of ballets, and of other approaches to dance history focused on a story of works. The dance or choreographic work-concept is arguably an even more recent concept than that of the musical work: it becomes dominant – or acquires regulative force – only with the development of modernist ballet and modern dance, although its reach extends also through subsequent dance practice. Only with the work of artists such as Michel Fokine, Vaslav Nijinsky and Martha Graham does a strong concept of choreographic authorship begin to consistently align with the expectation that choreographic structures remain stable across different instantiations, those structures governing performance interpretation and being treated as relatively permanent objects or persistent works. This is not to say, of course, that earlier centuries did not produce dances and composite entities involving dance (nor indeed that the work-concept governs all twentieth-century dance): rather, the specific configuration of related concepts which together make up the dance work-concept as it has been understood in the late modern period becomes a dominant way of thinking about dance's products only in the early twentieth century.

If this is right, then the application of the dance work-concept to earlier dance phenomena is anachronistic: they are conceived in terms that would not have been available to those responsible for their creation. Pre-twentieth-century dance works would in fact not really *be* dance works, at least for those who made and appreciated them. An approach like Lincoln Kirstein's (1984), which treats them as choreographic works in the same sense as twentieth-century ballets, risks focusing attention on features that the dances may not have had or exhibited in their own time. And the continuities between past and recent dances are overemphasized at the expense of acknowledging the otherness of the earlier dances' contexts of emergence. Below, I flesh out this schematic argument through discussion of one early dance 'work', often claimed to be the first ballet in a tradition that extends from the sixteenth century to the present day.

The *Ballet Comique* as the 'first' ballet

Although not the first 'masterwork' in Lincoln Kirstein's chronology of seminal dances, the *Ballet Comique de la Royne Louise*[3] is included as one of ten pre-eighteenth-century productions. Kirstein describes it as 'one of the first efforts to realize a coherent choreographic spectacle' (1984: 54), even though he recognizes that there are few dances and it seems closer generically to *opéra-comique* than *ballet de cour*. Elsewhere, he claims it 'can safely be labeled the "first" ballet, as we still read the term' (1969 [1935]: 151). Arnold Haskell also suggests it was '[t]he first dramatic ballet of importance from which the history of the art may be said to begin' (Haskell 1951: 17) and Richard Kraus, Walter Sorrell and Selma Jeanne Cohen all make similar claims (Chapman 1979: 259–60).

Why is the *Ballet Comique* accorded this status? Even a cursory perusal of its published record (Beaujoyeulx 1982) reveals this to be a very different sort of spectacle to later works in the ballet tradition: for a start, it is clearly a composite spectacle (as, indeed, Kirstein acknowledges) involving declamation, singing, instrumental music and machinery as well as dance. Yet the term 'ballet' in the title perhaps encourages an assumption of conceptual continuity between this and later works, that term carrying 'psychological, if not historical, force', as John Chapman suggests (1979: 259). Barbara Sparti (2011) speculates that Beaujoyeux may merely have used the term 'ballet' because it was difficult to find a word to describe this kind of composite spectacle. The term then lacked the associations – and particularly the connection with the idea of the autonomous dance work – which it subsequently acquired, and was perhaps just one among a variety of possible ways of characterizing the production. Sparti wonders whether this 'work' would have attracted the same degree of attention from dance historians had it borne the (perfectly plausible) title 'Allegory of Circé' without any mention of it being a 'ballet' (207). Selma Jeanne Cohen too notes that the accuracy of commonplace reference to this as the first ballet 'depends largely on the definition used' (Cohen 1992: 8). In short, being called a 'ballet' does not make the *Ballet Comique* a choreographic work as such works are conceptualized by later generations.

The unprecedented prominence that the *Ballet Comique* accords to its dance element is often cited as a mark of its dance historical significance. Beaujoyeux claims in the preface to his publication to have given 'first place and honour to the dance' (McClintock and McClintock 1971: 33). Yet, as even Kirstein acknowledges, the number of dances in this court spectacle is actually quite limited and Beaujoyeux's written accounts of them 'spare and non-specific', while also lacking iconographic illustration (Sparti 2011: 309–10). What is more, the idea that Beaujoyeux was a dancing master lacks supporting evidence: other sources suggest that he was Catherine de Medici's *valet de chambre*; and, while the dedicatory poem by Billard suggests he invented the *geometry* of the dance content, this does not necessarily imply that he was its choreographer as that role has been understood more recently to include responsibility for movement composition alongside overall design (Sparti 2011: 307). Thus to suggest that this is the first 'work' created by a dancing master or choreographer *and therefore* also the first to give such prominence to dance is misleading. It is clear neither that Beaujoyeux was a dancing master nor that he achieved what he claimed in the published preface regarding concentration on the dance content. The idea that the *Ballet* somehow sets a precedent for later choreographic works in which the dance element takes priority therefore also seems difficult to sustain.

The supposed influence of the *Ballet Comique* is also typically connected to the ballet's dramatic coherence. The spectacle has a dramatic through-line with clear political significance; indeed (as with other court ballets) the political function of the performance event itself shapes the thematic content of the production. The action concerns the enchantress Circe, who has enslaved the king's followers, transforming them into beasts held captive in her garden. The ballet begins with a 'fugitive gentleman' approaching King Henri III (seated in the audience) to plead for his aid. Angry Circe herself makes an *entrée*, followed by a tiered fountain carrying twelve naiads, all played by noblewomen and led by Queen Louise. They descend from the fountain to perform a dance of geometrical figures, interrupted by Circe stilling each with her rod. The enchantment is lifted by the descent of the god Mercury and the dance resumes, only to be stilled again by an increasingly enraged Circe, who enslaves Mercury himself and is then revealed presiding over her garden. Seated directly opposite King Henri in the audience, Circe embodies a challenge to his power, and the ballet thus sets up the dichotomy between good and evil that dominates the scenario. Satyrs, dryads, the gods Pan and Jupiter and the goddess Minerva all figure and, through uniting under the banner and good grace of the king, ultimately defeat the enchantress. The naiads reappear to dance a *grand ballet*, following which they present allegorical emblems to the king and his lords, who are then led in the *Grand Bal* which concludes the performance event.

The ballet's coherence around this dramatic through-line is often cited as the mark of its historical significance: 'breaking with the tradition of combining unrelated interludes of music and dance, [Beaujoyeux] used recitation, song and movement to convey a single storyline' (Cohen 1992: 8). As Cohen acknowledges, however, the production's lavish expense attracted much more contemporary attention than this dramatic cohesion. Picking up on the point, Chapman questions whether the ballet could have influenced subsequent works' aspiration towards coherence, given sixteenth-century witnesses' lack of interest in its dramaturgical construction: the *Ballet* 'lived in [these witnesses] and if they did not recognize or value dramatic coherence, then it simply was not historically important' (1979: 260). In Chapman's view, dance historians have overstated those features of the *Ballet Comique* which align with twentieth-century aesthetic values in order to position the 'work' in a narrative of evolution towards the present. And Sparti similarly criticizes more recent preoccupation with the ballet's unified plot, suggesting the need for reconsideration: '[t]his aesthetic value continues to give an unquestioned place of honor to unified works as being superior to those composed of episodes' (2011: 318). Again, then, it seems that a later concept of the dance work – as an autonomous entity cohering around a central theme or message – is applied to a phenomenon not created under that concept.

Indeed, several properties of the *Ballet Comique* seem out of kilter with the more recent conception of what a choreographic work is. Not only is the ballet in mixed mode – a composite and hybrid spectacle, as suggested earlier – but also it is participatory in a manner atypical of later choreography, where the division between performers and audience becomes more clear-cut. In the *Ballet Comique* members of the nobility performed and even those watching the earlier scenes joined in the final *grand bal* at the end. This feature connects with the ballet's explicitly political and ritual function to bring together the community while reinforcing the authority of the king. As Margaret McGowan comments, 'the power struggle between good and evil, between order and disorder, is not simply happening in a world of metaphor [. . .] but in another part of the real universe'; thus the ballet does not merely aestheticize troublesome political reality but discovers a 'different part of reality, which reflects the lived reality, and has the power to transmute it' (McGowan 1982: 33).

The *Ballet* thus clearly predates later beliefs and practices centred around the autonomy of the aesthetic, and on which the choreographic work-concept (as it develops later) partly depends: works are envisaged as structures separated and isolated from practical and political life, self-contained worlds which might symbolically represent that life without intervening directly in it. Similarly, the fact that the *Ballet Comique* was made for a specific occasion and not envisaged as an object or structure that could be repeated or instanced in other contexts sets it apart from later autonomous works. The ballet may have had influence beyond the Valois court, as Anne Daye argues with respect to its effects on the Stuart masque (2014, 2015). Yet, as she makes clear, it functioned as a model for other, *new* occasion-specific productions, not as the template for new performances *of the same* ballet. Its text proved important in allowing the *Ballet Comique* to persist as a point of reference for later practitioners and historians. But that text does not articulate a structure with the intention of enabling future performance. In this, it is unlike later dances notated in the Beauchamps-Feuillet (early eighteenth-century) or Labanotation (twentieth-century) systems, where the text or score ensured persistence by enabling new performances of the *same* movement structure.

All of the properties just identified (mixed-mode, participatory dimension, extra-aesthetic function and occasion specificity) might be present in later dance products. Yet the status of those features relative to the category of the (modern) choreographic work is different to their status relative to the *ballet de cour* (and other related contemporaneous genres). And, as Kendall Walton argues, aesthetic properties and their perception are partly determined by whether features are standard, variable or contra-standard to particular categories of art (Walton 1970). Thus, being in mixed mode and having a participatory dimension are standard features of *ballet de cour* but variable or contra-standard with respect to twentieth- and twenty-first-century dance works. Jérôme Bel's *Véronique Doisneau* (2004), for example, involves the performer verbally addressing her audience at some length (like a kind of declamation, although the tone is very different), but this feature is deliberately contra-standard for works on the opera house stage; the meaning and effect of the piece depend on the dancer being given a voice in a context where typically she would not. Likewise, political function and occasion specificity are standard with respect to *ballets de cour* but variable or contra-standard for choreographic works: dance 'happenings' in the 1960s were both political and occasion-specific but strategically so, offering a self-conscious challenge to the standard properties of aesthetic autonomy and repeatability. Unless one acknowledges the degree to which features of past dances are typical or atypical of their genre or category, one risks subsuming those dances under inappropriate concepts which distort understanding of their properties more generally. To prioritize the *Ballet Comique*'s dance element and dramatic coherence is to define that ballet in terms of characteristics standard for later choreographic works, even though they were variable or contra-standard for the categories operative when the ballet was made.

Is it not possible, however, to acknowledge that creations like the *Ballet Comique* were produced under one conception (the *ballet de cour* or *opéra-comique*) but can still be fruitfully viewed as members also of another, more recent, category? Perhaps this is what Kirstein and his colleagues are doing when they discuss this ballet as an inaugural work of ballet history. Perhaps seeing the *Ballet Comique* in terms of later concepts of choreography and work reveals aesthetic properties which have subsequently become central to the art form, but which those creations' contemporaries (lacking hindsight) could not have seen. Indeed, the application of these later concepts to earlier phenomena appears part of a conscious strategy to construct a canon of dance achievement – an imaginary museum of dance works, which justifies the artistic interest and status of the twentieth-century works that historians like Kirstein promote. As a historiographic approach, however, the strategy presents early ballets as having aesthetic properties that they arguably do not have, at least following Walton's proposal that the category of a work – and not just those features immediately apparent on that work's aesthetic surface – partly determines its aesthetic properties. For Walton, there are four key considerations when determining in which category a work is correctly perceived: (1) whether the work has numerous features that are standard within that category; (2) whether the work appears better or more interesting when perceived in a particular category; (3) whether the artist intended it to be seen as a thing of that kind; and (4) whether that category was well established and recognized in the society from which the work emerged (1970: 357–8). So whereas the interest of the work under a particular categorical ascription – when treated as a modern choreographic work, say – might be relevant, it should be balanced against other considerations. The three considerations listed all require historicization of the dance product, and awareness of the categories operative at the moment of its creation or devising.

Dances which display contra-standard features relative to the categories of their time can inaugurate new categories in which those features become standard (see Walton 1970: 352–3). For example Jérôme Bel made numerous other solo works on/with particular dancers, subsequent to *Véronique Doisneau*, creating a new category of such works, where extensive verbal narration is a standard feature.[4] Is something similar true of the *Ballet Comique* – namely that it is the first ballet in the modern sense of the term because it inaugurates a new category in which prominence of dance content and dramatic coherence are standard? The argument is difficult to sustain because it is not clear that ballets in the immediate wake of the *Ballet Comique* also have those features, or have them as a result of its influence. Only after several centuries do choreographic focus and dramatic coherence begin to define the products of dance practice, rendering their connection back to Beaujoyeux's 'work' tenuous.

Giselle, ballet and ballet-pantomime

Maybe, then, Kirstein and his contemporaries could have evaded the charge of conceptual anachronism by beginning ballet history later, with the oldest dances that are still part of today's repertoire – that is with early nineteenth-century ballets, such as *La Sylphide* (1832) and *Giselle* (1841). Yet if, as argued earlier, the concept of the choreographic work comes to prominence only in the twentieth century, these ballets also predate its consolidation. Despite being widely considered classic works of the ballet heritage, they would not really be choreographic works in the modern sense. In what follows, I will sketch how this case might be argued with respect to the ballet *Giselle*.

Conventionally, the Romantic era is celebrated as laying the foundations for modern ballet by emphasizing dance autonomy in contrast to older models: it gives new prominence to dance itself as a storytelling medium, no longer reliant on accessory media to convey its dramatic content; and it also prefigures the development of abstract or 'pure' dance through the phenomenon of the *ballet blanc*. Kirstein, for example, claims that *Giselle* in particular, 'whose pretext is dancing itself, is a milestone in establishing choreography as autonomous speech' (1984: 150). Kirstein's judgement here echoes the earlier writings of André Levinson, who criticizes late eighteenth-century *ballet d'action* on the grounds that it sacrificed dance's 'independence, its intrinsic aesthetic value [. . .] to the expression of character and sentiment' (1983 [1927]: 51). For Levinson, the dancing of Marie Taglioni, particularly in her father's ballet *La Sylphide*, allowed dance to reassert that independence, sublimated as it was in the *ballet blanc* whose effects exceed its instrumental narrative role.

This conventional view has been undercut, however, by the work of Lisa Arkin and Marian Smith (1997), and subsequent writing by Smith (2000, 2012). They highlight the modern neglect of both national dance and pantomime as crucial elements of Romantic ballet. For all the stress placed by early twentieth-century historians on the ethereal and other-worldly elements of Romantic work, national dance was much more important in terms of frequency of inclusion and stage time than the *ballets blancs* which have come to symbolize the period (Arkin and Smith 1997: 12). Nineteenth-century audiences expected ballets to offer realistic and 'plausibly authentic' representations of different cultures through national dance, set and costume design (Arkin and Smith 1997: 26, 36). These established lifelike settings for the dramas enacted, functioned as effective means of characterization and had an expressive potency which some considered superior to that of the classical *pas* (Arkin and Smith 1997: 26–7). Although Levinson and later critics have tended to downplay or ignore the importance of national dance – Levinson, for example, claiming that folk dances can be elevated only by being inclined 'towards abstraction' (Arkin and Smith 1997: 56) – it was central to the value and appeal of ballet in the nineteenth century.

Smith's detailed analysis of musical scores and libretti also makes clear the essentially dramatic character of ballet 'works' of that era: *Giselle*, for example, emerges as primarily a dramatic work with a complicated plot, a raft of major and minor characters and a roughly equal balance in terms of stage time between mime and dance (Smith 2000: 167–200). Smith examines how the characters of Bertha and Hilarion, for example, are fleshed out in the original libretto, musical score and notes on the *répétiteurs*:[5] those performers playing the roles are given long mime scenes involving description of off-stage action, specific and precise communication of fears for the future and recollection of earlier onstage events. These contribute to depicting the characters as 'well-rounded linguistic people' (Smith 2000: 177), who disagree with others on grounds that are quite explicitly elaborated and who debate at some length the relative merit of different courses of action (Smith 2000: 177–91). Today's productions of *Giselle* excise all but a tiny portion of mime content in order to give more prominence to dancing, and as a result sacrifice the wealth of realistic detail in terms of characterization and setting which constitute the dramatic fabric of the 1841 ballet. Twentieth-century revivals and scholarship mislead in presenting the ballet as 'less a mimed musical drama with dancing than a danced work with a modicum of miming in which the music plays only a minor role' (Smith 2000: 177).

If the conventional view of Romantic ballet applies 'twentieth-century performance practice and aesthetic preference to our assessments of the past' (Arkin and Smith 1997: 13), it also seems anachronistically to employ the twentieth-century concept of the choreographic work when examining nineteenth-century practice in which other categories operated. In overemphasizing the importance of the *ballet blanc*, the autonomy of the 'pure' (verging on abstract) dance work is privileged over the hybridity of the ballet-pantomime combining dramatic, musical and choreographic elements. Again, the use of the term 'ballet' may foster a misconception of conceptual continuity. *Giselle* tends to be described as a 'ballet' rather than a 'ballet-pantomime'. This foreshortening of the generic label effectively erases reference to pantomime as an important feature of the production, indeed a standard property for works in this category. When the products of Romantic ballet are treated as ballets rather than as *ballets-pantomimes*, their dramatic and hybrid character is downplayed, predisposing audiences and readers to think of them as modern ballets in the same sense as the works of (say) Fokine and Balanchine.

The shift connects with modernist arguments about medium specificity: the notion that art forms should aspire to a concentration on the media specific to particular art forms, distinguishing them from others. Levinson's claims about dance being sacrificed to 'the expression of character and sentiment' in the *ballet d'action* suggest it is contaminated by theatrical and (by extension) verbal elements, the specificity of the dance medium residing partly in its non-verbal character (this being what distinguishes dance from theatre). Yet Smith's analysis reveals how 'language lurked just below the surface of the ballet pantomime, even though the performers never actually intoned words' (Smith 2000: xiv). Also 'ballet, like opera, was meant to tell the kinds of stories that lent themselves to (indeed *required*) detailed recounting in words' (123) – it was accompanied by detailed programme synopses, and devised in concert with music that served very specific dramatic functions.[6] When later historians and restagers prioritize 'pure' and 'autonomous' dance choreography, they imply the externality of the storytelling framework. Yet that narrative and dramatic structure was central to the very conception of the *ballet-pantomime* category.

Conclusion

Kirstein's construction of an imaginary museum of dance works implies continuity in the way the products of dance practices are conceived across history. I have suggested that assuming such continuity is problematic, and that the historian needs to recognize the changing nature of the concepts embodied in dance practice and production. In particular, I have argued that imposing a twentieth-century idea of the choreographic work on ballets from the sixteenth and nineteenth centuries misleads us about what was at stake in such practice. It is not simply the presence (or absence) of certain features of properties within the dance products of the past which matters; whether those features were standard, variable or contra-standard for the categories in play at that historical moment makes a difference to the aesthetic significance appropriately attributed to them in specific cases.

My argument also has philosophical implications. It seems premised on an ontology of dances (and cultural artefacts in general) where what the creator intends the thing to be in part determines what it is: early ballets cannot really be choreographic works (partly) because that work-concept was not available to their creators. This places a certain premium on the creator's intentions, although with respect to determining the art kind or category to which a dance belongs, rather than the dance's meaning. Because dances are social phenomena, it is inappropriate to conceive of them naturalistically, as though they were just *there*, their properties arrayed on their aesthetic surface. Following Walton, their properties are partly determined by the concepts that govern their creation. But my argument also implies the possibility of those concepts changing – of new categories being generated or coming to prominence at different historical moments. There is, then, a story to be told about the continuities between different concepts or categories, alongside any attempt to draw attention to their discontinuities. But in recognizing this, and trying to tell that story, we should guard against a form of present-oriented conceptual anachronism which unreflexively subsumes earlier dances under modern categories. We should avoid, in other words, constructing an imaginary museum where little thought is given to the nature of the display cases and accompanying labels which shape perception and interpretation of the dances exhibited.

Notes

1   See Pakes (forthcoming), Part 1, for a more detailed historicization of the dance work-concept. I offer merely a summary of those arguments here: they are better justified and supported by evidence in the longer discussion.
2   See, for example, Davies (2001), pp. 86–91; Hagberg (1994) and Sharpe (1993).

3   The *Ballet Comique de la Reine* (the spelling is often modernized) was performed in 1581 at the French court, as part and culmination of two weeks of festivities celebrating the marriage of the Duc de Joyeuse to Mademoiselle Vaudemont, half-sister to Queen Louise, who commissioned the ballet. A published account by the event's orchestrator, Balthazar de Beaujoyeux (the French form of his Italian name Baldassare de Belgiojoso), appeared in 1582 (Beaujoyeulx 1982; McClintock and McClintock 1971). See also Daye (2014, 2015) and Franko (2015 [1993]: 31–50) for detailed discussion.
4   For example *Lutz Förster* (2009) and *Cédric Andrieux* (2009), for the eponymous dancers from the Bausch and Cunningham companies respectively.
5   *Répétiteurs* are musical scores, reductions of full orchestral scores, used by ballet masters to restage ballets. Some surviving examples include fairly extensive notes appended to the music line by line, detailing the action and/or emotions which accompany those sections of the music. For an extended discussion of the nature, role and historical significance of the *répétiteur*, see Day (2008).
6   For a discussion of the narrative and dramatic functions of ballet-pantomime music generally, see Smith (2000), especially pp. 3–18, and Jordan (1981). Smith (2000) also includes an analysis of *Giselle* (pp. 167–200) which highlights the dramatic role of the music. See the essays by Butkas Ertz and Nørlyng in Smith (2012) for similar analyses of the musical scores for *La Sylphide*.

Bibliography

Arkin, Lisa and Marian Smith (1997) 'National Dance in the Romantic Ballet', in Lynn Garafola ed. *Rethinking the Sylph: New Perspectives on the Romantic Ballet*, Middletown: Wesleyan University Press, 11–56.

Beaujoyeulx, Balthazar de (1982) *Le Balet Comique by Balthazar de Beaujoyeulx, 1581*, facsimile with introduction by Margaret McGowan, Binghamton: Center for Medieval and Renaissance Studies.

Chapman, John (1979) 'The Aesthetic Interpretation of Dance History', *Dance Chronicle*, 3:3, 254–274.

Cohen, Selma Jeanne (1992) *Dance as a Theatre Art: Source Readings in Dance History from 1581 to the Present*, Princeton: Princeton Book.

Conroy, Renee (2012) 'Dance', in Anna Christina Ribeiro ed. *The Continuum Companion to Aesthetics*, London: Continuum, 156–170.

Davies, Stephen (2001) *Musical Works and Performances*, Oxford: Clarendon Press.

Day, David (2008) *The Annotated violon répétiteur and Early Romantic Ballet at the Théâtre Royal de Bruxelles (1815–1830)*, PhD thesis, New York: New York University.

Daye, Anne (2014) 'The Role of *Le Balet Comique* in Forging the Stuart Masque: Part 1, The Jacobean Initiative', *Dance Research*, 32:2, 185–207.
Daye, Anne (2015) 'The Role of *Le Balet Comique* in Forging the Stuart Masque: Part 2, Continuation', *Dance Research*, 33:1, 50–69.
Franko, Mark (2015 [1993]) *Dance as Text: Ideologies of the Baroque Body*, revised edition, New York: Oxford University Press.
Goehr, Lydia (2007) *The Imaginary Museum of Musical Works: An Essay in the Philosophy of Music*, revised edition (first ed. 1992), Oxford: Oxford University Press.
Hagberg, Garry L. (1994) 'Review: *The Imaginary Museum of Musical Works* by Lydia Goehr', *Journal of Aesthetic Education*, 28:4, 99–102.
Haskell, Arnold (1951) *Ballet, a Complete Guide to Appreciation: History, Aesthetics, Ballets, Dancers*, revised edition, Harmondsworth: Penguin.
Jordan, Stephanie (1981) 'The Role of the Ballet Composer at the Paris Opéra: 1820–1850', *Dance Chronicle*, 4:4, 374–388.
Jordan, Stephanie (2000) *Moving Music: Dialogues with Music in Twentieth-Century Ballet*, London: Dance Books.
Kirstein, Lincoln (1969 [1935]) *Dance: A Short History of Classical Theatrical Dancing* (first published in 1935), New York: Dance Horizons.
Kirstein, Lincoln (1984) *Four Centuries of Ballet: Fifty Masterworks*, revised edition (first ed. 1970), New York: Dover.
Levinson, André (1983 [1927]) 'The Idea of the Dance from Aristotle to Mallarmé', in Roger Copeland and Marshall Cohen eds. *What Is Dance?* Oxford: Oxford University Press, 47–55.
McClintock, Carol and Lander McClintock (1971) *Le Balet Comique de la Royne*, English translation, New York: American Institute of Musicology.
McGowan, Margaret (1982) 'Introduction', in Balthazar de Beaujoyeulx, *Le Balet Comique by Balthazar de Beaujoyeulx, 1581*, Binghamton: Center for Medieval and Renaissance Studies, 7–49.
Pakes, Anna (forthcoming) *Choreography Invisible: The Disappearing Work of Dance*, Oxford: Oxford University Press.
Sharpe, R. A. (1993) 'Review: *The Imaginary Museum of Musical Works* by Lydia Goehr', *British Journal of Aesthetics*, 33:3, 292–295.
Smith, Marian (2000) *Ballet and Opera in the Age of Giselle*, Princeton: Princeton University Press.
Smith, Marian (2012) 'Levinson's *Sylphide* and the Danseur's Bad Reputation', in Marian Smith ed. *La Sylphide: Paris 1832 and Beyond*, Alton: Dance Books, 258–290.
Smith, Marian ed. (2012) *La Sylphide: Paris 1832 and Beyond*, Alton: Dance Books.
Sparti, Barbara (2011) 'Dance and Historiography: *Le Balet Comique de la Royne*, an Italian Perspective', in Ann Buckley and Cynthia J. Cyrus eds. *Music, Dance and Society: Medieval and Renaissance Studies in Memory of Ingrid Brainard*, Kalamazoo: Western Michigan University Press, 304–322.
Walton, Kendall (1970) 'Categories of Art', *The Philosophical Review*, 79:3, 334–367.

Chapter 6

Reconstruction and dance as embodied textual practice[1]

HELEN THOMAS

Introduction

SINCE THE MID-1980s, we have witnessed an increasing concern to reconstruct and preserve dances from the early American modern dance era in particular, and early twentieth-century modern ballet (Copeland 1994). Canadian dance professionals have also sought to recover the barely documented Canadian modern dance tradition (Adams 1992). There has also been an interest in reconstructing the work of German modern dance innovators such as Rudolf Laban (Rubidge 1985), Mary Wigman (Manning 1993) and Kurt Jooss (Lidbury 2000). Increasingly, too, internationally renowned choreographers of today like Merce Cunningham and Paul Taylor set their earlier 'company made' dances on other contemporary dance companies across the globe, as well as on their own. Taylor and Cunningham have also set their work on classically based companies (Kane 2000). Dance preservation, in effect, has become a minor industry. This professional dance interest has been accompanied by the development of healthy debates within dance scholarship regarding the politics of reconstruction and preservation. For example, in 1984, *The Drama Review* produced a dedicated issue on reconstruction (in theatre, music and dance), which opened up the debate to a wider audience than the dance notation/reconstruction/history audience where it traditionally resided (*The Drama Review* 1984). The 1992 Society of Dance History Scholars Conference at Rutgers University, New Brunswick, entitled *Dance Reconstructed: Modern Dance Art, Past, Present, Future* (proceedings published in 1993), opened up a number of divergent practical and theoretical issues. These were developed further in the first major European conference on the topic, which was held at Roehampton Institute in London in 1997. The impetus for *Preservation Politics: Dance Revived, Reconstructed, Remade*, which addressed ballet and modern dance forms, stemmed from 'strong signals' emanating from both the profession and dance scholars (Jordan 2000). In this chapter, I explore some of the theoretical issues that dance scholars have raised in regard to reconstruction and preservation (see Thomas 2003 for a broader discussion of the issues).

The absence of a 'usable' past[2]

The first question we might want to ask is: why reconstruct past dances in the first place? The answer to this from the perspective of dance scholarship generally refers back to dance's ephemeral nature and the need to search for a usable past upon which to build a substantive tangible tradition. Dance, as a performance art, unlike fine art or literature, does not leave behind it material objects, which remain 'relatively' stable in the sense that they can be touched, felt or looked at in their extant context. Rather, dance, according to Marcia Siegel (1968: 1) 'is an event that disappears in the very act of materializing'. Despite advances in technologies for recording dance, the majority of dance events unfold in what phenomenologists term the 'vivid present' – the here and now. A few dances do 'live on' over time or at least for some time by being kept in repertory. These have mostly been passed down in a performative manner from dancer to dancer. Drama is also a performance art but it is possible, for the most part, to refer to a script upon which the 'original' performance was based (I will return to the question of 'the original' later). Western music, too, has a long-established 'universal' system of notation and composers and performers are musically literate. Many attempts have been made to develop movement notation systems over the past five centuries, some of which were published and were popular in their time, although they soon died out (Hutchinson 1977). The twentieth century witnessed the rise of various systems of notation, some of which gained a considerable impact in dance and related areas of movement (see Hutchinson Guest 1984 for a historical survey of dance notation and Davies 1975 for a survey of major systems of recording movement and dance developed in the twentieth century). As yet, there is no one universally accepted system of dance notation, although Choreology (devised by Joan and Rudolf Benesh [1956] for recording ballet) and Labanotation (US) or Kinetography Laban (Europe) (based on the system invented by Rudolf Laban [1928]), have made increasing gains in terms of development and usage since they were invented. Choreographers and dancers of today, unlike their counterparts in music, are generally not literate in movement notation (Van Zile 1985–6), although a few, such as Cunningham, prefer to develop a method for their own use. Moreover, choreographers are generally more interested in creating new works as opposed to reworking old ones.

The overwhelming fact is that the traces of thousands of past choreographies can be found in scattered fragments which marked the existence of the privileged few dancers/choreographers over the many: critical commentaries; treatises of the famous dancing masters; dance histories; photographs; snatches on film here and there; the bodily memories of dancers who performed in them (if they are still alive) and/or transmitted their bodily knowledge to other dancing bodies; the mind's eye of the audience members who witnessed them and so on.

It is hardly surprising, then, that the history of dance is generally viewed as a history of 'lost' dances. One of the positivist reasons offered for reconstructing past dances is that filling in the 'blanks' of the dance 'story' offers a more inclusive and therefore more truthful picture of dance history. On one level, this viewpoint seems more democratic in regard to, for example, excavating and revealing African American concert dance artists' contributions to the development of the mainstream concert dance tradition in America, a subject which has been shrouded in a veil of silence in dance history and criticism until recently. John Perpener's (2001) detailed history of the careers of eight African American concert dance artists, who were mostly written out of dance history, attempts to do just this (see also de Frantz 2002). In the process, he highlights the unspoken but embedded assumption in European–American aesthetics that 'whiteness was a prerequisite for the universality in *art*' (Perpener 2001: 203) [my emphasis]. 'Whiteness was the background against which all other points of view were projected in a dichotomy of superiority and inferiority' (Perpener 2001: 203).

But on another level, the concern to fill in the blanks of the dance story shows signs of exclusivity too. It is overwhelmingly theatrical, 'high art' past dances that are deemed suitable, worthy candidates for reconstruction. Thus, what gets reconstructed or preserved remains highly selective. This selective preservation is underpinned by a vertical (hierarchical) concept of culture, which stems from the 'culture and civilisation tradition' in which culture is defined as 'the best that has been thought and said'. In this case, high art *per se* is the yardstick by which all other cultural forms and practices are measured. Thus, it sustains the high art/popular cultural divide, which postmodernist cultural criticism has so thoroughly challenged in recent years. By contrast, there is a sustained history of recording social or 'folk' dance traditions in central and eastern Europe, which is underscored by a broader, horizontal model of culture, which has its roots in the folklorist tradition (see Felföldi 1999; Giurchescu 1999) and the notion of culture as a way of life of a people or 'folk'. In this chapter, the problematics of dance reconstruction will be aired with reference to the vertical dimension, with examples drawn from early modern dance and modern ballet. However, it should be noted that many of the key concerns regarding authenticity, reproducibility and interpretivity, which animate debates on the reconstruction of early modern dances and modern ballet, are also visible in the ethnochoreological tradition of central and eastern Europe.

Advocates of dance reconstruction/preservation often rationalise the venture on the grounds that it offers the possibility of a kind of permanency to this ephemeral form, which in turn will facilitate a continuing cycle of cultural reproduction and perhaps enhance dance's traditional lowly status as an art form. In so doing, they sometimes unwittingly shift from the particular to the general by appealing to a well-worn trope concerning the universality of dance. The following quotation is a case in point:

> Knowledge of our dance heritage – kinaesthetically, visually and culturally – gives meaning and context to the dance works of today. Dance has been an essential and significant part of man's past, and too often it has been undervalued because of its ephemeral nature and lack of appropriate technological and notation systems to document dance's rich contributions to culture. As an art form and cultural expression, dance deserves rightful recognition.
> (Pernod and Ginsberg 1997: 4)

The idea of permanence in regard to those other arts which advocates of reconstruction often invoke has, of course, already been questioned in music (see Taruskin 1995), literature (see Thompson 2000) and fine art also, as the intentionally temporary artworks and installations created by contemporary artists show only too well. I will return to the concern to create a usable past on which to establish a firm dance heritage later on in the chapter. Having explored the reasoning behind the desire to reconstruct dances in the first place, I now wish to consider why this minor dance preservation industry has arisen in recent years.

Sally Kriegsman (1993) suggests a number of related social, biological and artistic reasons for the drive towards reconstruction and preservation in the context of dance in the US. To begin with, HIV/AIDS has had a significant impact on the theatre arts community in general. A number of performers and choreographers have had their life cut short before they had the opportunity to fulfil their promise and have their work recorded. Second, as modern dance choreographers, dancers and teachers become old or die, the possibility of passing down dances is lost. But this is also the case with ballet. When Nancy Reynolds (2000: 52) embarked on her video programme to 'retrieve fragments of Balanchine choreography no longer performed', she went initially to older dancers such as Dame Alicia Markova who had worked with him, almost by chance rather than design. However, she soon found an increasing sense of urgency to work with older dancers when one of the three famous 'baby ballerinas' who performed with the Ballet Russe de Monte Carlo in the 1930s, Tamara Toumanova, died before she could assist Reynolds with the 'original' *Mozartiana*. Third, America historically is a polyglot culture and new immigrants to the US often seek to preserve their 'native' dance traditions in their new social setting and thereby pass on their cultural traditions. Fourth, the field of dance has become aware of the richness and diversity of 'home grown' dance forms. Kriegsman notes the desire to explore and celebrate the influences of African traditions on African American and 'mainstream' modern dance practices, which had previously gone unrecognised. In times of rapid change and fragmentation, she suggests, a search for 'roots' can offer a sense of continuity. Fifth, rapid developments in 'electronic reproduction' and computer technology have made it increasingly possible for choreographers and performers to have a record of their own work at little cost. As Kriegsman notes, 'a choreographer born today has a camera in her hands ready to record her first crawl' (p. 16). In so doing, choreographers and performers can 'own' their own heritage. Finally, public scrutiny and external validation have become increasingly important to artistic survival in contemporary culture. Electronic recording of created dance works may be offered as records of choreographic achievement through which the artistic value of a choreographer may be externally judged in the present and the future. I would also suggest that the increasing process of rationalisation into almost every crevice of everyday life is a contributing factor in the drive to reconstruct, preserve and catalogue dance history and bring it in line with the economics of exchange. This is particularly evident in regard to the increasing concern with 'intellectual' (or creative in this case) property rights.

Addressing the 'why now' question, as Kriegsman is only too aware, leads to a number of other related questions, some of which are implied earlier. For example, what and who gets performed and recorded? What are the political and ethical consequences of reconstructing past dances? In this chapter I address these and other questions which emerge out of the discussion. But perhaps we are running on ahead of ourselves here. There appears to be an implicit assumption as to what reconstruction is. I therefore commence the next section by trying to define reconstruction. As will become clear, this is not as simple as it first appears.

'What is in a name?' Revival, reconstruction, re-creation, co-authorship, reinvention . . .

Dance researchers often use the terms reconstruction, revival and re-creation interchangeably, although some have sought to make a clear distinction between them. For Selma Jeanne Cohen (1993), for example, a revival is carried out by the choreographer him/herself. A reconstruction is made by someone else who researches the 'work'. A re-creation is concerned to capture the 'spirit of the work'. Ann Hutchinson Guest (2000: 65), on the other hand, uses the term revival to refer to a work that has been brought to life by someone using a notated score, rather like 'a musician bringing a music composition to life from a notated music score'. Unusually, Hutchinson Guest is highly 'literate' in a number of movement notations. Vaslav Nijinsky, the legendary dancer and choreographer of Diaghilev's Ballets Russes, recorded his first ballet for Diaghilev, *L'Après Midi d'un Faune* (1912), in his own system of notation. The ballet, however, was handed down over the years from dancer to dancer, without reference to Nijinsky's complex notation score. Hutchinson Guest and Claudia Jeschke deciphered the original score and subsequently translated it into Labanotation in the late 1980s, which in turn led to 'revivals' of the ballet in Naples, Montreal and New York (Hutchinson Guest 1991).

A reconstruction, according to Hutchinson Guest (2000), involves 'constructing a work anew' from a wide range of 'sources' and information, with the intention of getting as close to the original as possible. Millicent Hodson and Kenneth Archer's staging of Nijinsky's *Le Sacre du Printemps* (1913) for the Joffrey Ballet in 1987 and *Jeux* (1913) in 1996 would fall into this category. Archer and Hodson's (2000: 1) primary concern is to 'preserve only masterworks' of the twentieth century that are historically relevant and have 'contemporary relevance'. They aim to 'ensure that the reconstruction is a reasonable facsimile of the original'. They insist that in order to take on the task of bringing 'lost jewels' back to life, they have to ensure that the end product (the reconstructed work) will be founded on at least 50 per cent 'hardcore evidence for dance and design' (p. 2). Robert Joffrey, who commissioned *Le Sacre*, estimated that the 1987 reconstruction represented 85 per cent of the original Ballets Russes production in Paris, which caused a riot when it was premiered in 1913.

A re-creation for Hutchinson Guest (2000) is based on an idea or a story of a ballet (or dance), which has been lost in the mists of time. The re-creation may involve using the original music or idea. This idea of re-creation roughly corresponds to Cohen's notion. In the late 1980s Eleanor King, who performed in the early Humphrey-Weidman company, staged two versions of an early but little-known Doris Humphrey solo, *The Banshee* (1927), largely based 'on her own memories and imagination' (Dils 1993: 225). Ann Dils considers that King's first re-creation of the solo, which was performed by Dawn De Angelo, 'seemed very close to Humphrey's dances from the period' with its abstract choreographic scaffolding and 'the steely revelation of body parts . . . that builds a sense of dread in the audience, rather than being an imitation of a banshee' (p. 226). De Angelo performed the solo in leotard and tights. King's other version, the Kabuki banshee, performed by Mino Nicholas, was very different. Here the banshee was stylistically presented like a Kabuki actor. Nicholas's 'face was painted white and his eyes were outlined in red' and he donned a 'long white wig, cut to form a mane like a Kabuki lion' (Dils 1993: 225). This costume was in stark contrast to that worn by De Angelo, which in itself was different from the 'moldy green costume described in Humphrey's letters' (Dils 1993: 225). In 1927, Humphrey was attempting to distance her dancing from the orientalism of Denishawn. Thus the costuming and makeup used in the Kabuki version seems somewhat at odds with Humphrey's ideas when she created the solo. There were also differences in the stylistic qualities of the movement. In the Kabuki version, Dils argues, King built the dance around the specificities of Nicholas's movement tendencies and his muscularity. The dance, according to Dils, 'was changed to meet the performer, instead of expanding the dancer's movement range and stretching the audience's perceptions to see a tenuous female sprite actualized by a bulky male performer' (Dils 1993: 225). While King's first version might be considered a re-creation in the spirit outlined earlier, it may also be seen as a 'co-authored' work, as it was based on King's embodied memories of Humphrey's early style and her imagination. The Kabuki version, on the other hand, could be viewed as a 're-invention' (see Franko 1995) of Humphrey's 1927 solo for today's audiences. Perhaps through her extensive experience as a choreographer in her own right, King defamiliarised or distanced herself from the Humphrey solo as she had known it and on which she also based her first re-creation for De Angelo, to make something anew for Nicholas. Dils suggests that the Kabuki version is less valuable than the first re-creation because it shaped the dance to the demands of the performer rather than expanding the vision of the performer to the emergent Humphrey style of the late 1920s. Paying attention to the performative elements of reconstruction, Dils argues, presents present-day dancers with new challenges and 'expands the possibilities of dance moving beyond what is comfortable and expected to ways of performing that are essentially new and surprising for current audiences' (1993: 227). At the same time, however, it could also be argued that King's two very different versions of *The Banshee* reveal that 'authoring' and therefore the question of ownership of intellectual or creative property rights, is a more complex story than we might at first imagine.

There is no doubt in Hutchinson Guest's mind that the revival is the nearest to the 'original' dance work, because it is 'authored' by the choreographer's own hand through the notated score. From her perspective, the productions of *L'Après Midi d'un Faune*, based on her translation of Nijinsky's score, fit the criteria for a revival of the original production performed in Paris in 1912. In other words, they constitute 'the real thing', whereas reconstructions are less authentic. Indeed, she suggests that reconstructions might be better thought of as 'reconstitutions'. She further suggests that, for the sake of accuracy, reconstructions such as Hodson and Archer's 1996 version of Nijinsky's *Jeux* (1916) should read 'Choreography by Millicent Hodson based on existing evidence of Nijinsky's original ballet', not 'choreography by Vaslav Nijinsky' (Hutchinson Guest 2000: 66). She also proposes that ballets that have been passed on through memory, as with the numerous handed-down productions over the years of *Faune*, should indicate this in the programme notes.

As shown earlier, there are different terms used to speak about the activity of taking dances out of the shadows of time and putting them on to the stage. Although I have only scratched the surface of the debates, it should be evident that behind almost every discussion of reconstruction, revival, and so on, are assumptions (implicit and explicit) regarding authenticity, reproducibility and interpretivity.

Authenticity, reproducibility, interpretivity and *The Dying Swan*

In this section I am using the term 'reconstruction' in the broadest sense of the word to refer to bringing back past dances (lost and found and preserved) to the stage, or in some cases on the page. As indicated at the beginning of the chapter, the debates on reconstruction have usually been conducted in relation to early modern dance or early twentieth-century 'modern' ballet. I have chosen to focus on a particular case study of a now classic short ballet solo, *The Dying Swan*, choreographed by Mikhail Fokine in 1905, to shed light on questions of authenticity, reproducibility and interpretivity.

In the latter part of the 1990s, Fokine's granddaughter, Isabelle Fokine, was hired to teach her 'version' of *The Dying Swan* to the Kirov Ballet, who have had their own proud tradition of performing Fokine's ballets, including *The Dying Swan*, over many decades. In 1997, Isabelle Fokine was the central protagonist in a weekend arts television programme, *The 'Dying Swan' Legacy* (Fox 1997), which explored her sense of how this dance and others choreographed by her grandfather, such as *Spectre de la Rose* (1913), should be performed. Her convictions and rationale were set against the views of critics, historians, former ballerinas and members of the Kirov Ballet. The programme provides a fascinating example of competing perspectives on authenticity and their ramifications, despite the fact that *The Dying Swan* is not considered to be a particularly 'revolutionary' ballet. Indeed, as the critic Clement Crisp notes in the television programme, it has become something of a cliché. Unless otherwise stated, all references to this discussion of *The Dying Swan* are drawn from the programme. The words and views of the various critics, historians and dancers on the ballet cited in this discussion are also taken from the programme.

At the beginning of the programme, Isabelle Fokine asserts that her version of *The Dying Swan* and her approach to teaching it stems from her 'upbringing as a dancer' and her 'own family's beliefs' and 'family heritage'. Isabelle Fokine situates her claim to the authenticity of her *Dying Swan* in terms of her own performance practice and, more importantly, in the fact that she has privileged access to Fokine's ideas, notes etc., which he passed down to his son, who in turn passed them down to her. In other words, she has direct access to 'the oracle' for performing and teaching purposes. *The Dying Swan*, as Isabelle Fokine notes, does not make 'enormous technical demands' on a dancer but it does make 'enormous artistic ones because every movement and every gesture should signify a different experience', which is 'emerging from someone who is attempting to escape death' (Fox 1997). *The Dying Swan*, however, is probably associated more with the acclaimed early twentieth-century ballerina, Anna Pavlova, for whom the dance was created, than with the choreographer. Pavlova popularised the dance through her numerous tours, which were received by enthusiastic audiences across the globe for over twenty years. A film of her dancing *The Dying Swan* was made in 1924. Judith Mackrell, the dance critic, points out that because the ballet was made on Pavlova's body, the 'bird-like quality' of her movement for which she was noted became part of the choreography. Irina Baronova, also one of the three 'baby ballerinas' who performed with Ballet Russe de Monte Carlo from 1932 to 1940, notes that she considered the ballet to be closely connected to Pavlova — so much so that she never wanted to dance it herself, although she performed all the other roles that other great ballerinas before her had danced. *The Dying Swan*, according to Baronova, belonged to Pavlova; it was 'her very special thing' (Pavlova asked to be buried in the costume). Hence, both Baronova and Mackrell propose that Pavlova played a large part in the creation of the dance and its subsequent development through her continuous performance of it.

As Crisp notes, it would be impossible to obtain an accurate sense of what the dance looked like when it was first performed in 1905. The Hollywood film of Pavlova performing the ballet was taken many years later. If, as seems likely, Pavlova altered the dance over time to accommodate changes in her style and her ageing dancing body, then a large question is left hovering over the idea of an original authentic version and the likelihood of reproducing this or any other dance exactly 'as it was'. Many other leading ballerinas have also performed the ballet over the years, including Fokine's wife, Vera Fokina. Can we say with any confidence if their interpretations were more authentic or inauthentic than Pavlova's?

According to Isabelle Fokine, the way in which her grandfather had choreographed and recorded *The Dying Swan* is significantly different from the manner in which it is performed today. Her aim is to restore it to its original state. The ballet, she observes, often appears as if it is a variation of *Swan Lake* (Pepita-Ivanov version 1895); 'it looks like Odette at death's door'. However, she argues, the ballet 'in essence' is 'not about the beauty of a ballerina' being able 'to transform herself into a figure of a swan'. The ballet, she maintains, 'is *not* about a swan, it is about *death* and the swan is simply a metaphor for that' [my emphasis]. She continues:

> So what the *original* choreography offers the ballerina in general doing her own series of gestures, is a very textured piece . . . There are moments when the gestures express extreme fragility, her vulnerability, her surrender, her longing, her desperation, her yearning for love.
> [my emphasis]

Isabelle Fokine reasons that if her grandfather had genuinely considered this dance to be an improvisation, then 'he would not have recorded it in the great detail that he did'. Fokine, however, did not record the dance in 1905. It was recorded later and was published in 1925. Fokine, as indicated earlier, worked with other dancers and, as Crisp suggests, his restaging of the dance for Markova in 1941–42 could be deemed to be his '*last* thoughts' [my emphasis] on the subject. According to Markova, her version differed significantly from previous versions in that it was danced 'completely *en pointe de bourrée*'. Crisp implies that the notion of a definitive version of *The Dying Swan* is simply a Fokine invention.

The Kirov presented two versions of *The Dying Swan* at the Coliseum in London on two successive evenings in 1997. We are informed that these were their own and Isabelle Fokine's respectively. According to the dance critic Debra Craine, they were remarkably different. The first performance, according to Craine, was more like Odette in *Swan Lake*, while the second performance was more dramatic. Isabelle Fokine claims that she sought to offer the Kirov an 'authentic alternative' to their interpretation of the ballet. The Kirov, on the other hand, as Craine points out, retains *The Dying Swan* and other Fokine ballets, such as the *Polovtsian Dances* (1909), in the repertoire. As such, she notes, 'they have decades of performing these dances and they would need to be convinced as to the accuracy of Isabelle Fokine's version'. From the confrontations between the Kirov dancers and Isabelle Fokine evidenced in the programme, particularly in regard to the *Polovtsian Dances*, it is clear that the dancers had not been convinced. On several occasions in the programme the dancers openly protest that Isabelle Fokine's version of the dance is contrary to the way they have 'always danced it'. The Kirov dancers consider that their approach to Fokine is faithful to their tradition, which has been passed down from dancer to dancer. Isabelle Fokine, however, argues that the Kirov dancers' performance could be enriched 'with a degree of authenticity', which she could 'bring to their production'. Relying on memory to pass on dances, she suggests, is fallible, while she can return to the choreographer's sources and notations. These notations etc., to a large extent, become in the end the definitive 'dance text'. Isabelle Fokine's assertion that 'there is a definitive version of *The Dying Swan* because of the detailed records he [Fokine] left' is given a legal edge in the credits of the programme, which inform us that 'Fokine Ballets are protected by international copyright law and cannot be performed without a licence from the Fokine Estate Archive'.

Conclusion

This story of the legacy of *The Dying Swan* raises questions about the origin of a work of art and the search for a definitive, authentic version. It also shows that the attempt to reconstruct a dance on the basis of the choreographer's intentions is just as problematic, despite the fact that in this instance the choreographer maintained that his description of the ballet is the definitive version as he taught it to Madame Pavlova (Fokine 1925). Vera Fokina, not Pavlova, executed the 36 poses from the ballet, which accompanied Fokine's 'detailed description' of the dance, which was published twenty years after the first performance. The extent to which the choreographer is the sole 'author' of the work is also questioned here. Choreographers do not generally construct dances in the abstract, even although some may now work with computers and virtual bodies. Dancers are not simply vehicles for expressing the choreographer's intentions. There is of necessity a degree of collaboration between choreographer and dancer, if not always co-authorship in the creative process. The ownership of the work, however, mostly remains firmly in the hands of the choreographer. In an increasingly commodified and bureaucratised system of exchange, intellectual property rights are progressively mapping on to the agenda of contemporary performance practices. The case study shows that a dance work is not 'fixed' in either performance or in writing and that through the process of handing down dances from one dancer to another or by working from a dance script, description or score, different, often competing, interpretations emerge. This, then, challenges the drive towards reproducing a dance in the image of the 'original', which, as I have suggested, is bound more by myth than fact. Attempts to capture and to 'freeze frame' dances in their time may assist dancers and researchers to understand to some extent what a dance might have felt like to perform and witness and, in turn, may add to the knowledge base of the tradition. But that knowledge base, like the tradition, is always partial (biased and selective) and in light of the foregoing discussion I suggest that it is important to be reflexive about this in the process of reviving, reconstructing, re-creating or reinventing the dance 'stories' of the past. The construct of tradition with which I would want to work is one that lives and breathes through embodied textual practice (on or off the stage), not one that is locked up in 'performance museums' (Franko 1993).

Note

1 This essay is reprinted from the first edition of *Rethinking Dance History* (2004).
2 The American cultural commentator Van Wick Brooks coined the term 'usable past' in his writings on American culture in the early twentieth century. Aaron Copland used the term to describe his concern in the 1920s to search out former American composers who explored 'the American scene' in order to find a basis for developing a style of music that would be recognised as American in character.

Bibliography

Adams, L. (1992) 'The Value of Dance', *Dance Connection*, 10, 3: 24–6.
Archer, K. and Hodson, M. (2000) 'Confronting Oblivion: Keynote Address and Lecture Demonstration on Reconstructing Ballets', in S. Jordan (ed.), *Preservation Politics, Dance Revived, Reconstructed, Remade*, London: Dance Books.
Benesh, J. and Benesh, R. (1956) *Introduction to the Benesh Dance Notation*, London: A & C Black.
Berg, S. (1993) 'The Real Thing: Authenticity and Dance at the Approach of the Millennium', *Dance Reconstructed: Modern Dance Art, Past, Present, Future*, Proceedings of Society of Dance History Scholars Sixteenth Annual Conference, Rutgers University, New Brunswick: SDHS.

Cohen, S. J. (1993) 'Dance Reconstructed', *Dance Research Journal*, 25, 2(Fall): 54–5.

Copeland, R. (1994) 'Reflections on Revival and Reconstruction', *Dance Theatre Journal*, 11, 3: 18–20.

Davies, M. (1975) *Towards Understanding the Intrinsic in Body Movement*, New York: Arno Press.

De Frantz, T. (ed.) (2002) *Dancing Many Drums: Excavations in African American Dance*, Madison: University of Wisconsin Press.

Dils, A. (1993) 'Performance Practice and Humphrey Reconstruction', *SDHS, Dance Reconstructed: Modern Dance Art, Past, Present, Future*, Proceedings of Society of Dance History Scholars Sixteenth Annual Conference, Rutgers University, New Brunswick: SDHS.

The Drama Review (1984) 'Reconstruction Issue', 28: 3, 2–98.

Felföldi, L. (1999) 'Folk Dance Research in Hungary: Relations among Theory, Fieldwork and the Archive', in T. J. Buckland (ed.), *Dance in the Field: Theory, Methods and Issues in Dance Ethnography*, Basingstoke: Macmillan.

Fokine, M. (1925) *The Dying Swan, Music by C. Saint-Saëns: Detailed Description of the Dance by Michel Fokine; Thirty-Six Photographs from Poses by Vera Fokina*, New York: J. Fischer & Brother.

Fox, G. (1997) *The 'Dying Swan' Legacy*, produced and directed by Gerald Fox, London Weekend Television: South Bank Show.

Franko, M. (1993) *Dance as Text: Ideologies of the Baroque Body*, Cambridge: Cambridge University Press.

—— (1995) *Dancing Modernism / Performing Politics*, Bloomington, IN: Indiana University Press.

Giurchescu, A. (1999) 'Past and Present Field Research', in T. J. Buckland (ed.), *Dance in the Field: Theory, Methods and Issues in Dance Ethnography*, Basingstoke: Macmillan.

Hutchinson, A. (1977) *Labanotation, or Kinetography Laban: The System of Analyzing and Recording Movement*, illustrated by D. Anderson, New York: Theatre Arts Books.

Hutchinson Guest, A. (1984) *Dance Notation: The Process of Recording Movement on Paper*, London: Dance Books.

—— (1991) 'Nijinsky's *Faune*', *Choreography and Dance*, 1: 3–34.

—— (2000) 'Is Authenticity to Be Had?', in S. Jordan (ed.), *Preservation Politics: Dance Revived, Reconstructed, Remade*, London: Dance Books.

Jordan, S. (ed.) (2000) *Preservation Politics: Dance Revived, Reconstructed, Remade*, London: Dance Books.

Kane, A. (2000) 'Issues of Authenticity and Identity in the Restaging of Paul Taylor's *Airs*', in S. Jordan (ed.), *Preservation Politics: Dance Revived, Reconstructed, Remade*, London: Dance Books.

Kriegsman, S. A. (1993) 'Dance Reconstructed: Modern Dance Art, Present and Future', *Ballett International*, 6: 15–17.

Laban, R. von (1928) *Schrifttanz: Kinetographie Methodik*, Vienna: Universal Edition.

Lidbury, C. (2000) 'The Preservation of the Ballets of Kurt Jooss', in S. Jordan (ed.), *Preservation Politics: Dance Revived, Reconstructed, Remade*, London: Dance Books.

Manning, S. A. (1993) *Ecstasy and the Demon: Feminism and Nationalism in the Dances of Mary Wigman*, Berkeley, CA: University of California Press.

Pernod, J. and Ginsberg, A. (1997) 'Dialogue: New Work and Reconstructed Work in the Context of Dance Repertory', *Dance Research Journal*, 29, 1: 1–5.

Perpener, J. O. (2001) *African-American Concert Dance: The Harlem Renaissance and beyond*, Urbana: University of Illinois Press.

Reynolds, N. (2000) 'Inside Artistry: The George Balanchine Foundation', in S. Jordan (ed.), *Preservation Politics: Dance Revived, Reconstructed, Remade*, London: Dance Books.

Rubidge, S. (1985) 'Old Modern Dances Revived', *Dance Theatre Journal*, 3, 4: 38–9.

SDHS (Society of Dance History Scholars) (1993) *Dance Reconstructed: Modern Dance Art, Past, Present, Future*, Proceedings of Society of Dance History Scholars Sixteenth Annual Conference, Rutgers University, New Brunswick: SDHS.

Siegel, M. B. (1968) *At the Vanishing Point: A Critic Looks at Dance*, New York: Saturday Review Press.

Taruskin, R. (1995) *Text as Act: Essays on Performance*, Oxford: Oxford University Press.

Thomas, H. (2003) *The Body, Dance and Cultural Theory*, Palgrave: Basingstoke.

Thompson, A. (2000) 'Shakespeare: Preservation and/or Reinvention', in S. Jordan (ed.), *Preservation Politics: Dance Revived, Reconstructed, Remade*, London: Dance Books.

Van Zile, J. (1985–6) 'What Is the Dance? Implications for Dance Notation', *Dance Research Journal*, 17, 2 and 18, 1: 41–7.

Chapter 7

Preserving the repertory and extending the heritage of Merce Cunningham

KAREN ELIOT

Introduction

WHEN THE *EVENT* concluded on 31 December 2011, fourteen dancers exited the cavernous space at the Park Avenue Armory in New York City, and the Merce Cunningham Dance Company ceased to exist.[1] Cunningham had earlier made public his decision that after his death the company should embark on a two-year world tour, dubbed the 'Legacy Tour', and disband after a series of *Events* – the flexible, ninety-minute performance vehicles he inaugurated in 1964 – to be performed in the city he called home.[2] It might then have appeared inevitable that the company's abundant repertory, created over more than five decades, should simply dissipate. As if defying this gesture's seeming finality, the writer and choreographer Wendy Perron responded in her blog the following day that 'There's a piece of Merce in all of us', implying that Cunningham's artistic impact was by now so widely pervasive that it could scarcely be disentangled from all the ways that contemporary dance is envisioned, performed and viewed in the twenty-first century ([2012] 2013: 316). Still, to many devotees, Cunningham's decision to disband his company, the living repository of his work, looked like an unprecedented act of artistic annihilation. Without the active engagement of a troupe of dancers selected and trained by the choreographer himself, it seemed implausible that the legacy of works, those consistently inventive, 'disintegrated spectacles', might continue to exist (Vaughan 1974–75: 138).

In spite of the notable success of Alvin Ailey's American Dance Theatre under the direction of Judith Jamison, and recently, Robert Battle, other efforts to sustain dance companies and repertories after the deaths of major twentieth-century choreographers have been flawed. As Alastair Macaulay put it, 'How well [the New York] City Ballet has served Balanchine's dances has been a matter of fierce and lasting disagreement for over 20 years' (2014). With the death of Martha Graham in 1991, the dance world was shaken by a highly visible and long, drawn-out legal battle between Ron Protas, the choreographer's heir, and the dancers of the Martha Graham Dance Company, who fought over the rights to perform that choreographer's historic repertory. Recent efforts to preserve choreographic legacies may prove more fruitful: the choreographer Paul Taylor declared his intention to transform his company into a repertory ensemble. The newly minted Paul Taylor's American Modern Dance Company will preserve the works of Taylor along with those of other American choreographers, and the seven members of Trisha Brown's troupe announced plans to maintain Brown's work by remounting her choreographies in appropriate site-specific locations around the world (Kourlas 2016).

At the time of the concluding Armory *Event*, however, many in the dance world were unaware of the plans that had been laid out in the years leading up to Cunningham's death, by the choreographer himself, and by the Cunningham Dance Foundation staff, to create a unique model for preserving and promoting the further dissemination of the Cunningham repertory, a model that, as I shall argue, allows the dances to continue to circulate – as digital and physical artefacts – while the dancers who embody the work have assumed the tasks of teaching the technique and training others in Cunningham's unique approach to creation and performance.

'The Legacy Plan: A Case Study/Cunningham Dance Foundation', written jointly by members of the Cunningham Foundation and the writer and dance educator Bonnie Brooks, serves as an online case study available for consultation by arts organisations facing similar circumstances. According to the study, in response to the changing climate for touring at the end of the twentieth century, the Cunningham Foundation sought, and in 1990 was awarded, a major Challenge Grant from the National Endowment for the Arts to expand its Repertory Understudy Group, a move that promoted the dissemination of repertory to other companies, and that facilitated an increase in the number of film and video projects undertaken by the Merce Cunningham Dance Company. In this way, Cunningham staff began early on to devote attention to issues of preservation and dissemination, and to lay the groundwork for programmes that would be useful after the choreographer's death. Over time other plans were set in place: financial assistance would be provided to the dancers and staff members as they embarked on their subsequent careers; establishment of the Merce Cunningham Trust would allow that body to 'own and regulate the rights' to Cunningham's choreographies after his death (Cunningham Dance Foundation n.d.: 12). The extensive dance archives overseen by the company's archivist, David Vaughan, were transferred to the New York Public Library and, in a move that has proven significant for restagers and scholars alike, funds were raised to support the creation of eighty-six digital 'Dance Capsules', each 'providing an array of assets essential to the study and reconstruction of this iconic artist's choreographic work'.[3] Containing both public and private assets, these capsules contain films, videotaped performances and rehearsal tapes of the selected dances, and include as well all other available components of the work, such as Cunningham's choreographic notes, and information on design and musical elements.

If the Dance Capsules provide an invaluable resource to scholars, and to former company dancers who restage the choreography, the issue of preserving and disseminating the legacy of an artist often associated with the experimental and the unconventional is itself paradoxical. In 2013, two years after the final Armory *Event* performance, Carrie Noland (2013) explored this paradox in 'Inheriting the Avant-Garde: Merce Cunningham, Marcel Duchamp, and the Legacy Plan'. As Noland put it, the members of the Cunningham Trust would face contradictory impulses in their efforts to shape a legacy – that is to historicise the dances – of a choreographer whose career was devoted to experiment and to challenging assumptions about dance and art. 'To preserve a legacy', writes Noland, 'is implicitly an attempt to perpetuate a certain look and a certain praxis from one generation to the next (and the next and the next and the next . . .)' (2013: 86).

How have the Cunningham 'look' and the choreographic 'praxis' been preserved, and have they been preserved at the expense of what Noland calls Cunningham's 'unconventional approach to aesthetic production' (2013: 86)? I propose that the open-endedness with which the dancers and the Trust have handled the paradox of preserving and extending the repertory after Cunningham's death mirrors the choreographer's unconventional aesthetics. The repertory, having undergone a number of transitions over the course of the choreographer's lifetime, entered a new phase after his death. While the long-term future of the Cunningham repertory is – and has always been – unpredictable, the present moment is vibrant with vital, conscientious work being undertaken by former company dancers to teach the technique and restage the Cunningham repertory so as to keep alive Cunningham's own protean approach to his creations. Since 2011, the teaching of Cunningham technique and repertory in schools, conservatories and university dance programmes has expanded,[4] dance scholars have gained access to many of the public assets archived in the Dance Capsules, and the Trust's project to administer the Choreographic Fellowship[5] workshops has benefited restagers and the numerous pre-professional and professional freelance dancers who participate. Workshop performances as well as related panel discussions about individual works are offered on a regular basis in New York and occasionally elsewhere.[6] These initiatives have thus facilitated dissemination of the work, and the evolving approach to restaging Cunningham's corpus issues a challenge to established notions of legacy wherein restagers might aim chiefly to preserve what is assumed to be the authentic texts of historic choreography. The approaches employed by the current crop of Cunningham restagers demonstrate their dedication to enabling contemporary dancers to inhabit a world and to embody a technique distinct from their own. However, the flexibility with which Cunningham restagers approach the work suggests new ways to think about the endurance of a dance tradition.

The preservation and evolution of style

Although as Perron acknowledged, Cunningham's teaching and choreographic methods – often employing chance operations – have been infused throughout much contemporary dance practice today, what seems in jeopardy are the unique characteristics of Cunningham style that might become diffuse without the restager's careful oversight. But Cunningham's style, while always identifiable, continued to evolve during his lifetime. David Vaughan, whose association with Cunningham began in the 1960s and who served as the company archivist until 2011, noted that a significant juncture had been reached when the company was renamed in the 1970s, and the troupe first known as Merce Cunningham and Dance Company became the Merce Cunningham Dance Company. According to Vaughan, although the change in title was small, it nevertheless served to indicate Cunningham's shift in emphasis from his role as a soloist with a company to one in which his primary aim was to choreograph for his expanded troupe of dancers. Vaughan points out that in working with the larger group, Cunningham became more interested in 'mass effects', as seen in works in which 'longer passages of unison choreography occur, or in which individuals do not stand out even when everyone on stage is doing something different' (1979: 4). Still, Vaughan writes, it was the individuality that his dancers brought to the choreography that most interested him:

> As Cunningham says, everyone in the world walks according to the same mechanism, but no two people walk alike, and that is what constitutes 'expression'. Like many great choreographers, Cunningham wants to get at that individuality, to draw it out, and draw on it, in the act of creating movement.
>
> (1979: 5)

Cunningham, too, spoke of an evolution in his choreographic career, describing the 'four events that have led to large discoveries' ([1994] 1997), four major turning points in his career that shifted his approach to his work and altered the look of the choreography as well as the practice in daily technique classes. According to Cunningham, the first event occurred as early as the 1940s, when, inspired by his partner, the musician John Cage, he made the decision to separate music and dance, and to maintain the 'clarity and interdependence' between the two elements. The second was his choice to employ chance operations; the third came about when he began to experiment with video and film; and finally, the fourth occurred with his use of the LifeForms computer program to create movement phrases that could be stored in a memory bank, and examined from any angle. Cunningham described it as an ongoing journey towards finding new possibilities: 'My work', he wrote, 'has always been in process. Finishing a dance has left me with the idea, often slim in the beginning, for the next one. In that way, I do not think of each dance as an object, rather a short stop on the way' ([1994] 1997: 276).

As Cunningham's repertory evolved over time, so too did the training adapt to reflect his shifting choreographic concerns. Although students of Cunningham technique speak of specific changes manifested in the training over time – the later technique became 'more balletic', 'more codified', arms were more positional and the earlier links to Graham training were less prominent[7] – there are identifiable, constant features of Cunningham technique that link a dance made in the 1950s with one made late in the choreographer's life.[8] According to Pat Catterson, a New York City-based choreographer/dancer and educator, and a regular student of Cunningham technique from the 1960s on, the classes taught by early company members, including Barbara Lloyd Dilley (whose years in the company were 1963–68), Albert Reid (1964–68), Sandra Neels (1963–1973) and especially Viola Farber (1953–65/1970), were less codified than those of later generations; they allowed for greater indeterminacy, and seemed more individually distinct. Although the technique became more refined and more systematised over the years, says Catterson, there remain recognisable Cunningham features, including an emphasis on fast weight shifts and body isolations, a preference for volume in movement, attention to three-dimensionality, and what she calls a 'clarity of the destination of movement' (Pat Catterson 2016, pers. comm., 28 March). Susan Foster describes the unique look of the dancer executing Cunningham's choreography as straightforward, with an intense focus on the movement: 'Because movement represents nothing other than itself, the dance points up an expressiveness in movement itself and seems to empower it with a compelling and passionate logic all its own' (1986: 34). These elements of clarity and focus underlie the training and must be present in any staging of a Cunningham work: they effectively signal to viewers that they have entered a Cunningham landscape.

Undeniably, dancers attempting to learn Cunningham repertory need to come to the work with a strong underlying technical base. In the case of Cunningham repertory, this means they must have core stability as well as a highly mobile torso, a physical awareness of space, accurate and deft footwork, the ability to carve clear shapes with their limbs, a strong internal sense of rhythm, and an ability to move out in space. And yet, as I have found in my own experience of teaching American university students for almost two decades, and as has been confirmed in my conversations with other former Cunningham dancers who teach the technique and restage the repertory, technical skill alone does not ensure that a dancer can achieve that Cunningham look and praxis.

Preservation of the Cunningham legacy, then, requires that dancers assimilate a unique approach to the movement, a praxis that includes an appetite for risk taking. This approach to learning Cunningham's repertory requires the dancer to maintain an eagerness about experimenting with movement possibilities, a sense of responsibility to the work, and an excitement about embodying the challenges the movement affords. Such qualities, while they may be difficult to quantify, were absorbed and embraced by company dancers who trained under the supervision of Cunningham himself. They constitute what Jennifer Goggans (2000–2011), the Trust's current studio administrator, calls the 'institutional knowledge' that students of Cunningham learned from watching him and from hearing his vocal encouragements as they attempted to master what sometimes seemed the impossible technical challenges he set (Jennifer Goggans 2016, pers. comm., 27 April). Foster's impression is that in Cunningham's work, 'both subject and body are assimilated into the experience of physical articulation, an experience that is mindful and passionate' (1986: 52). Mindful passion is an important common denominator in the approach to learning Cunningham technique and repertory that the current crop of restagers is eager to transmit.

Reconstructing the steps and rediscovering the spirit

In 1998, Cunningham invited dancer Carolyn Brown (1953–1972) to assist in the reconstruction of *Summerspace* (1958), a beautiful, sun-drenched, spare dance that emphasises turning, and incorporates long, spacious phrases of movement featuring leaps and arabesques. Brown set to work with Robert Swinston (1980–2011), then the assistant to the choreographer, wading through Cunningham's notes, as well as those of later restagers, and watching early films and videotapes of more recent performances. It was, says Brown, 'A wealth of contradictory material, all of which added to our befuddlement in attempting to reconstruct the piece in as close to its original form as possible' (2002: 75).

In my observation of the work currently underway by former company members who teach Cunningham repertory to students and professional companies, however, the 'befuddlement' Brown speaks of when she confronted the array of sources has in fact proven to be one of the greatest benefits of the Trust's approach. The array of seemingly contradictory resources has allowed this restaging process to remain true to Cunningham's own openness to change, and his eagerness to embrace new possibilities. Gaining access to multiple versions of a dance, available through the Dance Capsules website, gives scholars and restagers alike a sense of historical change in the performances of individual works. Cunningham's decisions to alter his choreography over time become visible; restagers are afforded greater choice in selecting versions of the choreography which may be more appropriate to the dancers with whom they are working; and they gain a larger view of the possibilities within the performance of a work. For scholars and students interested in analysing Cunningham's choreography, such multiplicity highlights the dynamism of the choreography and affords insight into the contributions made by the unique qualities and physicalities of individual dancers.[9] Meanwhile, as Patricia Lent (1984–1993), the Trust's director of licensing, emphasised to me, each restaging project reflects the subjective approach of the restager. The restager, one who has benefited from training with Cunningham himself and who thus has a profound knowledge of dancing his choreography, is faced with a baffling array of sources; yet, on the basis of this deep, physical experience, she makes decisions about how the dancers should undertake the complex movement phrases and about what the eventual product should look like (Patricia Lent 2016, pers. comm., 30 March). The range of possibilities available to scholar and restager alike thus reflects Cunningham's enthusiasm for seeing his own works in new ways – as, for example, when new dancers assumed roles created for other bodies, or when excerpts of works were spliced into seamless *Events*, affording them altered contexts – different lighting, decor, costumes and music.

As Carolyn Brown put it, in staging *Summerspace*, she aimed to 'rediscover the initial spirit that informed the dance in the process of its creation' (2002: 75). Likewise, Lent suggested that while it is important to arrive at a strong and accurate version of a dance, she values allowing the dancers to participate in a process like that informing the first rehearsals when the piece was made. 'For me', says Lent,

> how [the dance] looks from Row G in the audience is of least interest. What's of most interest to me is that [the dancers and restagers] have an experience of the process of putting the dance together, in as authentic *a way* as possible.
> (Patricia Lent 2016, pers. comm., 30 March)

The experience of teaching the movement and the dancers' processes in learning it are the most important aspects of the transmission and teaching, she said. As a restager, 'you get to wherever you get, but in getting there you share the process, so there's something real that's happened. That to me reads, and you know, when someone comes to see it, they might say, "Oh, the arm should be here or it should be there", but in the end, there's some real experience', and it is communicated to the viewers and to the dancers involved (Patricia Lent 2016, pers. comm., 30 March). In other words, the dance's technical details are important to the end product, but the process of learning a dance in the way that Cunningham first taught it fosters the dancers' understanding of the work's 'spirit'.

Recapturing special moments

'You're not going to bring the Cunningham Company back', says Goggans, 'but you do want [the resulting performance] to be at a certain level of professionalism' (Jennifer Goggans 2016, pers. comm., 27 April). The challenge for restagers, she suggests, is to realise what might be possible to achieve in an individual situation, and to understand that in each case, the process involves allowing the dance to come alive in and through the bodies of the dancers in the room. At the time of writing, such projects are being undertaken in schools, university dance programmes and conservatories, in workshops with pre-professional and professional freelance dancers and in major touring companies in Europe and the United States; each project, says Goggans, presents its own challenge. With student dancers, there may be technical hurdles to overcome, physical and mental challenges in the choreography that can be mastered only through the dancers' daily, rigorous practice of the movement with attention to rhythm and time. On the other hand, for ballet dancers who may have strong foot- and legwork, there are other concerns. Goggans finds that she frequently coaches ballet dancers to move with larger sweep and momentum into space, and to take risks by extending their energy beyond the defined range of their limbs. Ballet dancers may be uncomfortable with unpredictable transitions and irregular rhythms and may require additional coaching to effect the quick weight shifts and sharp changes in focus and direction that make up Cunningham's style. 'Ballet dancers are trained to be perfect', and, according to Goggans, 'that wasn't always the goal with Merce' (Jennifer Goggans 2016, pers. comm., 27 April). Dancers need the encouragement that Cunningham gave his own dancers: to take on technical difficulties, assume risks and avoid smoothing out movement or blurring details, making the choreography appear overly easy or graceful.

Goggans spoke enthusiastically of two recent projects she felt were highly successful: at the Julliard School in New York, where she was impressed by the students' extraordinary discipline and commitment, and at the Lyons Opera Ballet, where the dancers achieved an assured and subtly nuanced performance of *Winterbranch* (1964). In the latter instance, Goggans said, the work itself presented few technical challenges to the Lyons dancers as it is made up of basic, task-like movement phrases. In working with these accomplished professionals, she opted to give them a broader experience of Cunningham's technique so as to promote a sense of the scope of his choreography. At the start of each rehearsal, she taught travelling phrases, adding some complicated arm gestures that constituted important physical knowledge for the dancers to acquire. Her goal was to allow the dancers to become 'more informed about the whole experience of dancing a Cunningham work. I try to give them something of Merce!' she said (Jennifer Goggans 2016, pers. comm., 27 April).

For Daniel Roberts (2000–2005), any effort to restage Cunningham's work imposes tremendous obligation on the restager, and for him, one of the most important qualities to impart to dancers is the work ethic and sense of responsibility that Cunningham and his dancers displayed (Daniel Roberts 2016, pers. comm., 27 April). In recreating in his rehearsal studio the process he underwent when he learned a dance from Cunningham, Roberts places demands on himself to first gain mastery of the movement, and to be able to present it clearly and coach it thoroughly to his dancers. The restager assumes the task of organising rehearsals and 'being on top of' all the movement material that is to be taught. Importantly, he spends considerable time outside of rehearsals learning each dancer's movement, and preparing himself to be able to teach it in a manner consistent with Cunningham's own clear and straightforward instructions. Never, he insists, would he ask the dancers to learn their movement from videotape; instead, all participants in the process assume the tasks attendant on their roles. For the dancer, this means there must be time set aside for independent practice, outside of rehearsal time, to gain some degree of mastery over the work's technical demands, and to shape a unique and individual execution of the very complex phrases.

Dancers who engage with the Cunningham repertory benefit in a number of ways: they gain greater technical expertise, and they become more fluent in remembering long sequences of complexly layered movement material. I have observed that students, and pre-professional dancers, often develop a more powerful performance presence as they learn to invest themselves fully in dancing a work that is devoid of narrative, music and any theatrical elements that might otherwise shield the dancer. Beyond these obvious gains, though, for Roberts it is that work ethic and sense of individual responsibility that make the experience of learning Cunningham repertory so rewarding for the dancers who participate.

In his work with the Kansas City Ballet and others, restaging *Totem Ancestor* (1942), a viscerally powerful solo that Cunningham created for himself, Roberts says he has tried to 'remember the special moments inside' the work. He recalls being coached in the solo by Cunningham, whose comments encouraged him to trust his instincts about the dance. These days, whether he is teaching repertory to professional dancers or to students, it is the uniqueness of that process that he aims to recapture. 'Merce always gave you the feeling that it was in your grasp as you learned', says Roberts. 'Yes', agrees Goggans, 'he always spoke to you as if you could do anything that he asked, so you never failed that'.[10]

'A short stop on the way'

Lizzie Feidelson, a New York-based dancer, writer and choreographer, has described the omnipresence of Cunningham's legacy in dance classes as they continue after his death. No longer housed in the Westbeth Studio in lower Manhattan, classes today occur in dance studios dispersed across New York, and in university dance programmes and conservatories elsewhere.[11] A regular student of Cunningham technique, Feidelson identifies herself as the granddaughter of an early company member (Marianne Preger-Simon, 1950–1958), and a one-time staff member in the Cunningham Foundation. The classes she attends today, as taught by former company dancers, continue to evoke the wisdom and physical presence of

Cunningham himself in one of his most important roles, as the teacher in the studio. 'Cunningham's presence hovers over the lessons given by his former dancers', she writes. 'From memory, they quote his advice on dancing, imitating his gravelly voice. In their stories, he's a wise and personable presence, like a relative students have never met' (2013: 16).

At the time of writing, Cunningham's presence remains vivid and palpable in a large segment of the dance world. Cunningham technique and repertory are not in jeopardy of imminently disappearing for they are taught, viewed, analysed and discussed by scholars and the public alike. However, the long-term future of the work remains as fluid and protean as it was during the choreographer's lifetime. As the last company dancers who were trained by the choreographer begin to age out of teaching, the Cunningham repertory will reflect this change and will enter, as Patricia Lent told me, 'another phase'. 'From my point of view', she said, the Cunningham legacy 'has already changed radically. It changed radically a whole bunch of times. It changed when Merce stopped dancing. It changed radically when the company closed and it's going to keep changing' (Patricia Lent 2016, pers. comm., 30 March). The future is open and will be in the hands of those who cherish the work and believe in its power to communicate to future generations of dancers and viewers. I am reminded of Wendy Perron's point that Cunningham's approach and training have now been disseminated throughout much of contemporary dance. Resisting any course that might fix the repertory in such a way that it might become historicised, Cunningham dancers and the Cunningham Trust have allowed instead for a unique approach to archive and legacy. The current impetus is not towards creating and preserving authorised and stable versions of Cunningham's choreography; rather, the trajectory is towards further dissemination of the choreographer's ideas and ethos. The true Cunningham legacy may well be in what Goggans calls the 'institutional knowledge' that Cunningham's dancers absorbed and incorporated through Cunningham's own strong model. It may well be located in what Carolyn Brown terms 'the spirit' of the original, and what Roberts and Lent say is most truthful about the process of learning the dances. The real legacy of Cunningham, then, may be in teaching dancers how to work, live and exist in the world of a dance. As Cunningham himself would have said, you take a step and then you take another, and you find out something new in the process.

Notes

1   See Merce Cunningham Dance Company Park Avenue Armory Events. Cunningham Dance Foundation and ARTPIX 2012.
2   Merce Cunningham was born in Centralia, Washington, on 16 April 1919. He died in New York City on 26 July 2009.

3 Some assets are protected and available only to restagers, but many afford public access. The Dance Capsules are available at: dancecapsules.mercecunningham.org.

4 According to Patricia Lent, the Cunningham Trust's director of licensing, in 2016 Cunningham technique is being taught across the United States, Canada, the UK and France, including at: The Julliard School, the Joffrey Ballet School, NYU Tisch School of the Arts in New York, the London Contemporary Dance School and Trinity Laban Conservatoire in the UK, Simon Fraser University in Canada, CNSMD in Paris, and my own institution, The Ohio State University in Columbus, Ohio.

5 The Choreographic Fellowship program, instituted in 2011, furthers the Trust's mission to teach, revive and stage Cunningham's works. Fellows, selected by audition, participate in multi-week intensives that include rehearsals and technique classes. See mercecunningham.org/fellowship-program/. Archival videos are available through the NYU Tisch Dance and New Media Program.

6 Panel discussions are moderated by Alastair Macaulay, the dance critic for the *New York Times*, and by Patricia Lent and are archived at: tischdanceandnewmedia.com.

7 Links to Graham technique are rarely noted in reconstructions today, although they are observable in the early solos that Cunningham created for himself. The 1942 *Totem Ancestor*, for example, demands propulsive jumps that initiate from a kneeling position, and incorporates the staccato impulse of the Graham back contraction. However, this lineage was no longer emphasised during my training with Cunningham in the 1980s.

8 In my interview with Jennifer Goggans and Daniel Roberts on 27 April 2016, they referred to Cunningham's '80s movement to indicate large moving phrases that travelled and carved out the space, and demanded deft footwork along with powerful, outward extensions of the limbs.

9 Some film recordings made in the early decades of Cunningham's career are available. It is worth noting, though, that because video equipment was not widely available before the 1980s, many dancers' contributions have not been recorded on film. The technological advances of the last decades have privileged the performances of Cunningham's later company dancers.

10 Goggans and Roberts collaborated on a restaging of *Split Sides* (2003) as part of the Choreographic Fellowship program. The work, danced by pre-professional students, was streamed live on 12 June 2015 at the New York City Center Studios. See the Film+Media link at merce.cunningham.org for archived recordings of all workshop performances.

11 The Cunningham Foundation, now the Cunningham Trust, no longer resides at the Westbeth Studio in lower Manhattan. The space is now occupied by the Martha Graham Dance Company.

Bibliography

Brown, C. (2002) 'Summerspace: Three Revivals', *Dance Research Journal*, 34:1, 74–82.

Cunningham, M. ([1994] 1997) 'Four Events That Have Led to Large Discoveries', in D. Vaughan ed., *Merce Cunningham: Fifty Years*, New York: Aperture, 276.

Cunningham Dance Foundation (n.d.) *The Legacy Plan: A Case Study/Cunningham DanceFoundation*, Cunningham Trust. Available from: www.mercecunningham.org/history/case-study/.

Feidelson, L. (2013) 'The Merce Cunningham Archives: The Dancer or the Dance?', *Double Bind*, 16:2–16. Available from: https://nplusonemag.com/ [accessed 1 February, 2016].

Foster, S. (1986) *Reading Dancing: Bodies and Subjects in Contemporary American Dance*, Berkeley: University of California Press.

Kourlas, G. (2016) 'Sending a Legacy Back into the World', *Sunday New York Times*, 24 January, AR, 8.

Macaulay, A. (2014) 'There Is So Much That Must Live On: Merce Cunningham's DanceLegacy', *New York Times*, 18 July. Available from: www.nytimes.com [accessed 5 April 2016].

Noland, C. (2013) 'Inheriting the Avant-Garde: Merce Cunningham, Marcel Duchamp, and the Legacy Plan', *Dance Research Journal*, 45:2, 85–122.

Perron, W. ([2012] 2013) 'Merce's Other Legacy', in *Through the Eyes of a Dancer: Selected Writings*, Middletown: Wesleyan University Press, 316–317.

Vaughan, D. (1974–75) 'Diaghilev/Cunningham', *Art Journal*, 34:2, 135–140.

Vaughan, D. (1979) 'Retrospect and Prospect', *Performing Arts Journal*, 3:3, 3–14.

Chapter 8

Making dance history live – performing the past

HENRIETTA BANNERMAN

IN THIS ESSAY I aim to take up a question posed by Anne Makkonen and Hanna Järvinen, who asked, 'Can we dance history?' (2010: 19), or more specifically is 'critical embodiment of a past practice [. . .] a real possibility?' (2010: 20). I want to continue these questions by pursuing the extent to which young dancers embody older works and what kind of historical knowledge they acquire when theory is combined with practice.

The dances with which I am concerned are those in the western canon created and performed from the mid- to late twentieth century, dances with movement vocabularies and styles of performance that are unfamiliar or even foreign to present-day dancers. As L. P. Hartley famously wrote in the prologue to his novel *The Go-Between* (1953), 'the past is a foreign country: they do things differently there' (1997: 5) a notion challenged by T. S. Eliot, for whom 'the conscious present is an awareness of the past' (1986: 19). Makkonen and Järvinen echo Eliot in claiming that 'the past is present in each one of us' (2010: 19). Following Hartley and drawing on my experience as a dance lecturer, I question the idea that the 'past,' in this case older styles or ways of dancing, readily or naturally inhabits the sensibilities and bodies of young people. As time moves on and the field of contemporary dance and its sociocultural context expand exponentially, the gap widens – for example between dance as it was understood and practised in the early years of the twentieth century and how it appears to dancers in current times. I am also drawn again towards Hartley's description of the past as a foreign country in the light of remarks by those such as Joan McNamara, who in 1999 wrote, 'Discussing the Judson Church Dance Theater in a dance history class, a student wonders: "What was it like to dance in New York in the early 1960s, and to be part of the social milieu of that time?"' (1999: 162).

These queries lead me to argue that if we are to provide young dancers with the insight they require into historical milestones that have shaped our current practices we need to listen to the voices of dancers who speak in the present about their experience of the past and thereby impart knowledge concerning not only the physicality of the movement but also the philosophy, intention and artistic environment of the choreographers with whom they had personal interaction and whose dances they performed. Such specialist tutors can tell their students what it was like to be part of this or that group at a particular point in time. In the absence of such inside information, one can fail to convince young people why they should be interested in older dances. I recall, for example, showing a video of Medea's solo from *Cave of the Heart* (1946), Martha Graham's retelling of Euripides's *Medea*. For me, this vitriolic 'dance of vengeance' was mesmerising when I saw it performed by Helen McGehee in New York in 1964. At the time I was studying at the Graham studio and thoroughly immersed in the atmosphere of the work and it stands to reason that I experienced a kinaesthetic rapport with the dancing I saw on stage. However, screening a video of this visceral solo four decades later to teenage students, I was dismayed that it met not with wonder and awe but with titters and giggles. Educated at best in classroom Graham or more often in cooler dance techniques, for these young people it was far too emotionally fraught and histrionic. But what if we were to rethink methods of history teaching and provide opportunities for dance students not only to study in seminars but also to practise her dances in the studio? If they learned the repertory from a Graham expert for themselves, they might better appreciate Graham's dance theatre, a topic to which I return later.

First, however, I consider the term 'embodiment' and refer en route to Birmingham Royal Ballet dancers in 1994 learning and performing Ashton's *Enigma Variations* (1968). I then devote attention to the historical project offered to second-year students at Trinity Laban (then Laban)[1] and their experience of performing Graham and Robert Cohan choreography. Finally I consider the restaging of Siobhan Davies's *Bank* (1997) for London Contemporary Dance School's (LCDS) postgraduate company, EDge in 2015. In this last case, I am interested in the notion of a living archive and what emerging professional dancers discovered when they experienced the historical dimension of British contemporary dance. However, I continue now by considering ways in which we understand the notion of embodiment.

Embodiment

Writing on the concept of embodiment, Jane Carr finds that this is a term which 'has become increasingly popular in the discourses of dance and particularly in those that draw on the traditions of modern dance developed in America and Europe in the early twentieth century' (2013: 63). She goes on to comment that when teaching at Trinity Laban in the early 2000s, 'embodying dance material was a taken for granted aim of many students and their teachers' (2013: 63). As a member of the faculty from 1999–2005, I testify to the fact that we sought to encourage a form of embodiment described by Sheets-Johnstone (1979) as 'consciousness-body.' As she writes, 'Fundamentally, man is not an objective structure to be known, but a unique existential being, a unity of consciousness-body, which itself knows' (1979: 12).

I do not hold, however, that we can intuit or *know* dances made in a time or social context outside our own experience. Thus I would argue that in the context of embodying older dances, the psychophysical as represented by Sheets-Johnstone's principle of consciousness-body is gained from personal interaction between a young dancer and an experienced performer. Consciousness-body or embodiment occurs only at that point of fusion between thought and action or learning and doing. It is not enough to learn 'about' a dance which, as Sarah Rubidge points out, 'is articulated in the form of propositions which describe, explain, or otherwise articulate ideas about the work' (1999: n.p.). I borrow Rubidge's notion of 'thinking *in* the work' (1999: n.p.) to theorise a type of embodiment according to which an older dance is rediscovered, remade and experienced anew. We return, then, to the idea of the voices referred to earlier and to a form of oral history, a place where 'history [is written] with evidence gathered from a living person, rather than from a written document' (Prins 1991: 114). Within many academic disciplines, oral history has received much criticism, as noted by Prins: 'Historians in modern, mass-literate, industrial societies – that is, most professional historians – are generally pretty sceptical about the value of oral sources in reconstructing the past' (Prins 1991: 114). This comment, I propose, is not relevant to a practice such as dance because dance scholars and academics have long appreciated the value of an oral tradition when passing dances from one generation to another. Even in cases where a work is taught to dancers from a notated score, it is common practice for those inheriting roles to be coached by experienced dancers, as is clear when Peter Wright talks about the way in which Birmingham Royal Ballet [BRB] brought Ashton's *Enigma Variations* (1968) 'to life' in 1994. This revival took place under Michael Somes's supervision and with the assistance of original performers, including 'Anthony Dowell, Antoinette Sibley, Monica Mason and Deanne Bergsma' (Wright 1996: 207).

Wright touches on the sort of sociocultural knowledge that the younger generation of BRB dancers had to absorb. Set in Edward Elgar's house and garden during the 1890s, Ashton presents a set of vivid 'character studies' based on the composer and his close friends (Craine and Mackrell 2000: 165–166). When talking about the duet between the ballet's 'young lovers,'[2] Isabel Fitton and Richard Arnold (1996: 208), Wright explained that Fitton 'was always described as young and romantic' and Richard Arnold (Matthew Arnold's son) as 'a fairly studious scholar, quite serious but obviously very much in love.' Geraldine Morris writes that in *Enigma Variations*, Ashton's characters 'are real flesh and blood' (2012: 174). Yet in 1994, this duet with its nineteenth-century sensibility was difficult to realise as such: 'Fred's idea was about love shining through the restraints of the period. Today we tend to go for it, and relationships develop very fast' (Wright 1996: 208). Nineteenth-century social mores, which called for discreet behaviour and restraint, were difficult to manifest stylistically and, according to Wright, 'harder than doing everything full out' (Wright 1996: 208). Abandoning their modern no-holds barred approach and tapping into the foreign world of the past meant that the dancers had to 'unlearn' what they knew about life in order to 'relearn' (Wright 1996: 208) or rediscover past ways of being. It is also interesting that Wright did not consider that full embodiment occurred until the dancers were on stage performing:

> [Y]ou learn and discover by performing [. . .] it is not until you get on stage with the audience that you really understand, get your timing right. There are a lot of interesting things in this duet: Ashton's use of music, phrasing, playing with the music.
> (Wright 1996: 208)

We understand that fostering the dancers' embodiment of the world that Ashton portrayed for his audiences required 'more than getting movement into the performers' bodies, more than their physical muscle, bone and skin' (Preston-Dunlop and Sanchez-Colberg 2002: 7). This was embodiment as a process which was not only a matter of absorbing information passed on to the dancers orally by specialists in Ashton's choreographic style and musicality, but also a process that reached its zenith in the actual act of performance on stage. Preston-Dunlop chimes with Sheets-Johnstone's consciousness-body when she writes, 'Embodiment of movement involves the whole person, a person conscious of being a living body, living that experience, giving intention to the movement material' (Preston-Dunlop and Sanchez-Colberg 2002: 7).

Performing Ashton's choreography for *Enigma Variations* includes attending to nuances of his distinctive style (Morris 2012), but also an awareness of the Edwardian society he portrayed. The expert tuition of Somes and the original cast members provided the BRB dancers with the opportunity to relive Ashton's choreography and thereby portray the nostalgia and characterisation required for the ballet. In order to shed further light on the advantages of the oral transmission and performance experience involved in rethinking methods of passing on older dances to new generations, I return to the historical project as taught at Trinity Laban from 2002.

The historical project 2002 and on

In the early 2000s, Trinity Laban introduced the historical project, a programme of study that since its inception has been followed in various forms by the school's second-year students.[3] In an attempt to redress the otherness of older dances we realised that the students could make better sense of what appeared to be the separate strands of technical and academic studies if they learned to perform the dances discussed and analysed in the lecture room. Rather than relying on watching dances on a screen, they performed extracts from them in an attempt to fuse experiential and cognitive aspects of learning and teaching. The idea of the fully integrated experience was to pursue the premise that practical and theoretical awareness of a choreographer's style operates in tandem to produce embodied knowledge.

The historical works that Trinity Laban students have studied and performed over the years include extracts from the 'Daughters of the Night' chorus from *Night Journey* (1947)[4] and the Furies' dances from *Clytemnestra* (1958).[5] Classes in Graham technique were (and continue to be) included in the school's technical dance training, but when learning the repertory, the students appreciated the extent to which the movements they practised in class became the means of conveying the emotional and psychological narratives they studied in history lectures and seminars. What was most often in their view a demanding form of classroom exercise became a transformative opportunity as they physically encountered the dramatic expression inherent within Graham's choreography. As one second-year put it, the historical project:

> was an experience of a truly modern technique, a journey back to a revolutionary period of dance. Now, I am able to find the links with the reading I do about Martha Graham, and the technique that I learn in class.
>
> (Author's notes 2002)

Another commented on her experience of Graham's theatricality, 'it was really fun to dance in the long skirts and having to put on the dramatic make up and hairdo allowed me to get into character' (Author's notes 2002). An understanding of Graham through theatrical play differs markedly from listening to the history teacher. Fully embodying a Graham work includes looking and feeling like one of her dancers. By donning the signature Graham skirt, applying the dramatic make-up and pulling the hair back from the face into a chignon worn high at the back of the head, the students physically inhabited the Graham dancer's world, tasting what it was like to be part of Martha Graham's company. As far as the men were concerned, they reported on the ample opportunity they had to increase their athleticism and to develop partnering skills when performing duets from *Diversion of Angels* (1948).

Related to but considerably later in time than the Graham dances is Robert Cohan's *Stabat Mater* (1975), inspired by Vivaldi's 1712 composition for solo voice and orchestra. Similarly to the BRB dancers, the Trinity Laban students first encountered this work from notation, taking careful note in the studio of the movement vocabulary, choreographic structure and musical phrasing. They also amassed a store of information in the lecture room about the genesis and context of *Stabat Mater*, but several of the students were from non-western backgrounds and had little comprehension of the work's biblical theme and air of spirituality.[6] Cohan's technically demanding choreography for *Stabat*, with its linear, sustained movements, I claim, is difficult for twenty-first-century dancers, accustomed as they are to speedy and physically extreme styles of movement. However, it was not until the ex-LCDT dancer Anne Donnelly (formerly Went) arrived in the studio that the dance came alive for these young dancers. In addition to coaching their technical rendition of the movement, she fed their imaginations by telling them about the emotional intensity and the religious symbolism woven into the choreography. Cohan is aware of the difficulty when transferring 'the original meaning of the movement onto the new person':

> Usually, the choreographer remembers the sensation of every step they have ever made [. . .] you will remember why you did that step thirty years ago and you will know if it is right from the sensation, not the movement. That is the difficulty of transmitting work and moving it on, and why you cannot learn from a video.
>
> (in Jackson 2013: 196–197)

Donnelly performed *Stabat Mater* throughout her career in LCDT (1981–1992) and like Wright, who, as we saw earlier, holds that the dancer fully embodies a dance only by performing it, she points out that embodiment involves more than 'just the choreography' (Donnelly 2015):

> [T]he lighting is important, the spacing, the design, the structure, the way the dresses move, the way we stand with the dresses being aware of where the lights were – how a lighting cue corresponds to the choreography, they all have to be part of the learning experience. That's the sort of thing that's very difficult for somebody to understand if they have not been involved with it or if they are looking at only one thing such as the choreography – it is the whole theatrical aspect of a work that is so important for the young dancer to comprehend and experience.
>
> (Donnelly 2015)

Once again the expert guidance of experienced dancers in the studio provides the range of information required by dancers if they are to comprehend artistic intention and thus embody choreographic authenticity and performance values. Moreover, it is in the act of performance that all theatrical elements cohere to enable young dancers to sample what it meant to perform Cohan repertory in a company like LCDT.[7]

Whether they study works from the distant or recent past, opportunities such as those extended to young dancers by Trinity Laban's historical project sow the seeds for the continued presence on stage of older dances, and thereby form the establishment of a living archive, as I go on to discuss below.

EDge 2015 – the living archive

For the purposes of this essay, the living archive represents the way in which young dancers perform older works that fall out of the repertory and perform them for new audiences, thereby maintaining a dance heritage. I have argued for the full embodiment of these older dances as characterised by 'thinking *in* the work' rather than *about* it (Rubidge 1999) and I continue to argue that in the case of an embodied art like dance, information gathered in the history lecture is better understood when it is augmented and concretised by performing the choreographer's work. Even in a situation, for example, where a young dancer is familiar with the history and context of a particular choreographer, performing an entire dance once part of the repertory can be new and surprising. Such was the case for Iris Chan of EDge (2015), as she explains:

> As an undergraduate student at Surrey in 2008 I learnt a solo from Davies's *Wyoming* (1988) for my final assessment and from 2006 I took classes from many of the Siobhan Davies Company dancers.[8] Nevertheless learning the complete *Bank* from 1997 was of course a new experience.[9]
> (Interview 2016)

Sophia Sednova was also on relatively familiar ground, having trained at the University of Iowa, United States, where she studied Limón technique and performed Trisha Brown's work:

> *Bank* wasn't that unfamiliar to me in terms of movement material, although for me Davies's movement is much more athletic than Trisha Brown's in terms of the physicality of it and the endurance needed to get through it physically, but it didn't feel foreign on my body; rather it felt quite natural. There were other pieces in the repertory where I felt out of place but Siobhan Davies felt nearer to my training and experience.
> (Sednova interview with author 2016)

Although for dancers like Chan and Sednova, *Bank* seemed contemporary, I refer to it in this essay as 'historical' because it is almost twenty years since it was first given by the Siobhan Davies Company and apart from its inclusion in the repertory of EDge 2006 and 2015, the work has not been restaged for British audiences. From 1999 Davies abandoned proscenium arch performances, concentrating instead on presenting her dances in art galleries and developing her interest in film. Aside from the fact that we have access to the excellent facility of the Siobhan Davies Replay website, there is little opportunity for new audiences to witness live performances of works such as *Bank*.

Dancers like Chan could not know the world of the 1997 *Bank*. Indeed she thinks of this work as 'a mark in British modern dance history' (interview 2016), especially as from 2001–2008, it became a model for the extended education of many professional contemporary dancers:

> [H]eralded as the first of its kind [. . .]. Between August and October 2001, *Bank* provided a unique opportunity for six dancers to 'explore, extend and enrich their own dance language'. They traced the journey taken by the original Siobhan Davies dancers when *Bank* was first created in 1997; with the project culminating in four very different performance experiences across the South East.
>
> (Chappell 2010)[10]

This model provided the basis on which Gill Clarke, in collaboration with Trinity Laban, instituted the Independent Dance MA Creative Practice in 2011;[11] thus throughout the recent past, *Bank*, and particularly the choreographic process according to which it was created, has acquired a history in the sense that it became the means of professional development experience for many dancers who have gone on to independent careers and teaching practices.

The restaging of *Bank* for EDge in 2015 was overseen by Davies but the dancers were also fortunate in being coached by Deborah Saxon, one of the original six dancers in *Bank* and a member of the Siobhan Davies Company from 1991. The level of authentic embodiment required for the work was further assured when, rather than EDge's own rehearsal director, 'Sasha Roubicek continued to rehearse *Bank* after Saxon left because of her experience and understanding as a company dancer with Davies (1999–2007)' (Chan interview 2016).

In common with Wright (together with his BRB colleagues), Donnelly, Saxon and Roubicek speak to their students from the position of those who are highly experienced performers and teachers. As Sednova remarks, '*Bank* felt very alive and present because Deborah made it ours to enjoy and encouraged us to play with the choreography within the structure of the work' (interview 2016). Clearly there was artistic freedom for the EDge dancers as there was for Davies's company. Nevertheless, Chan points out that:

> the level of detail and precision demanded of us was incredibly high [. . .] we had to fully develop embodied understanding rather than immediately replicate the steps that we learnt from the video. This

understanding was formed through a process of investing in time, practice, and patience.

(Interview 2016)

According to Chan most of the EDge dancers found *Bank* 'unusually challenging from a cardio vascular point of view':

> It's thirty minutes long and we are on the move all the time, running and walking and dodging around each other. The level of stamina needed to perform *Bank* required a method of breathing that sustained us throughout the dance, compared for example to other works we performed where you did thirty seconds of very intense, high-powered movement and then sat on the floor for two minutes.
>
> (Interview 2016)

Davies's 'slippery, organic way of moving' (Roy 2009) was influenced by release work incorporated into her practice after her sabbatical in the United States in 1988 (Clarke 1998). A release approach to movement engenders 'an exploration of the sensations of movement from the smallest parts to the largest holistic connections and total body use' (Clarke 1998: 2), principles that were not familiar to all the EDge 2015 dancers, some of whom came from a background of codified modern dance techniques. Even Chan and Sednova, who were accustomed to release-based techniques, found that for *Bank* they had to locate a surprisingly low and transferable sense of gravity, one in which the dancer 'poured weight and ease of movement through your joints and allowed weight through your limbs so that your centre could transfer forward into your arm as if you are tilting' (Chan interview 2016).

Bank might be described as a dance about dance itself in that the choreography does not reach beyond the presentation of geometric patterns, rhythmic complexity and the interweaving trajectories of its six dancers. As Chan points out,

> The choreography is intricate and precise and it doesn't demand expression – it is understated. It requires concentration and awareness of the group and of yourself within the performance. Some of the feedback that Sue [Siobhan Davies] gave us contained ideas such as thinking of *Bank* as an invitation to see people working and working together rather than a demonstration or presentation.
>
> (Interview 2016)

The dancers had only four weeks into which they had to squeeze a process that is normally twice as long and, despite these time constraints, Saxon considered that it was vital to reproduce Davies's creative process, at least 'on a micro-scale so that we had some idea of what it was like to be in that process' (Chan 2016):

> Deborah brought books with illustrations of African textiles, Chinese calligraphy, black and white prints from various historical periods and we used these to create what she called little 'events'; thus we used these patterns to build little phrases and some of it did go into what we learnt from the video.
>
> (Chan 2016)

Thus, by working through choreographic tasks the dancers 'explore[d] different avenues of moving' – the intention was not to fulfil the tasks *per se* but to experience the 'sensations and resultant form of the movement generated by them' (Clarke 1998: 2). The individuality and creative energy of a Siobhan Davies dancer were further emphasised when Saxon cast the EDge dancers in accordance with the material they produced during the first two days of creative process:

> When Deb taught me Sarah Warsop's solo she said, 'this is in the realm of what you did when you were showing me the pattern you were working on,' so she referred to things that she had noticed about us during the creative process. In the cases of myself and the other dancer who performed this solo, there were bits that were our own material, and on the videos, you can see slight differences between our versions of this solo because we danced our own input into it.
>
> (Chan 2016)

These dancers learned many of the principles which can be discussed when analysing Davies's choreography in the seminar room, but by thinking and doing in the studio, and over time in performance, they discovered for themselves what it was like to experience her demanding creative process and to sustain the stamina and energy required for dancing *Bank* on stage. As Chan rather touchingly puts it, 'I had even more respect for the original dancers because they were already perhaps in their mid-thirties when they were performing and to realise that they were dancing at that kind of level and speed was really humbling' (Chan 2016).

In this essay, I have argued that the opportunity to learn and perform historical modern dance repertory from specialist practitioners is an important stage in the training and performance experience of present-day and future dancers. Whether these works are from the more distant past, as is the case with Graham repertory studied and performed by Trinity Laban undergraduates, or they are relatively recent, such as *Bank* for the EDge dancers, full embodiment involves physically knowing that work from *within* as well as understanding *about* it. I claim that the examples of this type of psychophysical learning that I have cited demonstrate that it is possible to dance history from the perspective of a critical form of embodiment. Moreover young dancers welcome the opportunity to embody choreography that is fast disappearing from the contemporary dance stage, as Chan explains when reflecting on her performances of *Bank*:

> I wish that there was a dance like that happening now and also having done workshops with Trisha Brown dancers I really crave this kind of work, and I don't think that in current British contemporary dance it is easy to find. Some of the contemporary dance that I see now is either spectacular or virtuosic and acrobatic – it's often more like a sport or how far the human body can go.
> (interview with author 2016)

It was not my intention in this essay to claim that dancers in the twenty-first century performing older works capture the precise nuances of their original styles characterised as they are by technical and stylistic niceties and various types of otherness. It is more a matter of young dancers deepening and extending their current practice through experiencing the past canon. It is the storehouse of practical and cultural knowledge that they access from older dances that is of vital importance and the ways in which this information is passed on to them: *how* they learn about what it was like to be immersed in the works and to perform them onstage. I claim that dancers at various points in their careers benefit from acquiring knowledge about their heritage and perhaps even more importantly embodying this knowledge through performance on stage for present-day and future audiences.

Notes

1. The long-established Laban (Laban Centre) and Trinity College of Music merged in 2005 to become a leading music and dance conservatoire. Based in the Deptford area of London and housed in purpose-built headquarters, Trinity Laban dance school trains professional dancers and choreographers. Among its alumni is the internationally renowned Matthew Bourne.
2. See Morris (2012: 112).
3. Colin Bourne, Laban's head of undergraduate studies, explains that in recent times, the second-year students continue to research an aspect of the work they learn in the studio and use this research 'as a starting point to reflect on their participation in, and understanding of, the process [involved in creating and performing that work]' (Bourne 2015).
4. Graham's one-act dance drama based on Sophocles's *Oedipus Rex*.
5. *Clytemnestra* is Graham's full evening dance drama based on Aeschylus's *The Oresteia*.

6   *Stabat Mater* is based on Mary's sorrowing at Christ's crucifixion.
7   Over the years Laban's historical project has diversified and more recently the repertory has included Lea Anderson's *Smithereens*, Wayne McGregor's *Polar Sequences* (2003) and *Women* (2009) by Sasha Waltz. Colin Bourne explains that the decision to include less historic dances is 'not to deny the validity of the students understanding and embodying truly historic works' but rather to select dances that 'have a relevance to where our graduates might actually be working' when they enter the dance profession (Bourne 2015). See also O'Brien (2015).
8   Chan worked at the Siobhan Davies Company's studios in an administrative capacity from 2008 to 2013, also attending classes and workshops with company dancers.
9   EDge (2015) danced *Bank* to Matteo Fargion's accompaniment beaten out on cardboard boxes. The costumes were specially designed to tone with the grey floor on which the work was originally performed and with the light background. On account of the uncertainty of venues during the EDge touring schedule and the inability to travel with more than one lino floor, the company danced on their standard black floor and with a black backdrop. Saxon chose colours for the costumes to go with the grey floor but was concerned that they would be too dark in the black setting so Lucy Hanson increased the intensity of the lighting, which she had redesigned based on what she could fathom from the original video of *Bank* and in accordance with notes about the original lighting design – the actual plot was lost (Sednova 2016).
10 See also: 'six dancers were selected by the Company to recreate *Bank* and given the opportunity to introduce their own new material [. . .] the six dancers had the opportunity to experience the creative and working methods of one of the UK's leading contemporary dance companies' (Siobhandaviesreplay n.d.).
11 The programme titled 'MA Creative Practice: Dance Professional Practice' started in the academic year 2010/2011. Independent Dance and Siobhan Davies Dance run the MA in partnership with Trinity Laban (Alexander email communication 2016).

Bibliography

Alexander, K. (2016). Kirsty Alexander email communication with the author, 20 May.
Author's notes (2002). Notes compiled whilst tutoring second year BA Trinity Laban students in preparation for a presentation about the project.
Bourne, C. (2015). Colin Bourne email communication with the author, 20 November.
Carr, J. (2013). 'Embodiment and dance: Puzzles of consciousness and agency,' in J. Bunker, A. Pakes and B. Rowell (eds.). *Thinking through Dance*. London: Dance Books, 63–81.

Chan, I. (2016). Interview with Iris Chan conducted by the author at London Contemporary Dance School, 20 January.

Chappell, K. (2010). *Feature: Siobhan Davies Dance Company CPD Programme.* Available from: http://londondance.com/articles/features/siobhan-davies-dance-company-cpd-programme

Clarke, M. (1998). *Understanding the Choreographic Approach of Siobhan Davies.* Available from: www.siobhandaviesreplay.com/media2/UserT/. . ./00002716.pdfype

Craine, D. and J. Mackrell (2000). *Oxford Dictionary of Dance.* Oxford: Oxford University Press.

Donnelly, A. (2015). Interview with Ann Donnelly conducted by the author at London Contemporary Dance School, 22 October.

Eliot, T.S. (1986). 'Tradition and the Individual Talent.' *Selected Essays.* London: Faber and Faber, 13–22.

Hartley, L. P. (1997) *The Go-Between.* London: Penguin Books.

Jackson, P. (2013). *The Last Guru.* London: Dance Books.

Makkonen, A. and H. Järvinen (2010). *Can We Dance History? The Presence of History in Dance Practice.* Available from: http://sdr-uk.org/wp/wp-content/uploads/2014/10/2010_SDR_dance_history_symposium_proceedings.pdf

McNamara, J. (1999). 'Dance in the hermeneutic circle,' in S. Horton Fraleigh and P. Hanstein (eds.). *Researching Dance.* London: Dance Books, 162–187.

Morris, G. (2012). *Frederick Ashton's Ballets.* Alton: Dance Books.

O'Brien, B. (producer and director) (2015). Dance rebels: A story of modern dance. *BBC* 4: 13 December 9 p.m.

Preston-Dunlop, V. and A. Sanchez-Colberg (2002). 'Chapter 2 – Core Concepts of a Choreological Perspective,' in V. Preston-Dunlop and A. Sanchez-Colberg (eds.). *Dance and the Performative.* London: Verve, 7–37.

Prins, G. (1991). 'Oral history,' in P. Burke (ed.). *New Perspectives on Historical Writing.* Oxford: Polity Press, 114–139.

Roy, S. (2009). *Step-by-Step Guide to Dance: Siobhan Davies.* Available from: www.theguardian.com/stage/2009/mar24/guide-dance-siobhan-davies

Rubidge, S. (1999). *Embodying Theory.* Available from: www.sensedigital.co.uk/writing/EmbodTheory.pdf

Sednova, S. (2016). Interview with Sophia Sednova conducted by the author at London Contemporary Dance School, 22 October.

Sheets-Johnstone, M. (1979). *The Phenomenology of Dance.* London: Dance Books.

Siobhandaviesreplay. (n.d.) *Dance Works.* Available from: www.siobhandaviesreplay.com/

Wright, P. (1996). 'Excerpts from enigma variations,' in S. Jordan and A. Grau (eds). *Following Sir Fred's Steps.* London: Dance Books, 206–219.

Part 2

Researching and writing

Introduction to Part 2
Researching and writing

GERALDINE MORRIS AND LARRAINE NICHOLAS

WHILE PART 1 WAS CONCERNED, though not exclusively, with the initial approach to history, Part 2 is more methodological, in the sense that it deals with some of the details of historical work, in researching and communicating the results of research. The product of our research is most frequently realised in written history, but this could just as easily be seen as the 'writing on the body' of a danced outcome. Akram Khan's approach to choreographing his *Giselle*, for example (Ch. 3), could be argued as a process of research and communication very much equivalent to the traditional written communication of historical research we are mainly concerned with here.

Part 2 essays emanate from considerable research in various dance contexts. The essays are not only transdisciplinary but also transnational and reflect the expanding field of historical research. The reader will find topics from diverse dance genres: dances of India and China; ballet from America and nineteenth-century France; the 'Judson' influence in America and Europe; dances on film and video; aspirations of Swedish artists to archive their work. In addition, the essays have been grouped to raise discussion about methodological issues in researching and writing dance history. This introduction will outline these main ones: the role of the historian; the use and creation of archival sources; the new insights gained by adopting different theoretical frameworks; and some of the ways of structuring an historical account. They do not in any way exhaust the possibilities.

The role of the historian

Alexandra Carter (Ch. 9) introduces the business of the historian as a creative activity involving 'new ways of looking'. Our views of the past are not fixed in time but subject to 'shifting perspectives' as new ways of understanding the past come into historical discourse. She deals with the status of 'a fact', how we use sources, how we view our own biases and the privileging of certain kinds of knowledge. All require reflexive thinking about the nature of historical knowledge, how we arrive at it and how it is communicated. Writing on reflexivity and its epistemological framework, Simon Gunn argues that

> It directs historians towards a consideration of the grounds on which interpretations, including their own, are conducted. It involves a recognition that historical interpretation is not merely a question of 'giving voice' to the sources but that it involves . . . a methodological operation which transmutes information from one order of knowledge (that of archives) to another (that of scholarly narrative or explanation).
> (Gunn, 2006: 195)

As some essays in this volume demonstrate, 'scholarly narrative or explanation' also has an ethical dimension.

Sources

Cara Traders made an appearance in Part 1 (Ch. 2). Here we should note how her 'autobiography' is structured with selected archival sources that both inform it and supply a parallel voice from the historical context of this life. Appropriately, in Chapter 11, Lena Hammergren asks, 'how do we conceive of sources and what can we make of them?' (p. 136). She questions the convention of dividing sources into 'primary' and 'secondary' as if some sources hold unmediated truths. Even documents in archives have already been given significance by their conditions of preservation. Hammergren includes case studies on dancers' life stories and a richly theoretical discussion in which she argues for sources to be seen as profoundly ambiguous, needing to be read for their multiple meanings and generic codes from their sociocultural contexts.

Hammergren's case studies are from what we might now call traditional archive sources, but in the digital age the expectation is that archives should at least to some extent improve accessibility, with Internet access and databases. Such projects are invariably expensive and time-consuming, 'big dreams' in terms of small-scale artists. In Chapter 12, Astrid von Rosen reflects on some such projects in Sweden, considering how they have worked from the perspective of the local dance community. As she highlights, methods of structuring the digital collection can cause significant absences and distort the record of local dance history. She sees the goal of archiving and history-making, with and for the local dance community, as an aspect of artistic empowerment and political activism which must not be divorced from the community itself, whose members are themselves embodied historical sources (see Chs. 7–8). The 'impossibility of archiving (in a traditional manner) embodied dance knowledge' (p. 157) opens new opportunities for technologies to enable public engagement with the heritage.

Theoretical frameworks

Different theoretical frameworks bring to light new interpretations of our dance contexts. Even changing the perspective a little can radically alter the interpretation. This is what Geraldine Morris achieves (Ch. 19) in her examination of *Giselle* (1841). Long considered the archetypal 'romantic' ballet of love beyond the grave, there is evidence that in its time it was more Gothic in atmosphere. She draws out connections between characters and plot in *Giselle* and in *Great Expectations* (Charles Dickens, 1860) which certainly indicate some cultural commonalities. Seeing *Giselle* in the light of a Gothic sensibility, she argues, brings out the much darker undertones of the tale – the vengefulness of the wilis, the eroticism of the story and societal attitudes towards unmarried or fallen women. It may bring us closer to the experience of the first audiences.

Prarthana Purkayastha (Ch. 10) highlights the role of ideology in allowing some voices to be heard and suppressing others. Her insights from postcolonial theory are applied to the history of dance in India (as they could be in many other places), showing how colonialism created the conditions which would lead to two kinds of 'invisible violence': that of Orientalism (favouring western 'oriental' dancers, such as Ruth St Denis) and that of Indian cultural nationalism (favouring the reconstructed 'classical' dance forms). In both, race, class and gender were brought to bear in granting cultural status to some dancing bodies and not to others. Asking how we can decolonise dance history, she agrees with Sanjay Seth that 'it is through being vigilant to particular codes of history [. . .], codes that are time and culture-specific rather than universal, that we can continue to decolonize dance history' (p. 111).

Cultural values are specifically located geographically and not neutral or universal, as Emily Wilcox agrees in her work on dance in China (Ch. 13). In the twentieth century it was globalisation that threatened the development of the dance there. Linked with the US hegemony over global markets and Cold War ideology of freedom and individualism, globalisation privileged the export of modern and postmodern dance worldwide. She offsets the power of globalisation with that of 'provincialisation'. To see Europe and America as also 'provincial' takes away the determinism of the cultural values of 'centre' holding sway over the 'periphery' in geographical terms. Her research uncovers resistance to the adoption of American modern dance in the 1950s when China was developing its own indigenous dance theatre forms.

Perspectives from gender studies continue to have high relevance in dance history. For example the unequal representation of female choreographers in ballet, both in the historical canon and the present, continues to concern dance writers and inspire feminist explanations. Joellen Meglin (Ch. 17) takes a 'materialist feminist' approach in her research on the American choreographer Ruth Page. This means a close analysis of some of Page's works, the sources she used and other texts coexistent with her. Meglin shows how Page approached her choreographic work from the position of her own feminine subjectivity. One of her examples is *American Pattern* (1937), about the trap of female domesticity, arguably the first feminist ballet in the United States. Page's work is re-evaluated, consistent with other feminist texts of its time. By her crossing of generic boundaries (generic subversion), across other dance genres and between other art forms, we can interpret her work as modernist.

Ballet in particular is known for a strong division between male and female performers, in technique, physique and stage presentation. For some commentators this seems a problem in the twenty-first century, when gender issues have expanded far beyond notions of masculinities and femininities, to include homosexual, transgender and gender-neutral issues. Jill Nunes Jensen (Ch. 18) examines Alonzo King's work on his company, Alonzo King LINES Ballet. She argues that his style has developed to subvert some of the gender-based assumptions of classical ballet, to project a predominantly non-dyadic version of gender roles. This is to be seen in costume and movement qualities which allow his male and female dancers to move between expressions of power and grace and to relate to each other in non-stereotypical ways. Nunes Jensen considers a short timescale, but one in which she has seen King's work steer in this direction. This raises questions for the future of ballet as well as about the historical binary of continuity and change. 'Is it possible for ballet bodies not to mimic sociological presumptions of difference and still keep the form largely intact?' (p. 228).

Structuring historical narratives

How does change occur over time? Or indeed how do we account for continuities? A familiar linking structure in historical narratives is that of 'causation', conceived of as a chain of developments, rather like the 'family trees' once popular as ways of explaining American modern dance, tinged with unreflective suggestions of inevitable progress. As an alternative, Linda Tomko (Ch. 14) invokes Michel Foucault's bracketing of causation to explore the emergence of a group of female dance pioneers in early twentieth-century America. Exploring 'conditions of possibility' rather than simple causation changes the focus to an array of societal changes that gave support to women such as Loie Fuller, Isadora Duncan and Ruth St Denis. In particular, she focuses on the 'separate spheres' ideology that allowed groups of well-placed women to claim philanthropic and education reform as their own legitimate public spheres, so raising the possibility of women claiming cultural authority. In conclusion, though, Tomko suggests that we should not give up on causation and individual agency but see the potential for their interaction with conditions of possibility.

The plotting of a dance historical narrative can take a number of temporal pathways, focusing on short to very long time spans. Arguably, with long time spans it is possible to gloss over conditions of possibility, or to give insufficient weight to continuities as well as change. Including a large part of the twentieth century, Beth Genné (Ch. 15) takes the long view of the 'street dance', dances from film or video performed on city streets, featuring dancers such as Fred Astaire, Gene Kelly and Michael Jackson. This is a tightly focused but temporarily expansive narrative about the genre in which she establishes the continuities within the genre, an established iconography, in which later exponents paid homage to their predecessors. But, as she points out, the safe streets of the early part of the century change into the urban jungle in which Michael Jackson dances and his references to the earlier dance scenes serve to point out the cultural reversal. This is not just a history of a dance but dance as sociocultural history.

Also taking a longitudinal view, Marcia Siegel (Ch. 16) traces the influence of Judson forwards from the 1960s. Even though it took place in 'a culture utterly different from what provokes art today' (p. 197), its presence is still felt in the work of Victoria Marks and Anne Teresa De Keersmaeker as they work with minimalism and non-professional performers. More significantly for our concepts of time and history, De Keersmaeker in her open-access Rosas Remix Project (recalling her *Rosas Danst Rosas*, 1983) and Yvonne Rainer in her *RoS Indexical* (2007, referencing the Nijnsky *Sacre du Printemps*, 1913) illustrate how past and present leach into each other in what Siegel astutely titles 'the porous nature of dance history' (p. 207).

In writing about dance history, the absence of the dancing body should remind us of the absence of the thing we are writing about. Siegel's essay demonstrates how the dancing body can be brought to life on the page through beautifully observed movement description.

Bibliography

Gunn, Simon (2006) *History and Cultural Theory*, Harlow: Pearson Longman.

Chapter 9

Destabilising the discipline
Critical debates about history and their impact on the study of dance[1]

ALEXANDRA CARTER

DANCE HISTORY IS NOW WELL established as a vital component of dance studies. Whether engaged with as a 'named' course or integrated within broader fields of study, it is a part of the curriculum at many levels of dance education and training. Paradoxically, the traditional discipline of history has come under attack from critical and cultural theories which question the very nature and status of knowledge, and how that knowledge is retrieved, organised, recorded and received. These debates about the construction and reception of knowledge arose from postmodern, poststructuralist and feminist theories. Although the challenges to the accepted modes of engaging with history which are presented by these critical perspectives have, in themselves, been challenged (see Appleby et al. 1994), my purpose here is to identify their relevance to the teaching and learning of dance history – that is how theoretical debates about history might impact on the pedagogy of dance history. The examples are drawn from western theatre dance but the general principles are relevant to an engagement with the histories of all dance forms.

Debates about the nature of knowledge have arisen from a variety of critical and cultural perspectives. Poststructuralist thought has influenced our conception of the very nature of 'history' itself, such as the assumption that the historical endeavour coheres around the retrieval of 'facts' which are, in themselves, 'true'. The postmodern attitude to the role of the 'author' has given rise to a questioning of the role of the historian, who is now seen not as neutral recorder of events but as active creator of them. Discourse theories have exposed how knowledge is constituted not by limited logocentric modes of engagement with the world but by a vast variety of influences; this calls into question the reliance on written sources as privileged evidence for recreating the past. Cultural studies impacted on traditional thinking about the hierarchy of knowledge in which certain events are deemed more significant than others. Similarly, attacks on his-story came from feminist writers who exposed the gendered nature of historical construction. In all, the gaps and silences in historical records have been exposed not as 'empty' or unworthy of research but as a product of culturally constructed, hierarchical perspectives on the 'what', 'who', 'when' and 'how' of the past.

In terms of the teaching and learning of dance history, these challenges can be explored in relation to:

- the totalising nature of history and the status of 'facts';
- the role of the historian;
- the nature of and attitudes towards sources; and
- the privileging of certain kinds of 'knowledge'.

The totalising nature of history and the status of 'facts'

The writing of history is the writing of stories about the past. These are narratives, which imply a traditional narrative structure of beginning, middle and end. This structure is a way of 'using story to give shape to experiences as a way of understanding them' (Husbands 1996: 46). But it also, argues Hutcheon, 'imparts meaning as well as order' (1989: 62). The packaging of dance history into neat periods or 'shapes' with a beginning, middle and end not only enables the organisation of a curriculum ('next week we'll do the Romantic period') but also gives meaning to those periods, making them discrete and self-contained in the specificity of their characteristics. The dangers inherent in this packaging are that those activities, those periods of time, which don't fall neatly under prescribed labels don't fall anywhere at all. They are less researched, under-recorded, not studied. Why is *Coppélia*, a very popular ballet in our repertoire, far less well known and less written about than *Giselle* or *The Sleeping Beauty*? Might it be that, created in 1870, it is on the cusp of the waning Romantic era and the impending neoclassical age of the Russian Imperial ballet – but it doesn't fall neatly into either? We all know that modern dance started in Britain in the mid-1960s with the policy change of Ballet Rambert and the establishment of London Contemporary Dance Theatre and School – but did it? The history of modern dance in Britain is far richer than this commonly accepted 'starting point' suggests. Of course we need to organise our teaching and learning and our textbooks, for there are clusters of characteristics which can be ascribed to particular times and phenomena – certain conditions of production and reception which result in particular kinds of dance works. But we also need to be conscious that nothing neatly starts or finishes. There are dance works which sit firmly within a period but don't conform to the characteristics which have been identified. For example our notion of the Romantic period is based on the supernatural ballets of spirits and sylphs, and we tend to forget all the 'national' ballets presented during the same period which were different in their aesthetic concerns. One of the historian's problems, therefore, is 'to decide how and where to insert an analytic knife into the seamlessness of time, and to recognise the motivations for whatever incision is made' (Southgate 1996: 113). We need to define parameters, 'the Romantic period', the 'Neoclassical', the 'Modern', the 'Postmodern', but we need to be aware of the flawed finality indicated by these capital letters and the fact that these packages are tied by historians, not necessarily produced by neat, all-inclusive, clusterings of events themselves.

Implicit in the foregoing debate is the notion of continuity – that is a sensitivity to traces left behind and embedded in what is to come. But the postmodern challenge to totalisation also rejects the imperative of continuity. As Hutcheon, drawing on Foucault, suggests,

> instead of seeking common denominators and homogeneous networks of causality and analogy, historians have been freed . . . to note the dispersing interplay of different, heterogeneous discourses that acknowledge the undecidable in both the past and our knowledge of the past.
> (Hutcheon 1989: 66)

In our own learning, teaching and research, we can acknowledge that events, or repertoire, might not 'fit in' to a linear notion of history. We tend to see the past as a line stretching back from the present. As Chapman says in relation to ballet history,

> the dance historian sets off on a voyage through the past with the rudder of his modern prejudices steering his course. He seeks significance in terms of what he knows of the theatrical dance of today. His explanation of historical development is couched in terms of the progressive accumulation of traits similar to the major features of twentieth-century ballet.
> (Chapman 1979/80: 256)

It is a fascinating project, for example, to look at a reconstruction of the *ballets de cours* of the seventeenth century and identify features which can be 'traced through' to our ballet vocabulary and repertoire today. This helps to enhance appreciation of why we are studying history at all. But history is not just a line from past to present; it is a web, a 'dispersing interplay' of discourses. (See Tomko, this volume, for an extension of this debate.) As such, our histories can accommodate activities which do not seem to contribute in any obvious ways to the 'development' of the art form but, in their time, were a vital part of it. My own work on the ballet in London in the Victorian era is a case in point. Although I would argue strongly that this period disrupts the notion that British ballet was 'born' in the 1930s, the ballets were also, in their own right, a central part of the entertainment scene of London and many provincial cities. As such, they are worthy of study not for their place in the continuum but for their place in their time.

We can argue, therefore, that the study of history comprises not the study of neat boxes of knowledge, which embody uncontested facts, but is analogous to the study of clouds. Clouds have the capacity to change shape, to present different images, depending on who is looking at them, and when and why.

The role of the historian

'History is a shifting discourse constructed by historians and . . . from the existence of the past no one reading is entailed: change the gaze, shift the perspective and new readings appear' (Jenkins 1991: 14). This is what can make the study of dance so vital; it is not just that new sources are found which lead us to reformulate our accounts, but new ways of looking, 'shifting perspectives' which can offer new readings of old sources. As Jenkins argues, sources in themselves don't say anything: 'The claim that bias can be expunged by attending to "what the sources say" is undercut by the fact that sources are mute. It is historians who articulate whatever the "sources say"' (Jenkins 1991: 38). The biases in historical record are strengths, so long as we are aware of what they are. It is the biases, the different perspectives on the past, that stop it solidifying. Ramsay Burt's *The Male Dancer* (1995) could not have been written twenty years ago,[2] or certainly would have been written differently, for the explanatory models which he uses to grant meaning to the past (Hutcheon 1989) did not exist. As a result, we see the male dancer afresh.

The difference between the traditional model of history which strives for an unachievable neutrality and objectivity and more recent models is that the latter acknowledge their bias: 'What is foregrounded in postmodern theory and practice is the self-conscious inscription within history of the existing, but usually concealed, attitude of historians towards their material' (Hutcheon 1989: 74). This notion does not, of course, make the endeavour a free-for-all, but it develops a consciousness that the study of history is a creative activity – created, that is, by both the historian and by the recipient. It involves the imaginative piecing together of various accounts in order to produce meanings; it may necessitate speculation where there are gaps and asking questions as to why there are gaps. In our studies, one of the key questions we can ask is: who wrote this? Why is Nijinsky so privileged in primary source accounts of the Ballets Russes, and Karsavina barely mentioned? Why was Nijinska, until recently, written out of these accounts? We might ask who wrote them, what were their sexual proclivities, what attracted them to the performers and how has that personal attraction become embodied in seemingly neutral accounts of the Ballets Russes? Sally Banes's book (1998) is not really about 'dancing women'; it is about dancing women in America – because the author is American and that is her realm of expertise. Not much, if anything, may be known about the writers whose works we study but a quick look at their autobiography on the flyleaf will indicate nationality, gender, profession. This information does not invalidate their writing; it just alerts us to where the authors are 'coming from'. Historians make meaning; we need to be aware of who is making the meaning and from what perspective that meaning is made.

Attitudes towards sources

Although a case has been made that dance poses a special challenge to the historian because of its ephemerality (see e.g. Berg in Fraleigh and Hanstein 1999), such a claim is only partially tenable, for all of the past is ephemeral; it exists only in records of the events, not in the events themselves. As suggested, 'hard' evidence, such as artefacts or documents, does not have meaning in itself, for meaning is ascribed through various interpretative frameworks or points of view. While we might be personally better informed if we could have seen Nijinsky dance, it is the exploration of what that dancing might have 'meant' and how it meant different things to different people which is the interrogative and imaginative task of the historian.

Writers and readers of history, therefore, make meaning from sources, for 'the development of historical understanding is always the result of an active dialogue between ourselves, in the present, and the evidence in whatever form the past has left behind' (Husbands 1996: 13). In an ideal world, those who learn about dance history should be able to juxtapose those sources, compare them, consider their biases, their explicit or otherwise theoretical frameworks. What, for example, are the different stances taken by David Vaughan in his *Frederick Ashton and His Ballets* ([1977] 1999) and Julie Kavanagh in *Secret Muses* (1996)? What do these books tell us, in their different ways, not only about Ashton but also about the changing nature of biography? But we do not work in an ideal world and it is not always possible to compare sources critically. What can be done, as already suggested, is to consider the nature of the source as well as its content, even at a simple level. Who wrote it, when and where? If distinguishing a theoretical stance is not always easy, discerning a personal bias is easier. How useful is the source? Are there chapter headings, a contents page, an index, a bibliography? For whom is it written – the intended recipient? It is becoming more common now to tackle educational assignments which address the nature of the sources, or the research methods, rather than the rewriting of history culled unimaginatively from books. It isn't easy, however, to be persuaded by the validity of these tasks. For a history module I teach in a university, an essay assignment demands a critical analysis of selected historical sources. A monitoring questionnaire on the module produced the comment that 'it was a pity that the assignment did not relate to history'.

In most history curricula, time is short and there will be a tension between how much of it we spend on engaging with historical methods and how much on historical content; there's not much point in establishing Ivor Guest's credentials if you don't know what Ivor Guest has written about. But on the other hand, a critical approach to sources is a lifelong, transferable skill which has the potential to inform how we read the daily newspaper, watch the television news, hear the political broadcast. A healthy scepticism about 'facts', about 'truth', about how these are constructed and by whom, will stand scholars in good stead as discriminating citizens.

A key source in the study of dance, however, is not the traditional written one but the visual: the dance itself. Here, the adoption of a critical attitude towards the works we see is still vital – no, that's not Coralli/Perrot's version of *Giselle* we're viewing but Grigorovitch's new choreography of 1990, based on Petipa's of 1884 and Coralli and Perrot's of 1841. Marwick in 1989 (p. 323) devotes a page to the use of visual sources as if they are a novel idea. Ten years later, Simon Schama, in a Radio 3 talk in November 1999 (Schama 1999), is still calling for a wide variety of source material as well as 'text-bound' research. It is in the use of visual sources where dance study has the edge over many other disciplinary endeavours.

The privileging of 'knowledge'

A further debate in macro-history which inevitably impacts on dance concerns the notion that historiography is not value-free. It privileges certain kinds of people and activities and it is these that constitute the canon. As Laakkonen says, 'Canons guide our thinking of what is considered to be good and worth knowing . . . our way of writing and interpreting history' (2000: 60).[3] She claims, however, that canonisation and its implicit rules have resulted in a limited understanding of our past. Traditional history has been accused of celebrating 'the achievements of . . . dead white European males rather than showing the contribution of women, minorities, gays or other oppressed and excluded groups' (Appleby et al. 1994: 5). Now, as Hutcheon claims for a postmodernist perspective, we can consider 'the histories . . . of the losers as well as the winners, of the regional . . . as well as the centrist, of the unsung many as well as the much sung few' (Hutcheon 1989: 66). This is now happening in our dance literature: Burt and Kavanagh have written about homosexuality and the dance artist; Lynn Garafola rescued Nijinska (1987/88). She also, in her extensive account of the Ballets Russes (1989), put audiences back into the picture, thus explicitly acknowledging the full interplay of people and events, the range of discourses which produce historical phenomena. But that interplay is still limited. Although Jowitt (1988), for example, looks at the working lives of performers, the whole notion that dance performance is a job is still underexplored. The glamour of the ballerina is fascinating, but so too is the question 'how much did she get paid?' We know about the big names, and we will probably never know the actual small names, but we can be alert to the notion that the dance event is produced not only by individual creative artists but also by unacknowledged armies of dancers, walk-ons, administrators, scene builders and movers, front-of-house, publicity and marketing people and so on. We cannot, as said, name all these but we can acknowledge that context is not just background, but context is what produces the artistic event, and shapes our perception of it. The state of an employment market at a particular time, the financial imperatives – if Terpsichore was in sneakers in America in the 1960s (Banes 1986), it was not just an aesthetic choice but also an economic one – all this impacts on how dance is produced and received. This information can be found in our dance books, as history cross-fertilises with other disciplinary perspectives, such as sociology, cultural studies and ethnography, but it is not easy to disentangle. Nevertheless, by being alert to the notion that history is produced by this interplay of a huge variety of discourses, we can bring it closer, acknowledging it as part of everyday life that was – and is.

In conclusion, one of the attacks upon postmodern and other critical perspectives is that they result in a deep cynicism of the whole historical project. They appear to unravel the nature of historical knowledge until we can't see what is left; they seem to undermine the professionalism of historians, trivialise the value of their archival research and doubt the integrity of all sources. But there is a difference between cynicism and scepticism. As Appleby et al. (1994: 6) point out, 'skepticism is an approach to learning as well as a philosophical stance' but 'complete skepticism . . . is debilitating, because it casts doubt on the ability to draw judgments and make conclusions'. Part of the skill of a historian is the ability to 'draw judgments and make conclusions', for history is not an exercise where all is relative and anything goes. But we can, perhaps, promote the development of a questioning attitude. As postmodern dance is an attitude to dance making, not a predetermined set of procedures and outcomes, so with history. An awareness of the debates would encourage the loss of a 'theoretical innocence' (Jenkins 1997: 2) about history and nurture an incredulity towards its metanarratives (Lyotard, in Jenkins 1997). We may not, or cannot, change the syllabus content but we can introduce a critical engagement with sources. It is important to be realistic, of course; as I've said, it's a struggle sometimes to read one source, let alone engage with several. But even that one book or article can be read with an inquiring mind about not just its content but also its status as a source. The role of the historian can be invested with qualities of both reason and imagination; students of all ages can see that they, too, are historians. They can learn that dance history is produced by many other histories and, in turn, has the potential to contribute to those other histories.

Students have so much to learn and teachers have so much to offer, in so little time; we have to be realistic about what can and cannot be done. It is not possible to argue or make judgements if there is no awareness of the nature or sides of the argument; the engagement with historical content is paramount. But it is possible to argue, for historical theory is necessarily imbued in its content; it is just a question of whether we choose to disentangle it. As Geyl (in Southgate 1996: 109) claimed, 'History is argument without end'. By nurturing an inquiring attitude towards how history is made, by whom and for what purpose, we can see our own creative role within it. History is an essentially human endeavour in which we attempt to make sense, with the emphasis on 'make', of what Simon Schama describes as 'the past, in all its splendid messiness' (1991).

Notes

1   This chapter is based on 'Partners in Time: A Critical Examination of the Changing Nature of "History" as a Discipline', a paper given to the European Society of Dance Historians Conference, Twickenham (Carter 2000). In its present form the essay was published in the first edition of *Rethinking Dance History* (2004) and is reproduced here with minor editing necessitated by different content in the previous volume.
2   Carter was writing for the first edition in 2004.
3   In her paper (2000), Laakkonen disentangles the various means by which the canon is constituted.

Bibliography

Appleby, J., Hunt, L. and Jacob, M. (1994) *Telling the Truth about History*, New York: W. W. Norton.

Banes, S. (1986) *Terpsichore in Sneakers: Postmodern Dance*, Middletown, CT: Wesleyan University Press.

—— (1998) *Dancing Women: Female Bodies on Stage*, London: Routledge.

Burt, R. (1995) *The Male Dancer: Bodies, Spectacle, Sexualities*, London: Routledge.

Carter, A. (2000) 'Partners in Time: A Critical Examination of the Changing Nature of "History" as a Discipline', in *Dance History: The Teaching and Learning of Dance History*, Conference Proceedings of the European Association of Dance Historians, Twickenham: EADH.

Chapman, J. (1979/80) 'The Aesthetic Interpretation of Dance History', *Dance Chronicle*, 3:3, 254–74.

Fraleigh, S. and Hanstein, P. (eds.) (1999) *Researching Dance: Evolving Modes of Enquiry*, London: Dance Books.

Garafola, L. (1987/8) 'Bronislava Nijinska: A Legacy Uncovered', *Women and Performance*, 3:6, 78–88.

—— (1989) *Diaghilev's Ballets Russes*, Oxford: Oxford University Press.

Husbands, C. (1996) *What Is History Teaching? Language, Ideas and Meaning in Learning about the Past*, Buckingham: Open University Press.

Hutcheon, L. (1989) *The Politics of Postmodernism*, London: Routledge.

Jenkins, K. (1991) *Rethinking History*, London: Routledge.

—— (ed.) (1997) *The Postmodern History Reader*, London: Routledge.

Jowitt, D. (1988) *Time and the Dancing Image*, Berkeley, CA: University of California Press.

Kavanagh, J. (1996) *Secret Muses: The Life of Frederick Ashton*, London: Faber.

Laakkonen, J. (2000) 'The Problem of Canon in Writing and Teaching Dance History', in *Dance History: The Teaching and Learning of Dance History*, Conference Proceedings of the European Association of Dance Historians, Twickenham: EADH.

Marwick, A. (1989) *The Nature of History*, 2nd edn, London: Macmillan.

Schama, S. (1991) 'A Room with No View', *Guardian*, 26 September, p. 12.

Schama, S. (1999) 'Sounds of the Century' lecture, BBC Radio 3, 13 November.

Southgate, B. (1996) *History: What and Why? Ancient, Modern and Postmodern Perspectives*, London: Routledge.

Vaughan, D. ([1977] 1999) *Frederick Ashton and His Ballets*, London: Dance Books.

Chapter 10

Decolonising dance history

PRARTHANA PURKAYASTHA

Introduction

WHAT MAKES THE PAST OF DANCE so important to our present? Is the history of a dance form limited to its context, its specific sociocultural meanings, to the understanding of a particular community of people, their heritage and their behaviours? Or is that history part of an intricate web of other histories that interconnect to form a complex network of meanings? In historical accounts of dance, whose dancing bodies are remembered, and whose forgotten? And *why* are the memories of some dances or dancers preserved, while others are erased from the pages of history? Ultimately, what and whose project does dance history serve? Or what are the ideological underpinnings of processes that produce histories? Several dance history scholars have grappled with these questions in recent decades, and this essay attends to this set of queries through a focus on dances of the Indian subcontinent. In reviewing seminal scholarship and practices from South Asia and the global diaspora, the essay explores how dance history can become a particularly potent and valuable site through which social, cultural and political knowledge production can be studied.

It is important to review some of the major shifts that have occurred in Indian dance history writing in recent years, and there are three main emergent themes that I would like to consider here. First and foremost is interdisciplinarity in dance history. Recent scholarship has shown how Indian dance history has become a vibrant area of academic enquiry, dialoguing with multiple disciplines of research and thinking, ranging from law (Banerji 2010) to transnational citizenship and neoliberalism (Kedhar 2014). Historical writings on dance have not been limited to a study of why, how or when people danced, but have shown how dance history can provide us with important tools, conceptual and methodological, to help understand other fields of knowledge. Not only has Indian dance history uncovered new insights into the past of dance, but also it has generated new frameworks of thinking in fields such as national politics, race and immigration studies (Srinivasan 2012) and popular culture (Chakravorty 2010).

The second major theme to have emerged in dance historical research is transnationalism. For many years, dance history as a discipline had been concerned with exploring and documenting forms, practices and specific case studies that remained somewhat tethered to the idea of a particular nation or community. In recent years, there has been a noticeable shift from the idea of dance as an embodiment of 'pure' or 'authentic' culture to the notion that dance forms often reflect or signify the flow and exchange of movements and ideas across nations and cultures (Srinivasan 2012; Purkayastha 2014). Historical writing today is therefore attentive to both national and transnational movements of dancing bodies across linguistic, political and geographical borders, and the repercussions these may have on the complexly 'impure' realities of dance forms.

The third theme relates to the notion of ideology and the ways in which it informs and even produces certain histories, and ignores or suppresses others. Several dance historical projects focused on dance in and from India have suggested how the discipline of history as a written account of past events can be subjective, selective and ultimately limited in its scope. Ideological frameworks – national, political, social, cultural or racial – governing any historical discourse often encourage the act of privileging certain dance practices and practitioners while silencing others. As evidenced in the work of South Asian scholar Davesh Soneji (2012) among many others from and of the Indian subcontinent, the task of an ethical and critical dance history is to be alert to the ways in which the embodied past represents not simply those in positions of power, mobility or privilege but also those without.

These three themes intersect and interweave throughout this essay to produce a complex picture of Indian dance history, one in which questions of heritage, authenticity and identity are intimately tied to nationalism and nationhood, race and class, power and disenfranchisement. In the next section, a critical examination of selected dance practices from India is offered, through which the dancing body's links to colonial and postcolonial history are explored.

Dance in India: colonial and postcolonial legacies

For the purpose of a sustained focus, this essay will discuss dance in the late colonial and postcolonial periods, a window of time which offers a glimpse into complex processes of cultural identity formation during a volatile political period in India's history. The dance forms included in this discussion are what are now commonly known as Indian classical dances, folk dances and Indian modern dances.

The problematic and tokenistic use of categories and labels, such as 'classical', 'folk' and 'modern' in the context of Indian dance, has been critiqued by several scholars (see Vatsyayan 1974; Coorlawala 1994; Bose 2001; Lopez y Royo 2003; Purkayastha 2014). Without reiterating this well-rehearsed narrative, the discussion here aims to highlight the historical conditions through which these categories of dance came to be constituted and popularised, and signpost major historical projects that have upset certain conservative assumptions about Indian dance heritage.

Our history of dance begins at the turn of the nineteenth and the beginning of the twentieth centuries, in a colonised India that was witnessing a steady upsurge in nationalist and anti-colonial movements. The British Empire had tightened its grip on the subcontinent, one of its most economically profitable colonies, and the Empire's reach and domination had by this time pervaded many aspects of Indian life, from infrastructure and governance to education and cultural practices. Under Queen Victoria's Crown, the British 'Raj' or rule continued the work of the British East India Company, which preceded it, and from 1858 onwards the Raj symbolised the absolute power of Britain over India, power that was accumulated through an appropriation of local history and knowledge. In Ranajit Guha's seminal work *Dominance without Hegemony: History and Power in Colonial India* (1997), the author offers an articulate and incisive critique of India's colonial past, suggesting how the commissioning of local histories by the British administration was a means to gather information on landed property and inheritance. Guha's discussion of cultural difference and how it impacted on the construction of history is quoted at length here:

> Indian history, assimilated thereby to the history of Great Britain, would henceforth be used as a comprehensive measure of difference between the people of these two countries. Politically that difference was spelled out as one between rulers and the ruled; ethnically, between a white *Herrenvolk* and blacks; materially, between a prosperous Western power and its poor Asian subjects; culturally, between higher and lower levels of civilization, between the superior religion of Christianity and the indigenous belief systems made up of superstition and barbarism – all adding up to an irreconcilable difference between colonizer and colonized. The Indian past was thus painted red.
>
> However, the appropriation of a past by conquest carries with it the risk of rebounding upon the conquerors. It can end up by sacralizing the past for the subject people and encouraging them to use it in their effort to define and affirm their own identity. This, no doubt, was what happened [. . .], and the appropriated past came to serve as the sign of the Other not only for the colonizers but, ironically, for the colonized as well. The colonized, in their turn reconstructed their past for purposes opposed to those of their rulers and made it the ground

for marking out their differences in cultural and political terms. History became thus a game for two to play as the alien colonialist project of appropriation was matched by an indigenous nationalist project of counter-appropriation.

(1997: 3)

It is through these notions of *reconstruction* and *counter-appropriation* of the past posited by Guha earlier that we can understand the processes through which many Indian dance forms were resurrected from near oblivion and legal prohibition under colonial law to become the embodiment of a national 'non-Western' culture. For instance, many of the temple dance forms in southern India, involving the dedication of underage or prepuberty girls called *devadasis* (servants of gods) to the temple deities through marriage rituals, became associated with prostitution and therefore banned by law. The first anti-dedication movement began in 1882; the Devadasi Abolition Bill was proposed in 1929 and passed as the Anti-Devadasi Act in 1947, the year of India's independence from British rule (see Kersenboom-Story 1987; Soneji 2012). The *devadasis* became the embodiment of schizophrenic sociocultural tensions in the emergent Indian nation state. On the one hand, they appeared to be objects of male sexual predatory behaviour that were sanctified and validated by patriarchal Hindu religious institutions. On the other hand, records suggest that the *devadasi* dancers' access to education (many of them were literate), wealth (many were gifted and owned land) and social power or status (many had the ability to choose their sexual partners) was something denied to many middle-class Indian women or even English women in the Victorian era. As such, *devadasis* presented to the British colonial rulers and to a large section of the Indian bourgeoisie a severe challenge, since they subverted normative codes of gender and sexuality. Their dances were threatened with abolition and extinction.

Since the 1980s, historical writings on Indian dance have been particularly suspicious of a grand nationalist discourse. Amrit Srinivasan (1985) importantly pointed out that practices of dance forms such as the *sadir* (trans. 'to present') by the *devadasis* were subjected to the two contradictory forces of reform and revival. The anti-*nautch* campaign of the late nineteenth century in Bombay and South India was unleashed by Hindu reformists, while a public *sadir* dance recital was given in 1926 by the Madras High Court advocate E. V. Krishna Iyer, one of the revivalists, wearing a *devadasi* costume. By 1936, the revivalists managed to halt *sadir*'s extinction, but only in a newly reconstructed form called 'bharatanatyam'. Avanthi Meduri (2005) suggests how women pioneers, such as Rukmini Devi Arundale (1904–1986), a revivalist associated with the Theosophical Society of India, which strongly advocated home rule for India, played an important role in conceptualising a new dramaturgical route for *bharatanatyam*, highlighting the importance of gender in the nation-building process. Meanwhile, Janet O'Shea (2007: 10) reminds us how *bharatanatyam* practitioners 'aligned their projects with political discourses through an explicit and selective engagement with the dance form's past', and how this selectiveness favoured certain practices while suppressing others.

The reconstruction and counter-appropriation of Indian history also occurred through other dance forms that were similarly in decline owing to the direct rule of the British Raj and the loss of arts patronage from royal courts and landowners that occurred as a result of an overhaul of property and inheritance laws. Pallabi Chakravorty's in-depth historical research in her book *Bells of Change: Kathak Dance, Women and Modernity in India* (2008) not only provides an excellent analysis of the nationalist revival of the northern Indian dance form *kathak*, but also challenges orthodox historical accounts of the form's rootedness in male authorship and hereditary knowledge. By excavating the narratives of women dancers and courtesans (the *tawaifs* and *baijis*, who like the *devadasis*, also came to be associated with moral depravity under British rule) and locating *kathak*'s past within female hereditary practices, Chakravorty successfully highlights the importance of women's embodied agency in colonial and postcolonial India, and produces a new legacy and repertoire of female-centred dance knowledge.

Similarly, other critical histories of Indian dance, such as *odissi* (Chatterjea 2004), have been set in motion, valuable in terms of their re-evaluation of existing historical material, and significant for the ways in which they question colonial discourses and legacies of thinking about Indian dancing bodies. A postcolonial legacy of critical historical thinking has been particularly attentive to the relational categories of gender, race and class that have intersected to produce a complex picture of India's danced past. Indian dances became major symbols of an embodied national heritage that was consciously constructed to counteract the violence of colonialism in the early twentieth century, and a postcolonial history is committed to a close understanding of those violent systems that produced such heritages.

Subaltern dances: histories of violence, appropriation and erasure

If the violence of empire (actual and visible) produced embodied forms of Indian national heritage among colonised subjects, then these newly constituted heritage forms also put into motion other violence (symbolic and invisible) on minority groups within that same nation space. The creation of a collective national memory came at the cost of erasing some dancers' bodies and their work. Two main forms of invisible violence constructed Indian dance heritage, both for the world and for the newly emerging Indian nation state in the late nineteenth and early twentieth centuries. The first was the violence of Orientalism, a Euro-American project famously described by Edward Said as imperialism's 'monstrous chain of command' which managed and even produced the 'Orient' (1995: 45). India was one of the Orient's most popular products, created, marketed and consumed largely by a western imagination. Its dances were either accepted or rejected by that imagination depending on how successfully they whetted the western appetite for an exotic Orient. The second form of invisible violence was Indian cultural nationalism, which legitimised and bureaucratised certain dance practices in the interest of a national heritage, while marginalising others.

To better understand the invisible violence of Orientalism on Indian dance practices, one should turn to Priya Srinivasan's excellent scholarly work in *Sweating Saris: Indian Dance as Transnational Labor* (2012). Through painstaking archival research, Srinivasan uncovers the forgotten stories of dancers who travelled from India to North America to perform in impresario Augustin Daly's production *Zanina* in New York in 1881. Srinivasan's findings reveal that these dancers were not the main performers in the production, even though their arrival caused much excitement and anticipation in New York's press – the main roles were played by White actresses in brownface. Despite generating much curiosity, archived performance reviews show that the female dancers Sahebjan, Oomdah, Bhoori, Ala Bundi and Vagoir failed to woo their audiences in New York. As Srinivasan suggests,

> Audiences had imagined Oriental bodies of temple and court dancers, swathed in jewels and rich silks, doing sexy, erotic dances to tantalize men. Women of color (particularly Asian women) were hypersexualized within the discourse of both orientalism and U.S. racialization. Indian dancers did not live up to that expectation because they remained more covered than expected. While 'otherness' had been an attraction before the dancers' arrival, the dark, unsexy Indian dancers proved not to live up to the terms of Oriental otherness.
>
> (Srinivasan 2012: 58)

We gather from Srinivasan's meticulous analysis of archived material that the bodies of these Indian female dancers, loosely defined as '*nautch*' dancers, were considered too grotesque, unsophisticated and therefore unpalatable for North American audiences, reflecting clearly a pattern of racialisation of bodies in the United States. As these dancers vanished into oblivion (the show they were in was replaced by another after a very short run), history chose to forget their dance, along with the fact that one of these dancers (Ala Bundi) died on American soil, and one (Sahebjan) gave birth to a baby who also died, aged only a few days old. Srinivasan's research also reveals that while one kind of Oriental body was a failure on the North American stage, another kind, that of White American dancer Ruth St Denis (1879–1968), rose to stardom not long after these *nautch* dancers departed. Heralded as a pioneer of North American modern dance, St Denis's career featured unequal, and at times unethical, collaborations with visiting performers from India, whose dances (along with the dances of many other Asian cultures) she appropriated to carve a unique position for herself as an independent modern dance artist (see Chapter 3 in Srinivasan 2012).

The invisible violence of Orientalism not only erased the memories of certain Indian dancers from the pages of dance history but also produced two distinct dance heritages – a heritage of North American modern dance, with dancers such as Ruth St Denis as its forbearer, and a heritage of Indian traditional dance, which dancers from Euro-American soil would seek out, validate and fetishise. Western dance modernity had no place for the bodies of dancers from India, even though this modernity was founded on embodied material from the so-called Orient.

The invisible violence of Indian cultural nationalism, on the other hand, continued this binary of a modern West and a non-modern East, and displayed a similar tendency to grant cultural legitimacy to certain bodies, while denying it to others. While the reconstructed classical dance forms became constitutive of a national heritage, several dancers and their practices remained under the radar of cultural bureaucrats. One such group of dancers who have received attention in recent years from scholars, such as Ananya Chatterjea (2009) and Urmimala Sarkar Munsi (2010) among others, is the *nachni*, who perform mainly in rural circuits in eastern India in the states of Bengal, Bihar and Odisha. The *nachni* are women dancers who embody a long legacy of dance practice that can be traced back to the courts of local kings and feudal lords. With the waning of royal patronage after India's independence in 1947, the fate of the *nachni* was and continues to be decided mainly by their male co-performer, the *rasik*. Sarkar Munsi provides a fascinating glimpse into the life of a *nachni*, who usually hails from some of the most impoverished sections of society.

> The women who are lured into the profession or brought into it perforce or against payment to their family become social outcasts. The family observes *shradh* (last rites) and *kaman* (religious shaving of facial hair and head) ceremonies according to the Hindu rules of rites of passage once a girl leaves her family to become a *nachni*. The *nachni* has to wear *sindur* or red vermillion powder on her head to ensure a long life for her [r]*asik* and has to observe all norms of a married woman although she has no position in her *rasik*'s family. She cannot enter the main house of the *rasik*. The *rasik* can be married and have a family of his own. But the *nachni* has to live the life of a concubine in an outhouse provided by the *rasik*. She or her children do not have any right to the *rasik*'s property, and the children cannot use their father's name. Yet she has to observe all the rituals of a widow once the *rasik* dies.
>
> (Sarkar Munsi 2010: 249)

Sarkar Munsi's account provides an important view of established dance practices in India that continue to be framed by precarity – cultural, social and economic.

The acute contradictions that define the life of the *nachnis* are startling: these women are dead to their families, but alive in their dances, have earning power but are economically reliant on their male partners, can enjoy familial bonds but move outside a patrilineal system of inheritance. What kind of dance history or heritage is being written for these dancers? Ananya Chatterjea similarly asks some hard questions of the *nachni*'s journey through history:

> Recently recognized as a 'folk dance' form, a necessary classification if the state is to allocate any resources to it, is this rural entertainment form going to be appropriated by city women searching for a 'new' form that will mark their dancing careers? Will it be cast as a little-known village form that needs to be 'cleansed' and 'sophisticated' to become acceptable? [. . .] I cannot help but remember how 'classical' dances were repeatedly legitimized through appropriation by the urban elite, and how ultimately these forms, instead of simply becoming accepted in the public domain as performance traditions, really entered the cultural market as representations of 'tradition' that could be brokered primarily by performers from the upper classes. Can we witness the performances of such subalterns on their own terms?
>
> (Chatterjea 2009: 132–3)

Chatterjea's questions and indeed a history of *nachnis* can be read within the context of an established body of subaltern studies scholarship, which has provided postcolonial theory with much fodder for discussion over the decades. It is useful to remind ourselves that the term 'subaltern' (person of low rank or in a subordinate position) was used by the Italian Marxist theorist Antonio Gramsci (1891–1937) to discuss the politicisation of unorganised populations necessary for any social revolution. Gramsci's writings reflected on the role of the oppressed peasantry in Fascist Italy, but his theories found a new home in the work of Indian postcolonial scholars in the 1980s. One of the major contributions to Indian subaltern studies, apart from Ranajit Guha's historiographical work (1982), was made by Gayatri Chakravorty Spivak and her seminal essay 'Can the Subaltern Speak?' (1988), in which she questioned the role of the intellectual in becoming the mouthpiece of the disenfranchised. Spivak warns the postcolonial scholar of fetishising or romanticising the subaltern condition, suggesting that the historian-intellectual's giving of voice to the oppressed invariably replicates the colonialist discourse, since the historian 'speaks for' the subalterns rather than allowing the subalterns to speak for themselves. Spivak's essay ends with the conclusion that the subaltern cannot speak, since whatever mobilises the subaltern, be it education or political/social organisation, ultimately transforms the subaltern's condition and swallows it into the gut of the dominant.

If we, as dance historians and intellectuals sensitive to the condition of forgotten or marginalised dancers, ultimately become their mouthpieces and speak on their behalf, then can the subaltern dance? Do the dance history projects of Srinivasan and Soneji, Sarkar Munsi and Chatterjea end up fetishising or romanticising the subaltern dancing bodies of the *nautch* dancers, *devadasis* and *nachnis*? What do these histories achieve for those who are written about? What does witnessing the performances of the subalterns 'on their own terms', as Chatterjea suggests earlier, really entail? These are complex questions which refuse to yield straightforward answers. I would like to suggest, however, that taken as a cumulative whole, the work of the Indian dance historians mentioned earlier, and many others who work in the field (including myself), remains incredibly significant in terms of revealing hidden and sometimes uncomfortable facts in dance historiography, and in exposing the palimpsestic layers in historical narratives. And a major difference does lie between the subaltern as a speaker and the subaltern as a dancer or doer – that difference is the moving body, which carries within it an agency, the potential for transformation and also the impossibility of being wholly remembered or documented due to its evanescent nature. This perhaps makes the most well-intentioned of liberal intellectual translations or histories of subaltern dances ultimately a failure, but nonetheless a productive failure that is necessary to the historian's experience.

A heritage of revolutionary dance

Many dance heritages have emerged from the Indian subcontinent since the collapse of the British Empire and the birth of the new Indian nation on 15 August 1947. Some of these embodied heritage forms were commissioned, authorised and legitimised by nation builders, cultural policymakers and bureaucrats. The classical dances fall under this category of 'authentic' heritage, and represent an 'Incredible India' to tourists, both domestic and international, and audiences both at home and abroad. Some other Indian dance heritages are less written about, since they did not uphold the idea of an unbroken tradition, but instead embraced change, improvisation and discontinuity. I have written about the history of a modern dance movement in India elsewhere (Purkayastha 2014, 2015), a history that allows us to understand that experimental, avant-garde and socially conscious choreographies came out of India at the same time as classical dances were being reconstructed. In this penultimate section, I would like to return briefly to one of my case studies, the Indian People's Theatre Association (IPTA), a nationwide cultural movement led by the Communist Party of India.

Instead of speaking about IPTA's dances from my removed position as a historian, I privilege here the voice of a former IPTA activist-dancer, Reba Roy Chowdhury (1925–2007), who has left behind her memories of dancing and performing in India at a time when anti-colonial revolution took centre stage across the nation. Roy Chowdhury joined the IPTA's Central Ballet Troupe in Bombay, working under the artistic directorship of Shanti Bardhan (1916–1954), before returning to Calcutta in February 1947, six months before India's independence from British rule. The following short excerpts are taken from Roy Chowdhury's autobiography, published in Bengali in 1999. Here she discusses her life as a dancer and performer in Calcutta and on tour across several regions of eastern India:

> On contacting the Party's headquarters on Decker's Lane, I found out that dance rehearsals were in progress in Shyambazar's Bangiyo Kalalaya. I joined in. [. . .] It was decided that I would teach some of the dance pieces from the Central Ballet Troupe's repertoire. Enthusiastically, I started to teach the dances *Ramlila, Holi, Kashmir, Lambadi, Call of the Drum*. [. . .] Alongside these, rehearsals also began for the shadow-play *Shohider Daak* [*Martyr's Call*]. Benoy [her brother] was the Secretary of the group. We began to prepare for a tour of East Bengal, North Bengal and Assam.
>
> [. . .] Around mid-1947, we left for Barisal [in present-day Bangladesh] on tour with *Martyr's Call*. [. . .] I remember that we had to perform in a hall made of tin in tremendous heat. After every dance piece, we would step out for a breath of fresh air. Those of us who were dancing were in a woeful condition. Our makeup melted down our faces. We looked like ghouls. But we garnered a lot of praise for our show.
>
> [. . .] We reached Bogra. There were no arrangements in place. There were so many of us – but we were young, and there was no end to our enthusiasm. Now that we had arrived, we had to perform. We managed to find an accommodation. But what about our meals? Santosh-da brought some firewood from the jungle. We hired some utensils. Kalyani and I made some *khichudi*. Sajal and Salil went with a loudspeaker on a rickshaw to advertise the show. In those years, Boguda was a conservative place. We met the organisers after quite a while. They could not get us a hall to perform in. But we had to do the show! Next to us was a huge warehouse for storing rice, made of tin, where we built a stage and started our show. It started to rain. We could not hear a thing with the noise of rain falling on the tin. Water started leaking indoors. The huge white screen used in *Martyr's Call* became completely drenched. We had to stop the performance. On the audience's request, we had to perform again the following day. This is how popular we were.
>
> [. . .] I will not forget our show in Nagaon, Assam. During that time, there was a lot of anti-Communist sentiment in the area. Our conservative organisers would not allow men and women to perform together in the show. There was a huge crowd in front of the hall. After a lot of persuasion, the organisers suggested that they would allow one performance. If it did not go well, they would cancel the other shows.

At the end of our performance, the organisers were mesmerized and congratulated us heartily. We performed the show twice the following day. Our humility, hard work and commitment had won them over.
(Roy Chowdhury 1999: 27–31; my translation)

These short autobiographical excerpts provide a useful glimpse into the lives of IPTA dancers and performers who gave hundreds of performances across India in the lead-up to Indian independence in August 1947. Such remembered histories are priceless accounts of the role of a dancer's labour, toil and sweat during periods of political revolution, of the significance of dancing bodies as they breathlessly stamped, turned and weaved their way between villages, towns and linguistic territories, in the process not only propagating socialist agendas but also changing and resisting deeply conservative views on gendered social relations. For a historian seeking to reanimate the past of dance, such alternative heritages become profoundly important in understanding dance's impact on social, political and cultural transformation.

Conclusion: decolonising history

What lies ahead for any historian studying dance practices from or of the Indian subcontinent, or indeed of any of the other previously colonised countries of the world? How has the discipline of history itself shifted, rolled or pirouetted out of its earlier Eurocentric positions to include new thinking about dances past? How do we decolonise the field of dance history, which has for decades perpetuated an oppositional relationship, a binary, between eastern and western dance heritages? Perhaps Sanjay Seth's brilliant essay 'Which Past? Whose Transcendental Presupposition?' (2008) can provide the historian with some useful insights. Seth argues convincingly that post-Enlightenment historiography fosters a 'transcendental narcissism' through which the 'modern West creates and secures the anthropological/ humanist theme that Man is the source and origin of meaning and value and hence the subject of history' (2008: 224), but that this may not be useful or relevant in the writing of an Indian past. Seth further writes that

> the code of history is but one way of representing the past, and a recent one. It is eminently useful even where anachronistic, for, when written in a hermeneutic mode, it can be a way of engaging, better understanding, and developing and refurbishing the intellectual tradition(s) to which we belong, and out of which we reason. But this is only true where the code of history is applied to the pasts out of which this code itself developed; applied to other pasts, it is neither the 'right'

way of recounting these pasts, nor does it illuminate the traditions of the peoples whose pasts these are.

(2008: 224)

Perhaps it is through being vigilant to particular codes of history as Seth points out earlier, codes that are time- and culture-specific rather than universal, that we can continue to decolonise dance history. A decolonised dance history field is one which resists the fetishisation of non-western heritage forms, challenges dance history conferences to rethink their 'world' or 'ethnic' dance panels, and enables future scholars to engage with the 'impure' traces of dances that emerge out of unfamiliar bodies, illegitimate archives and forgotten histories.

Acknowledgements

I would like to sincerely thank my colleagues in the dance field Royona Mitra and Melissa Blanco Borelli for their advice and support, which helped in the writing of this chapter.

Bibliography

Banerji, A. (2010) *Odissi Dance: Paratopic Performances of Gender, Law, and Nation*, Unpublished PhD dissertation, New York: New York University.

Bose, M. (2001) *Speaking of Dance: The Indian Critique*, New Delhi: D.K. Printword (P).

Chakravorty, P. (2008) *Bells of Change: Kathak Dance, Women and Modernity in India*, Calcutta: Seagull Books.

Chakravorty, P. (2010) 'Remixed Practice: Bollywood Dance and the Global Indian', in P. Chakravorty and N. Gupta, eds., *Dance Matters: Performing India*, New Delhi: Oxford University Press.

Chatterjea, A. (2004) 'Contestations: Constructing a Historical Narrative for Odissi', in A. Carter, ed., *Rethinking Dance History: A Reader*, London: Routledge, 143–156.

Chatterjea, A. (2009) 'Red-Stained Feet: Probing the Ground on Which Women Dance in Contemporary Bengal', in S.L. Foster, ed., *Worlding Dance*, Basingstoke: Palgrave Macmillan.

Coorlawala, U.A. (1994) *Classical and Contemporary Indian Dance: Overview, Criteria and a Choreographic Analysis*, PhD thesis, New York: New York University.

Gramsci, A. (1971) *Selections from the Prison Notebooks*, edited and translated by Q. Hoare and G.N. Smith, London: Lawrence and Wishart.

Guha, R. ed. (1982) *Subaltern Studies: Writings on South Asian Society and History*, New Delhi: Oxford University Press.

Guha, R. ed. (1997) *Dominance without Hegemony: History and Power in Colonial India*, Cambridge, MA: Harvard University Press.

Kedhar, A. (2014) 'Flexibility and Its Bodily Limits: Transnational South Asian Dancers in an Age of Neoliberalism', *Dance Research Journal*, 46:1, 23–40.

Kersenboom-Story, S.C. (1987) *Nityasumangali: Devadasi Tradition in South Asia*, New Delhi: Motilal Banarsidass.

Lopez y Royo, A. (2003) 'Classicism, Post-Classicism and Ranjabati Sircar's Work: Redefining the Terms of Indian Contemporary Dance Discourses', *South Asia Research*, 23:1, 153–169.

Meduri, A. (2005) *Rukmini Devi Arundale (1904–1986): A Visionary Architect of Indian Culture and the Performing Arts*, New Delhi: Motilal Banarsidass.

O'Shea, J. (2007) *At Home in the World: Bharata Natyam on the Global Stage*, Middletown: Wesleyan University Press.

Purkayastha, P. (2014) *Indian Modern Dance, Feminism and Transnationalism*, Basingstoke: Palgrave Macmillan.

Purkayastha, P. (2015) 'Women in Revolutionary Theatre: IPTA, Labor, and Performance', *Asian Theatre Journal*, 32:2, 518–535.

Roy Chowdhury, R. (1999) *Jibaner Taney Shilper Taney*, Calcutta: Thema.

Said, E.W. (1995) *Orientalism*, New York: Vintage Books.

Sarkar Munsi, U. (2010) 'Tale of the Professional Woman Dancer in Folk Traditions in India: Commodification of Dance and the Traditional Dancing Women', in B. Dutt and U. Sarkar Munsi, eds., *Engendering Performance: Indian Women Performers in Search of an Identity*, New Delhi: SAGE.

Seth, S. (2008) 'Which Past? Whose Transcendental Presupposition?', *Postcolonial Studies*, 11:2, 215–226.

Soneji, D. (2012) *Unfinished Gestures: Devadasis, Memory, and Modernity in South India*, Chicago: University of Chicago Press.

Spivak, G.C. (1988) 'Can the Subaltern Speak', in C. Nelson and L. Grossberg, eds., *Marxism and the Interpretation of Culture*, Urbana: University of Illinois Press, 271–313.

Srinivasan, A. (1985) 'Reform and Revival: The Devadasi and Her Dance', *Economic and Political Weekly*, 20:44, 2 November: 1869–1876.

Srinivasan, P. (2012) *Sweating Saris: Indian Dance as Transnational Labor*, Philadelphia: Temple University Press.

Vatsyayan, K. (1974) *Indian Classical Dance*, New Delhi: Ministry of Information and Broadcasting, Govt. of India.

Chapter 11

Many sources, many voices

LENA HAMMERGREN[1]

WHY HISTORY? KEITH JENKINS reflects upon this question in his thought-provoking book written at the end of the last century (Jenkins 1999). He concludes that we no longer need history as we have known it; we do 'not need to go to history' in order to find 'all the imaginaries we need to think the future' (Jenkins 1999: 199–200). In this statement, he refers to what historians have usually considered the primary goal of any historical study of a reflective nature: we investigate the past in order to learn about the future. Inspired by his intention (although not fully by his conclusions, since I still believe that certain conceptualizations of the past help us to think about the future) I will focus this text on the question: why source material? Or, to formulate it more precisely, how do we conceive of sources and what can we make of them? To raise these questions is to highlight a part of the process of constructing historical narratives that we sometimes regard as less 'problematic' in nature compared to the more troublesome undertaking of applying theories. In this chapter I will query the process of assembling, choosing and interpreting documents from which dance histories can be told.

Source criticism

Every scholar who has spent hours in archives will be aware of the daunting task of conflating often disparate sources into a single, unified history. One of the traditional tools historians use to address this problem is source criticism, a process which often starts by dividing source material into primary and secondary sources. The former category generally includes material that is 'close' in time to the object of study and may be considered 'raw material' (e.g. diaries and dance performances); the latter involves sources produced 'farther away' in time, and they emphasize interpretation (e.g. history books and performance reviews). Historians also propose a hierarchical relation between these two categories, deeming primary sources to have the potential of being more 'true' to the object than secondary sources. In this view, a personal letter and a dance written and performed respectively by Isadora Duncan are more likely to reveal her intentions or aesthetic ideals than would an analysis of her work by a dance historian, written several years later.

Yet we find an intriguing contradiction inherent in this view, and it has to do with how time is supposed to affect the historian's ability to evaluate the importance of events or the agency of an individual artist. The German historian Oskar Bie has provided us with a good example of how time might change our evaluation of a dancer. In 1906 he published his first version of *Der Tanz* (The Dance), and in 1919 he wrote a second, revised edition. In the two editions we find interesting changes concerning Bie's judgement of Isadora Duncan's importance. In 1906 he rejects her influence on modern dance (Bie [1906] 1919: 305). In the later edition he gives voice to an altered opinion, and argues that she did indeed lead dance into a new phase of development, even though she never fully realized her intentions (Bie [1906] 1919: 362). We might explain this evaluative turn as a result of the passage of time in between the two editions. In 1919 Bie would have had more sources supporting the judgement of Duncan's influence on contemporary dance than in 1906, a year perhaps too close in time to her breakthrough as an artist. However, because we lack enough information on exactly why Bie changed his mind (was he influenced by other critics' opinions, had the audiences' reception changed, or had he simply watched more performances by Duncan?), we might, instead of deeming him wrong in 1906, look at the two editions as equally 'true'.

This view could direct our interest to focus on the question of when and why an individual artist becomes part of the dance canon rather than on the historian's ability to make the right evaluations or whether the sources are primary or secondary. It is quite interesting to note that some of today's historians use German dance histories from the 1920s as 'evidence' when they are referring to Duncan's influence in Germany during the early years of the twentieth century (e.g. Partsch-Bergsohn 1994: 3–4). This is not wrong, but Bie provides one example of how differently we could interpret the reception of Duncan in Germany if we were to choose a source from an earlier date, more contemporary in time to the object of study.

From an international perspective it is also important to stress the need for analyses of local sources. We often use a shared canon of source material, which can be reinterpreted many times in different contexts, but national or regional sources hitherto not investigated or not addressed by international dance histories can offer us possibilities for new interpretations or complementary analyses. Amy Koritz has emphasized these circumstances in her cogent research on dance and literature in early twentieth-century British culture. From a British perspective, she addresses the historical stature accorded to Maud Allan in comparison to some other contemporary dance artists. Koritz argues that 'a dance history written from the point of view of the English public would not give the same status to St Denis, or to Duncan . . . as either is commonly accorded in the United States' (Koritz 1995: 31–2). Thus, it is easy to understand that the way we choose and use source material might result in many different historical narratives.

Sources as social constructions

Instead of trying to distinguish between sources' classification as primary or secondary, we can look at them as parts of discourses. The word discourse has multiple meanings, and I use it here to signify the codes and conceptual systems by which we manifest and make understandable different aspects of our lives, to ourselves and to others. Thus, we can distinguish between discursive topics (the subjects that we are 'talking' about), discursive media (the documents in which the discourse is manifested), and the set of codes and conventions forming the discourse. If the development of dance is the chosen topic, we may find it in discursive media or sources such as history books, encyclopedias, or oral statements. In order to analyse the discourse, we then need to look at each discursive medium's particular manner of expressing the discourse.

One excellent application of this view has been made by David E. Nye in the field of the history of science (Nye 1983). He assumes that 'all evidence has been given a form', which is connected to the sociocultural systems that produced the sources (p. 12). Our contemporary view on historiography has made us aware of the role of the historian's interpretation of sources. The questions we put to the documents affect the answers we receive. But Nye clarifies one additionally important aspect to the commonly expressed notion that sources are 'mute'. An object is imbued with patterns of meaning already in the act of becoming a document, for example when it is included in an archive or inserted into the layout of a newspaper. As a result, primary sources cannot be perceived as 'raw material' in comparison to the assumed interpreted nature of secondary sources.

Let me give as an example two different collections of dance reviews, and how the act of collecting gives rise to different interpretations of the reviews. Both collections are part of the Dance Museum's archive in Stockholm. The first is a collection made by the two Swedish sisters Marja and Rachel Björnström-Ottelin, who made careers as modern dancers in Europe during the 1920s and 1930s. In their scrapbooks, all the reviews are neatly arranged in chronological order, and most of the clippings come with a note from the agency providing the clipping service. This was a service available by subscription, and it reveals the sisters' awareness of the importance of documenting their careers. All the reviews in the collection have dates and names of newspapers, the kind of information you would usually expect in a proper documentation of press clippings. The second example is a scrapbook once belonging to Edgar Frank, who was a dancer in the German choreographer

Kurt Jooss's early company. The company visited Sweden for the first time in 1934, and in 1935 Edgar Frank returned as a Jewish refugee. Frank's clippings usually lack information either on the newspaper's name, its date or the name or byline of the critic who wrote the review. These informative details are often simply cut off as if they were judged unnecessary. In every review, however, one finds Frank's name underlined in red, regardless of how much or little is written about him and whether the criticism of his dancing is negative or positive.

Applying Nye's view on sources, let us focus our attention on the documents' different material forms, and on the acts of collecting and transforming the clippings into source material. The two collections represent contrasting strategies with regard to how they formulate dancing careers as expressions of individual differences, and as part of a specific time and sociocultural context. Edgar Frank was a dancer on the move. At the time of the Swedish performance, Jooss and his company had just left Germany because of the emerging Nazi politics. Based on this contextual information, Frank seems to need clippings as a mirror of his life. His name underlined in red exists as a vital link between a nomadic existence and a desire to belong, or to be at home within himself, regardless of the continuous change of geographical locations. Frank's clippings provided him with an image of permanence and stability, and because his future held uncertainty to such a high degree, that was perhaps all that was needed. Recording informative details on newspaper names and critics' signatures were deemed less important than identifying his own name, and marking it in bold red. The sisters' agenda was very different. Browsing through their collection of scrapbooks one gets an impression of the sisters acting as professional archivists of their own life stories. The meticulous documentation is a strong expression of the will to shape a career, an example of the sort of self-fashioning activity which is evident in other parts of the collection as well. One finds different versions of letters to agents, notes on spelling and translation. In an outline to a letter addressed to the German theatre director Max Reinhardt, someone has added the comment: 'Use a lighter and more original tone, and bear in mind that the man has to read several hundred [letters] per week.' So, in my interpretation, Frank's clippings speak of an existential need for permanence and equilibrium, whereas the sisters' manner of collecting documents is employed to improve their professional dance personas.

Because documents are saturated with such codes of meaning, Nye argues, there is no hierarchical distinction between primary and secondary sources. To dance scholars following in Nye's footsteps, this would mean that we do not privilege some documents over others. We do not make hierarchic choices between descriptions of a dance made by the choreographer, reconstructions of the same dance, photos of the original dancers, or personal reminiscences about the performance of the dance documented many years after its premiere. Rather, these different sources may render simultaneous versions of the dance under consideration. Given this situation, the historian will look for the particular relationships which can be found between the sources. In Nye's words, we search for 'patterns of translation, displacement, and contradiction' (Nye 1983: 18).

Accordingly, using the famous reconstruction of *Le Sacre du Printemps* by Millicent Hodson and Kenneth Archer as an example, it could be interpreted as a translation or a contradiction. Instead of searching for its degree of 'truthfulness', one would look into the notion that an assumed origin was created long after the premiere of the dance in 1913 (for this idea of an assumed origin, see Lion 2001). We may choose to conceive of the reconstruction as a translation of an origin in the sense that documents have been translated into movements, sound and stage setting. But because the origin is lost, that is, it has disappeared from repertory and the reconstruction has replaced it as another kind of 'authentic origin', we could perceive it as a contradiction in relation to the 1913 version. This is of course not the end of the story concerning *Le Sacre du Printemps*. With the use of different documentary realms, the dance(s) will take on other kinds of relationships. Using the many excellent workshops and writings on the method of reconstruction, produced by Hodson and Archer, as a distinct cluster of documents, dance as an object of study takes on another guise, namely that of a scientific method including source criticism (Archer and Hodson 1994). Here, we can speak of a relationship of displacement. *Le Sacre du Printemps* exists simultaneously as an example of Nijinsky's individual artistic talent, and as an instance of scientific research. In the first case the ballet is constructed as a high point in a developmental conceptualization of twentieth-century dance history; in the second, the ballet adds to the status of dance research as a respectable enterprise among other established academic disciplines. The 'same' ballet gives rise to several different but interrelated historical voices.

From a theoretical perspective, it is important to acknowledge that Nye includes the mapping of structural relationships between different realms of documents, in a framework of semiotic history, based on the linguist A. J. Greimas's semiotic square, a system of binary opposition. Written in the 1980s, Nye's book was to a large extent influenced by the writings of Hayden White (e.g. White 1973) and in particular his critical view on causation as historians' fundamental mode of explanation. Nye, in his turn, questioned traditional biography, hence he labelled his book an anti-biography. But he was also explicit in stating that a semiotic history was used only as a 'temporary weapon, helping to clear the ground for a new kind of history' (Nye 1983: 29). His emphasis on semiotics/structuralism, does not, I argue, disqualify Nye from being an inspiration today. His analytic treatment of source material is still valid as a methodological tool in an era of postmodern historiography.

Individual life stories

Some of the examples I have presented so far are generated within the area of biographical research, and this particular kind of study lends itself very well to reflections on the use of source material and the different historical narratives we can construct with the help of documents. One of the basic assumptions in this discussion is a slightly simplified notion, for argument's sake, of traditional biographies as texts applying 'unmasking, unveiling, and uncovering' as central, conceptual metaphors (Nye 1983: 24). In addition, they strive for biographical and historical realism by placing documents in chronological order, thus achieving the presentation of an individual as a unitary presence, and often disregarding contradictory tendencies and interpretations.

Intertextuality

If we look at memoirs and biographies as specific genres of historical narratives, we can apply intertextuality as one method with which we can escape the traditional typecasting of biographies as texts aiming at uncovering an individual's personality behind the public persona. The intertextual approach focuses on the object of analysis – for example a text, a dance, a film – in relation to other texts, dances etc., as well as in terms of the relationship between the interpreter and the object of study. One initial phase of intertextual methodology is the identification of intertexts, which are conceived as 'a corpus of texts, textual fragments, or textlike segments of the sociolect that shares a lexicon and . . . a syntax with the text we are reading' (Riffaterre 1984: 142). A sociolect is a kind of social 'dialect', used by a group sharing not only a lexicon and syntax, but also a culture's codes of conduct, values and myths. It is in this sense that we can argue that autobiographies and biographies are genres which make use of a shared set of narrative codes. These codes can in turn be worked upon in different ways, either by individual texts or by groups of texts. From this it follows that we can speak about generic codes as well as other kinds of intertexts interacting with the text we are studying, for example different critical theories, cultural practices of various sorts, and contextual material.

Several scholarly studies of autobiographies offer intriguing examples of how the narratives are adjusted to generic and time-specific conventions. In an analysis of nineteenth-century women's autobiographies, Thomas Postlewait has revealed how well they are adapted to narrative codes found in contemporary popular and picaresque novels (Postlewait 1991: 253–4). Likewise, David E. Nye points out how businessmen's careers in the nineteenth century were moulded after heroes in novels, the narratives typically describing how the person 'rose from obscurity and poverty to a promising position in middle class life, not through years of hard work, but through a single meritorious action' (Nye 1983: 107). With the help of a dramatic peripety, the businessmen's life completely changed after 'stopping a run-a-way [sic] horse, protecting a chest of money for a stranger, or saving a drowning child' (Nye 1983: 107).

In dancers' memoirs from the early twentieth century, we find striking similarities. Both Loie Fuller and Isadora Duncan begin their narratives by evoking childhood memories. Fuller describes a ball she attended as a baby, only six weeks old, and how she was carried from one person to another, enthralling everyone with her charm (Fuller 1908: 9–10). Duncan starts her story at an even earlier point, by remarking on how her mother's pregnancy affected her choice of career. Duncan vividly describes how she had already started dancing while in her mother's womb, as an effect of the only nourishment her mother could take – iced oysters and champagne, the glamorous food of the goddess Aphrodite (Duncan 1927: 9). Both Fuller and Duncan refer to images from a time they could not themselves have remembered, and they do so in a particularly artful manner.

To begin a life story with childhood reminiscences has long been a narrative convention. Most dance artists use it in the same manner as Fuller and Duncan in order to point out how their future careers were decided very early in life, and they depict dance as a kind of 'natural' or universal force impossible to avoid. An interesting exception to this generic convention is the American ballerina Gelsey Kirkland's autobiography. She also starts by telling the reader about her birth, but since her story is a tragedy marked by drug addiction and mental collapses, she uses a self-conscious and ironic tone and emphasizes her awkward appearance as a baby, indicating that she was fat and had a pear-shaped head, making a dancing career seem unlikely (Kirkland and Lawrence 1986). From a generic perspective, it is important to acknowledge that the confessional narrative mode, which could be used by a female dancer writing in the 1980s, was not part of the accepted literary codes for a woman writing an autobiography at the time around 1900.

Another generic tendency in both Fuller's and Duncan's memoirs is that, in contrast to autobiographies by nineteenth-century actresses, they give more room for their characters' agency. In nineteenth-century memoirs, one often finds stories about other people's agency and importance in changing the development of the author's career. Postlewait notes the recurring use of 'the crucial meeting – the encounter that provides the opportunity or catalyst for success' (Postlewait 1991: 260). Moreover, in women's memoirs these pivotal meetings occur with powerful men, who thereby take over the role of propelling the narrative forward. In Fuller's and Duncan's memoirs there are traces of this convention, but overall there is a much more outspoken agency directly linked to themselves.

Paying attention to autobiographies' literary or generic qualities does not mean that they can be used only for locating fragmentary pieces of factual information. Perceived as discourses giving voice to specific sociocultural codes and values, autobiographies are no less valid than other kinds of sources. On the contrary, they give us ample opportunity to compare and relate them to one another and to discover all those existing modes of producing an individual identity that can be found in the process of transforming documents into historical narratives.

Structure and agency

Intertextuality has been used here in order to highlight history's multiple voices. Its focus on generic relationships might, depending on the purpose of the research, need to be complemented by another perspective, that is an analytic approach that can emphasize the notion of individual agency but still give equal opportunity to multiple historical narratives. This perspective involves looking at the object of study from the viewpoint of structure and agency. Within the eclectic grouping of theories known as cultural studies, the tensions between structure and agency as explanatory and interpretative modes have been clearly outlined. This became particularly apparent when researchers turned to studies of popular culture and subcultures. In order to analyse these cultural fields, it was necessary to concentrate on how groups of people interact with sociocultural regulations. Studies like these often focused on themes of 'pleasure, empowerment, resistance and popular discrimination' (Storey 1993: 185). This became a contested area within cultural studies, and the problem can be summarized as follows. There are always social structures and rules governing an individual's actions within a society: economic, political, educational and gender systems, to name a few. But if this were true for all human actions, there would be hardly any possibility for individual agency. On the other hand, if we believe that agency is possible, how can we understand the workings of social structures and their regulative power? One way to address this problem has been to mediate between the two perspectives and be constantly aware of how they constitute each other. This mediation can be conceptualized in theoretical terms as a joining together of structuralism and hermeneutics. In short, the former focuses on society's structural grids and explains how they are constructed and function, and the latter focuses on the interpreter's or historical subject's process of understanding and communicating life and interpersonal relationships. Several instances of dance scholarship based on mediations between structure and agency could be mentioned in this context. One example is Nadine A. George's compelling article about the African American Whitman Sisters performing on the vaudeville stage in the beginning of 1900 (George 2002). She shows how the sisters cleverly undermined the contemporary fixed sexual, gender and racial identities, that is how different performance strategies were used in order to resist and upset audience expectations.

Structure, as it has been referred to so far, concerns larger social systems and practices. But I will also use it with a more stratified purport, to single out particular layers of meaning with regard to readings of different types of source material. I will exemplify it with a discussion of interviews employed as sources for interpretations of structure and agency. As Nye has remarked, memoirs and biographies can be said to reveal to their readers the private persona behind a public, professional individual. The same might be said about interviews, in which a reporter probes a person with questions aimed at getting behind the professional mask, of revealing how things 'really are'.

In the beginning of the twentieth century, interviews were still quite a novelty in European newspapers, having appeared as a true media genre only during the late nineteenth century. In Sweden, as in many other countries, whenever there was a guest performance, including a dancer with an assumed 'star quality', reporters stood in line in order to conduct their interviews. It is useful to investigate how individual dancers use the interview, that is how they express agency with regard to the interviews' structural feats of intimacy and news event. The famous French ballerina Cléo de Mérode (visiting Sweden in 1903 and 1904) readily answers many kinds of personal questions, which Isadora Duncan (visiting Sweden in 1906) refuses to do. She prefers to talk about her school in Germany, the importance of physical education, and about art. In this sense she reveals a clever marketing strategy, adapted to her professional persona. But de Mérode, who seemingly adjusts to the reporters' expectations, expresses agency of a different kind. She allows the reporters to sit in during her meetings with the theatre director as well, and shows a very strong-willed and efficient business mind. She is a career woman who is clearly aware of how she can make use of the reporters' interest in her private person. Both de Mérode and Duncan act on the 'rules' of the interview, albeit in different ways, and thereby transform a structure of assumed intimacy and unmasking into one that reveals the workings of clever, professional entrepreneurs.

The Canadian-born dancer Maud Allan exemplifies agency in a different manner. In an interview conducted by a Swedish journalist in 1908, Allan paints a nice and highly respectable picture of herself and her family, which artfully manipulates the truth. Had she revealed the true story, it would have been a journalistic scoop, since Allan's brother had been executed for murdering two girls in 1898. Allan's agency consists of creating a higher social, rather than artistic, status for female dance artists. Although her story is quite remarkable in its details, one can find many examples during the period under consideration in which interviews were used as a means to heighten social position.

Development over time

Having focused my discussion on the research of individual artists whose lives do not stretch too far over time, one might very well wonder what will happen once these multi-narrated biographies become included in other kinds of historical research spanning longer periods of time. Research on individual life stories is usually labelled a form of micro-history, thus it is reasonable to reflect upon the relation to its opposite category, macro-history.

Generally, construction of a narrative covering shorter or longer periods of time follows one of two different trajectories: a diachronic or synchronic perspective. The former focuses on long-term analyses of certain historical features (for example, tracing the development of classical ballet from the Renaissance to modern times);

the latter pays attention to relationships between specific features, often occurring during a shorter time-span (for example, the interrelation between different forms of theatrical dancing during the early twentieth century). These analytic perspectives also affect the way in which we use source material, and David E. Nye's views on sources could be neatly placed within the category of synchronic history. What diachronic and synchronic perspectives have in common, however, is that they both rely on some kind of tropological or discursive figure, that is figures of thought which underpin the entire conceptualization of the historical narrative. We are all familiar with the tropological figure of rise-and-fall used to describe the Romantic ballet in the nineteenth century, but there are other possibilities of narration. Deborah Jowitt has replaced that metaphor with the dichotomy of flesh and spirit, which thereby changes the reading of the period (Jowitt 1988). The development of western modern dance has often been conceptualized as a family tree, beginning with the pioneers and continuing with the first and second generation of modern dancers. Each group breaks away from its predecessors in order to shape its own dance aesthetics. In comparison, we can look at the development of theatre dance in Africa, which has been analysed as a continuous fusion of old and new movements (Adewole 2000: 126), or at history writing in India, which has been labelled a 'stratified stockpiling' (de Certeau 1988: 4). If we choose to emplot biographies of, for example, Fuller and Duncan as psychobiographies, using 'the true self' as the explanatory and narrative figure, we get a completely different narrative than we would if we were to use the opposition between dance as autonomous art and dance as popular culture, a recurring narrative motif in western dance history. If we use sources usually associated with 'unmasking' we find impressive manifestations of professionalism (for example, in responding successfully to a reporter). If we juxtapose the psychobiography with the cultural dichotomy of dance as art and dance as popular culture, we find everyday tactics of compromises, failures and triumphs in response to larger social structures. Every micro-history or biography can be read and contextualized in this manner. Thus it can be used to point out certain tendencies in macro-history.

The important task in rethinking dance history from this perspective is not to judge 'who is right', but to learn to discern the emplotment strategies used by historians, and how it affects the dance history being told. And, accordingly, to begin to understand and perceive sources as profoundly ambiguous, because they are part of a polysemic structure of meaning making. This involves an act of reading which emphasizes how a particular source always has more than one meaning, depending on the larger system into which it is activated.

Finally, I would like to return to Keith Jenkins and use one of his references concerning a more overarching view of history, which deals with the notion of historical time, and thus historical narratives, and present it as a kind of summary of this chapter. Jenkins cites Elizabeth Deeds Ermarth, who has provided perhaps the most compelling trope so far for dance scholars to be inspired by: rhythmic time. 'I swing therefore I am. In this conjugating rhythm, *each move forward is also digressive*, also a sideways move. A postmodern narrative . . . keeps alive . . . an awareness of multiple pathways and constantly crossing themes', (Ermarth cited in Jenkins 1999: 174). I swing – hence I will understand that the life of a historical subject is not a curriculum vitae but a series of paratactical moves with many beginnings, middles and ends.

Notes

1 This essay is reprinted from the first edition of *Rethinking Dance History* (2004).

Bibliography

Adewole, F. (2000) 'African Theatre Dance: Aesthetics, Discourses and the Stage', in *Dance History: The Teaching and Learning of Dance History*, Conference Proceedings, of the European Association of Dance Historians, Twickenham: EADH.

Archer, K. and Hodson, M. (1994) 'Ballets Lost and Found: Restoring the Twentieth-Century Repertoire', in J. Adshead-Lansdale and J. Layson (eds.) *Dance History: An Introduction*, London: Routledge.

Bie, O. ([1906] 1919) *Der Tanz*, 2nd edn, Berlin: Verlag Julius Bard.

De Certeau, M. (1988) *The Writing of History*, trans. T. Conley, New York: Columbia University Press.

Duncan, I. (1927) *My Life*, New York: Boni and Liveright.

Fuller, L. (1908) *Quinze Ans de ma Vie*, Paris: Librairie Félix Juven.

George, N. A. (2002) 'Dance and Identity Politics in American Negro Vaudeville: The Whitman Sisters, 1900–1935', in T. F. DeFrantz (ed.) *Dancing Many Drums: Excavations in African American Dance*, Madison: University of Wisconsin Press.

Jenkins, K. (1999) *Why History? Ethics and Postmodernity*, London: Routledge.

Jowitt, D. (1988) *Time and the Dancing Image*, New York: William Morrow.

Kirkland, G. and Lawrence, G. (1986) *Dancing on My Grave*, Garden City, NY: Doubleday.

Koritz, A. (1995) *Gendering Bodies/Performing Art: Dance and Literature in Early Twentieth-Century British Culture*, Ann Arbor, MI: Michigan University Press.

Lion, K. (2001) *Les Sacres: En Socio-kulturell Analys av tio Versioner av ett Våroffer*, PhD thesis with English summary, Stockholm: Theatron-serien.

Nye, D. E. (1983) *The Invented Self: An Anti-Biography from Documents of Thomas A. Edison*, Odense: Odense University Press.

Partsch-Bergsohn, I. (1994) *Modern Dance in Germany and the United States: Crosscurrents and Influences*, Choreography and Dance Studies Series, Volume 5, Chur, Switzerland: Harwood Academic.

Postlewait, T. (1991) 'Autobiography and Theatre History', in T. Postlewait and B. McConachie (eds.) *Interpreting the Theatrical Past: Essays in the Historiography of Performance*, 2nd edn, Iowa City, IA: University of Iowa Press.

Riffaterre, M. (1984) 'Intertextual Representations: On Mimesis and Interpretative Discourse', *Critical Inquiry*, September, 11, 1: 141–62.

Storey, J. (1993) *An Introductory Guide to Cultural Theory and Popular Culture*, London: Harvester Wheatsheaf.

White, H. (1973) *Metahistory: The Historical Imagination in the Nineteenth Century*, Baltimore, MD: Johns Hopkins University Press.

Chapter 12

'Dream no small dreams!'
Impossible archival imaginaries in dance community archiving in a digital age

ASTRID VON ROSEN

Introduction: who is allowed to dream big dreams?

'Dream no small dreams . . . (Goethe)

THE FOREGOING ADMONITION to dream big enough dreams opens the executive summary of a Vision 2020 document produced by the Dance Heritage Coalition.[1] Based in the United States, the coalition has long been a large and successful fixture within the field of dance archives. It not only dreams about but also actually plans to create a 'virtual *Digital Humanities Center* for dance' and has managed to link together major dance archives as well as develop archival consulting for dance companies with in-house archives (National Dance Heritage Leadership Forum 2010:8). It might be argued that such large, publicly accessible portals are intended, especially through their consulting and advice services, to help smaller, independent archives to get noticed, be listed on the portal and have material digitized and linked to from the portal; however, this is not always the case. In the somewhat different Swedish context where I am located, there is no equivalent to the Dance Heritage Coalition, and initiatives to create something similar, on either a national or regional level, have so far failed. For most small-scale independent dance companies, funding to digitize their materials cannot be found, their archives will not be linked to a public platform for a variety of reasons and efforts to achieve virtual archiving will remain scattered and lead to minimal results. So, one might ask, who is allowed to dream big dreams? Who may have large-scale imaginings, not only of relevant archives being assembled under a digital platform but also of scholars and practitioners arriving to explore those archives and create the histories of individuals, groups and communities, or to use the resources in other ways?

Furthermore, what is at stake when some great archival vision falls apart and may need to transform into something different and more possible to realize, if it is to survive at all?

Drawing on recent research at the University of Gothenburg and University College London, the aim of this chapter is to chart and theorize the challenges faced by local independent dance communities when it comes to realizing their archival dreams. After a brief section introducing the reader to recent developments within archival theory three case studies are presented, exploring how dance archives have been dreamt of as well as actually emerging in the city of Gothenburg, and how they are understood and used by the communities as well as by scholars investigating independent dance. The chapter concludes with arguments for a methodologically conscious, digitally engaged participatory approach ('dancing where we dig – digging where we dance') to dance archiving and archival research as a way of further augmenting the potentially productive role of dreaming big dreams.

Enter: the archival multiverse

From the 1990s and onwards the understanding of what an archive is and what it does has undergone considerable change, a process encompassing different world views and practices pertaining to diverging traditions and contexts across the globe. In particular postcolonial, human rights and social justice research has emphasized the need to re-imagine traditional notions of records as neutral containers of facts, to embrace contesting world views and acknowledge the perspectives of excluded groups and individuals. These changes have occurred in tandem with the development of digital technologies and their promise to enhance democratization of sources and knowledge.

As suggested by Anne Gilliland, the archival changes and developments can be understood by way of the *archival multiverse*, a pluralizing concept describing the infinite character of archives (in the broadest sense of the term) and emphasizing the critical potential of pluralization of contexts, perspectives and provenances (Gilliland 2017). Signifying a paradigm shift challenging both positivist and interpretivist mindsets, the archival multiverse has the potential to better acknowledge features such as 'oral forms of records, literature, art, artefacts, the built environment, landscape, dance, ceremonies, and rituals' hitherto by and large 'excluded from the professional meanings given to *record*, *archive*, and *archives*' (McKemmish 2011:123). Navigating through the multiverse, in my case studies I identify productive frictions between an unimaginative and essentially positivist understanding of archives and sources as plain containers of facts and the recognition that archival absences and imaginaries have the power to motivate research, propel change and stimulate the writing of new histories. I have found Gilliland and Michelle Caswell's terms 'impossible archival imaginaries' and 'imagined records' particularly useful, as they 'offer important affective counterbalances and sometimes resistance to dominant legal, bureaucratic, historical and forensic notions of evidence' (Gilliland and Caswell 2016:55). In resonance with participatory approaches to knowledge production, this stance calls for implementation of reflective methodologies. Hence, I will situate myself in relation to the dancers and dance groups I have engaged with in my research.

In my previous career as a professional classical and contemporary dancer, and now as a scholar, I have been deeply involved in what can be called the local dance community. As noted by Andrew Flinn, community is one of those slippery notions that take on different meanings depending on one's perspective and reason for using them (Flinn 2011:7–8). The independent dance community at the heart of this exploration is a rather large and somewhat cohesive grouping that in turn consists of smaller units whose members share some but not all artistic ideas, and take part in some but not all group activities. In particular I share their dreams and aspirations for dance archives and spaces to engage with history. I also share with Judith Hamera the view that dance and its communities form a 'vital urban infrastructure', rather than being something sealed off from society and thus considered irrelevant (Hamera 2011:xi).

Paraphrasing Anna Sexton on the impossibility of completely separating personal and scholarly roles when striving to be participatory, I can say that I have 'lived the research' presented in this article (Sexton 2015:18). My activity has oscillated between being immersive and more distanced, with implementation of feedback loops and consistent reflection on the research process. With this said, I will now move on to examine a big archival dream, one that contains both harsh failure and a strong manifestation of community engagement for local dance and its histories.

Case 1: dreaming of an all-embracing dance archive

In the late 1990s, when there was no official systematic approach to archiving independent dance in Gothenburg and the wider region (Västra Götaland), the idea of creating a Västsvenskt dansarkiv (West Swedish Dance Archive – WSDA) began to grow.[2] In its context, this was indeed a big dream. In the following I will outline some of the significant features of the WSDA project, which ran between 2000 and 2003, as a way of describing the local dance context and its archival aspirations. I draw on several sources, but an interesting as well as digitally accessible one (albeit in Swedish) is a twenty-minute talk outlining the WSDA project, given by dancer and choreographer Marika Hedemyr (Hedemyr 2013).

As explained by Hedemyr the main ambition of the WSDA project was first to create a virtual portal or platform for an extensive dance archive bringing together materials from institutions, such as museums, libraries and the university. The second step would be to develop this into a physical library, archive and research centre. After mapping other archival projects and performing a great deal of lobbying, the WSDA working group (consisting of Hedemyr and, among others, the well-established choreographer Gun Lund) applied for grants from several funding bodies, including in particular the regional authority (Västra Götaland). Despite an ambitious programme foreseeing that the archive would be used by practitioners, teachers, artists, scholars and others, all the applications were rejected. Apparently the WSDA group had imagined that the participating institutions could simply link up their systems to make dance literature and materials more accessible. But it was no big surprise that the proposed digital solution turned out to be far from compatible with the reality at the institutions involved. It is apparent that the symbolic (lawgiving, ordering) structure (funding bodies, institutions) did not view this particular regional/local dance as a worthy basis for an archival meta-structure, and the imaginary dream suffered great harm. However, this does not necessarily mean that the dream disappeared.

At this point it might be tempting to criticize the WSDA group for clinging to naïve ideas about digital technology, lacking knowledge about how institutions are structured and operate, not having recruited powerful enough representatives for its executive board and so forth. However, the failure of the project and the resulting impossibility of a West Swedish Dance Archive may have more complicated causes, and need not be seen as the end of the big dream. Following Gilliland and Caswell, for a great variety of communities and individuals seeking and needing change, affectively charged features, such as imagined and even impossible archives, are 'pregnant with the possibility of establishing a proof, a perspective, a justice that heretofore has remained unattainable' (Gilliland and Caswell 2016:72). For the local independent dance community, the struggle for recognition and respect for their art, for dance to be incorporated into the university and to receive fair payment for their work, as well as the longing for more research-based histories, was, I suggest, strongly linked with the big archival dream and carried forwards by it. It is worth noting here that independent dancers, and especially the many female practitioners, have notorious and well-documented difficulties making a living from their work and being accorded value and status by other actors in the cultural and political arena (Konstnärsnämnden och Kulturrådet 2015). It is in relation to these obstacles that the impossible imagined dance archive becomes a means to question or even surpass the often unstable and poor circumstances typical of the independent dance world. However, before looking more deeply into these potentialities, I will analyse a new digital actor arriving in the archival arena.

Case 2: getting a publicly funded database without a 'kitchen'

On the opening page of the online database Scenarkivet.se (Stage Archive.se) bold green letters state '*Vi skriver historia!*' ('We're writing history!'). In line with Gilliland

and Caswell's argument for 'taking affect seriously' in order to better engage collective imaginaries in relation to archives, the exclamation mark and the sense of engagement associated with it might contribute to encouraging the actual making of local history (Gilliland and Caswell 2016:73).

In contrast to WLDA's failure to attract support, in 2006 Scenarkivet.se received funding from Access, the Swedish Arts Council's project to promote employment within the cultural sector (Kulturrådets skriftserie 2010:1). The application was submitted by a different section of the local dance community, a venue that applied together with two similar venues in other Swedish cities, and the WLDA group was thus *not* actively part of the application. The overarching aim of the Access project was to make cultural materials stored at institutions publicly accessible by organizing and digitizing them. This time, venues for independent culture with a focus on dance were actually chosen by the symbolic structure (overarching regulating system). The particular mission for Scenarkivet.se was to document activities at the venues Atalante in Gothenburg, Moderna Dansteatern in Stockholm, and Dansstationen in Malmö, and make the materials searchable in a database. It was argued that handling the traces of twenty years of work at the three venues was a way of safeguarding 'a substantial part of the performing arts heritage in Sweden' (Scenarkivet.se, my translation). I will now turn to how the database functions (and does not function) in relation to potential ways of stimulating the production of local dance community history.

Scenarkivet.se offers a clear and easy-to-navigate system, where performances, groups and persons are searchable categories. Basic performance information is combined with such things as photographs, press clippings, posters, flyers and video (for copyright reasons seldom longer than two minutes). Even if there are obviously many gaps in what is presented, it no doubt contains much that can be useful in historical research. The documentation in the database also functions as a reservoir of memories for the people who were once part of the past events. While there are multiple ways of engaging with the database, I wanted to better examine its limits in terms of representing multiple aspects of the local dance context. My intention has not been to devalue what is there, but to chart important absences as a way of respecting what choreographers and dancers have talked with me about and described as aspects that are vital for the community (von Rosen 2013–16).

While exploring Scenarkivet.se, it soon becomes clear that neither dance performances at other venues or in hybrid spaces nor choreography for events labelled with another tag, such as 'theatre', has been included. Notably, important infrastructure, and in particular a large amount of work done by women choreographers and dancers, disappears for this reason. Yet another – crucial – aspect of the exclusive focus on one venue in each city (Atalante, in the case of Gothenburg) is that places and structures for education and training are lacking in the database. Moreover, Scenarkivet.se cannot in its current form historicize beyond the mid-1980s in terms of adding materials and information from previous years. This means that the important infrastructure consisting of different places and activities, and engaging a variety of groupings and individuals (of different ethnicity, race, gender, dance background and so forth), as well as imaginaries traversed by material and structural circumstances, is difficult to access.

Drawing on Baz Kershaw and Angela Piccini's distinction between 'integral' (all sorts of materials pertaining to process and performance) and 'external' (curated materials for the public to view) documentation, one might say that Scenarkivet.se contains and presents 'pure' materials, while what could be described as 'dirty' or messy is absent (Ledger et al. 2012:166). For example there are no messy, tangible or rough notes, sketches on napkins, inspiration photographs, precarious diary entries and so forth accessible in Scenarkivet.se. The external structure facilitates swift navigation, especially for scholars and others used to similar systems; it prompts or instructs people like me to apply habitual skills. Such systems are rooted in long-standing archival traditions and practices. Moreover, they form part of a positivist paradigm, where documents and objects by and large are conceived as containers of facts, meaning that many objects in the performing arts archives are both unimaginatively used and poorly theorized. While the current system at Scenarkivet.se does not necessarily prevent creative visitor engagement, participatory approaches, memory work and so forth, it does not offer specific functions for such approaches. What the structure does allow for is the continued production of more digital records, and I think it is fair to say that Scenarkivet.se will neither write (or otherwise construct) local dance history nor propel change for the community unless people get involved in more substantial ways. As demonstrated by Gilliland and Caswell (for the case of social justice records), having access to a plenitude of digital materials in processes aimed at change does not help much if the records – the things we see and how we interpret them – are not problematized and critically engaged with (Gilliland and Caswell 2016).

Sarah Whatley, in her work with the online archive Siobhan Davies Replay (SDR), provides an example where the positivist paradigm is at least partially transgressed in favour of more engaged and creative opportunities in and with archives. While SDR provides users with creative spaces and tools called 'kitchens', enabling them, among other options, to create their own collections, it has also been criticized for failing to fulfil its more traditional task of safeguarding the legacy of the artist. Despite these obstacles, Whatley argues that the kitchens provide 'a new kind of critical space for contemplating the complex relationships between artists, researchers, designers, and technologists, and provides a potent demonstration of how artists and researchers can work together' (Whatley 2013:177). Even if Scenarkivet.se differs significantly from SDR in many respects, I find Whatley's kitchens useful for engendering new ways of engaging with performance archives across all sorts of borders. I would say that the kitchen as metaphor and digital example can open up new imaginaries and perhaps even reactivate some features of the big archival dream, understood as a wish for pluralistic living history-making with and for the local dance community. Another component to be considered in relation to impossible archival imaginaries is activism. As previously hinted at, despite being initially turned down for funding, the local dance community's big dream did not disappear. Instead, as will be discussed in the following section, it transmuted and found new ways to exist.

Case 3: creating an activist dance community archive

My first substantial encounter with the 3rd Floor Dance Library and Dance Archive (3VDLDA, Tredje våningens dansbibliotek och arkiv) took place during a symposium called *Dance as Critical Heritage: Archives, Action, Access*, held in Gothenburg in October 2013. Planned together with representatives for the community and aiming to stimulate research on independent dance, the symposium welcomed thirty participants from outside and within the university. Among these were Gun Lund and her partner, medical doctor and dance producer Lars Persson. Arriving at the symposium venue, they carried two large binders, taking on the role of active participants, functioning as what Robin Bernstein calls 'scriptive things', items that prompt us to act according to existing cultural protocols (Bernstein 2009). Having conducted much archival research, I felt a clear urge to take on the task of exploring the binders – for example to chart the local dance infrastructure and get a better grip on the reception of the early independent dance interventions. The binders' rich historical content also testifies of a sense of collective achievement and belonging, as well as providing connections to the past in terms of attachment to place. Despite these qualities of the binders, I also was well aware that dance, as a living memory, would not be readily accessible through such an exploration. Several symposium participants demonstrated that dance knowledge is a practice and a process to be created and experienced in a collective and embodied space. Hence, the community generously offered several ways of accessing local dance history, in terms of engaging with their archives, both the collections and the bodies. I also became aware of the long-term archival passion that was an integral part of Lund's artistic persona and career. The binders came across as extensions of her, and she could more clearly be perceived as what Lepecki terms 'an endlessly creative, transformational archive' for dance practices and experiences (Lepecki 2010:46). When I have conducted what I term oral-corporeal history with Lund, she has physically demonstrated her memories of dance in resonance with my embodied responses, making me in turn part of a living archive.

During the symposium, Lund explained that one set of binders contains almost everything that has been written about dance in Gothenburg since the 1950s, and the other set almost everything that has been written about Lund and Rubicon (1978–98), the dance group she was part of as founder and choreographer. Belonging to a more extensive collection of materials, the binders are kept at the venue 3:e Våningen (3rd Floor) inaugurated in 2010 and run by Lund, Persson and now also their son, choreographer Olof Persson, and form part of what I term an activist dance community archive (here meaning an archive holding materials that provide access to many aspects of the community). This means not only that the archive is meant to propel political change for independent dance, so that both Lund's work and that of other dance groups and individuals can find ways of being acknowledged and better supported, but also that it is a product of a historical activist context. Persson described a political situation where many groups were collectively organized, and the unemployment office to a large extent provided the salaries for the dancers involved in Rubicon's projects for urban space. He linked this zeitgeist to the political context of 1968, saying that 'it was kind of a natural place to be, in the streets' and that 'the political fight was in the streets; why shouldn't art be in the streets?' Drawing on the ideas and actions of previous avant-garde movements, Persson explained that it is a very recognizable situation to have 'no money and no space' and to 'do art anyway' (Persson 2013). My intention by quoting this is not to romanticize or oversimplify the situation of underpaid dancers and choreographers, but to understand the activist world view that underpins the 3VDLDA archive and renders it different from Scenarkivet.se and institutional archives. While I am not seeking to create unproductive dichotomies between various mindsets and archival models, I do think that having a clearer understanding of what is at stake might be a better way of dreaming big dreams, imagining better futures and contributing to fashioning them.

Part of the explanation of why Lund and Persson have put so much effort into creating an activist archive and a physical space for researching is their need for direct access to their own materials and to be able to save what they value and use it as they please. Lund explains that there was a plan to donate materials to the Gothenburg Museum, but, echoing the experiences of many community-based archives and archivists when engaging with mainstream heritage institutions, she found it unacceptable to lose the ability to handle the materials as she pleased. When previously given an opportunity to donate parts of her archive to Scenarkivet.se, she chose not to do so, as too much unpaid work was required within that structure. Instead Lund and Persson have chosen by and large to work in activistic and self-organizing ways, sometimes with the help of small-scale grants. Recognizing that Lund and Persson belong to a first generation of independent dance pioneers and that the community now also consists of second- and third-generation groups and individuals struggling to find their place and make a living, it seems all the more urgent to at least try to come to terms with the local archival multiverse.

'Dancing where we dig!': from archival impotency to participatory activism

The case studies outlined earlier convey a somewhat fragmented archival picture, where funding bodies, organizations and individuals have different agendas and different understandings of what a dance archive is and how it can be used. It seems to me that 3VDLDA's move away from public authorities and overly formal or bureaucratic structures is also a move away from archival impotency towards a more powerful and active stance where the archival dream can live and stimulate research. Including Lund and Persson as living archives, the 3VDLDA provides access to a rich web of community history, and is indeed encouraging researchers and practitioners to 'dance where we dig!', or explore their own history.

Inspired by Sven Lindqvist's *Dig Where You Stand: How to Research a Job* (DWYS, *Gräv där du står: Hur man utforskar ett jobb*, 1978), Flinn and I have seen the potential for activist participatory research in the local dance context to be a possible way to produce history (Flinn and von Rosen 2016). Empowering cement workers to investigate their own workplaces as experts, Lindqvist's model for history from below became an important tool for communities not only for 'self-defence' when under attack but also as part of the process of transforming their current social and economic realities.[3] This need for a form of history able to serve as a powerful tool when striving to change difficult realities is precisely what continues to be at stake for the local dance community. While Lindqvist envisioned mostly men from one social group engaged in digging up industrial history, we imagine mostly female dance-workers, several of whom have been pioneers, bringing a cultural and artistic past into the present in practical and empowering ways.

Lindqvist's DWYS methodology was envisioned as contributing to the ongoing struggle for industrial and economic democracy above and beyond the political democracy of suffrage and representation. For this to happen, he argued, in order to conquer the company one must first create a new picture putting workers centre stage. This stance seems to be highly relevant for the dance community, both in terms of an imaginary picture – the big archival dream – and as an impetus to collaboratively start 'dancing where we dig – digging where we dance'. The ultimate reason for turning to Lindqvist's manual is the spirit and intention behind its combination of a politically conscious activist imperative, a DIY knowledge-production ethos and practical hands-on suggestions for how to go about doing the digging. In its thirty chapters, DWYS provides detailed instructions for exploring a job in such features as the world, a records office, school, memory, death, home and research. This, we argue, is clear and direct enough to be kept readily updated and attuned to contemporary research challenges, technological shifts and struggles for the places and functions of independent dance, art and creativity in society.

Calling into question the traditional understanding of archives as 'unconscious and therefore objective by-products of bureaucratic activity', this move towards an inclusive, participatory model of archival engagement instead views the keeping of records as 'a continually interacting and evolving set of contingent activities with individual, institutional and societal aspects' (McKemmish and Gilliland 2013:93). More specifically, in the dance context it is also a move towards processes of engaging with what Diana Taylor terms 'the repertoire' or embodied practices of memory (Taylor 2003). For a participatory approach to be able to function in the local community context I believe that the flexible and inclusive idea of the archival multiverse, allowing for a plurality of dance histories to emerge, will need some sort of symbolic (ordering and critically affirming) structure. One way of understanding such a symbolic order is as a dialogic partner that is always there – not a structure to be blindly consulted and obeyed, but an ordering feature that provides a strong point of reference while distributing the power to conduct research. The *Dig Where You Stand* book, motto and metaphor, has by and large taken on that function, and continues to script activist engagement to produce local dance history. Constructing a *dancing-digging-digital manual* in resonance with recent digital developments through a process of shared control between community and scholars would be a way of making this less abstract. Not only would such a moving manifestation of best practices enable more people to join in mapping, exploring, theorizing and interpreting local dance memories, but also it would function as a shared material as well as digital space for exchange and action. What I am looking for here is a unifying feature that at the same time allows for a plurality of voices and is not directly connected with or dependent on either the existing archives (databases and so forth) or the university. I think a jointly produced dig and dance manual could function as a symbolic structure that does not put constraints on imaginary powers, community and individual wishes, ideas and approaches, but embraces them and cares for them, while building trust and legitimacy. Importantly, a manual can provide guidance for continuing and even transforming the exploratory work and its dissemination, even if people come and go, support fluctuates and digital platforms change or disappear. One example of a challenging nexus that could be addressed in such a manual is the impossibility of archiving (in a traditional manner) embodied dance knowledge and the possibility of using new technology and mobile methodologies to enable a great variety of people to engage with dance as a powerful and critically constructive infrastructure and heritage.

Acknowledgements

I am thankful to Andrew Flinn and Anna Sexton for useful comments on the manuscript and to the Carina Ari Memorial Foundation for supporting my research. Thanks are also due to CIRN (Community Informatics Network) for permission to publish this essay, based on a longer paper presented at their 2016 conference in Prato, Italy and to be published in the CIRN context.

Notes

1   The quotation is attributed to Goethe by the authors of the Vision 2020 document, not by me.

2   Gothenburg is the second city of Sweden. It has an opera house with a resident ballet company, and two universities (but none of them holds a dance department).
3   We use the book as inspiration to find ways to explore the history of 'a dance job', as (potential) employment, task and meaning-making activity.

Bibliography

Bernstein, Robin (2009) 'Dances with Things: Material Culture and the Performance of Race', *Social Text*, 27:4, Winter, 67–94.

Flinn, Andrew (2011) 'Archival Activism: Independent and Community-Led Archives, Radical Public History and the Heritage Professions', *InterActions: UCLA Journal of Education and Information Studies*, 7:2, 1–21.

Flinn, Andrew and Astrid von Rosen (2016) 'Reading "Dig Where You Stand": Re-Imagining a 1978 Manual for Participatory Heritage Activism', conference presentation, *What Does Heritage Change?*, third biannual ACHS conference, Montreal June 3–8.

Gilliland, Anne (2017) 'Archival and Recordkeeping Traditions in the Multiverse and Their Importance for Researching Situations and Situating Research', in Anne J. Gilliland, Sue McKemmish and Andrew J. Lau, eds. *Research in the Archival Multiverse*, Clayton Victoria: Monash University, 31–73.

Gilliland, Anne and Michelle Caswell (2016) 'Records and Their Imaginaries: Imagining the Impossible, Making Possible the Imagined', *Archival Science*, 16:1, March, 53–75.

Hamera, Judith (2011) *Dancing Communities: Performance, Difference and Connection in the Global City*, Basingstoke: Palgrave Macmillan.

Hedemyr, Marika (2013) *Invigningstal 3 Våningen bibliotek och arkiv*, https://vimeo.com/user3065097/videos (accessed 26–06–2016).

Konstnärsnämnden och Kulturrådet (2015) *Översyn av statens nuvarande insatser inom dansområdet*, www.kulturradet.se/Documents/publikationer/2015/oversyn_dansomradet.pdf.

Kulturrådets skriftserie (2010:1) *Uppföljning av Access*, www.kulturradet.se/Documents/publikationer/2010/access_final.pdf (accessed 27–01–2016).

Ledger, Adam J., Simon K. Ellis and Fiona Wright (2011) 'The Question of Documentation: Creative Strategies in Performance Research', in Baz Kershaw and Helen Nicholson, eds. *Research Methods in Theatre and Performance*, Edinburgh: Edinburgh University Press, 162–185.

Lepecki, André (2010) 'The Body as Archive: Will to Re-Enact and the Afterlives of Dances', *Dance Research Journal*, 42:2, Winter, 28–48.

McKemmish, Sue (2011) 'Evidence of Me . . . in a Digital World', in Christopher A. Lee, ed. *I, Digital: Personal Collections in the Digital Era*, Chicago: Society of American Archivists, 115–148.

McKemmish, Sue and Anne Gilliland (2013) 'Chapter 4. Archival and Recordkeeping Research: Past, Present and Future', in Kristy Williamson and Graeme Johanson, eds. *Research Methods: Information, Systems, and Contexts*, Prahran, Victoria: Tilde, 79–112.

National Dance Heritage Leadership Forum (2010) *Vision 2020, Creating a New Place for Dance in the Public Imagination*, Dance Heritage Coalition, www.danceheritage.org/vision2020.pdf (accessed 26–04–2016).

Persson, Lars (2013) 'Personal presentation', *Dance as Critical Heritage: Archives, Access, Action*, Symposium 28–29 October, Critical Heritage Studies, University of Gothenburg.

von Rosen, Astrid, Interviews with dancers and choreographers conducted 2013–16 within the research project *Dance as Critical Heritage*. Notes from the interviews are kept by the researcher. Available on request.

Scenarkivet.se, www.scenarkivet.se/ (accessed on numerous occasions between 2013 and 2016).

Sexton, Anna (2015) *Archival Activism and Mental Health: Being Participatory, Sharing Control and Building Legitimacy* (PhD Diss.), London: University College London, http://discovery.ucl.ac.uk/1474368/1/A%20Sexton%20Thesis%20With%20Corrections.pdf (accessed 27–06–2016).

Taylor, Diana (2003) *The Archive and the Repertoire: Performing Cultural Memory in the Americas*, Durham: Duke University Press.

Whatley, Sarah (2013) 'Dance Encounters Online: Digital Archives and Performance', in Gunhild Borggreen and Rune Gade, eds. *Performing Archives/Archives of Performance*, Copenhagen: Museum Tusculanum Press and University of Copenhagen, 163–178.

Chapter 13

When place matters
Provincializing the 'global'

EMILY E. WILCOX

Introduction

IN THE FIRST EDITION of *Rethinking Dance History: A Reader*, Alexandra Carter discussed the need for new stories in dance history. In particular, she highlighted the importance of moving beyond linear narratives with clear endpoints in the present. '[O]ur histories can accommodate activities which do not seem to contribute in any obvious ways to the "development" of the art form but, in their time, were a vital part of it' (Carter 2004: 13; also this volume). As dance historians, Carter's critique helps us recognize that writing about dance history is important even when it does not validate today's artistic tastes and ideas. It suggests that such scholarship may be even more urgent, since it may help us overcome the biases of our own time.

Building on Carter's insights, I would like to suggest that it is not only temporal but also spatial and formal prejudices that call for new stories in dance history. Whereas Carter's concerns are with the problems of presentism – making dance history serve values and practices of the present – the concerns addressed in this essay are with problems of placeism – making dance history serve the values and practices of particular places or communities. Like time, place is entangled with issues of culture, and it is the organic combination of *where*, *how*, and *with whom* people dance that constitutes place in the context of dance history.[1] As I use it in this essay, 'place' is not limited to physical location, but includes translocal networks of dance communities defined by shared dance activities. To combat placeism in this sense means telling stories that are varied not just geographically but also in the types of dance spaces, practices, and communities they engage.

As a scholar of dance history specializing in China, my concerns about placeism are prompted by observations about the scholarly prejudices at work in my own field. Since the early 2000s, there has been an exciting growth in Anglophone scholarship dealing with dance history in China and the broader Sinophone world, including Hong Kong, Taiwan, and the Chinese diaspora. Thematically, however, this scholarship has been uneven in the spaces and communities with which it has engaged. Taken as a whole, its focus has been disproportionately on practitioners working within the broad category of modern and postmodern dance. Ensembles such as Cloud Gate Dance Theatre of Taiwan and City Contemporary Dance Company of Hong Kong and individuals such as Ts'ai Juehyüeh, Wu Xiaobang, H.T. Chen, Jin Xing, and Shen Wei have been privileged at the expense of companies and artists working in other media (e.g. Chen 2003, 2009; Kwan 2003, 2009, 2013; Lin 2004, 2010, 2016; Minarty 2005; Gerdes 2010; Seetoo 2013; Ma 2015, 2016). This has produced a placeist perspective in the field, which has limited the types of stories dance historians tell about the Sinophone world.[2]

In this essay, I consider how the concept of the 'global' has contributed to this kind of placeism in the writing of dance history. Since their popularization in the 1990s, the concepts of the 'global' and 'globalization' have been methodologically very productive. By mapping cultural flows through transnational exchange and diaspora, these ideas challenged earlier approaches that emphasized bounded communities and place-based identities (Appadurai 1996; Gupta and Furgeson 1997b). Later, by highlighting the agency of people and places outside the global North, they also helped complicate core-periphery models (Inda and Rosaldo 2002; Ong and Collier 2005). While the benefits of these approaches are clear, there is also a need for critical reflection on new prejudices they have introduced. In the field of dance scholarship, one such prejudice is the tendency to privilege practitioners of modern and postmodern dance in the writing of dance history most often described as 'global'. Such an approach is particularly troubling for dance historians, because it obscures alternative subjects and limits our understanding of dance practices present and past. In this sense, limited perceptions of what counts as 'global' promote placeism in the writing of dance history.

The tendency to equate modern and postmodern dance with the 'global' is not accidental. It reflects specific cultural, economic, and political conditions that define the historical phenomenon of globalization and discourses about the global in Anglophone academia. The English term 'globalization' first emerged in the 1960s and became commonplace in academic discussions from the 1990s onward (Dalby 2008). Although many features of late twentieth-century globalization appeared before the 1990s, the rise in popularity of globalization discourse, as well as the specific historical changes it has come to describe, dates to this period. Specifically, many aspects of what is now called 'globalization' and the 'global' relate directly to the new economic, political, and cultural conditions that emerged after the Cold War, in a new period marked by the merging of world markets and the unprecedented ascendance of US hegemony (Klein 2003).

The spread of US culture to places that had previously rejected it in favour of other transnational affiliations was an important feature of the 'global' moment of the 1990s. This was made possible, in part, by the enforcement of neoliberal economic doctrines – prepared for in the Cold War but realized during the Reagan-Thatcher era – which became an essential, if not defining, feature of globalization. Because the United States was their main promoter, these doctrines are also called 'the Washington consensus' (Dalby 2008: 430). Along with these economic changes came the widespread acceptance, even naturalization, of US ideology – a thought system hinged on values such as 'freedom' and 'individualism'. Perhaps the greatest impact of globalization in the sphere of culture has been the increasing impossibility of thinking outside these values, making it more difficult to reflect on their limitations.[3]

Dance history is not politically, economically, or culturally neutral and, therefore, cannot be separated from these broader historical events. Throughout the Cold War, the US State Department actively promoted modern and postmodern dance as embodiments of US culture, to 'contain' the spread of communism and promote US interests abroad (Kowal 2010; Croft 2015). By the 1990s, the advent of globalization made possible an even greater international spread of these dance forms, particularly in places like China that had once resisted them as embodiments of US imperialism (Ou 1995). Meanwhile, in dance scholarship the term 'global' increasingly came to refer to experiments that emerged from this new expansion of modern and postmodern dance around the world. The surge in research on modern and postmodern dance in the Sinophone sphere reflects both the historical phenomenon of globalization during the 1990s and the rise of the 'global' as a theme in dance studies.

Because of its historic importance during the Cold War as one of the most prominent ideological critics and opponents of US expansionism, China was one of the places where globalization had its greatest impact. Its history was different from that of Taiwan and Hong Kong, which had been allies of the United States during the Cold War. In China, there is a direct connection between globalization, US influence, and the spread of modern and postmodern dance. China's surge in modern and postmodern dance activities began in 1987, when the American Dance Festival and US-based Asian Cultural Council sent teachers to Guangdong, the area of China that was the first to enact economic liberalization policies and court foreign investment in the early stages of globalization. These efforts led to the founding of China's first officially recognized modern dance company, the Guangdong Modern Dance Company, in 1992 – just one year after the end of the Cold War. They also facilitated the training of China's first generation of modern and postmodern dance practitioners, including influential figures such as Jin Xing, Shen Wei, Wang Mei, Xing Liang, Ma Shouze, Yang Qiao, and others (Solomon and Solomon 1995). The explosion of companies specializing in modern and postmodern dance across

China during the 1990s and early 2000s was a direct result of increased exchange between dancers in China and the United States, which coincided with the expanding impact of US culture in China in nearly all other fields.

For the term 'global' to be used critically in the writing of dance history, it is essential that we move beyond the idea that modern dance and postmodern dance are culturally universal, neutral, or exempt from place-based identities and political histories. Building on the work of dance scholar Ananya Chatterjea and historian Dipesh Chakrabarty, and my own research on the history of dance in China, I argue that modern dance and postmodern dance are not neutral universals, but, rather, represent specific, place-based agendas that benefit from a myth of universalism. Before an effective reconceptualization of the 'global' can occur in dance history scholarship, modern and postmodern dance must be critically examined as place-based forms that promote culturally specific values.

One way of doing this critical work is by looking to moments in dance history when communities engaged in active resistance against the spread of modern and postmodern dance and explicitly described these forms as place-based political projects with non-neutral cultural values. This type of critical assessment occurred, I argue, among Chinese dancers during the 1950s, when socialist culture encouraged the principled rejection of US expansionism and Eurocentric cultural hierarchies. In today's post-globalization moment, when modern dance and postmodern dance enjoy increasingly hegemonic status in dance programming and scholarship around the world, investigating such historical voices is particularly urgent. By attending to communities who resisted, refused, and created their own alternatives to modern and postmodern dance, we can disrupt forms of placeism embedded in existing definitions of the 'global' in dance scholarship. In other words, we can acknowledge the fact that treating modern and postmodern dance as neutral universals is a form of placeism in itself.

The myth of neutrality: provincializing the global

There are good reasons why the language of the 'global' gained traction in dance scholarship. For many, the 'global' overcame problems inherent in an older concept of 'world dance', which had seemed to promote a 'West and the Rest' dichotomy for investigating dance history. Concepts of the 'global' recognized hybridity and interculturalism within the category of 'the West', while also breaking down perceived barriers around 'world' dance forms. For many, the formulation of 'global' was inherently non-hierarchical and inclusive, because it treated all dance forms as part of a shared sphere of cultural flows and interconnections, with none inherently privileged.

In a recent essay, Ananya Chatterjea (2013) contests this idealized conception of the global as an inclusive, non-hierarchical arena. In practice, Chatterjea argues, performance spaces marked as 'global' exhibit clear stylistic preferences:

> While the idea of the 'global' seems to offer the promise of a range of aesthetics and a range of bodies from different contexts marking widely different understandings of beauty and power, the reality of what materializes on stage seems to suggest that there are some unspoken conditions for participation on the global stage that ensure some kinds of conformity.
>
> (Chatterjea 2013: 12)

Chatterjea identifies a key ideological problem contributing to this culture of conformity in the global stage, especially as it relates to dances by Asian practitioners. According to her, many programmers and participants believe that modern dance and postmodern dance, unlike other dance forms, are free from cultural specificity and therefore more open to new identities and expressions. For this reason, they value the techniques and choreographic modes of modern and postmodern dance, believing them to be what Chatterjea calls a 'neutral universal':

> What seems to be increasingly popular in the sphere of Asian 'contemporary' dance is a kind of ventriloquism, where contemporary Asia finds its voice through the signifiers of the Euro-American modern/postmodern, the latter passing once again as the neutral universal, which is able to contain all difference.
>
> (2013: 11)

By using the term 'ventriloquism' here, Chatterjea attributes a cultural and place-based identity to the signifiers of modern and postmodern dance. Although these signifiers claim to be universal, she argues, they are in fact Euro-American. The phrase 'once again' also signals an important reference to historical repetition in Chatterjea's analysis: claiming universality for cultural forms that originated in the West is part of a repeating pattern: it appeared in colonialism, then in multiculturalism, and now in the global. Thus, Chatterjea warns, 'we need to be vigilant that these old violences are not perpetuated under the guise of "new" global ventures' (2013: 14). In other words, it is imperative that the 'global' not become a new way of retrenching old hierarchies.

One way to cultivate the vigilance Chatterjea calls for is by reinforcing the place-based histories of Euro-American cultural forms that are treated as universal. In his book *Provincializing Europe: Postcolonial Thought and Historical Difference*, Dipesh Chakrabarty (2000) provided a model for this type of critique, calling it 'to provincialize'. In its earliest usage, the word 'provincialize' meant to speak or write in a provincial dialect, or to make something seem provincial, as in 'of the provinces'. It was originally a sign of cultural backwardness. When mapped on a global scale during the time of Western colonialism, the colonies were equated with the provincial, while the European and North American metropoles were considered the centres of cultural sophistication.[4]

It was in a deliberate effort to overturn such colonial hierarchies that Chakrabarty called for the provincialization of Europe. He provocatively reversed the term's traditional values, insisting that Europe was provincial too. A historian by training, Chakrabarty made his critique by challenging the use of categories and trajectories derived from European history to write histories of the global South. Because actual history always exceeds these categories and trajectories, Chakrabarty argued, translating non-European phenomena through the categories and logics of an imagined Europe was highly problematic. To provincialize Europe, then, meant to strip away European culture's claim to universality and, furthermore, to recognize that furthering such claims only helped to promote Europe's power. According to Chakrabarty, Europe was just one corner of the world that gained power over other corners of the world, and claims to universality served this process.

To 'provincialize Europe' reterritorializes cultural norms and ideas that originated in Europe, recognizing two things in them simultaneously: (1) the universal presence they have attained as a result of modern world history and (2) their place-based origins. Explaining this method in a later essay, Chakrabarty wrote, 'To provincialize Europe was precisely to find out how and in what sense European ideas that were indeed universal were also, at one and the same time, drawn from particular intellectual and historical traditions that could not claim any universal validity' (2008: 96). Chakrabarty's point was that even though aspects of European culture have attained the capacity of universal application – due to colonialism, imperialism, and the spread of global capitalism – they are not inherently universal. Thus, their universality derives from the history of Western power, not from any actual capacity to contain all forms of difference.

The most salient example of this in *Provincializing Europe* is what Chakrabarty describes as the inability of modern European secular history to account for the agency of gods, something that appears frequently in local histories of South Asia. Translating such histories into a narrative that will satisfy the logical requirements of modern European historical thought necessarily requires loss – stories about gods and their agency must disappear. This process is what Chakrabarty calls 'the mediation of a universal, homogenizing middle term', in this case the middle term being secular history (2000: 85). By claiming to be universal, this process of translation denies the act of loss (the gods were never there to begin with, and they were not part of the true history), thereby erasing the evidence of its own inadequacy as a translation tool.

When modern dance and postmodern dance become universalized as a tool of expression for dancers around the world, a similar act of mediation takes place, enacting similar forms of power inequality and loss. In Anglophone dance scholarship, ballet has long been recognized as a product of European cultural values (Keali'inohomoku 1983[1969–70]). As such, the adoption of ballet by non-European dance communities has regularly been treated as a process of cultural translation (e.g. Reynoso 2014). The same has not been true, however, in most discussions of modern and postmodern dance, whose adoption by non-Western artists tends to be either normalized as a process of modernization or valued as an expression of freedom and individualism. Adopting modern and postmodern dance tends to be imagined as a departure from local constraints or 'cultural traditions' constructed variously as inauthentic, convention-bound, or otherwise limiting (e.g. Ou 1995). It is rarely characterized as submission to US hegemony or a product of neoliberalism. Such arguments actually reproduce the ideology of globalization, while de-legitimating dancers' choices when they do not fit this model.

To adapt Chatterjea's and Chakrabarty's insights into a methodology for dance history would be to recognize that modern dance and postmodern dance are not neutral mediators, and that they have a cultural context and political history that require critical reflection. To provincialize the global in dance history is to see modern and postmodern dance as carrying specific political and cultural values and having global relevance because of place-based histories, not because of their inherent artistic neutrality. As Chakrabarty proposes for the gods silenced by secular history, we must make space for the dancers and styles disappeared by the ascendance of modern and postmodern dance.

Resisting modern dance: recovering alternative voices

Throughout the Cold War, there were many who, for different reasons, expressed critical voices challenging modern and postmodern dance's claims to universalism.[5] One example of this challenge appeared in 1958 in the Beijing-based journal *Wudao* (*Dance*). Reflecting socialist ideals dominant in China at the time, a Chinese critic named Xia Yu made an argument against using modern dance as the basis for China's dance education.[6] Xia was responding to a proposal published two years earlier by Guo Mingda, a Chinese dancer who had studied modern dance in the United States and wanted to bring it to China.

Xia outlined several reasons for rejecting Guo's proposal. First, Xia argued that introducing modern dance would divert attention from creating new native dance forms, which was the focus of activity among Chinese choreographers at the time. 'Excuse me, but where does native dance stand in this scenario?' Xia asked (1958: 10).[7] Second, promoting modern dance would, according to Xia, support an ideological view that was fundamentally at odds with China's socialist values. Modern dance claimed to be, in Xia's words, 'beyond class and beyond ethnicity'

(Xia 1958: 10).Yet, class and ethnic identity were considered essential to socialist notions of progressive politics. This point led directly to the last problem, in which Xia identified modern dance as essentially foreign. Xia likened Guo's proposed adoption of modern dance in China to a type of 'cultural invasion' (Xia 1958: 10). Rather than seeing modern dance as neutral or universal, Xia viewed it as a threat to local culture that was potentially invasive.

Although the exponents of modern dance imagined that it could transcend cultural and political differences, critics like Xia did not accept this claim. Rather, Xia interpreted this argument as part of the ideology of American cultural imperialism, which attempted to obscure the cultural specificity of modern dance and promote the idea that US culture was good for everyone. Conveying scepticism about the cultural neutrality of modern dance, Xia wrote, 'Guo says "all roads lead to Beijing", but this is not true. Some people want their roads to lead to New York, London, or Paris; for them this is a well-travelled and familiar old path' (1958: 10). By calling roads that lead to New York, London, and Paris as a 'familiar old path', Xia indexed the colonial consciousness in which subjects of European and US colonialism idealized the culture of the Western metropoles and viewed it as more advanced or appealing than their own culture. Here, Xia suggests that Guo holds a naïve view that dismisses these historical inequalities, since Guo believes that adopting modern dance can lead to a spatial consciousness in which 'all roads lead to Beijing'. Adopting an anti-colonial logic, Xia argues that the only way to combat the 'familiar old path' is to actively revolt against it. Thus, for Xia China's resistance to modern dance is part of breaking a much larger pattern of historical inertia, one in which US and Western European metropoles like New York, London, and Paris continue to be treated as centres of cultural knowledge. Xia wanted to end this pattern, and he saw resistance to modern dance as one method to do so.

The personal biography of Guo Mingda helps to explain his knowledge of modern dance and his eagerness to introduce it to China. Guo was born in Sichuan, China, and graduated from National Central University, an institution affiliated with the Nationalist Party, the political group that the United States backed during China's civil war. In 1947, Guo travelled to the United States, where he pursued a master's degree at the University of Iowa and then spent seven years studying modern dance in New York, working largely with Alwin Nikolais (Feng 2006: 400).

When Guo returned to China in 1956, he encountered a new environment: the People's Republic of China, founded in 1949, had already established a large system of dance institutions and its own new dance styles adapted from indigenous performance (Wilcox 2011, 2012, 2016). The global network in which Chinese dancers participated was linked not to the United States and Western Europe, with which Guo was familiar, but to the Soviet Union, Eastern Europe, and the postcolonial Third World (Wilcox forthcoming). As a result, Guo's ideas about dance were very unfamiliar to the majority of Chinese dancers, as theirs were to Guo. Moreover, rather than seeing US culture as a source of artistic inspiration, most of Guo's

Chinese colleagues viewed the United States as an ideologically backwards country with little to offer in terms of progressive culture (Liu 2015: 12).

Guo's lack of knowledge about the new forms of Chinese dance was apparent in his proposal. With the exception of Russian director Konstantin Stanislavsky, the major figures informing Guo's proposal were Émile Jaques-Dalcroze and Rudolf von Laban, neither of whom were considered important in China's dance circles at the time (Guo 1956: 12). Even more problematic was Guo's suggestion that the new styles of Chinese classical and folk dance be categorized as 'traditional' and US modern dance as 'modern' (Guo 1956: 14). The dance forms that Guo labelled 'traditional' had been created during the nine years that he was studying in Iowa and New York and were actually newer than the ones Guo was proposing to import from abroad. Thus, this categorization made little sense to Chinese readers, who saw the new Chinese dance styles as expressions of a new, revolutionary society. As the product of a different place-based dance community – namely US modern dance circles – Guo's ideas failed to translate into the new context of socialist China. Hence, Xia wrote, '[Guo] is far too unfamiliar with his own national arts. I really wish he would go to the countryside and take a look around' (1958: 11). Rather than uncritically adopting Guo's teachings on US modern dance simply because they came from a Euro-American metropole, Xia turned Guo's proposal around, inviting Guo instead to learn from the new dance developments in socialist China.

When looking back on this historical moment, many today sympathize with Guo, viewing him as a righteous underdog who championed the 'freedom' of modern dance in the face of the 'tyranny' of socialist culture. This is the narrative that best serves the common US-centric perspective promoted during the Cold War, and it is increasingly one also adopted among Chinese scholars eager to criticize China's socialist past and embrace the post-Cold War world. For dance historians concerned with overcoming placeism and other problematic effects of globalization in dance scholarship, however, Xia's perspective is important to recover and consider. In the post-globalization moment, it is the voices of resistance and the once very real alternatives they presented that are increasingly obscured in historical memory, in addition to being too often dismissed politically, artistically, and ideologically. When viewed from today's perspective, Xia's voice may sound grating or even irrelevant. Yet, I argue that it is precisely this quality that makes Xia's voice important. In Chatterjea's words, it offers 'non-alignment/ mistranslation/ contamination' to 'create productive frictions and tensions' (2013: 19).

Conclusion

'Global' is not a neutral concept; it too has political and ideological implications. As Arif Dirlik writes, '[G]lobalization discourse is of obvious ideological utility in sugar-coating an unprecedented US corporate domination of the world' (2010: 5).

When using the term 'global' in dance history, it is important to be aware of these political and ideological implications and to avoid reproducing them uncritically. Promoting a form of 'global' dance history that focuses disproportionately on spaces and communities of modern and postmodern dance risks re-inscribing the agendas of globalization and their attendant place-based prejudices. It also risks obscuring the alternative global networks and challenges to US capitalist culture that thrived during the Cold War but ultimately disappeared in the new era of globalization. These networks are often obscured in dance historical work that ties the 'global' to connections to modern and postmodern dance.[8]

Far from being neutral, modern dance and postmodern dance advance place-based cultural agendas, and their universalization came with place-based costs. Asia is one of the places where the exercising of US power was felt most keenly in the decades of the Cold War. As Amy Kaplan points out, the markets of Asia were 'long the chief prize sought by advocates of [US] expansionism' (1993: 14). During the twentieth century Asia became the literal place in which US wars of influence were waged, often with extreme human, material, and cultural consequences (Klein 2003). Through colonization of the Philippines, nuclear bombing and occupation of Japan, support for martial law in Taiwan, engagement in the Korean and Vietnam Wars, and support for anti-government uprisings in China and Indonesia, US intervention in Asia was consistent, intensive, and often violent. When we write about dance history in Asia, it is important that we engage with these issues. Rather than being isolated from geopolitics, the history of modern and postmodern dance, in particular, is directly entwined with it.

In the post-globalization moment, it is especially important to recover spaces and communities that represent resistance to the current dominant geographical imaginaries and their related dance values. Examining these alternatives will help to undo the ideological work of globalization. It will open up new conversations about the costs of 'freedom', the limitations of the 'individual', and the violence of the 'universal'.

Notes

1   Here, I am drawing on the extensive anthropological literature on place-making. See for example Gupta and Furgeson (1997a).
2   There are, of course, exceptions to this pattern. What I am identifying here is a broader trend of the field as a whole.
3   For more on the culture of neoliberalism, see Brown (2015).
4   This definition is based on the entries for 'provincialize' and 'provincial' in the *Oxford English Dictionary*, 2nd ed., published by Oxford University Press in 1996.

5   Although ballet also claimed universal relevance in some contexts as a symbol of European elite culture, because ballet was promoted by both the United States and the Soviet Union, it was not as directly associated with Western capitalism. See Ezrahi (2012), Giersdorf (2013), and Croft (2015).
6   At the time, China's dance education included a blend of Soviet-style ballet and European character dance, Chinese opera training, and the newly created native dance styles of Chinese classical, folk, and ethnic dance.
7   Translations from Chinese are the author's own.
8   An example of this is the dance festivals hosted by the World Federation of Democratic Youth, which were widely attended by artists from the socialist and Third World countries. Chinese dancers regularly attended these festivals between 1949 and 1962, and they defined a form of 'global' aesthetics for Chinese dancers at this time.

Bibliography

Appadurai, Arjun (1996) *Modernity at Large: Cultural Dimensions of Globalization*. Minneapolis, MN: University of Minnesota Press.

Brown, Wendy (2015) *Undoing the Demos: Neoliberalism's Stealth Revolution*. New York: Zone Books.

Carter, Alexandra (2004) 'Destabilising the Discipline: Critical Debates about History and Their Impact on the Study of Dance.' In Alexandra Carter, ed., *Rethinking Dance History: A Reader*, London: Routledge, 10–19.

Chakrabarty, Dipesh (2000) *Provincializing Europe: Postcolonial Thought and Historical Difference*. Princeton: Princeton University Press.

———— (2008) 'In Defense of *Provincializing Europe: A Response to Carola Dietze*.' *History and Theory* 47:1, 85–96.

Chatterjea, Ananya (2013) 'On the Value of Mistranslations and Contaminations: The Category of "Contemporary Choreography" in Asian Dance.' *Dance Research Journal* 45:1, 4–21.

Chen, Ya-Ping (2003) 'Dance History and Cultural Politics: A Study of Contemporary Dance in Taiwan, 1930s–1997.' PhD dissertation. New York University, New York.

———— (2009) 'In Search of Asian Modernity: Cloud Gate Dance Theatre's Body Aesthetics in the Era of Globalisation.' In Jo Butterworth and Liesbeth Wildschut, eds., *Contemporary Choreography: A Critical Reader*, London: Routledge, 316–330.

Croft, Clare (2015) *Dancers as Diplomats: American Choreography in Cultural Exchange*. New York: Oxford University Press.

Dalby, Simon (2008) '"Global" Geopolitics.' In Kevin R. Cox, Murray Low, and Jennifer Robinson, eds., *The SAGE Handbook of Political Geography*, London: SAGE, 427–437.

Dirlik, Arif (2010) 'Asia Pacific Studies in an Age of Global Modernity,' In Terence Wesley-Smith and Jon Goss, eds., *Remaking Area Studies: Teaching and Learning across Asia and the Pacific*, Honolulu: University of Hawai'i Press, 5–23.

Ezrahi, Christina (2012) *Swans of the Kremlin: Ballet and Power in Soviet Russia*. Pittsburgh: University of Pittsburgh Press.

Feng, Shuangbai, Liu Chunxiang and Luo Xin, eds (2006) *Zhongguo wudaojia da cidian* [*Comprehensive Dictionary of Chinese Dance Artists*]. Beijing: Zhongguo wenlian chuban she.

Gerdes, Ellen (2010) 'Shen Wei Dance Arts: Chinese Philosophy in Body Calligraphy.' *Dance Chronicle* 33:2, 231–250.

Giersdorf, Jens Richard (2013) *The Body of the People: East German Dance Since 1945*. Madison: University of Wisconsin Press.

Guo, Mingda (1956) 'Yi ge wudao yishu jiaoyu xin tixi de niyi [A Proposal for a New System of Dance Education].' *Wudao tongxun* [*Dance News*] 12, 12–14.

Gupta, Akhil and James Furgeson, eds (1997a) *Culture, Power, Place: Explorations in Critical Anthropology*. Durham, NC: Duke University Press.

——— (1997b) *Anthropological Locations: Boundaries and Grounds of a Field Science*. Berkeley: University of California Press.

Inda, Jonathan Xavier and Renato Rosaldo (2002) *The Anthropology of Globalization: A Reader*. Malden, MA: Blackwell Publishers.

Kaplan, Amy (1993) '"Left Alone with America": The Absence of Empire in the Study of American Culture.' In Amy Kaplan and Donald Pease, eds., *Cultures of United States Imperialism*, Durham: Duke University Press, 3–21.

Keali'inohomoku, Joann Wheeler (1983[1969–70]) 'An Anthropologist Looks at Ballet as a Form of Ethnic Dance.' In Roger Copeland and Marshall Cohen, eds., *What Is Dance?*, Oxford: Oxford University Press, 533–549.

Klein, Christina (2003) *Cold War Orientalism: Asia in the Middlebrow Imagination, 1945–1961*. Berkeley: University of California Press.

Kowal, Rebekah J. (2010) *How to Do Things With Dance: Performing Change In Postwar America*. Middletown, CT: Wesleyan University Press.

Kwan, SanSan (2003) 'Choreographing Chineseness: Global Cities and the Performance of Ethnicity.' PhD dissertation. New York University, New York.

——— (2009) 'Jagged Presence in the Liquid City: Choreographing Hong Kong's Handover.' In André Lepecki and Jenn Joy, eds., *Planes of Composition: Dance, Theory, and the Global*, London: Seagull Books, 11–20.

——— (2013) *Kinesthetic City: Dance and Movement in Chinese Urban Spaces*. New York: Oxford University Press.

Lin, Yatin (2004) 'Choreographing a Flexible Taiwan: Cloud Gate Dance Theatre and Taiwan's Changing Identity, 1973–2003.' PhD dissertation. University of California, Riverside.

―――― (2010) 'Choreographing a Flexible Taiwan: Cloud Gate Dance Theatre and Taiwan's Changing Identity.' In Alexandra Carter and Janet O'Shea, eds., *The Routledge Dance Studies Reader*, 2nd ed., London: Routledge, 250–260.

―――― (2016) *Sino-Corporealities*. Taipei: Taiwan National University of the Arts Press.

Liu, Qingyi (2015) 'Guo Mingda yu Zhongguo xiandai wu [Guo Mingda and China's Modern Dance].' *Zhongguo yishu shikong* [*China Arts Space*] 11, 3–18.

Ma, Nan (2015) 'Dancing into Modernity: Kinesthesia, Narrative, and Revolutions in Modern China, 1900–1978.' PhD dissertation. University of Wisconsin, Madison.

―――― (2016) 'Transmediating Kinesthesia: Wu Xiaobang and Modern Dance in China, 1929–1939.' *Modern Chinese Literature and Culture* 28:1, 129–173.

Minarty, Helly (2005) 'Transculturating Bodies: Politics of Identity of Contemporary Dance in China.' *Identity, Culture and Politics: An Afro-Asian Dialogue* 6:2, 42–60.

Ong, Aihwa and Stephen Collier (2005) *Global Assemblages: Technology, Politics, and Ethics as Anthropological Problems*. Malden, MA: Blackwell.

Ou, Jian-ping (1995) 'From "Beasts" to "Flowers": Modern Dance in China.' In John Solomon and Ruth Solomon, eds., *East Meets West in Dance: Voices in the Cross-Cultural Dialogue*, New York: Harwood Academic, 29–35.

Reynoso, Jose (2014) 'Choreographing Modern Mexico: Anna Pavlova in Mexico City (1919).' *Modernist Cultures*, 9:1, 80–98.

Seetoo, Chiayi (2013) 'The Political Kinesthetics of Contemporary Dance: Taiwan in Transnational Perspective.' PhD dissertation, University of California, Berkeley.

Solomon, John and Ruth Solomon, eds. (1995) *East Meets West in Dance: Voices in the Cross-Cultural Dialogue*, 2nd ed. New York: Harwood Academic.

Wilcox, Emily E. (2011) 'The Dialectics of Virtuosity: Dance in the People's Republic of China, 1949–2009.' PhD dissertation, University of California, Berkeley.

―――― (2012) 'Han-Tang *Zhongguo Gudianwu* and the Problem of Chineseness in Contemporary Chinese Dance: Sixty Years of Controversy.' *Asian Theater Journal* 29:1, 206–232.

―――― (2016) 'Beyond Internal Orientalism: Dance and Nationality Discourse in the Early People's Republic of China, 1949–1954.' *The Journal of Asian Studies* 75:2, 363–386.

―――― (forthcoming) 'The Postcolonial Blind Spot: Chinese Dance in the Era of Third World-Ism, 1949–1965.' *positions: asia critique*.

Xia, Yu (1958) '*Women bu shi bozi!* [We Are Not Cripples!].' *Wudao* [*Dance*] 1, 9–11.

Chapter 14

Considering causation and conditions of possibility
Practitioners and patrons of new dance in progressive-era America[1]

LINDA J. TOMKO

FOR HISTORIANS, one of the most perplexing aspects of Michel Foucault's *The Order of Things* ([1966] 1971) was perhaps its bracketing of causation. Foucault neither exploded nor reinvigorated the search for causal explanation that was so typical of Euro-American historical inquiry in the nineteenth and twentieth centuries. He simply set aside the issue and turned to a different problem. *The Order of Things* pursued the notion of 'episteme' as a kind of master mode of knowing or apprehending, invoked by and characteristic of a given era, which was displaced by a different mode in a following era. Resemblance, the figure for the Renaissance, for example, gave way to classification or the taxonomic urge in the seventeenth and eighteenth centuries. Shifts between epistemes occurred by some sort of rupture; Foucault sought and proffered no reason for the change. Nor was he concerned to pinpoint agents of change. For twentieth-century studies of dances past, and dance's past, this sidelining of causation and agency presented a radical departure from what may be termed modernist models of analysis. In their search for origins and their tracings of 'influence' and teacher–student 'family trees', modernist dance studies have frequently sought to locate the sources of change, and principal actors, that shaped genres like ballet or modern dance.[2] For dance history in particular, adherence to Foucault's example seemed to require a break with principles of professional history just as the field was beginning to gain recognition as an academic discipline.

Displacing causation and agency, Foucault studied instead the conditions of possibility for relations and networks that framed social existence. In *The Order of Things* and other works, he scrutinized the constitution of knowledge, the circulation of power, and the designation of sameness and difference (Gordon 1980: 229–59). Foucault's reorientation of inquiry was liberating in several respects, and it intersected with other poststructuralist concerns. It abetted new interest in matters of representation – how representation worked, how its products circulated, how its operation participated in relations of domination and subordination. Interest in representation proved especially beneficial to studies that analysed dance practices as means through which people presented and interpreted themselves, *to* themselves. Jane Desmond's 'Dancing out the Difference' (1991), for example, read Ruth St Denis's dance drama *Radha* for its orientalizing effects. Susan Manning's 'Black Voices, White Bodies' (1998) parsed the metaphorical minstrelsy by which White women's modern dancing bodies on the concert stage stood in for absented African Americans. Foucault's redirection of inquiry also contributed to a larger reconsideration by poststructuralist writers, such as Judith Butler (1988), of the unitary, authentic self, and subjectivity. Such reconceptualization has proposed the self and subjectivity to be multiple, even fragmentary, and as constituted in several and varied kinds of relationships. This vein of theory has helped dance scholars to show ways in which performance and compositional strategies have troubled and challenged sanctioned modes for embodying cultural characteristics, such as gender roles, the sense of belonging to a nation, and class position. Mark Franko's 'Where He Danced', for instance, considered the potential of Kazuo Ohno's butoh work *Suiren* to provide an alternative registration of maleness via cross-dressing conceptualized as 'through dressing', suggesting a model of gender performance that allows gender attributes to recombine 'at uneven intervals and to unequal degrees' (Franko 1995: 107).

Foucault's liberating effect also extended to concern with identity, conceived as something comprised in and by its relation to something else. Identity has attracted increased scholarly attention as the understanding has dawned on researchers and general readers alike that, at the end of the millennium, flows of people, like flows of capital, technology, media, and ideas, are increasingly global in scope (Appadurai 1990). In 'Welcome to the Jungle: Identity and Diversity in Postmodern Politics', Kobena Mercer (1990) seconds the sense of key cultural studies writers that the relations and elements comprising identity are capable of varied or multiple accenting. 'Social identities are structured "like a language"', Mercer explains, 'in that they can be articulated into a range of contradictory positions from one discursive context to the next since each element in ideology and consciousness has no necessary belonging in any one political code or system of representation' (p. 57). Mercer cites 1980s Britain as a case in point, where the re-articulation of Black identity made it a force to be reckoned with. He quotes Stuart Hall on this point, emphasizing the possibility for *re*-articulation: 'What was being struggled over was not the "class belongingness" of the term [Black], but the inflexion it could be given, its connotative field of reference' (p. 57). For Americans, the much-discussed racial profile of golf champion Tiger Woods offers a ready example of variable accenting. With parents of Thai, African American, White, and American Indian heritage, Woods in the American South during the 1950s would have been immediately classified as Black. There, any Black heritage trumped all other heritage to legally designate a person Black. In 2002, Woods's multiple heritages are equally likely to be trumpeted, especially on the West Coast and in gateway cities for late twentieth-century immigration to the United States. Here the particular decade in the twentieth century, the region of the United States, and the metropolitan politics of immigration create the conditions of possibility for different inflection of Woods's identity. Recuperating neither causation nor agency *per se*, the attention scholars pay to conditions of possibility indexes a concern that – perhaps surprisingly – poststructuralist inquiry about identity shares with classical historical analysis: how change (or, here, variable accenting) occurs over time.

It is to conditions of possibility for new dance innovation that this essay turns. In the early twentieth-century United States, a cluster of women movement practitioners took the opportunity to press for and to fashion dance practices that contested and confirmed current cultural issues. The persons and practices of Loie Fuller, Isadora Duncan, and Ruth St Denis are not new to dance history and analysis. Until the advent of gender and feminist analysis, historians failed to make much of the shift in the sexual division of labour for dance that Fuller, Duncan, and St Denis catalysed. When they took unto themselves the right and responsibility to compose their own dances as well as perform them, these women redistributed, and regendered, the creative roles typically allocated to men in nineteenth-century commercial theatre. The impact of their assertions has been felt for a century. Further attention to matters of gender illuminates the salience of middle- and upper-class White women's reform and study movements in creating conditions of possibility for this significant shift in theatrical performance and representation.

Ideology and opportunity

The changes in dance practice launched by Duncan, St Denis, and Fuller in different ways capitalized on almost a century of vibrant efforts to parse women's roles in US society. A 'separate spheres' ideology of gender roles had circulated since the early nineteenth century, exerting powerful force. It assigned women to the private sphere of the home and family and men to the public world of work and politics. Although this formulation appeared to speak to and for all women and men, it patently ignored the situation of working-class women, slave women, and later free women of colour who toiled in the paid labour force. Despite this disjunction between its enunciation and its effective reach, separate spheres ideology proved quite powerful at organizing expectations about middle- and upper-class White women's appropriate activity. It charged women to be pious, pure, domestic, and submissive. It also assigned them the primary responsibility for nurturing children and maintaining the home. Potentially limiting, these charges in fact offered springboards for women's entry into certain kinds of public sphere activity.

In the early years of the nineteenth century, the renewed religious fervour of the Second Great Awakening added force to women's separate spheres responsibility for spiritual matters. It helped propel women to join and participate in tract and Bible study societies in the public sphere. By forming themselves into voluntary societies, such groups adopted a strategy for social action that others in the period had already come to recognize as distinctively American. Alexis de Tocqueville remarked in *Democracy in America*,

> Americans of all ages, all conditions, and all dispositions constantly form associations. They have not only commercial and manufacturing companies, in which all take part, but associations of a thousand other kinds, religious, moral, serious, futile, general or restricted, enormous or diminutive . . . Wherever at the head of some new undertaking you see the government in France, or a man of rank in England, in the United States you will be sure to find an association.
> (de Tocqueville [1840] 1945, 2: 114)

Using this strategy, women in the 1830s and 1840s formed societies to promote 'moral reform' — that is to expose, protest, and attempt to eliminate prostitution and the sexual double standard. They worked prodigiously in female anti-slavery societies of their own forming; in male-led abolitionist organizations they constituted a growing proportion of the membership and a crucial labour force for petition drives. Conflicts within mixed-sex anti-slavery societies over women's public speaking and potential leadership wracked the movement and helped precipitate women's formation of women's rights groups. In each of these types of activism, women capitalized on the responsibilities assigned to them by separate spheres ideology and entered the public sphere of social interaction to pursue those charges.

A similar pattern obtained with the Women's Christian Temperance Union (WCTU), which was the largest grassroots women's organization in the United States. Adopting a women's suffrage plank 'for home protection', the WCTU also established model eating houses, reading rooms, speakers' bureaus, and even temperance societies for children. It consistently played upon separate spheres expectations to validate and mobilize women's public sphere activity.

The several women's reform movements discussed earlier occupied different points on the continuum of period theorizings about the sources of social problems that women mobilized to address. Earlier in the nineteenth century, poor relief and moral reform societies typically identified the poor person or the prostitute as the source of his or her own predicament — the problem was one of individual personal morality. By the end of the nineteenth century, more and more reform movements subscribed to an environmental analysis. The country's shift to mass production industry in some cities while sweated labour continued in other areas, the nation's demographic shift from rural to urban settlement and crowding, and the persistence of ward politics began to receive credit as sources for turn-of-the-century problems, like crime, tenement decay, infant mortality, and continuing poverty and prostitution (Walters 1978: 192, 213–16). The perceived structural nature of social problems further enabled women's organizations to claim a 'municipal housekeeping' role for themselves, again extending the responsibility for family welfare to achievement of that goal through public sphere activity. Environmental analysis stimulated the US settlement house movement, which specifically addressed the needs and perceived problems that came with large flows of immigrant people from Central and Southern Europe. With women strongly represented, settlements constituted an early kind of social welfare network in a country whose government provided none.

Strands of the post-Civil War women's club movement responded in different ways to women's public sphere activity. Founded in 1868, Sorosis brought together professional women at a time when opportunities for higher education and professional training remained extremely limited for women. Also founded in 1868, the New England Women's Club tended to bring together middle-class women who did not work outside the home. Clubs like this one sprang up across the United States. Pursuing cultivation and self-improvement, they functioned as voluntary study clubs focusing on music, literature and poetry, painting, and drama. By the 1890s, women's culture clubs turned increasingly to municipal reform issues, without, however, relinquishing interest in culture study.

Opportunities seized: platforms and patrons

Fuller, St Denis, and Duncan seized the several opportunities afforded them by the women's reform and culture club movements in the late nineteenth century. The rationales for and social action by female voluntary society organizations provided the dance innovators with much-needed platforms for launching a performing career and, certainly for St Denis, even sustaining it. In addition, the voluntary organizations supplied a nexus in which women claimed new authority as artistic arbiters and cultural custodians at the turn of the century.

Loie Fuller

Of the three innovators, Loie Fuller capitalized on the potential available through women's social movements in perhaps the most specific and contained way. In the 1890s and early 1900s she achieved prominence for her daring combination of electrical light and sensuous fabrics that she undulated and manipulated (with help from concealed rods) to form moving images of fire, flowers, and streaming motion. She scrabbled hard to reach that point, however. Historical accounts have frequently made mention of Fuller's early temperance lecturing, but without pursuing it further, when they cited the emerging artist's early stints in breeches roles, temperance dramas, and stock theatre. It was historian Sally Sommer, however, who voiced two additional, important insights. She noted the capacity of temperance's 'moral instruction' to mediate the suspect qualities of women's theatrical performance, and she discerned the value that Fuller attached to the power she was able to wield in the very process of performing (Sommer 1979). These insights enable a much more nuanced reading of Fuller's autobiographical account of her early temperance identification. In unpublished writings – possibly drafts for her *Fifteen Years of a Dancer's Life* – Fuller recounted a temperance lecture she single-handedly conducted in Monmouth, Illinois.[3] Having newly taken up residence there with her family, Fuller says she scouted the town and decided out of the blue to book an available hall and publicize a speech to be given by herself. An audience arrived at the appointed hour, she claims, and listened to her discourse on everyday matters, and then traditional temperance topics and some ad hoc extensions of the same. For example she reports that she queried the audience whether saucy children or debtors fleeing their obligations should be considered intemperate. By the conclusion of her two-hour talk she earned $85, which she said she gave to her father.

This early temperance lecture may have actually taken place. Or the report of it may have been apocryphal, a retrospective construction that Fuller used to fashion a self-portrait that exuded agency and control. If the lecture took place as reported, Fuller drew cannily on the model of female temperance speakers who preceded her in order to constitute herself as a legitimate public performer. And she drew from subject matter that their reform movement had already validated in order to attract a bona fide audience. These would have been fine skills to hone for the later stints of temperance lecturing that have not been questioned as part of her career. If the Monmouth scenario is a retrospective fiction, it nonetheless illuminates ways in which temperance as a social movement offered women a template with which to conceptualize parts or dimensions of their lives. For Loie Fuller, the temperance connection offered an instrument with which to authorize herself as a performer, at a very early age, when female stage performance still struck many as illicit. Further, the way in which she used these tools to author her own coming-to-be highlights the self-fashioning that this reform movement made possible for women during a particular period in American life, a salience that we have only recently been able to discern.

Ruth St Denis

Ruth St Denis's interaction with women's voluntary organizations advanced the cultural claims of both parties. The aspiring actress and dancer incorporated backbends and fabric manipulation characteristic of 'skirt dancing' in the 'eastern'-inflected dances she created for her own solo performance. As Suzanne Shelton (1981) pointed out, St Denis had clearly absorbed the vogue for things oriental that swept nineteenth-century America, and she pursued further reading of her own. Following employment in David Belasco's commercial theatre productions, she was determined to present her own production of *Radha*. This she styled an East Indian dance drama. Through a connection found by her mother's friend, St Denis presented a private performance of *Radha* for Mrs Kate Dalliba and her salon guests, and she received several society invitations to perform as a result. Still with her mother, she made the rounds of theatrical managers, seeking a theatrical engagement. She won the interest of theatre manager Henry B. Harris. Harris presented her in a showcase concert to an audience of male managers. Among appearances that St Denis garnered from this were 'two-a-day' stints at Proctor's Theatre. This vaudeville job was not her desideratum, but there Mrs Orlando Rouland, wife of the painter and enthusiastic orientalist, viewed her performance. Mrs Rouland took up the cause of securing a 'legitimate' theatre gig for St Denis, soliciting the financial support of numerous friends. The result was their rental of the Hudson Theatre and sponsorship of a ladies' matinee performance. For this March 1906 show, St Denis performed *Radha*, *The Cobras*, and *Incense*.[4]

In response, Harris himself booked St Denis for engagements during the next months at the Hudson Theatre. At the same time, the matinee's success prompted a spate of engagements by women's culture clubs, reform groups, and society hostesses. These included an appearance sponsored by Mrs Herbert Saterlee, the daughter of financier J. Pierpont Morgan, for the meeting of the Thursday evening club, a Manhattan arts and literature study club. St Denis was one of several performers for a membership that included architect Sanford White and society leader Mrs Cadwalader Jones. In April St Denis appeared in a benefit for the People's Symphony, held at the Waldorf Astoria. Several days later in Washington, DC, she performed in a benefit sponsored by Mrs A. C. Barney. The event raised funds for a settlement house – the Barney Neighborhood Club – and the Hospital for Incurables. In May she appeared at Fenway Court, the Boston home of society leader Isabel Stuart Gardner. This evening benefited the Holy Ghost Local Hospital for Incurables in Cambridge, and it was Mrs Gardner who recommended that St Denis be invited to perform. The patrons cited for the latter performance illuminate the confluence of society figures, professional men, and reform-oriented women. Charles Eliot, president of Harvard, and Charles Eliot Norton, professor and vice president of the hospital, were patrons together with Reverend Samuel Crothers. The programme was coordinated by Norton's daughter Elizabeth. Lady patronesses included Mrs J. J. Storrow, wife of the financier and herself a supporter of the settlement house movement, arts and crafts proceedings, and, later, the playground and Girl Scout movements. Additional patronesses drew from Boston's artistic and financial elite: Mrs R. H. Dana, wife of the writer; Mrs William Wharton, wife of the financier; and Mrs Rudolphe Agassiz, wife of the academic. These examples from New York, Boston, and Washington illuminate the range of performance platforms that the female network of culture clubs, reform, and charity organizations created for St Denis. The visibility they provided was matchless.

In June 1906 she sailed to Europe, and the next two years saw the consolidation of her reputation as an artist of the first water. When she returned to the United States, Harris booked St Denis for concerts in his Hudson Theatre and backed production of the new work *Egypta*. Harris also underwrote St Denis's tour to Midwest and East Coast cities with the 'Indian' solos and a cross-country tour of *Egypta*. He lost money on both ventures. To repay him St Denis turned to vaudeville and secured more salon dates. Harris lost his life, and St Denis her chief sponsor, when the *Titanic* sank, and St Denis again turned for support to a network of female patrons. Some patrons engaged her purely to provide novel entertainment for guests; the reform and study club connection was manifest in other gigs. In Chicago, she was persuaded to donate or forgo her fee to dance at the annual charity ball sponsored by Mrs Potter Palmer. The press coverage was outstanding and the proceeds of the event went to support an array of reform and charitable projects. In March 1914, back in New York, St Denis danced at a birthday party given for Anna Howard Shaw, leader of the National American Women's Suffrage Association, in New York City.

St Denis recast her career when she joined forces with Ted Shawn and in 1915 formed the Denishawn school and dance company. She would not have survived the turbulent years as a solo artist had she not drawn on the support networks offered by women's clubs, reform groups, and society salon engagements. These offered a third type of performance platform that handily troubled the burgeoning polarity between 'high-culture' legitimate theatre gigs and 'low-culture' vaudeville jobs that subsequently characterized modernist rankings of aesthetic production. At the most fundamental level, women's organizations and society gatherings supplied crucial platforms for performance that sustained St Denis's innovations as a choreographer and dancer.

In turn, the female patronage network supplied an arena in which female sponsors actively claimed a role as arbiters of American culture. In newspaper coverage of the ladies' matinee sponsored by Mrs Rouland and friends, one jaundiced reporter explicitly connected interest in St Denis's production with ongoing investment by women's culture clubs in orientalist literature and other fare (*New York Times* 1906). In another account, the comments of a named sponsor voiced the express commitment and undeniable excitement of sponsoring something new and offering new standards of taste:

> 'She is a genius', declared Mrs [Charles C.] Worthington, 'and too imaginative and original for the vaudeville, it seemed to us, though if our taking her up gives her a "boost" – is that what you call it? – in the business way, why, we are more than pleased. And it's such fun to be in on something absolutely new – as this certainly is, for she has gotten it all up herself, out of books and things. I believe she has never been abroad.'[5]

For women to lay claim to aesthetic leadership was something new in late nineteenth- and early twentieth-century America, where men typically took the lead in planning and funding the new libraries, symphonies, and museums of the era. What seems clear about cultural leadership at the turn of the century is that while men participated strongly in launching edifices for new arts enterprises, women were claiming a place in the sun via their culture club concerns, their growing representation in arts and crafts societies, and, particularly germane here, their sponsorship of new dance practices. Offering performance platforms to St Denis at crucial junctures in her sojourn as a soloist, female American patrons rewrote their gender roles and reconstituted their social agency to include cultural arbitership.

Isadora Duncan

Isadora Duncan primarily pursued her career outside the United States after 1900. The tours and return visits to America that she made in the next decades registered indelibly, but it was in the earliest stages of her career that she took advantage of the support offered by women's patronage networks.

As both Fuller and St Denis had to do, Duncan spent some time working in commercial theatre productions, in this case in plays and pantomimes, and touring with the company of Augustin Daly. Located in New York, Duncan and family members conducted a teaching enterprise while she pursued engagements as a solo dancer. The slender documentation from this period in her career illuminates the transition she made from commercial theatre performer to the composer and performer of her own movement invention. In one early performance, she appeared as a supporting artist in a concert by composer and pianist Ethelbert Nevin. She danced to 'water scenes' music in Nevin's *Narcissus*, *Water Nymphs*, and *Ophelia* before an audience 'well-filled with fashionable people' (*New York Times* 1898). Duncan (1928) later claimed that this appearance spurred invitations from society women to perform in their drawing rooms. The surge of interest in Duncan as a performer was confirmed by a mention of the emerging dancer in the March 1898 issue of *The Director*. Oriented to dance teachers and their students, this magazine observed that 'Miss Duncan is a professional entertainer, and she has been taken up extensively by well-known society women' ('Emotional Expression' in *The Director* 1898: 109).[6]

Duncan asserts in *My Life* (1928) that society matrons of Mrs William Astor's ilk secured her performance at their summer residences in Newport, Rhode Island. Documentation survives for one such occasion, when Miss Ellen Mason of Boston hosted a piano recital on the lawn of her Newport home in summer 1898. The event patrons were all female and included Mrs Potter Palmer and Mrs William Astor, recognized leaders of Chicago and New York elite society. To text recited by sister Elizabeth Duncan, and violin and piano played by John Mullaly and Duncan's mother, the dancer presented the *Rubaiyat of Omar Khayyam* 'done into dance' – that is accompanied and interpreted in movement by Duncan.[7] When Duncan again danced the *Rubaiyat* in March 1899, a *New York Times* account reported that the Carnegie Lyceum event, managed by society figure Mrs Robert Osborn, 'was under the patronage of a number of well-known women' (*New York Times* 1899). The Duncan family belongings were destroyed in a fire at the Windsor Hotel several days later, and in April society women again supported her, this time by sponsoring a benefit performance for the fire victim. Again newspaper reportage cited the elite status of her sponsors, who included women 'from the inner ranks of the 150 of New York, San Francisco, Tuxedo [sic], and Chicago'.[8] Shortly thereafter, Duncan sailed for London and began a different phase of her career.

Although data from this period is thin, period accounts linked Duncan's name with those of the leaders of New York and Chicago society – the Astors, the Vanderbilts, and the Palmers. For the monied New York women involved, society competition offered a potent vehicle for contesting class leadership within a felt and actual scenario of long-term, waning influence of the Knickerbocker elite, the earliest leaders in the city's colonial days (Jaher 1972, 1973). The competition played out by hostesses through dinner stylings and salon engagements, and their related sponsorship of matinee and recital events, created conditions of possibility for innovation by the emerging dancer at a key point in her career.

The practitioners and patrons considered earlier troubled and pressed against prevailing definitions of the ways in which artistic dancing could signify and the realms in which women could exert public leadership. It must be acknowledged that these two types of activism won gains primarily for White, middle- and upper-class women. St Denis's refashionings of orientalist source materials certainly furthered the 'othering' – the reifying and derogation – of other cultures accomplished by western representations of Indian and Egyptian cultures that Edward Said so cogently identified in connection with the Middle East. As well, the women's acts of recasting failed to bridge American racial divides of the era and secure presentation or reception for women of colour. With these substantial limits noted, we should credit the ways in which female practitioners and patrons seized the moment to stage themselves as creators and arbiters possessing cultural authority.

Causes and agents or systems of relations?

The interpretive tradition in academic history has been relatively slow to invoke the insights that critical theory might afford for both the posing of historical questions and the framing of conclusions. Foucault's bracketing of causation and agency in *The Order of Things* jolted historians, seeming as it did to erase first principles of inquiry about the past. To work one's way through the 'conditions of possibility' in a specific historical situation, as in this chapter, provides a useful perspective on distinctions that critical theory has drawn between causation and agency, on the one hand, and conditions of possibility, on the other. Causal analysis that emphasizes individuals as agents of change does embrace, it must be said, a kind of romantic faith in the individual that has characterized much western social thinking since the Enlightenment. Foucault's focus on networks and circulation privileges a systems orientation and bespeaks, it is fair to say, a scholarly investment in structural relationships as the features in society and history that matter most – and that offer the entering wedge for resistance. Foucault's sidelining of causation and agency literally helped create intellectual space for other notions of social change and operation to gain hearings. What should be the outcome of this period for reconsideration and potential recalibration of analysis? To place all analytical weight on individual actors as primary causal agents is, perhaps, hopelessly romantic, and also naïve with regard to structured inequalities that have operated over time. To place all analytical weight on system relationships and structures in a given period is to draw nigh to determinism. Neither of these alternatives alone offers viable motion. A path to pursue, I submit, is first to release the brackets tethering causation and agency. Then we need to think through the ways in which causation, agency, and conditions of possibility may be necessary to each other, even constitutive of each other – and also ways in which they are not. People and/or groups actualize the potential available in conditions of possibility; they can and do turn potentials to different account. Equally important, particular historical surrounds help conceptualize, condition, and shade the perceptions people form and choices they make. It is not too much to consider agents, causes, and conditions of possibility as different registrations or enactments of the structures and dynamism compelling change that both are capable of accessing. In the foregoing account, nineteenth-century separate spheres ideology could very well have limited White, middle- and upper-class American women to a private space materially realized as 'the home'. We need to assess the interaction of agents, causes, and conditions of possibility to parse how it is that prescriptions can be upended, representations redirected, rights and power reconceptualized. Network or discourse analyses, and causal analyses acknowledging agency, are necessary to sorting out how our societies arrived at their current conjunctures. Both are necessary to forging twenty-first-century action.

Notes

This chapter is based in part on research discussed in L. Tomko (1999) *Dancing Class: Gender, Ethnicity, and Social Divides in American Dance, 1890–1920*, Bloomington: Indiana University Press.

1   This essay is reprinted from the first edition of *Rethinking Dance History* (2004).

2   Two works that deployed the family tree strategy were Guest (1976), with articles written by Moore from the 1940s through the 1960s, and McDonagh (1977).
3   Fuller (1913) does not mention this early lecture nor temperance speaking during 1875–77. See Loie Fuller, holograph page, no title, n.d., Loie Fuller Papers 1892–1913, folder 34, Jerome Robbins Dance Division, New York Public Library for the Performing Arts (hereafter DDNYPL); and Loie Fuller, 'Before Many Years Were Over, I Had Attended Many Lectures', unpublished autobiography typescript and holograph pages, n.d., Loie Fuller Papers 1914–28, folder 204, DDNYPL.
4   On St Denis's performing career see also Schlundt (1962), St Denis (1989: 74–5) and Tomko (1999). On the March matinee, see for example *New York Times* (1906).
5   H. Tyrell (1906) 'Yes, Society DID Gasp When "Radha" in Incense-Laden Air "Threw off the Bondage of the Earthly Senses"', *The World*, March 25, in Denishawn Collection – Scrapbooks – Clippings, DDNYPL.
6   Additional data on Duncan's female sponsors is given in (1898) 'Narcissus and Other Scenes', *The Director*, October–November: 272.
7   Program (1898) 'Rubaiyat of Omar Khayyam Done into Dance by Isadora Duncan, Newport, September 8, 1898', in Duncan, Isadora/Programs 1898–1929, DDNYPL; *The Director* (1898), September: 254.
8   'A Soulful Function', unidentified newspaper clipping, hand-dated April 19, 1899, in Duncan, Isadora, Reserve Dance Clippings file, DDNYPL.

Bibliography

Appadurai, A. (1990) "Disjunctures and Difference in the Global Cultural Economy", *Public Culture*, 2, 2: 1–24.
Butler, J. (1988) "Performative Acts and Gender Constitution: An Essay in Phenomenology and Feminist Theory", *Theatre Journal*, December, 40, 4: 519–31.
Desmond, J. (1991) "Dancing out the Difference: Cultural Imperialism and Ruth St Denis' 'Radha' of 1906", *Signs*, Autumn, 17, 1: 28–49.
De Tocqueville, A. ([1840] 1945) *Democracy in America*, originally published as 2 volumes in 1835 and 1840, this edition reprinted in 1945 and edited by P. Bradley, New York: Vintage Books.
The Director (1898) undated reprint of this magazine's December 1897 to November 1898 run, New York: Dance Horizons.
Duncan, I. (1928) *My Life*, London: Victor Gollancz.
Foucault, M. ([1966] 1971) *The Order of Things: An Archaeology of the Human Sciences*, reprinted 1973, New York: Vintage Books.

Franko, M. (1995) "Where He Danced", in M. Franko (ed.), *Dancing Modernism / Performing Politics*, Bloomington, IN: Indiana University Press, 93–107.

Fuller, L. (1913) *Fifteen Years of a Dancer's Life, with Some Account of Her Distinguished Friends*, Boston, MA: Small, Maynard.

Gordon, C. (1980) "Afterword", in C. Gordon (ed.), *Power/Knowledge: Selected Interviews and Other Writings 1972–1977 by Michel Foucault*, trans. C. Gordon, L. Marshall, J. Mepham and K. Soper, New York: Pantheon Books, 229–259.

Guest, I. (ed.) (1976) *Echoes of American Ballet: A Collection of Seventeen Articles Written and Selected by Lillian Moore*, New York: Dance Horizons.

Jaher, F. C. (1972) "Nineteenth-Century Elites in New York and Boston", *Journal of Social History*, 6: 32–77.

—— (1973) "Style and Status: High Society in Late Nineteenth-Century New York", in F. Jaher (ed.), *The Rich, the Well Born, and the Powerful*, Urbana, IL: University of Illinois Press, 258–284.

Manning, S. (1998) "Black Voices, White Bodies: The Performance of Race and Gender in *How Long Brethren*", *American Quarterly*, 50, 1: 24–46.

McDonagh, D. (1977) *The Complete Guide to Modern Dance*, New York: Popular Library.

Mercer, K. (1990) "Welcome to the Jungle: Identity and Diversity in Postmodern Politics", in J. Rutherford (ed.), *Identity: Community, Culture, Difference*, London: Lawrence & Wishart, 43–71.

New York Times (1898) "Society Notes", 25 March: 7.

—— (1899) "What Is Doing in Society", 15 March: 7.

—— (1906) "Bringing Temple Dances from the Orient to Broadway", 25 March, 2nd magazine section: 2.

Rutherford, J. (ed.) (1990) *Identity: Community, Culture, Difference*, London: Lawrence & Wishart.

Schlundt, C. L. (1962) *The Professional Appearances of Ruth St Denis and Ted Shawn: A Chronology and an Index of Dances 1906–1932*, New York: New York Public Library.

Shelton, S. (1981) *Divine Dancer: A Biography of Ruth St Denis*, Garden City, NY: Doubleday.

Sommer, S. R. (1979) "Loie Fuller: From the Theater of Popular Entertainment to the Parisian Avant-Garde", unpublished PhD dissertation, New York: New York University.

St Denis, R. (1989) *An Unfinished Life*, New York: Harper & Bros.

Tomko, L. J. (1999) *Dancing Class: Gender, Ethnicity, and Social Divides in American Dance, 1890–1920*, Bloomington, IN: Indiana University Press.

Walters, R. G. (1978) *American Reformers 1815–1860*, New York: Hill and Wang.

Chapter 15

'Dancin' in the street'
Street dancing on film and video from Fred Astaire to Michael Jackson[1]

BETH GENNÉ

THE BIRTH OF SOUND FILM also saw the birth of a new site for dance – and with it a new dance genre. The "street dance", as I will call it, takes film dance off the stage, out of the ballroom and into the everyday life of the city street. The street dance also resulted in a reconceptualization of film dance as directors and choreographers began to realize that the camera as well as the dancer could be choreographed to create a new kind of dance – cinema. And, of course, the genre is transformed over time in response to the changing social and political climate of America's street life.

Established by Fred Astaire with Hermes Pan in the 1930s and developed by Gene Kelly with Stanley Donen and Vincente Minnelli in the 1940s and early 1950s, the street genre continued through the 1960s, most notably in Jerome Robbins's choreography for the film *West Side Story*. In the second half of the twentieth century, the street dance moved, for the most part, to video as dancers like Michael and Janet Jackson and their choreographers and directors took the form in new directions to fit the concerns of contemporary audiences and the changing urban environment.

The street dance has roots in the early 1930s in films of René Clair, Ernst Lubitsch and Rouben Mamoulian. In Mamoulian's landmark musical *Love Me Tonight* (1932), Maurice Chevalier, a carefree young tailor, strolls to work through the busy streets of his *quartier*. His walk is engagingly rhythmic and he salutes his neighbors in song. He's not exactly *dancing* but he is awfully close, and his music and movement poeticize early morning workaday Paris.

Fred Astaire also turned walking into a form of dance. George Gershwin, inspired by his elegant but carefree style, wrote music to accompany Astaire's shipboard stroll with Rogers in the "walking the dog" sequence in *Shall We Dance* (1937). It is also Fred Astaire who really begins to *dance* in the street in *Damsel in Distress* (1937) when he performs amidst a traffic-filled London thoroughfare for an audience of delighted pedestrians and hops a moving bus for a finale.

But long before Astaire was filming his street dances in London-recreated studio lots, African American dancers were dancing on real urban streets. From New York to Philadelphia to Kansas City, jazz tap dancers were developing their art on busy street corners and in urban alleyways. As dancer Sandman Sims and others tell it, city streets had become open air dance schools where young and old dancers could meet, challenge and learn from each other (Nierenberg 1979). Certain street corners in Philadelphia were known for their exceptional dancers. Though these dances did not enter mainstream films, the lucky pedestrians who stopped to gape at them undoubtedly witnessed some of the greatest dancing of the era.

In another part of Pennsylvania, on the streets of Pittsburgh, Gene Kelly would learn from these marvelous dancers and from Astaire. Kelly would definitively establish the street dance genre in films, from the dockland streets of Brooklyn in *Cover Girl* (1944) to the rain-washed streets of Hollywood in *Singin' in the Rain* (1953). In his first major street dance in *Cover Girl*, Kelly, Rita Hayworth and Phil Silvers transform Brooklyn streets with their antics. The bright, confident tone of Jerome Kern's song "Make Way for Tomorrow" musically reflects Ira Gershwin's lyrics, with their clever internal rhymes expressing the three friends' optimism just as the dance reflects their youthful enthusiasm and camaraderie (see Kimball 1993: 310). They begin in a small, dockyard Brooklyn restaurant then continue outdoors, commandeering street paraphernalia to dance with. Silvers makes cymbals of dustbin lids, Kelly drums on a bucket and Hayworth uses a breadstick as an imaginary flute. Silvers rhythmically bails out an imaginary boat which Hayworth and Kelly row vigorously. A passing policeman twirling his nightstick puts a temporary stop to the fun, but the trio explode again into dance when they turn the corner out of his view. Passers-by join the fun: a milkman participates in a spirited reel, the neighborhood drunk's staggering steps unsteadily counterpoint the dancers. The policeman's reappearance forces a finale to this early Kelly street dance and they tiptoe indoors to the woozy applause of the drunk.

"Make Way for Tomorrow" establishes an iconography that will recur in whole or in part in many street dances to come: an urban or suburban street, choreography based on variants of walking, skipping and running steps or children's street games and the transformation of ordinary street objects such as stairs, curbs, gutters and lamp posts into dancing partners. Part of the street dance, too, are passers-by who may, like the milkman, enter into the dance, or like the drunk form a delighted audience. The policeman will reappear too, most notably in "Singin' in the Rain". He helps to emphasize the idea of the dancers as *enfants terribles* who, in response to music and their own high spirits, temporarily become children in an adult world, flouting convention by transforming the street into a musical playground.

Kelly also uses the long narrow street shape, to reconceptualize his dance space and explore the possibilities of the cinematic medium by choreographing for the camera as well as the dancers. He uses the moving camera and editing not only to record but enhance the dance. In the street dance in *Damsel in Distress* Astaire uses the camera mostly to document his movements. The street becomes a stage; the camera takes the position of the audience in a theatre. We view Astaire from the front and the camera remains relatively stationary in front of him, moving only slightly so that in Arlene Croce's words 'one has the impression of watching every moment from an ideally placed seat in a theatre' (1972: 126). But although many of Astaire's dances were conceptualized with the stage–audience relationship in mind, Astaire didn't always use the full-frontal format and these exceptions would become models for Kelly and his colleague Stanley Donen. In another section of *Damsel in Distress*, "Things are Looking Up", Astaire is tracked by a moving camera as he walk dances Joan Fontaine down a wooded path. In *Carefree* (1938), the moving camera follows a procession of dancers from a country-club dance floor along a curving path as they try out "The Yam". These are the precedents that Kelly and his colleagues Stanley Donen and Vincente Minnelli would follow, explore and develop for their dance on film (Genné 1984: 170–207).

Around the same time as *Cover Girl*, Minnelli's choreography for the camera in the dance sequences in *Meet Me in St Louis* (1944) and for Fred Astaire and Lucille Bremer in *The Ziegfeld Follies* (1944) and *Yolanda and the Thief* (1945) would also prove that the dance and the choreographed moving camera could be extraordinary partners. Minnelli was particularly interested in the possibilities of what was called the boom camera: a camera mounted on wheels and attached to a crane, allowing the camera to move in height as well as on the ground. Minnelli working with Kelly would bring an exciting new dimension to dances manipulating the boom camera in ever more daring ways (Genné 1984: 234–62).

A good example is the street dance "'S Wonderful" in *An American in Paris*, directed by Vincente Minnelli and choreographed by Gene Kelly. By the time of *An American in Paris*, Minnelli's skill with the boom had become something of a legend among film makers and technicians. Only a handful of directors and their camera operators had mastered the technique of using it effectively. Directors too often used boom shots gratuitously, employing them solely for their breathtaking effect with no real relationship to the dramatic action. Walter Strohm, head of MGM's production department, notes this as he pays tribute to Minnelli's virtuoso use of the boom:

> Minnelli loved to be on the boom and was very astute in using it, although it's a time consuming and costly thing because you could take a whole day just to rehearse and shoot one boom shot.
>
> Sometimes he did a whole day's work in one shot, which is rather interesting. Some days he would be on the boom all day rehearsing, riding it, and, when the end of the day came they would make the shot and that would be the whole scene. Well, there are very few directors you could allow to do that because they are not capable of visualizing

and timing boom shots. They become very awkward and mechanical, and you become conscious of the boom and not the action. Booms are deadly to most directors. In fact, we had a rule – people hated it, but we had to have it because everybody wasn't Minnelli and everybody didn't know how to use the boom – so directors couldn't use the boom without my okay . . . But, with Minnelli, some of his great boom shots were classic. I just used to love to watch his boom shots. The one he did on "'S Wonderful" with Gene is just a classic.

(Strohm, in Knox 1973: 109)

The boom shot to which Strohm refers is the final shot of the "'S Wonderful" street dance sequence. Kelly and Georges Guetary start the song seated in a sidewalk café then stroll rhythmically down the street. The camera, on a level with them, parallels their movement, gliding precisely in tempo, pausing briefly while Kelly dances and Guetary sings to an audience of pedestrians. The song is a compendium of slang superlatives that climaxes as each singer outdoes the other in finding the adjective that describes the emotional "high" he feels for the girl he loves, moving chromatically up the scale with every new adjective.

Kelly's choreography and Minnelli's boom camera work parallel this crescendo of emotion, music, and lyric. The singers move in opposite directions down the street, shouting to be heard over the people and traffic as Minnelli's camera glides back and up to capture them. The pull-back of the camera, precisely coordinated with the music, becomes a visual metaphor for the crescendo of sound and emotion that conclude the song. The camera's highest point coincides with the song's final note, then hangs in the air as people in the street are carefully positioned to form, in color and compositional arrangement, a dynamic diagonal across the screen. At either end of this the two singers stand, applauding their impromptu performance.

Following Kelly's experiences with Minnelli in *An American in Paris*, Kelly and Donen's moving boom camera achieves a new level of fluidity and expansiveness, demonstrated in the most famous street dance in all films. "Singin' in the Rain" incorporates almost every Kelly convention: a "street" dance, it expresses the hero's euphoric response to falling in love and it makes use of a dance vocabulary of typical Kelly vernacular movements. "Singin' in the Rain" is also a kind of children's dance. Kelly performs a set of variations on the theme of playing in the rain as, drenched and euphoric, he abandons all sense of decorum and dances in the driving rain. He uses his umbrella as a dancer's prop rather than protection as he balances on the curb, dances under a downspout and, for a finale, stomps and splashes ecstatically in the street's deepest puddle. The appearance of a policeman, like his counterpart in *Cover Girl*, puts an end to his musical games.

The song starts quietly. At first, the camera simply glides in front of Kelly as he strolls towards it. It becomes more active, however, after the dancer abandons himself to the rain, shuts his umbrella, and begins to sing. When Kelly suddenly vaults a lamp post in his excitement, the camera (equally suddenly and exhilaratingly) pulls back and up, then swoops in to capture, in close-up, his euphoric smile as he dismounts and leans drunkenly against the post. This camera gesture is repeated a few steps further down the street when he opens his arms in an invitation to the heavens to soak him, and the camera responds by swooping low over his upturned face. At the emotional and musical climax of the dance, the camera sweeps exhilaratingly back, up, and around as Kelly catapults off the sidewalk and, using his open umbrella as a sail, traces a circle on the street while brass and percussion forcefully state the song.[2] The final camera gesture we have seen at the end of "'S Wonderful" in *An American In Paris*, but here it parallels (equally effectively) a *diminuendo*: the camera pulls back and up slowly to give us a full view of the final poetic moment – the black-slickered policeman watching Kelly skip off down the street (Genné 1984: 375). Kelly pauses briefly to hand his closed umbrella to a passer-by who is hunched over to protect himself from the downpour. He opens the umbrella, then hurriedly moves on as Kelly, drenched and happy, skips off.

In addition to the reconceptualization of the relationship of camera work and dance, the street dance genre was ideally suited to the new, "ordinary" American that Kelly portrays in *Cover Girl* and would develop throughout his career. The street dance was the perfect answer to Kelly's wish to create a new kind of dance with which ordinary working-class Americans could identify. "Dance for the common man" was a phrase the young Kelly used a lot when describing his ideals to his friends, the playwright Dick Dwenger and his future wife Betsy Blair.[3] Kelly's ideas about the social role of dance were honed during his years as a student at the University of Pittsburgh and continued in New York where he participated excitedly in groups of socially minded intellectuals and artists like William Saroyan in whose play, *The Time of Your Life* (1939), Kelly first appeared as the down and out dancer Harry the Hoofer. These utopian ideals were in line with the increased social consciousness reflected throughout American arts and letters beginning in the 1930s in response to the great depression. Kelly's interest in the "common man" was also a part of the burgeoning interest in developing a new and specifically American subject and style for dance, an interest he shared with fellow choreographers working at the same time such as Ruth Page, Martha Graham, George Balanchine, Eugene Loring, Lew Christiansen, Doris Humphrey and Charles Weidman and others whom he knew and admired (Genné 2001: 87).

Following *The Time of Your Life*, Kelly made a tremendous impact on Broadway playing a new American character type for musicals in Rodgers and Hart's *Pal Joey* (1940). Street smart, cocky, depression-hardened Joey was diametrically opposed to the idealistic romantic juveniles on Broadway or the dapper, offhandedly elegant American type modeled by Fred Astaire. Kelly's stocky, compact frame suited this character and the street choreography he would later devise for himself – choreography he infuses with a distinctively aggressive energy that differs radically from Astaire's casual, seemingly effortless dancing nonchalance. Kelly's body was ideal for his vision of dance: it is a body with which a worker can identify and he looks right in shirt and pants. "Put me in a tuxedo," Kelly once remarked, "and I look like a truck driver going to Mass on Sunday."[4]

The choreography that Kelly devises for his street dances is more overtly based on ordinary gesture than is Astaire's complex, multilayered choreography or the intricate elegant patterning of jazz tappers like John Bubbles or the Nicholas Brothers. To be sure, Astaire and jazz tap dancers often began their dances with a simple walk, which is basically a street gesture, but that walk would soon develop into a complex, multilayered series of rhythmic foot movements. Kelly's "walk" is simple, down-to-earth and purposeful and he combines it with a repertory of movements derived from the children's street games he played in the streets of Pittsburgh. These are movements with which any urban American can identify: teetering on the curb, vaulting fire hydrants, skipping along the sidewalk, swinging on lamp posts, splashing in the gutter, roller skating. In *Living in a Big Way* (1945), for example, Kelly leads a group of kids over a construction site balancing on beams and swinging on rafters. In *It's Always Fair Weather* (1955), Kelly glides through the streets on roller skates captured by a swift moving camera. In *On the Town*, Kelly and Donen use brilliant jump cut editing wed to music and the actors' movements to transform an out-of-town sightseer's exuberant, wide-eyed, and bewildered walking tour into a kind of dance. (Kelly and Donen's editing for this sequence would have a tremendous impact not only on future musicals, but on French new wave film making, and you can also see influences in Richard Lester's editing for the Beatles' musicals *A Hard Day's Night* and *Help!* (Delameter 1981: 460).)

Kelly saw a strong link between his choreography and sports, especially urban "street" sports. Sports movements give his dances the "vernacular" flavor that so suit his character type and the street dance itself (Genné 1996: 644). Kelly said that when he was "groping for an American style",

> the closest thing I could get was how American men moved in the field of sports . . . If you were raised in a poor neighborhood you don't grow up with a tennis racquet or golf club in your hand . . . Soccer is a poor man's sport because you don't have to have anything but newspaper to kick around . . .[5]

Kelly doesn't mention it but the most basic "poor kid's street sport" is simple competition: Who can vault the highest over the fire hydrant? Who is most agile at curb balancing? Who can jump off the curb and swing with impunity into the forbidden territory of that street your mother won't let you cross? Who can get away with stunts without incurring the wrath of the cop on the beat? In "Singin' in the Rain" and in other street dances, Kelly turns this urban child's sport into art and proves he is the very best kid on the block.

But urban streets have changed. In most of Kelly's street dances, the city is benign and his use of street props is playful. He stops short of disrupting the passers-by and vandalizing the objects on the street. The street dances that follow, in line with growing class unrest and the developing drug culture, increasingly portray American streets as places of danger rather than delight. In *On the Town* (1949), New York and its citizens are bright and cheerful. We don't see vagrants or drug sellers and the policemen are stern but benevolent. However, in two instances Kelly departs from this benign model. The Alter Ego dance in *Cover Girl* and the drunk dances in *It's Always Fair Weather* become more threatening and the dances are used to express the dark side of human nature: anger, jealousy and despair. In the Alter Ego dance Kelly works over his complex and conflicting feelings of jealousy by dancing down a deserted, rundown street with a transparent image of himself (the "alter ego"). The dance ends when Kelly angrily shatters the plate glass window of an empty store front to destroy his reflected image. In *It's Always Fair Weather* (1955) three soldiers, panicked at facing their new lives at the end of World War II, reel drunkenly down 3rd Avenue, commandeer a taxi, shake up its driver and dance noisily with garbage can lids in a forbidding street shadowed by the elevated tracks.

Six years after *It's Always Fair Weather* the film version of *West Side Story* (1961) made its debut. In it Jerome Robbins adapts and expands Kelly's cinematic street dance traditions using a brilliantly choreographed mobile camera on a crane and exciting rhythmic cutting to enhance the dance's excitement. But now the street dancers dance to demonstrate their domination of the city streets they skim across and the fire hydrants they leap over. Gang warfare and racial tension are transformed into dance. The passers-by look upon them with fear and despair rather than delight as they disrupt traffic and steal street vendors' wares to fight their enemies. The littered rundown streets, with their broken windows and graffiti-defaced walls, reveal a society at war with itself and the distinctive energy that Kelly used to portray enthusiasm and joy in "Make Way for Tomorrow" and "Singin' in the Rain" is now transformed into something darker: a combination of anger and alienation. The policemen who break up *West Side Story*'s dance – fight are anything but benevolent: they threaten the boys and use them as pawns in a race war, offering to help the white gang, the Jets, clean up their rivals, the Puerto Rican Sharks.

By 1960 the terms "juvenile delinquency" and "street gang" warfare had become buzz phrases in the American media. New York increasingly came to be seen as a frightening and dangerous place. My research has shown that the rise of popular interest in the subject of urban teenage gangs is dramatic. A search of *New York Times* articles from 1870 to the present under the key words "juvenile delinquency", "street gangs" or indeed any combination of a word and gangs reveals relatively few articles on the subject between 1929 and 1945. After that articles about street gangs increase steadily, peaking in the late 1950s and early 1960s. A search of the *Reader's Guide to Periodical Literature* covers a wider range of popular magazines and reveals a similar trend.

The decline of the film musical as a form also contributed to the temporary disappearance of the street dance in movies. There were exceptions. Bob Fosse carries on the Astaire–Kelly–Robbins tradition with his own distinctive accent in *Sweet Charity* (1968). But the most popular street dance of the era takes place not in America, but in Austria. Julie Andrews leads her troupe of children through the sunny streets of Salzburg and the surrounding countryside, singing "Do Re Mi" in *The Sound of Music* (1965). "Do Re Mi" also owes a lot to the walking tour opening of *On the Town*, but its roots are also in *West Side Story*. Robert Wise, who also directed *West Side Story*, directed *The Sound of Music*. It was Wise who conceived the opening sequence of the former leading into Robbins's dance in which a camera moving above the city streets leads us from the tip of Manhattan to the upper west side. He duplicates that idea in the opening of *The Sound of Music*, but we've left the littered streets of New York for a more pastoral landscape: the green and majestic mountains of Austria.

Saturday Night Fever, the big hit of 1977, gave the street dance new life. John Travolta is a direct descendant of Maurice Chevalier in *Love Me Tonight*, taking us on a rhythmical walking tour of his urban neighborhood. His director, John Badham, employs a new variation for dance with his tracking camera. It glides along the sidewalks on a level with Travolta's feet pulling us along in tempo just ahead of the young dancer. Travolta's walk and the music of the Bee Gees captures the distinctive temper of this young character and his time, just as Rodgers did for Chevalier in *Love Me Tonight* and Gershwin for the elegant Astaire and Rogers in *Shall We Dance?*

Around this time, the film street dance also received another powerful infusion from the 'real' streets where African American hip hop culture and the various forms of street dancing it engendered (B-Boy dancing resulting in breakdance, popping, locking and other forms) would give street dances a new look (see Banes 1994: 126–58). The immensely popular *Flashdance* (1983) brought breakdancing into mainstream films such as *Wild Style* (1982) and *Beat Street* (1984). Mostly, however, movie street dances in the second half of the century come in the form of *homages* (tributes) to the earlier ones and they are few and far between. In 1967 French new wave director Jacques Demy paid tribute to Gene Kelly in *Les Demoiselles de Rochefort* in which Kelly, as choreographer and star, reprises the street dance form in the French port town of Rochefort. In Martin Scorsese's *New York, New York* we catch a glimpse of a sailor and his girl dancing under the elevated tracks. Billy Crystal and Woody Allen "quote" the romantic quay side dance "Our Love is Here to Stay", from *An American in Paris*, in their films *Forget Paris* and *Everybody Says I Love You*. And Baz Luhrman, who seems to be the director most interested in reviving the musical film, has his dancers perform above the street under a glittering sign in *Strictly Ballroom*.

In the latter part of the twentieth century the street dance moves to another visual medium, that of video/dvd. Again the immediate influence is African American hip hop culture, but the roots of video dance in African American jazz dance and in the Astaire–Kelly–Robbins street dances are still visible. Michael Jackson and his choreographers and directors build on the camera movement and editing innovations of his film musical predecessors, adding new tools from the computer age. In Jackson's early videos *Thriller* (1983) and *Beat It* (1984), choreographer Michael Peters, an admirer of Jerome Robbins, draws directly on his own experience as a dancer in *West Side Story*. The gang dances in *Bad* (directed by Martin Scorsese and choreography by Gregg Burge and Jeffrey Daniels) are not too distant relatives of the *West Side Story* dances, in particular "Cool", danced in an underground garage. In *Bad* the dancers dance *under* the streets in the New York subways.

Reflecting an urban culture where children carry uzis and kill over designer clothing, Michael Jackson's street dances get progressively more surreal and frightening. Even love dances are scary. In *Thriller*, a chorus of the dancing dead led by a Zombie-like Jackson, captured by the moving camera of director Michael Landis, transforms an after-the-movie stroll into an unforgettable experience for Jackson's terrified date. In *The Way You Make Me Feel* (1987), choreographed by Vincent Paterson, Jackson dances through the streets singing of the same euphoric feelings as Kelly in *Singin' in the Rain*, but the streets through which he dances are run down and graffiti-littered as are the eerie surrealistic city scapes of *Billie Jean*. Urban poverty is brought up close and personal. And Kelly's childlike games and innocent enthusiasm are transformed into dancing with a real edge. Jackson aggressively taunts his would-be lover and his openly erotic gestures have an undertone of anger. The finale of *The Way You Make Me Feel* resonates with *Singin' in the Rain*'s waterlogged ending. This time a fire hydrant explodes in the heat of the summer: the arc of glimmering water is as beautiful as the backlit rain in Kelly's street dance. And the Place de La Concorde sequence in *An American in Paris* is a direct ancestor of this moment when the girl finally succumbs to Jackson's wooing and we see them embrace in silhouette against a tapestry of vapor clouds. But the image is also a reminder, albeit unconscious, of those hot summer days when the poor migrate to the streets to get relief and have to vandalize city property to do so. (Think of Spike Lee's *Do the Right Thing* which similarly evokes a hot summer night.)

In the street dance section of Jackson's "Black or White" race issues are directly addressed, as they are in *West Side Story*, but this time on a global scale. Jackson dances with a classical Indian dancer on a busy highway and moves to various locations around the globe where his choreography reflects a variety of folk forms. Both Kelly and Astaire are referenced in this video: in one street scene, Jackson combines an elegant hands-in-his-pocket nonchalance with intricate footwork that has roots in Astaire's moves although they are used along with crotch-grabbing gestures Astaire wouldn't consider. Kelly's final window-smashing gesture in the Alter Ego sequence and Astaire's drunk dance in *The Sky's the Limit* (1943) are also in the background of this dance but without the clear dramatic motivation. Jackson vandalizes a car, resulting in an extended and violent glass-shattering sequence that concludes with the heaving of a barrel through a plate glass window that duplicates the climactic gesture of the Alter Ego dance. He follows this with a very dark take on Kelly's ecstatic splashing at the end of the "Singin' in the Rain" street dance.

It is no secret that Jackson idolized Astaire. He and his sister, Janet Jackson, grew up on the "street dance" musicals of the first half of the century. Janet Jackson pays direct homage to these roots and to other of her African American dance predecessors in her video, *It's Alright*. And, as in her brother's work, digital imagery is added to the arsenal of tools used to enhance the scope and drama of the dance. In *It's Alright*, The Nicholas Brothers, Cyd Charisse, and Cab Calloway appear with Jackson and Heavy D as they dance through the busy city streets, captured by a choreographed and extremely mobile camera which sweeps over the streets on a level with the dancer and, at times, hovers in the air above them.

The popularity of the street dance shows no signs of waning and we can expect that there will be dancing in the streets way into the twenty-first century. There is a lot more to be said about video street dancing since Michael Jackson, but that will have to be left to another article. In the meantime, it is clear that the dance genre that grew up in the movies has now found a home in video and on dvd. It seems likely to continue so long as we have streets to walk on and to dance through.

Notes

1   This essay is reprinted from the first edition of *Rethinking Dance History* (2004).
2   The grandest camera gesture of the entire sequence relates to the climactic gesture in the courtship dance "You Were Meant for Me" (and also to a gesture in the "Olivera Street" sequence in *Anchors Aweigh*).
3   Beth Genné interview with Betsy Blair, London, 1998. Some of the material on Gene Kelly in this section has been published in my article on Kelly in *Envisioning Dance on Film and Video* (Genné 2002).
4   Gene Kelly interviewed by John Russell Taylor, National Film Theatre, London, May 20, 1980.
5   Gene Kelly interviewed by Marilyn Hunt, Los Angeles, 1975.

Bibliography

Banes, S. (1994) *Writing Dancing in the Age of Postmodernism*, Hanover: Wesleyan University Press.
Croce, A. (1972) *The Fred Astaire and Ginger Rogers Book*, New York: Galahad.
Delameter, J. (1981) *Dance in the Hollywood Musical*, Ann Arbor, MI: UMI Research Press.

Genné, B. (1984) *The Film Musicals of Vincente Minnelli and the Team of Gene Kelly and Stanley Donen (1944–1958)*, University of Michigan doctoral dissertation, Ann Arbor: University Microfilms.
—— (1996) "Gene Kelly", *Dancing Times*, April: 643–9.
—— (2001) "Freedom Incarnate': Jerome Robbins, Gene Kelly and The Dancing Sailor as an American Icon in World War II", *Dance Chronicle*, 24, 1: 83–103.
—— (2002) "Dancin' in the Rain: Gene Kelly and Musical Films", in J. Mitoma (ed.) *Envisioning Dance on Film and Video*, London: Routledge, 71–7.
Kimball, R. (ed.) (1993) *The Complete Lyrics of Ira Gershwin*, New York: Knopf.
Knox, D. (1973) *The Magic Factory: How MGM Made "An American in Paris"*, New York: Praeger.
Mueller, J. (1985) *Astaire Dancing*, New York: Knopf.
Nierenberg, G. T., dir. (1979) *No Maps on My Taps* (film), Milestone Films.

Chapter 16

Judson
Redux and remix

MARCIA B. SIEGEL

JUDSON DANCE THEATER in New York in the 1960s has become a well-worn topic as the source of contemporary dance. The name shadows everything, half a century after the idea of Judson dance has dissolved into the sensibilities of its many adherents. Scholars and critics have focused on the sociocultural issues of race, gender and ethnicity as the product of Judson dance. But these issues didn't become important until the 1980s, when Judson's first radical choices had opened the way to further experiments in chance, minimalism and improvisation. In the broadest terms Judson dance was a revolution against modern dance and ballet, as well as an attack on all the conventions of mainstream art and performance. Judson dance came at the outset of the counterculture, a massive shift in art and social life, and we can't really assess it without considering the world in which it happened, a culture utterly different from what provokes art today.

One reason for the reductive way Judson dance is portrayed is that so little of it can be studied. Judson's dances were intentionally ephemeral. Repertory in a formal sense, and the permanent dance company needed to implement repertory, was considered a hindrance to creativity. We find it hard to imagine a world with no Internet, computers or readily available recording devices. Technological refinements have facilitated not only a much more complete documentation of dances but also a revising of the documents that do exist. Dancer Elaine Summers filmed much of the Judson activity, and she crafted the footage into an 'intermedia' piece, *Fantastic Gardens*, and several documentary films (Summers 2009: 136–141). Editing in those days was done by literally cutting the film and glueing it back together. Much original footage was probably lost in the process. Today's recordings can be easily doctored to eliminate the boring parts and leave in the exemplary parts. For historical accuracy, the boring parts would have been just as informative as the exciting ones.

Yvonne Rainer's *Trio A* has become a touchstone of postmodern dance teaching and scholarship, largely, I think, because of two documents. The '60s dancers insisted that the non-verbal had to be given its due in an overwhelmingly verbal universe of meaning. But when the non-verbal artefacts were no longer present, the dancers' own written statements have stood in for the actual work. Yvonne Rainer's NO manifesto (Rainer 1974: 51) has come to represent the whole 'Judson' movement, even though she herself said at the time of its publication that she intended it to reflect her immediate working concerns. Assuming NO was the whole of the Judson aesthetic diminishes the work and its influence. Or perhaps we have become so familiar with the anti-heroic and anti-magical as working tools that today's experiments have become heroic and magical. I'm thinking of the star-power of the subjects of Jérôme Bel's films *Cédric Andrieux* and *Véronique Doisneau*, for example, or Rainer herself in the film of *Trio A*.

The other thing that cemented Rainer and *Trio A* in postmodern dance's anti-canonical canon is the film that dance critic/historian Sally Banes made of Rainer performing the dance in a studio in 1978. But this isn't the dance as made by Rainer in 1966. The first performance was literally a trio. Rainer performed it with David Gordon and Steve Paxton at Judson Church in January 1966 (photo in Rainer 1974: 307). As Rainer reported later, Alex Hay threw hundreds of wooden slats down on them from the choir loft at regular intervals (Rainer 2006: 270). *Trio A* has had a long life, mutating into different modes, media and castings without losing its own identity.[1] Months after its premiere, Rainer taught it to ballet-trained Peter Saul, inserting pirouettes and jumps (Rainer 2006: 273). She performed it alone after serious surgery in 1967, as *Convalescent Dance* (Rainer 2006: 279). From the first, Rainer was interested in the differences among individuals performing the same material.

The idea of defamiliarizing a dance by drastically changing the circumstances of its performance – the number of performers, the previous training required, the surroundings in which they do it – is a way of downplaying a work's canonical stature. Ironically, this dance itself became canonic. Rainer's choreography, sometimes misread as improvisation, consisted of moves she made up that were not supposed to look like modern dance or ballet moves. The moves seem simple but aren't easy to execute. In the first sequence of the Banes film, Rainer begins with legs slightly bent, her arms swinging two and a half times across the body; she places one foot behind the other and rotates her arms from the shoulders twice, straight out to the sides. She takes one step, remains on the standing foot and, leading with one hand, tilts forwards into a lunge that ends with her still standing, facing the floor. Five minutes more of non sequiturs follow this.

All the sequences are performed continuously, at low energy, and the dancer avoids making eye contact with the camera, even when it means adding a turn of the head to accomplish this. Rainer doesn't repeat any of the sequences in the dance, though some of the phrases have repeated moves built in. The idea was to perform them without expressive nuance or performing enhancements, and to avoid engaging with the audience visually. Few choreographers have evaded the effects of previously codified movement as successfully as Rainer did.

One aim of the Judson and post-Judson followers was to reset the ways of thinking about dance, as well as to redefine the idea of dance itself. In this they have succeeded, impacting even the latter-day traditional theatre forms. During the great cultural shifts of the '60s, Judson dancers shared reformist aesthetics with artists and musicians who were their frequent collaborators. Where movement came from and how it was put together were key elements for them in making dances. *Trio A*'s movement might have originated intuitively, out of Rainer's desire to avoid anything familiar. Some of her other early dances derived from the movement of dealing with objects (mattresses and other mundane props for instance), or from game-like gambits (falling and catching one another unexpectedly). *Trio A* looks ordinary, not because of the movement itself but because of the way Rainer performed it. Pedestrian movement, in one form or another, became a staple of the Judson and post-Judson dancers as they distinguished themselves from the heroic, romanticized movement of the modern dancers. Rainer's hilarious attempts to teach *Trio A* to an uncomprehending Martha Graham as impersonated by Richard Move is captured in the 2002 film *Rainer Variations* by Charles Atlas.[2]

Trio A also illustrated one solution to the problem of suppressing the artist's personal style. By the time of Judson, Merce Cunningham was using chance operations to avoid imposing his personal preferences on his movement, but he continued to make discrete dances and to train a company of dancers to perform them. He came to have a recognizable style, one that evolved gradually over the years but was distinctly his. Rainer didn't seek the personal longevity inherent in preserving a repertory, or the branding implied by having her own dance company with classes in her own 'technique'. Her movement for *Trio A* was deliberately chosen but she didn't shape it choreographically.

The experimenters wanted to jolt the audience out of comfortable reactions. With the exception of Trisha Brown, none of the Judson or post-Judson dancers attempted to create an original dance vocabulary. What most of them have done is to appropriate other movement languages in whole or in part, or, like Deborah Hay and Lucinda Childs, they've used the everyday vernacular of walking, running and turning as a primary source of movement. David Gordon and Steve Paxton often borrowed moves from sports. Instead of inventing entirely new vocabularies, they could repeat these familiar movements so many times that they no longer carried any automatic meaning, or began to acquire new meanings. Composting dance from many non-dance sources became an approved way of getting around the ego investment of creating one's own technique. There have been idiosyncratic movers (e.g. Douglas Dunn) but they usually pursue their work from one project to the next, creating the vocabulary needed for each undertaking. Though many post-Judsonites teach dance, few of them have codified a personal technique. In fact, Judson's anti-modern dance crusade has succeeded to the extent that 'modern dance' as a category has mostly been superseded by 'contemporary dance', an eclectic mix based on many sources.

*

Two decades into post-Judson reductionism, the young American modern dancer Victoria Marks was teaching on a Fulbright Fellowship at London Contemporary Dance School when she made *Dancing to Music* for four students. She had a piece of music in hand, *Casting No Shadow*, a meditative score for voice and piano by Wim Mertens. Marks was wondering if one could dance to a piece of music with your eyes: 'Could your experience of seeing be choreographed?'[3] Her question eventually turned into a dance about looking. The women essentially remained in place for eleven and a half minutes, turning their heads. They stood side by side, facing the audience, looking in different directions on counts determined by Marks. She mapped the head moves directionally – side to side, up and down – and added a limited number of associated possibilities – reaching out with one hand, clasping both hands in front of the body, a step forwards or back. All of the actions could expand and combine. Everything was choreographed and set. Marks instructed the dancers to move as if they were producing Mertens's sound.

The performed dance was mesmerizing. As the dancers turned their heads, in unison or in counterpoint, the simple moves became invested with the personal act of seeing, and the seeing became invested with the women's relation to each other. When Marks returned to New York, where she had her own small company of dancers, she set the piece on herself and three companions, Hetty King, Barbara Canner and Nancy Ohrenstein. On a return visit to London in 1992, she taught it to four generations of women affiliated with London Contemporary Dance Theatre: the veteran modern dancer Jane Dudley, Louise McDonald, pianist and composer Judyth Knight and a student. After that, Marks says, 'it became this *thing*'. She had many requests from other groups to perform the dance, and it has been set on Taipei's Cloudgate II, Dance Alloy Theater, Liz Lerman Dance Exchange and AXIS Dance Company. Invited back to the Place in 2010, she set *Dancing to Music* for four men.

Each iteration of the dance looked different, but Marks, Canner, King and Ohrenstein's performance, recorded at Dance Theater Workshop on 26 November 1988, reflects Marks's intentions well. The women perform at low intensity, with calm expressions on their faces. Without exaggerating, they register the contacts they make with each other. The head turnings and hand touches occur on the downbeat of Mertens's music. At rare intervals they spread the move over two beats, or hesitate and quickly repeat within one beat. The women don't always move in unison. In fact, some form of counterpoint occurs most of the time, so that they're not all looking in the same direction at the same time. They bring their weight into play, dropping their heads or their arms heavily. The direction and movement changes vary in intensity, but only towards the end of the dance does abruptness become urgency.

These manipulations lose their neutrality almost at once. The moves that begin as head turnings become looks, and the looks are meaningful depending on who is looking at whom and with what timing. Some eye contacts occur suddenly; others are gradual. Sometimes someone's focus will turn inward, withdrawing from contact. Hands are clasped formally in front of the body; at some point one of the women reaches out and clasps the hand of the woman next to her. At another point they all unclasp their hands at the same time, letting them drop and dangle. Towards the end of the dance, one woman turns away from the audience with a single step. This precipitates a stir of action among the others, who step and face upstage together. They bring the first woman front again, and in their original line they gradually look at each other and very gradually smile, inching slightly closer together.

I've tried to describe this in objective terms but, in fact, the women take on separate identities and roles during the course of the dance. Who are they and why are they together there? What is their relation to each other? The dance becomes dramatic even if it started out as an objective exercise. The extraordinary thing about this is that when shown the video without any preamble, viewers come up with different interpretations, different roles.

*

No one has succeeded in making a comprehensive definition of minimalism. In some ways, the idea is circular. To deal with the least amount of anything possible is to leave so much unused, and so many openings for further investigations. What minimalism made possible in dance is more, not less. The limitations minimalism places on the performers and the audience have the effect of magnifying the smallest changes, intensifying perception and allowing for dance that is more diverse.

Minimalism in music is associated with the composers Steve Reich, Philip Glass and Terry Riley, and maybe even Asian chants and drones. In dance it can mean reducing the movement possibilities to simple actions, like walking, standing and turning the head, or subtle signifying acts, like eye blinks or weight shifts. It can refer to the dynamics with which any movement is executed; moves can be imperceptibly slow or can be carried out at an even pace without dynamic accents. The duration of a given movement event can be stretched out, suspended or even held still for long periods of time. Minimalism can apply to how the movement sequence is structured, with lots of repetition or none at all. Rainer's invented vocabulary wasn't physically minimal, but the way she performed it had a reduced range of options.

Judson dance opened up the question of what a dance is. If a dance could be the kind of understated performance Rainer advocated, it followed that ordinary persons without formal dance training could be dancers. A video made for television as part of *Dance in America*, 'Beyond the Mainstream', in 1980 put together a continuous performance of *Trio A* shared serially by modern dancer Sara Rudner, ballet dancer Bart Cook and non-dancer Frank Conversano. Whatever shape a person was in, that person could dance. A dance could take place outside of a proscenium theatre. It could be planned and rehearsed in advance or improvised on the spot; it could include both rehearsed and improvised movements. Besides music and design, a dance could incorporate words, spoken or projected. It could make use of sophisticated technology, and by the 2010s it could become a video or a livestream event, or even a web artefact without live performers. Minimalistic practices have informed large spectacles and community events. They have facilitated community rituals and events aimed at implementing personal interaction. In America post-Judson dancers have brought their work into museums, galleries and the anti-gravity environments of aerial dance.

*

The European dance scene absorbed Judson ideas from visiting artists, subsidized teaching residencies and commissioned works. Europeans were drawn to New York to study with the post-Judson dancers and attend their performances. The Belgian choreographer Anne Teresa De Keersmaeker studied at Maurice Béjart's school, Mudra, in Brussels, and then in 1980 she attended New York University. Two decades into the Judson era, Judsonites Trisha Brown and Lucinda Childs and other postmodernists had begun working independently. De Keersmaeker saw their performances. She was strongly influenced by the musical minimalist Steve Reich, who had developed much of his own early work in collaboration with the dancer Laura Dean. De Keersmaeker choreographed an impressive solo to Reich's *Violin Phase* in 1981. The fifteen-minute dance consisted of only two movements: stepping and swinging the arms. But by making small shifts within this limitation, she created a hypnotic dance that traced a mandala on the floor and crescendoed into an ecstasy of spinning.[4] De Keersmaeker followed this with three other early Reich works that were performed together with *Violin Phase* as *Fase* (1982).

When De Keersmaeker returned to Europe she formed her own company, Rosas. Instead of severe step dancing, as in the Reich pieces, she began making more conventional theatre dances, but she still used the minimalist tactic of repeated movements in series. Rosas's first dance, *Rosas Danst Rosas* (1983), was an evening-length structure in four parts that featured the four women in the company and a score by Thierry de Mey and Peter Vermeersch. De Mey filmed a fifty-four-minute version of the dance in 1996 in Leuven, Belgium, in the deserted corridors and courtyards of the RITO technical school, a historically important building designed by the noted art-nouveau architect Henry van de Velde.[5]

For *Rosas Danst Rosas* De Keersmaeker borrowed some of the tropes that were becoming signatures of Pina Bausch's Tanztheater: lines of chairs, skimpy costumes, self-conscious gestures. She differed from Bausch, though, in using these devices as structural elements, not as triggers for social interactions. There's no immediate drama in a theatrical sense, as there is in Bausch, but De Keersmaeker's dance becomes expressive as a whole, when the repetition invokes the viewer's visceral and imaginative response. De Keersmaeker's dancers seldom related to each other, neither touching nor interacting except to make momentary eye contact. Her use of repetition differs significantly from that of Victoria Marks in *Dancing to Music*. Where Marks uses very simple movements and gradually attaches meaning to them, De Keersmaeker begins with loaded moves and gestures. Used as compositional elements and repeated until they become value-free, they can be manipulated according to minimalist procedures. Expressive resonance arises from the spiralling dynamics and spatial changes.

Rosas Danst Rosas begins in silence.[6] The women, wearing grey T-shirts and skirts over tights, with socks and heavy shoes, stand in a line with their backs to the audience; they topple over backwards and begin a long sequence on the floor. They roll halfway over, sit up on their heels, and lower themselves to the floor again. Prone, they lift their chests very slowly, leaning on their forearms, turn their heads without looking at each other, lower their faces to the floor again. Slowly they raise one hand to touch their heads. All these gestures are elements of a lexicon that will be used in the later sections of the dance.

In Part 2 the women take possession of ordinary chairs. Seated, they perform strings of gestures: flinging their arms across their bodies, swooping forwards so that their long hair falls over their heads, touching a breast, tugging at the neck of their jerseys, crossing one leg over the other. Most of the gestures carry the freight of 'feminine' provocation, but they don't progress into sexual play.

A rhythmic tapping sound has begun in Part 1. The rhythm changes to a different pattern; from a quiet scratching, the score gradually accumulates instruments (clarinets, saxophones, more percussion) and the rhythm is embellished and made more complicated. The change in the sound throws the women into locomotion and turning. With each further alteration in the music, the camera finds the dancers in a new space. At the music's most dense, the dancers are outside in a courtyard, at night. This is when the dance reaches its highest intensity, but other than drawing them into group formations, the movement doesn't extend to personal seduction. The music thins out and the women gesture in a squared-off floor pattern. Later, the light comes up, suggesting dawn, and then daylight, and the camera moves in close enough to the dancers to hear their breathing. The narrative energy descends into exhaustion.

Rosas was successful immediately, and after making several more dances, the company was given a fifteen-year residency at the Théâtre Royal de la Monnaie in Brussels, from 1992 to 2007.[7] This prestigious appointment gave De Keersmaeker the opportunity to create more repertory and an international school, P.A.R.T.S. (Performing Arts Research & Training Studios). After completing the residency at the Monnaie, the company continued to pursue its now-important career.

*

In 2011 De Keersmaeker engaged in a brief legal dispute with the pop star Beyoncé, who may have plagiarized Rosas's dances for one of her music videos. Deflecting the Beyoncé issue, De Keersmaeker claimed that even schoolchildren could do her moves, and invited anyone to make their own facsimile. According to Judith Mackrell of the Guardian, 1,500 people answered the call.[8] De Keersmaeker formalized the experiment with the website 'The fABULEUS Rosas Remix Project', based on *Rosas Danst Rosas*.[9] It turned out to be one of the most imaginative of many egalitarian efforts mounted in the post-Judson era.

The Rosas Remix Project uses the gestural vocabulary of Part 2 of the dance. The Remix home page contains a typewritten message of welcome by De Keersmaeker, encouraging the public to participate in the project. Separate pages on the site lead the user to instructions for the six gestures of the dance, a surprisingly elaborate explanation by De Keersmaeker of how she structured the choreography, and a three-and-a-half-minute demonstration of the sequence done in various canons and reversals by four members of the company. In her welcome talk, the choreographer opens the work to any adaptation. Participants can change the order of the movements, the music, the number of dancers. 'The only thing you need is a chair', she says. The website also includes a recording of the original fifteen-minute score and a convenient box in which to register and upload your own version.

As this is being written, 357 groups have posted their own Remix performances. The groups participating display a remarkable range of interpretations that retain the basic gestures. Number 1, 'Yukio yoshida danst Rosas', has four women seated on chairs in a gym. Spectators off camera contribute the sounds of an audience in loud conversation. This bare-bones version is followed by Number 2, 'Ursulinen Mechelen dansen Rosas'. Four girls perform in a classroom, possibly in a parochial school. Standing, each girl gives an introduction, and then sits in her chair. When all four have done this, they go through the gesture sequence in immaculate unison. They're accompanied at first by the original score; halfway through their two-minute performance, a female pop song plays. At the end, they self-consciously receive prolonged applause from what must be their friends in the back of the classroom.

From these early postings, the dance becomes more ambitious. Number 12, 'Danse Madi (Rosas)', is a solo done by a man with a chair in front of what looks like a large woodshed. He elaborates, extends and repeats the original vocabulary, using the chair as a prop. At the end of four minutes, he drags the chair out of the frame. He's made a rather conventional dance.

In keeping with the twenty-first century's casual use or neglect of information, most of the entries have little or no identification. They take place in rooms, on stages and outdoors. Number 350, 'dans les bois', is set in a forest where chairs are strewn around. The nine-minute dance begins with men and women walking through the woods, listening to bird calls and other natural sounds. Each person takes possession of a chair; the music begins and the dancers start the sequence together. After a certain number of cycles, they get up and move almost stealthily through the undergrowth to rearrange the chairs and begin the sequence again. The sunlight and shade, and the restless camera, make it hard to tell how many dancers there are.

Minimalism can have a super-serious effect. De Keersmaeker performs and teaches with a neutral demeanour, but the idea of the Remix Project is playful, welcoming and respectful of any contribution anyone would like to make. Some entries are goofy. Number 13, 'Frauen danst Frauen', features two women and two dogs. The women may be improvising on the gestures, and one of them keeps her eye on a laptop perched open in front of them. Neither of them pays any attention to the dogs. The main dog looks interested but mystified.

A classroom full of what may be 10-year-olds ('Voltaire Danst Rosas', Number 276) is divided into docile groups with a stern teacher conducting them. When she turns away to face the chalkboard, the class rebels. Defeated, the teacher collapses into a chair. The children celebrate. In another classroom, Number 343, nine uniformed Korean girls sit at their desks, going through the sequence as two male monitors patrol among them. An appended note says the website was used to teach the students contemporary dance for the first time.

Some of the groups perform on stages, with or without an audience. Some see theatrical uses for the gestures. Two women wait for a subway train (Number 106, 'Rosas Danst Aspudden'). Seated on a bench, they begin the gestures. When the head-turns bring them into eye contact, there's a hint of speculation. They may recognize each other, or they may be imagining a more intimate encounter. But they continue the sequence impersonally until the train comes. One woman gets on; the other remains on the bench. The woman on the train smiles over her shoulder as the train pulls out.

Work preoccupies some of the entries. In Number 107, 'Pleinair', a man in a business suit wanders through the woods until he comes upon an old-fashioned computer and a copy machine in a clearing. Discarding his jacket and tie, he tries to operate the machines. Unsuccessful, he sits in a chair, gestures in despair or defeat, and finally, folding over weightily, he falls to the ground.

I didn't look at every entry, but I was particularly taken with Number 212, 'BAM danst Rosas (New York)'. In this one some twenty people sit on the steps of Brooklyn Academy of Music. The performers are the staff of BAM. They execute the sequence in different spaces of the famous performance venue, home of the Next Wave, where I've seen Pina Bausch's Wuppertal Tanztheater and Rosas, and innumerable other post-Judson works.

Most of the videos are chamber-sized works, but a few encompass whole schools or communities. Number 346, 'Requiem for Rosas', divides forty to fifty students into large counterpoint groups in a large field. Depersonalized, they might be performing a movement choir.

*

The Remix Project is only one of several De Keersmaeker ideas built around community outreach and outside-the-proscenium events. In the spring of 2016 she posted a website, 'My Walking Is My Dancing',[10] calling for people to join 'an ultra-long flashmob' through the streets of Brussels in honour of Dance Day. Like the Remix site, this gave meticulous but readily understandable instructions for joining the walk. It included an animated map of the city showing the five starting points and predicting the approximate time and location as the groups would progress after the 11 a.m. starting time. The goal was to converge in the city centre, where the choreographer, with members of the company and students of P.A.R.T.S., would be giving a workshop and dance jam for all. The walk would take five hours, at an estimated speed of five metres per minute.

De Keersmaeker expected that the walk would bring people together after the disastrous terrorist attacks in the city. The minimalist practice of extremely sloweddown walking would act as a kind of meditation. On the website De Keersmaeker says, 'Rosas wants to pause and reflect on the city and attempt to make it part of us again through the most basic form of movement conceivable: walking'.[11]

In 1992, during her second Fulbright residency in London, Victoria Marks continued her career in collaboration with filmmaker Margaret Williams. They made *Outside In* for the disabled and non-disabled dancers of CandoCo company in London.[12] This led Marks into choreographing for community groups and unconventional performers, a direction she's pursued ever since in addition to choreographing stage dances. Marks said that the thirteen-minute CandoCo project challenged her to change the way the public thinks about disability. Instead of taking the traditional choreographer's role of bringing in her own ideas, she began to approach her work as a listener. She wanted to represent the needs of the subjects as well as her own. Ultimately, she started calling her work 'choreo-portraiture' (Marks and Bench 2015).

Later still, she began working with distinct groups of people – veterans of the Iraq War with PTSD, young female dropouts and adult women in Vermont. With individuals or groups who hadn't known each other before, Marks uses improvisation exercises to bring about interactions and understandings nonverbally, and to preserve that sense of discovery once the dance is performed or filmed. Her essay 'Against Improvisation', a contribution to an anthology devoted to dance improvisation (2003: 134–139), demonstrates Marks's unconventional approach to choreography. She combines the democratic instincts of the postmodernists with the discipline and personal investment of a modern dancer.

Yvonne Rainer returned to choreographing in 2000 after two decades of making films, on the invitation of Mikhail Baryshnikov to contribute something for his White Oak Dance Project. In 2008 she revisited her NO manifesto and ratified a few of its edicts, debunked a few and offered qualifications to the rest (Rainer 2013). 'NO to spectacle . . . Avoid if at all possible', it begins. In her latter-day choreography she rejected the idea of through-composition as much as she had initially, relying on short, disconnected phrases of movement. A collagist, Rainer looks ironically at serious ideas and sidesteps personal expression. Her recent dances have pointedly quoted from other performance works, including her own, and from important verbal texts, but she's not known for inventing her own movement vocabulary.

In 2007, as part of the Performa biennial in New York, Rainer created *RoS Indexical*, reflecting on the great unknown ballet of 1913, *Le Sacre du Printemps* (Rainer 2009: 102–108). The Nijinsky/Stravinsky ballet caused a celebrated scandal at its premiere. It disappeared after a few performances in Paris and London but survived afterwards as a glamorous myth. Acknowledging the layers of interpretation that have accumulated over the *Rite*, Rainer set the Nijinsky movements, as reconstructed in 1987 by Millicent Hodson, on four women. They danced the phrases accompanied by the music that was played on the soundtrack to the British movie *Riot at the Rite*, an imagined dramatization of the ballet's premiere. The film alternated scenes of the Paris audience with clips from a Finnish National Ballet production of Hodson's *Rite*. Rainer didn't use the film itself, but only its soundtrack, including the indignant actors' voices. Instead of a complete version of the 'original' choreography, she inserted sections of it against other movement sequences, including *Trio A*. The whole long piece was a kind of burlesque, but also a serious commentary on the porous nature of dance history.

Notes

1. Rainer's own chronology of the versions of the dance up to 2002 appears on the Video Data Bank listing for *Trio A* (www.vdb.org/titles/trio).
2. *Rainer Variations*. For comments by filmmaker Charles Atlas and Rainer: www.vdb.org/titles/rainer-variations.
3. Victoria Marks in conversation with author, 17 March 2016.
4. De Keersmaeker was filmed in a later performance of *Violin Phase* (https://vimeo.com/88903141), which included overhead shots that showed her step patterns as she traced a circle in white sand.
5. A fifty-seven-minute film directed in 1996 by Thierry de Mey is posted (with Luke Jennings's review of a 2009 performance at Sadler's Wells Theatre in London) at www.ubu.com/dance/keers_rosas.html.
6. I refer principally to de Mey's film in this account.

7   The state-sponsored Monnaie had been the home of Maurice Béjart, whose company was succeeded by that of Mark Morris (1988–1991).
8   'Beyoncé, De Keersmaeker – and a dance reinvented by everyone,' www.theguardian.com/stage/2013/oct/09/beyonce-de-keersmaeker-technology-dance.
9   'Re:Rosas!' www.rosasdanstrosas.be/en-home. A split-screen video of the Beyoncé piece together with scenes from De Keersmaeker's dances, plus a long list of viewer comments, is at www.youtube.com/watch?v=PDT0m514TMw.
10 'My Walking is My Dancing,' www.mywalking.be/en.
11 'SLOW WALK BRUSSELS Anne Teresa de Keersmaeker 24/04/2016,' www.youtube.com/watch?v=h-Jd7DQ-IF0 www.youtube.com/watch?v=MH9GHbTJKMo.
12 Marks and Williams discuss their collaboration in separate essays in the anthology *Envisioning Dance*. Excerpts from *Outside In* and *Mothers & Daughters* are included in the DVD that accompanies the book.

Bibliography

Banes, Sally (1979) *Terpsichore in Sneakers: Post-Modern Dance*, Boston: Houghton Mifflin.
Banes, Sally (1993) *Democracy's Body: Judson Dance Theater, 1992–1964*, Durham: Duke University Press.
Banes, Sally (1998) 'Envoi' in *Dancing Women: Female Bodies on Stage*, London: Routledge, 215–231.
Banes, Sally (ed.) (2003) *Reinventing Dance in the 1960s: Everything Was Possible*, Madison: University of Wisconsin Press.
Burke, Siobhan (2011) 'Circling Back in Time with Anne Teresa De Keersmaeker', *Dance Magazine*, Feb. 17, http://dancemagazine.com/news/Circling_Back_in_Time_with_Anne_Teresa_De_Keersmaeker
Crimp, Douglas (2012) 'Dance Mom: Yvonne Rainer', *Interview*, 27 Dec., www.interviewmagazine.com/culture/dance-mom-yvonne-rainer
Daly, Ann (2002) *Critical Gestures: Writings on Dance and Culture*, Middletown: Wesleyan University Press.
Danspace Project Platform 2012 (2012) *Judson Now*, New York: Danspace Project.
De Keersmaeker, Anne Teresa and Charles Aubin (2016) 'In conversation', *Performa Magazine*, Feb. 18, http://performa-arts.org/magazine/entry/anne-teresa-de-keersmaeker-and-charles-aubin-in-conversation
De Mey, Thierry (n.d.) film of *Rosas Danst Rosas*, www.ubu.com/dance/keers_rosas.html
Greenspan, Karen (2015) 'The Early Work of Anne Teresa De Keersmaeker', *Ballet Review*, 43:1, 46–51.

Jennings, Luke (2009) Review of *Rosas Danst Rosas* at Sadler's Wells, *The Observer*, Sept. 12, www.theguardian.com/stage/2009/sep/13/de-keersmaeker-rosas-sadlers-wells

Mackrell, Judith (2009) Review of *Rosas Danst Rosas* at Sadler's Wells, *The Guardian*, Sept. 9, www.theguardian.com/stage/2009/sep/09/rosas-review

Marks, Victoria (2002) 'Portraits in Celluloid', in Judy Mitoma, ed. *Envisioning Dance on Film and Video*, New York: Routledge, 207–210.

Marks, Victoria (2003) 'Against Improvisation', in Ann Cooper Albright and David Gere, eds. *Taken By Surprise: A Dance Improvisation Reader*, Middletown: Wesleyan University Press, 134–139.

Marks, Victoria and Harmony Bench (2015) 'Mobilizing Subjectivity', *International Journal of Screendance*, 5, http://screendancejournal.org/article/view/4662/3846#.V5ecXK50Fj0

Rainer, Yvonne (1974) *Work 1961–1973*, Halifax: Press of the Nova Scotia College of Art and Design and New York University Press.

Rainer, Yvonne (2006) *Feelings Are Facts: A Life*, Cambridge, MA: MIT Press.

Rainer, Yvonne (2009) '*RoS Indexical* by Yvonne Rainer', in RoseLee Goldberg, ed. *Everywhere and All at Once: An Anthology of Writings on Performa 07*, Zurich: Performa, 102–109.

Rainer, Yvonne (2013) 'Yvonne Rainer's Manifesto', *Lavender Review: Lesbian Poetry & Art*, 8, www.lavrev.net/2013/12/issue-8-dance-contents.html

Siegel, Marcia B. (1991) *The Tail of the Dragon: New Dance 1976–1982*, Durham: Duke University Press.

Siegel, Marcia B. (2008) 'Pomo Retro Rite', *Hudson Review*, Spring, 158–164.

Summers, Elaine and Lana Wilson (2009) 'Elaine Summers in Conversation with Lana Wilson', in Rose Lee Goldberg, ed. *Everywhere and All at Once: An Anthology of Writings on Performa 07*, Zurich: Performa, 136–141.

Williams, Margaret (2002) 'Making Dance Films with Victoria Marks', in Judy Mitoma, ed. *Envisioning Dance on Film and Video*, New York: Routledge, 211–215.

Zimmer, Elizabeth (2016) 'Reimagining *Rosas Danst Rosas*', *Dance Studio Life*, 21, February, www.dancestudiolife.com/february-2016-remagining-rosas-danst-rosas

Chapter 17

Ruth Page, feminine subjectivity, and generic subversion

JOELLEN A. MEGLIN

IN AN ESSAY ENTITLED 'Where Are Ballet's Women Choreographers?' Lynn Garafola counts on one hand the number of women who have entered the pantheon of ballet choreographers: Bronislava Nijinska, Agnes de Mille, Andrée Howard, Ninette de Valois, and Ruth Page (2005: 215). She goes on to question a number of misleading assumptions inherent in our genealogical narratives of ballet history: for example, that authorship has always been acknowledged; and that the bulk of ballet choreography originated as self-sufficient works presented at the opera house – rather than as diversions in spectacular extravaganzas, incidental ballets inlaid in operas, or popular entertainments presented in less prestigious venues. As a case in point, Garafola shows that women choreographers abounded in late nineteenth-century and early twentieth-century Paris, although their work was relegated to the Opéra-Comique (rather than the well-subsidised Palais Garnier) or to provincial opera houses, music halls, and boulevard theaters. Hence, in order to recover women's choreographic achievements on the periphery of the *danse d'école*, the dance historian must exert special efforts.

Similar patterns prevail today in the United States. In the line-up of institutional and guest choreographers for the premier American ballet companies – New York City Ballet (NYCB) and American Ballet Theatre (ABT) – one often looks in vain for female choreographers.[1] *New York Times* music and dance reporter Michael Cooper recently wrote that NYCB 'performed 58 ballets this season, including seven world premieres – and not one was by a woman'.[2] Historically, in the United States, women like Page and de Mille were excluded from the ranks of well-subsidised institutional choreographers, such as George Balanchine, Lew Christensen, and Jerome Robbins. The disparity becomes even more disturbing when one considers the crucial roles played by women in the founding of upper-echelon companies: Lucia Chase and ABT, Barbara Weisberger and the Pennsylvania Ballet, and Tatiana

Semenova and the Houston Ballet. Even where women served as grassroots founders and innovators, once the power and prestige of the established institutions came into play, men took the helm as artistic directors.

While premises that women do not have the spatiotemporal, musical, or abstract thinking abilities to be top-rank choreographers would be considered sexist today, the fact remains that few women hold positions as artistic directors of, or resident choreographers in, major ballet companies (Marshall 2010; Meglin and Brooks 2012: 2). And this is true in spite of the fact that women have constituted the vast majority of founding directors of regional ballet companies in the United States – companies they created, in connection with schools they headed, to meet the needs of their students for performance opportunities (Garafola 2005: 225). It is a familiar picture: women's handiwork, men's genius. A complex array of factors contributes to the status quo of the exclusion of women from high-profile, and well-paying, opportunities, including the adoption of corporate business models among non-profit organisations, and the existence of 'old boys' networks among ballet administrators, philanthropic organisations, company directors, and dance critics (Marshall 2010).

Recently, dance and arts writer Gia Kourlas interviewed a number of 'ballet luminaries' – male and female – on the question of the lack of female choreographers associated with major ballet companies.[3] The idea emerged more than once that ballet demands more of women than men as a result of *pointe* work and, even more importantly, the sheer number of corps and soloist roles, with women frequently performing in two or three ballets a night. Thus, the reasoning goes, women have no time to pursue choreography, as men do in their free time. One might reasonably inquire whether these workingwomen receive higher pay for more highly skilled labour or greater quantities of it. Further, do the women receive some kind of recompense for the release time they subsidise for men?

One of the obstacles to parity, I propose, in a *materialist feminist* approach,[4] is dance criticism that, in creating a canon of ballet masterworks, has historically obviated a woman's subject position. Might a reconsideration of women choreographers' ballets – in specific terms of their feminine subjectivity and potential for generic subversion – reveal some gems? Might it facilitate a more inclusive and expansive repertory that would enhance ballet's enduring legacy?

In *The Feminist Spectator as Critic*, performance studies scholar Jill Dolan explains how aesthetic canons relate to hegemonic systems of power (1988: 19–40). Through claims of a work's universality, or its ability to transcend particular historical/ material circumstances, critics construct its entry into the canon. But this very criterion, which implies 'the ability to speak to the generic spectator' (34), works to suppress alternative discourses or value systems, which emerge inevitably from the material circumstances of an individual's 'situatedness' – her class, ethnic identifications, sexual orientation, political allegiances, and so forth. Dolan quotes playwright Marsha Norman: 'The theatre says, Who lives today? Whose stories matter?' (36).

By suppressing some points of view – feminist, African American, Latino, Asian American, LGBTQ – canons can subtly communicate whose stories do not count.

Further, in mystifying the power-brokering process through which they are created, canons set up an aura of incontestability:

> From a revisionist perspective, cultural authorities have determined the canon's selection and then mystified its terms, so that this reified body of work seems to have always been in place. The invisibility of both its constructors and the origins of its construction renders the canon peculiarly (but purposefully) remote from question or attack.
> (Dolan 1988: 31)

Hence, demystifying ballet's canon, particularly how it has been established, is an important project to feminist inquiry. Ballet historian Andrea Harris argues that by mid-century, American and British critics had crowned Balanchine's 'neoclassical modernism' as the pre-eminent form of ballet in the United States, as synonymous with the Americanisation of ballet (2007: 145). She notes that, in the 1930s and early 1940s, the prototypical American ballet incorporated dramatic narratives, character studies, pantomime, and 'a stylistically hybrid movement vocabulary' in a primarily representational mode (142). The goal was to render the off-the-cuff, ingenious, and smart-alecky spirit of screen characters like Fred Astaire and Ginger Rogers in order to create a unique American art form with broad popular appeal: or so expounded Lincoln Kirstein, the impresario who brought Balanchine to America (Kirstein 1967: 45). This was a mode in which women like Page and de Mille (and men like Christensen and Robbins) could make their mark. But, as Harris argues, by the post-war period, within the context of Cold War anxieties about Soviet aggression, the spread of communism, and atomic incineration, 'common-man' characters and narratives of the people – so pervasive during the leftward-leaning 1930s – became suspect (139–55). Even as abstract expressionism achieved primacy in the art world, and neoclassicism became a stylistic pillar in music, neoclassical ballet – stripped of narrative and external referents (abstracted), pointing to the intrinsic elements of the medium and the formal manipulation of the ballet lexicon – became king. Critics identified Balanchine as neoclassicism's leading exponent, relegating other choreographic modes to the margins and their practitioners to the ranks of minor choreographers.

My own research on the Ford Foundation's grants, in 1959 and 1963, to 'professionalise' ballet suggests that technical excellence – the artistic correlate of technological advancement – reigned supreme in the post-war 'Age of Anxiety', which saw the advent of the nuclear armament build-up and the coinage of the term 'military-industrial complex'.[5] While Harris points out the parallels between the 'time-space compression' of Fordism (the Ford Motor Company's model of mass production) and Balanchine's style (151), the connections between these institutions go far beyond aesthetic ones alone. The Ford Foundation's huge subsidies of the New York City Ballet, its affiliated School of American Ballet, and satellite Balanchine companies like the Pennsylvania Ballet legitimated, crystallised, and underwrote the process of canonisation of neoclassicism over the next decade.

* * * * *

This essay addresses the question of how, given such obstacles, the dance historian can locate a woman's distinct subject position, or subjectivity, in a particular ballet. Using the case study of Ruth Page, a Chicago choreographer and artistic director who was prolific in the period 1926–1971, I closely read two ballets: *An American Pattern* and *Frankie and Johnny*, co-choreographed by Page and her dancing partner Bentley Stone in 1937 and 1938, respectively. Not only do these ballets stem from a woman's subjectivity, I argue, but also, through their *generic subversion*, they exhibit a core principle of twentieth-century modernism.[6] By the end of this essay, I shall arrive at a proposition for what generic subversion might encompass in ballet. For now, let us assume that, when a work tests and crosses the boundaries of its implicit genre by incorporating lexicons and generative structures from other genres, it practices generic subversion.[7] My purpose is to explore how widening the canon with the paradigm of feminine subjectivity could, ultimately, expand the relevance of ballet as an art form.

In my long-term research project on Ruth Page, I have discovered two potent means to excavate a woman's subjectivity. The first involves intertextual analysis of performance texts vis-à-vis literary texts that the choreographer has adapted, used in spoken or musical scores, or alluded to indirectly. Comparisons across texts may focus on performed personae; poetic imagery, irony, and rhythms; or narrative and thematic material related to women's situation in the twentieth century.

For example, during World War II, Page created an innovative concert vehicle in which she performed an entire programme of 'danced poems'.[8] Instead of dancing to recordings of the poems or to someone else's live recitation, she intoned the words herself as she danced. In other words, she experimented with the embodied connection between speaking and moving, as she self-accompanied her movements with a verbal sound score. Not only did this hybrid performance form subvert stereotypes of lack of intelligence in women, or their reduction to mindless bodies, but also it declared that poetry was within women's professional grasp, and that dancing, like poetry, was high art.

What is more, in each instance, Page inscribed her voice as a woman into the poem. For example, Federico García Lorca's *Lament for Ignacio Sánchez Mejías* is clearly an elegy written by a male poet for a male bullfighter. But Page feminised the poem's subjectivity by changing the gender and dramatic role of the enunciator's voice to that of a bereft lover or widow. Addressed to audiences largely composed of women – wartime women, at that, who had known or feared loss and grief – this approach personalised the poem and made its rhythms and imagery transparent and visceral.

More importantly, Page highlighted feminine subjectivity through her choice of poems written by Dorothy Parker and Edna St. Vincent Millay. Well known for 'her witty satires on the American Girl',[9] Parker's stories and poems were intimate, acerbically witty, and full of modern feminine satire. Literary critic and feminist theorist Regina Barreca encapsulates Parker's agenda: 'Her business was to make fun of the ideal, whatever it was, and [to] trace the split between the vision of a woman's life as put forth by the social script and the way real women lived real lives' (1995: xii). Rendering Parker's poems 'A Fairly Sad Tale', 'Inventory', and 'Unfortunate Coincidence', Page physicalised the changeable moods and dissonant rhythms, the non sequitur, the exaggerated impulses, the irony and self-satire.

In this solo program, Page also performed a number of poems appealing to a child's-eye view, such as e. e. cummings's 'hist whist'. Carried along by alliteration, internal rhyme, onomatopoeia, and exclamation, this poem seems to delight in its very sound-making capacity, much like children. Such unconventional subject matter for a solo concert touring programme spoke to Page's understanding of one of women's deepest wartime concerns: the well-being of children.

Yet, when Page asked *New York Times* critic John Martin, who could not attend her New York performance of the danced poems, whether the idea piqued his interest, he replied, 'yes, . . . it was possible but certainly not probable'.[10]

Page always sought new adventures of immersion in modern music, literature, and fine arts; hence, finding source texts for her ballet adaptations is not difficult. However, in some instances one must go beyond adapted texts to probe the larger milieu of literary modernism, particularly its feminist threads. Such is the case with *An American Pattern*. For this work, Page wrote, with her trusted collaborator Nicolai Remisoff, an original libretto that arguably laid the groundwork for the first feminist ballet in the United States. Moreover, she assembled a team of collaborators with diverse perspectives: Remisoff, the Russian American painter, muralist, and designer; Jerome Moross, the Jewish American composer; and Bentley Stone, the gay dancer who would go on to operate, with his life partner Walter Camryn, the famous Stone Camryn School of Ballet in Chicago.

In the first place, Page's highly collaborative process earmarked her approach to ballet making as interactional and far from domineering and hierarchical. In the second place, the distinct feminist subject matter of this ballet reflected women's concerns at the time: their disenchantment with, and alienation from, marriage and a lack of meaningful alternatives or options for women in society. It cannot be coincidental that, as we know from Susan Jones, modern women writers, such as Virginia Woolf, expressed their anxieties about women's loss of autonomy in marriage. In fact, Jones links Nijinka's 1923 ballet *Les Noces* to such feminist concerns voiced in modern British literature (2013: 117–50).

An early draft of programme notes for *American Pattern* questions the whole institution of marriage from a middle-class woman's perspective: 'Her husband, being himself satisfied with the limitations of American business success, has little meaning for her as a woman, so that in the end they are strangers. There seems to be nothing ahead for her except dull routine, to which she succumbs'.[11] In the ballet's narrative, the young woman turns from one false icon or empty ecstasy to another: sex, money, mysticism, and mob – each represented by a male power figure. Neither acquiescing to convention nor flouting it with behaviour that counters society's mores offers a solution. 'Her life is tragic because she has failed to find herself – her soul'. The woman finds neither meaningful purpose nor meaningful relationships; it is truly an existential crisis without the prospect of educational or professional growth, self-development, or transformation.[12]

The opening scene could not differ more from the wedding scene that culminates the typical marriage-plot ballet: after dancing with each of three clone-like men, the young woman 'grabs' one and 'stands motionless with him'. Her choice results in a physical freezing – an emotional numbing – symbolised by a complete absence of motion. A procession files, as if by rote, across the stage, accompanied by a 'sarcastic' wedding march, and, after the husband drops a coin into an automat, a marriage certificate appears.[13] Husband and wife move in stilted, marionette style: marriage as a *ballet mécanique*.

The 'Domestic Scene' that follows may have been the most personally terrifying to Page.[14] Enter three women in black, 'very domestically dressed', 'representing good standing [in] society, good citizens, clubwomen, etc.'.[15] As the ballet progresses, they hover in the background, stalking the heroine like the Fates. In this scene, hands clasped at diaphragms, they walk on half-toe with militaristic stiffness, before coercing the heroine to execute an endless succession of repetitive, boring, and isolated housekeeping tasks.

In the scenes that follow, the ballet theatricalises the social upheavals of the 1930s in a spectacle of class distinctions, from high-society rituals to workers' strikes and communist rallies. In the end, the conflict between 'union strikers' and 'the National Guard' scares the protagonist and, 'torn between [the Militant Idealist's] lofty ideals' and the numbing security of the housewife's conventional life, she 'succumbs to the inevitability of the American pattern'.[16] In the last few moments of the ballet, Stone, as the Militant Idealist, becomes a towering figure, held aloft by four men, while the three Matrons bring Page, as The Girl, to her knees, pinioning her arms to a horizontal, as if she were martyred to domesticity.

While leftist, agitprop dance was fairly common – at least in New York throughout the 1930s (Graff 1997) – in very few such works did a feminist perspective take precedence over a proletarian one. Leftist modern dancers saw feminist issues as subsumed by workers' issues. What was so unusual about *American Pattern* was that the woman's plight as a woman, not a stand-in for humanity, took centre stage. Moreover, the introspective tone of a woman's self-examination and complicity in the co-optation of her own freedom points to something new, something original in the ballet.

One critic praised the choreography as 'full of intriguing dance incidents and fluid in design', though he thought the scenario of the bored wife trite.[17] How the story of a wife's rebellion read as trite, particularly in the context of the American ballet, is difficult to imagine. However, women's oppression by, and escape from, marriage – a celebrated subject of European literature since the second half of the nineteenth century (cf. Flaubert's *Madame Bovary* and Ibsen's *A Doll's House*) – had been taken up with force by American novelist Sinclair Lewis in his 1920 blockbuster *Main Street* and by American journalist Sophie Treadwell in her 1928 play *Machinal*. A biting satire of American conservatism, conformity, self-complacency, provincialism, and xenophobia, *Main Street* follows its heroine, Carol Kennicott, '[determined] to be class-conscious without discovering the class of which she was to be conscious' (Lewis 1992: 285), through various attempts to cure her malaise, including flirtations with cultural uplift, 'parlour socialism', and employment in the nation's capital. Ultimately, she returns to her husband and succumbs to domesticity in Gopher Prairie.

Supported by an avant-garde sound score of machine noise and dramatised in the Expressionist style, *Machinal* evokes the coercive, mechanised structures of patriarchal society that subjugate women at work; in marriage, childbirth, and the legal system; and through the unresponsive ritual-speak of religion. The feminine subject presents herself as an exile in this world, with its oppressive institutions, automaton-like people, and clichéd, repetitive language. Comparisons of *American Pattern* and feminist works like *Main Street* and *Machinal* yield much to ponder. But the great originality of *American Pattern* lay precisely in the adaptation of these women-centred political issues to the rarefied medium of ballet.

Thus, intertextual analysis can illuminate the ballet's store of meaning glossed over by dismissive critics. But an equally potent mode of locating a woman's subjectivity or distinct subject position seeks answers in historically situated feminisms. Hence, I turn to Simone de Beauvoir's *The Second Sex*, that masterpiece of phenomenological-existential analysis of what it means to be a woman, written within ten or eleven years of Page's feminist ballet and published in 1949. De Beauvoir begins with a premise from the perspective of 'existentialist ethics': life's meaning issues from the human subject's 'undefined need to transcend [herself]' – to seek liberty; to make difficult choices; and 'to engage in freely chosen projects' (Beauvoir 1989: xl–xli). Abdicating this central task of the self in order to avoid the anxiety inherent in freedom represents 'bad faith' (655 fn.). According to de Beauvoir, woman's predicament arises from the contradictions and conflict inherent in being a subject, who, by definition, strives towards a self that is essential – an agent of action, the centre of a life – and the situation that society structures for a woman as an inessential, peripheral Other (xli).

In the chapter 'The Woman in Love', de Beauvoir argues that a woman structures her life *pour-autrui* (in relation to others) as opposed to *pour-soi* (in relation to herself) (1989: 668). By submerging her identity in that of an essential male subject and failing to attain her own subjectivity, a woman 'creates a [dependent] hell for herself' (654). Placing *American Pattern* against the backdrop of de Beauvoir's mid-century inquiry into woman's second-class status and her thwarted subjectivity permits us to consider the ballet's deeply feminist message. The American pattern is The Girl's acceptance of a subsidiary, vicarious existence: a pro forma marriage; mystical and sexual encounters in search of self-worth; an embrace of the sociopolitical causes of a dominant male rather than the invention of her own commitments. Although the critique of women's choices seems harsh in both the philosophical tract and the ballet narrative, ultimately, such critique is empowering because it implies that the means of change lies in women's hands: women must become the transformative inventors of themselves, the active agents in their lives. This is the 'soul' that eludes The Girl.

Of course, the ability to read the ballet in such a manner would require critics to have some knowledge of women's studies, cultural studies, or at least modernist literature with feminist overtones. While such an expectation may at first seem unreasonable, one quickly thinks of how cultural knowledge presents the key to unlocking understanding in critical assessments of non-Western dance forms. The real question is, why should a rigorous standard of cosmopolitanism, and a willingness to research different modes and circumstances of creation (inevitably situated in time, place, gender constructs, and culture), *not* be required of critics who review works in major metropolitan areas?

In spite of her ballet about an unrealised life, a contingent self, a soul that buds without blossoming, Ruth Page led a remarkable life, creating scores of ballets for her own and other companies, including the Federal Theatre Project, the Ballet Russe de Monte Carlo, Les Ballets des Champs-Élysées, the London Festival Ballet, and the Chicago Opera Ballet.[18] Moreover, from the beginning to the end of her choreographic career, she explored various forms of generic subversion to challenge narrow boundaries in ballet. Her first substantial choreography, *The Flapper and the Quarterback* (1926), incorporated movements from the Charleston and other African American vernacular dances; her ballet *La Guiablesse* (1933) featured a whole troupe of African American dancers, including a young Katherine Dunham; and *Americans in Paris* (1936), choreographed to George Gershwin's tone poem, spotlighted four African American tap steppers.

During the same decade, Page crossed boundaries of genre, gender, and geopolitics in a four-year touring partnership with German Expressionist dancer Harald Kreutzberg, embracing modern dance practices and manner of performance (Meglin 2009: 52–75). Garafola posits that 'contact with "modern" forms of movement', such as eurhythmics, 'Greek' dancing, and Central European dance, stimulated women like Rambert, de Valois, and Nijinska to choreograph. Outside the ballet establishment, in the marginalised spaces of modern dance and the avant-garde, not only did women act as innovators but also they placed 'a premium on dance making' (Garafola 2005: 223). Such a milieu served as an incubator in which women could develop their craft as choreographers. It is hardly a coincidence that many of the American women whose works *did* eventually make it into the repertories of major ballet companies spent their formative years in the modern dance world: Valerie Bettis, Twyla Tharp, Lucinda Childs, and Trisha Brown.

Page and Stone's ballet *Frankie and Johnny* provides a third example of generic subversion that went hand in hand with a woman's subjectivity. In this case, the innovations derived from source material originating in African American culture: a ballad about life in the red-light district of St. Louis that had become an American icon. While Page did not employ African American dancers as she had done in her earlier ballets, she did import signs of African American's culture in an unusual way. First of all, the ballet dealt with street characters, street culture, and street style. Secondly, the intermingling of jazz, tap, and modern dance idioms in *Frankie* contested its very framing as a ballet. The main characters embodied a 'cool' counterculture – one that satirised the sanctimony of Main Street, White, reformist culture.[19] Similarly, Moross incorporated into his ballet score African American musical forms, such as a stomp, the blues, two rags, a foxtrot, and a one-step.

A description of Frankie's solo when she discovers Johnny's infidelity with Nellie Bly shows the extent to which Page mixed incongruous vocabularies to experiment with genre.[20] Frankie (Page) makes a series of modern, molten shapes and strikes everything at hand; her dance is almost flamenco in its arching *renversés* and body percussion. She hangs her back over the railing, slaps the banister with her hands, beats the ground with her feet. She suspends, arched backwards on one leg, then falls, and, pinioned to the ground by that same leg, stamps in deep lunges with the other. Her fists beat her thighs and she develops the jazz motif called 'The Itch' into a percussive cadenza of angst.[21] Finally, she rolls across the stage until her body wraps around the lamp post. Her mind made up, she runs in the direction of Nellie's room and drops into a *bourrée* on the knees; lumbers up the stairs on hands and feet and pounds on the door. It is Martha Graham without the abstraction – a histrionic use of literal gesture and popular motif, delivered with seriocomic intent.

Frankie the ballet was as ingenious as the ballad in its compact narration of a story of love, infidelity, and murderous rage with an ironic twist: a woman emerges not as a victim but as the hand of poetic justice. The reversal of the usual state of affairs – the punishment of a pimp rather than the women he exploits – also contributed to the sense of fair play.

Viewing the production of *Frankie* mounted on the Ballet Russe de Monte Carlo, Martin pronounced it 'the best ballet of the [1944–1945 New York] season', with its racy theatricality and break from the 'set formulas' of ballet (1945: 44). Later, he crystallised the ballet's tragicomic import: 'it captures completely the raucous, grotesque, but basically tragic quality of the true ballad. It convinces you of its human truth even while you are chortling at its crude and uninhibited sentimentalities'. And he dubbed it 'one of the most genuine and perceptive pieces of Americana that the ballet repertoire has yet achieved' (1947: 16). The *New York Times* critic's accolades are impressive, coming after the successes of Eugene Loring's *Billy the Kid*

(1938), de Mille's *Rodeo* (1942), and Robbins's *Fancy Free* (1944). But Martin's assessment was by no means universal. *New York Herald Tribune* critic Edwin Denby found the protagonists' duet mere 'high school "necking"' and the group dances just so much 'milling about the stage' (1968: 103). Once again, the paradigm of feminine subjectivity and generic subversion can help critics, scholars, and dance aficionados to evaluate the ballet in a more informed manner.

Throughout her lifetime, Page pursued transformative experiences, chiefly in the form of artistic collaborations with composers, such as Moross, William Grant Still, Aaron Copland, and Darius Milhaud; visual artists, including Isamu Noguchi, Pavel Tchelitchew, and Antoni Clavé; and dance partners, like Kreutzberg and Stone. She continued to explore innovative formats, adapting opera into ballet and depicting complex women like Azucena, Carmen, Sonia, and Camille. One of her last choreographies, *Alice in the Garden* (1970), bent gender mercilessly. The Chicago ballerina took ballet class well into her eighties.

For a complex set of reasons, some of which have been outlined here, Page's choreographies were never enshrined in a ballet company that outlived her and kept her repertory alive. 'Most choreographers seem to think that your voice leaves you once you get into toe shoes', she quipped about the typical separation between voice and body in ballet (Page 1978: 108). On another level, one can read into this statement – as well as the extent of her choreographic output – Page's refusal to subscribe to the stereotype of the ballerina's muted voice and dampened authority. Moreover, when a female choreographer writes her own ballet librettos and programme notes; when she documents her dances meticulously in scrapbook, film, and notebook; when she crafts essays revealing her opinions, observations from the field, and personal reminiscences; and further, when she makes all this and more accessible to forthcoming generations of researchers, she leaves the traces of her unique voice and situated subjectivity for the dance historian to retrieve.

Precisely because women's work has been relegated to the margins of the *danse d'école* and institutionalised dance, women hold a stake in generic subversion. These subversions may take the form of inter-medial or mixed-media interventions, narrative aberrations and anomalies, intercultural experiments, infusions of popular culture, displacements and distortions of the ballet lexicon, whatever you can imagine to upend and refurbish ballet as a living art form that ought to emerge from diverse and varied perspectives and situations. As de Beauvoir knew, what prevents a woman from developing a transcendent self is not her essence but rather the lack of parity in education, opportunities, and expectations. A word to the wise . . .

Notes

1   For example, see '2015–2016 Season New York City Ballet' [brochure]; and 'American Ballet Theatre: 2016 Spring Season, Metropolitan Opera House' [brochure].

2   Michael Cooper, 'Breaking the Glass Slipper', *New York Times*, June 26, 2016, AR 1, 12.
3   Gia Kourlas, 'Weighing in on a Conspicuous Absence', *New York Times*, June 26, 2016, AR, 13.
4   For an explanation of materialist feminism, see Dolan (1988).
5   'Grants-in-Aid Program for Young Ballet Dancers', Sept. 11, 1959, Folder 'Ballet Society, Inc. – General, 1958–1962', Box 43, Series XIII: Program files, Educational and Public Policy Program, Office of the Arts, FA640, Ford Foundation records, Rockefeller Archive Center; and 'Grant Request: Humanities and the Arts', Nov. 14, 1963, Folder 'Ballet Development Program Background, 1962–1963', ibid. President Dwight D. Eisenhower coined the term 'military-industrial complex', delivered with a cautionary tone, in his farewell address to the nation in 1961.
6   On generic subversion and modernism, see Susan Jones (2013) and Carol J. Oja (2000).
7   Various framing conventions and/or the venue in which a work appears communicate an implicit genre.
8   For a thorough study of Page's danced poems, see Meglin (2012: 22–56).
9   'Eau Claire State Teachers College Presents Ruth Page' [program], Jan. 31, 1944, Ruth Page Scrapbooks – 10, Jerome Robbins Dance Division, New York Public Library of the Performing Arts (hereafter, NYPL–PA).
10 Ruth Page to Marian Heinley Page, April 7 and 16, 1943, and undated [1943], Folder 43C3, Ruth Page Collection (hereafter, RPC), NYPL–PA.
11 Early drafts of programme notes for the ballet, originally titled 'An American Woman', indicate Page and Remisoff as co-authors of the scenario. 'An American Pattern', P25 [Programme notes, 1936–37], RPC.
12 For a full analysis of this ballet in the context of Ruth Page's life and work, see Meglin (forthcoming).
13 Ruth Page, M30 [Manuscript scenario for *An American Pattern*], RPC. A streaming video of a 1938 performance of *An American Pattern* is available online at the Chicago Film Archives website, www.chicagofilmarchives.org/collections/index.php/Detail/Object/Show/object_id/8680.
14 Ruth Page, N13 [Notebook 1937], RPC.
15 Page, M30.
16 Page, M30.
17 Robert Pollak, 'Josephine La Placa Bows in "Rigoletto"', undated clipping, Ruth Page Scrapbooks – 8, NYPL–PA.
18 For a biographical essay on Page's career and life, see Joellen A. Meglin, 'Ruth Page: Early Architect of the American Ballet', Dance Heritage Coalition, *America's Irreplaceable Dance Treasures: The First 113* [online exhibit], 'Ruth Page' www.danceheritage.org/page.html (accessed June 2, 2016).
19 For a full analysis and history of this ballet, see Meglin (forthcoming).

20 Online access to *Frankie and Johnny* [1938, Chicago, Great Northern Theatre production] is available at the Chicago Film Archives website: www.chicagofilmarchives.org/collections/index.php/Detail/Object/Show/object_id/8709.
21 Two African American dancers performing 'The Itch' can be seen on King Vidor, *Hallelujah* [DVD], Metro-Goldwyn-Mayer, 1929.

Bibliography

Alterowitz, Gretchen (2014) 'Embodying a Queer Worldview: The Contemporary Ballets of Katy Pyle and Deborah Lohse', *Dance Chronicle*, 37:3, 335–366.
Barreca, Regina (1995) 'Introduction', in Colleen Breese, ed., *Dorothy Parker: Complete Stories*, New York: Penguin Books, vii–xix.
Beauvoir, Simone de (French ed. 1949; 1953; 1989) *The Second Sex*, trans. and ed. Howard M. Parshley, New York: Vintage Books.
Denby, Edwin (1968) 'Frankie and Johnny, an Indecent Ballet?' (March 4, 1945), in *Looking at the Dance*, New York: Popular Library, 103–105.
Dolan, Jill (1988) *The Feminist Spectator as Critic*, Ann Arbor, MI: UMI Research Press.
Garafola, Lynn (2005) 'Where Are Ballet's Women Choreographers?', in *Legacies of Twentieth-Century Dance*, Middletown, CT: Wesleyan University Press, 215–228.
Graff, Ellen (1997) *Stepping Left: Dance and Politics in New York City, 1928–1942*, Durham, NC: Duke University Press.
Harris, Andrea (2007) 'Choreographing America: Redefining American Ballet in the Age of Consensus', in William W. Demastes and Iris Smith Fischer, eds., *Interrogating America through Theatre and Performance*, New York: Palgrave Macmillan 139–155.
Heil, Johanna (2016) 'Exercises in Discipline and Freedom? The Graham Technique', *Dance Chronicle*, 39:2, 123–152.
Jones, Susan (2013) *Literature, Modernism, and Dance*, Oxford: Oxford University Press.
Kirstein, Lincoln (1967) 'Blast at Ballet: A Corrective for the American Audience [1938]', in *Three Pamphlets Collected*, Brooklyn: Dance Horizon, 1–128.
Lewis, Sinclair (1992) *Main Street & Babbitt*, New York: The Library of America.
Marshall, Lea (2010) 'Ballet Is Woman? Not in the Artistic Director's Office', *Dance Magazine*, May 4, www.dancemagazine.com/blogs/guest-blog/3349 (accessed Dec. 7, 2011).
Martin, John (1945) 'The Dance Annual Award', *New York Times*, Aug. 5, p. 44.
Martin, John (1947) '"Frankie, Johnny" Leads Dance Bill', *New York Times*, Feb. 21, p. 16.

Meglin, Joellen A. (2009) 'Blurring the Boundaries of Genre, Gender, and Geopolitics: Ruth Page and Harald Kreutzberg's Transatlantic Collaboration in the 1930s', *Dance Research Journal*, 41:2, 52–75.

Meglin, Joellen A. (2012) 'Victory Garden: Ruth Page's Danced Poems in the Time of World War II', *Dance Research: The Journal of the Society for Dance Research*, 30:1, 22–56.

Meglin, Joellen A. (forthcoming) *Ruth Page: The Woman in the Work*, New York: Oxford University Press.

Meglin, Joellen A. and Lynn Matluck Brooks (2012) 'Where Are All the Women Choreographers in Ballet?', *Dance Chronicle,* 35:1, 1–7.

Oja, Carol J. (2000) *Making Music Modern: New York in the 1920s*, New York: Oxford University Press.

Page, Ruth (1978) 'The Use of the Speaking Voice with Dance Movement', speech given at Jacob's Pillow, Aug. 16, 1948, rpt. in Ruth Page, *Page by Page*, ed. Andrew Mark Wentink, Brooklyn: Dance Horizons.

Chapter 18

Extensions
Alonzo King and Ballet's LINES

JILL NUNES JENSEN

MY RESEARCH ON SAN FRANCISCO choreographer Alonzo King and his company, Alonzo King LINES Ballet (AKLB), began just into the twenty-first century. At that time, dance studies did not appear to offer much hope for the ballerina's subjectivity, or the confidence that ballet had the ability to do away with tired mores from its history and still maintain a distinguishable identity. Although it seemed somewhat common to view interventions in gender patterns in the creations of choreographers working for European ballet companies – for instance Nacho Duato, Mats Ek, William Forsythe, and Jiří Kylián – when it came to the US ballet scene, new approaches to partnerships were not as easily locatable. In spite of this, I clung to the belief that there must be choreography within the US ballet idiom that presented an alternative for the ballerina and possibility for the form. Unconvinced that the female had no option but to dance her own objectification vis-à-vis the genre's hierarchical paradigm, I came to view King's work as affording a possible rewrite to the narrative described earlier.

What made King's ballets unique in my eyes had little to do with racial and ethnic diversity, even though these were the reasons that began to earn his work critical response; rather my interest stemmed from the dancers' constant movement and distinctive interactions.[1] The agility and flexibility demonstrated by the company undoubtedly privileged technique but not in the same vein as many have come to conjure with the use of such terminology in the ballet world. In place of defined shapes there was a suspension of fear and assumption of risk as dancers defied fundamental ballet vocabulary and token heterogeneous partnerships. As a consequence, his choreography was forging a new aesthetic, one that would present moving bodies with little regard for fixed notions of gender. Decades later his dances continue to look distinct; this is arguably due in large part to the development and performance of non-dyadic relationships within a genre that has for centuries upheld beliefs to the contrary. By choreographing movements that do not have particular and specific attachments to dancers through the created categories of masculine and feminine, King has contributed to the changing course of ballet.

The following pages suggest a model for the inculcation of non-normative gender roles in ballet. This would tactically allow ballet dancers, both male and female, the potential to escape archetypes and assist in engendering contemporary choreographies. As many in the new millennium have questioned ballet's relevancy and sustainability, dance theorists have been tasked to provide tangible examples of rejuvenating material within the form. Recognizing the limits bifurcated gender dynamics uphold in ballet, this essay centralizes a methodology of choreographing movement to challenge such divides. King's work is relied on as exemplar here, not because the vocabulary used is drastically different from his artistic colleagues, but because of how the women and men of his company receive, internalize and dance those movements. His aesthetic teeters between new and old as it replicates balletic positions known for centuries, yet it does so with rearticulated attention towards spirituality and gender. The philosophy undergirding (the) movement takes precedence, making the work new and likewise setting it apart from many who have actively embraced a similar vocabulary since the late twentieth century.

As an African American choreographer working on the West Coast, King has consistently met ballet's discriminating heritage head on – he learned this from his parents and family, who were instrumental leaders in the civil rights movement. Claiming his first forays into both dance and choreography came from time spent moving alone to music rather than the structured classes he would come to participate in, it is clear his influences are many. As a result, King repeatedly questions the term 'ballet' and substitutes 'Western Classical Dance' in its place. In doing so he affirms the belief that even with ballet's hierarchical heritage, the vocabulary still has the capacity for effective communication. King's approach to choreography encourages the audience to reflect rather than simply observe. He has regularly found productivity in the process of collaboration and has built a career working with a variety of artists for whom ballet is not their primary method of investigation. The repertoire taken as a whole confirms that King asks dancers to extend their reach as performers in order to show qualities typically masked in ballet. In a King piece, much like the foundational philosophies of modern dance in the United States, choreography is inextricably linked to meaning rather than superficial effect and the priority of the dancer is to be open and honest while being precise and placed. This is a crucial distinction, for King is not devaluing technique for a separate notion of artistry. As an alternative he is asking his dancers to find their art in ballet based movement. In addition though there is rarely discussion of the choreographic or performative experience as being a spiritual one, that is undoubtedly present for the dancers of this company and their audiences. The search for choreography that manifests 'truth' and 'light' is part of King's purpose that he passes along to the dancers. This ultimately yields ballets rooted in concepts of spirituality, and reveals reimagined male/female gender roles that disregard a history of parsed-out functions for men and women.[2]

A close American contemporary of King would be William Forsythe. King is, too, a theorist – one who is keenly aware of movement – but his ballets have a syncretic[3] underpinning that is not brought up in current critiques of Forsythe.[4] King's is a small chamber-sized company that operates more in line with non-balletic troupes in the United States: no ranks, a director who values contribution, and a belief that the dancers will strive to display perfection albeit construed in another way. He demands exactness but it is not via the faultless demonstration of recognizable tricks; on the contrary it is an ideal state wherein clarity and communication are crucial. This interplay is fundamental to King and his company's history; many who see the dances believe there is a great deal of improvisation – due to the lack of unison/synchronicity among the ensemble and the extreme quickness with which they move – yet this is another way by which his approach to choreography is marked as distinct.

The refutation of inessential material is visually demonstrated by the company's costuming – often leotards and bare legs for the women and briefs with sheer tunics or skirts for the men. The outfits worn by the dancers problematize dyadic understanding, as the women retain aspects of the gendered attire of the ballerina – namely leotards and pointe shoes – while the men seem to embrace androgyny.[5] What this does is create the occasion for men to dance with greater latitude, absent 'masculine' and 'feminine' epitomes. In concurrent fashion, the women are emboldened by the physical reach afforded by pointe shoes and the lack of encumbering clothing. The costuming effectively helps viewers see beyond the conformity that gender suggests and to watch ballets that do not adhere to identity tropes. The company programming reinforces this as many ballets choreographed do not utilize pointe shoes for the ballerinas (and if they do, they are usually juxtaposed with a flat shoe piece on the same bill). Still, technical prowess aside, there is something that keeps conventional ballet-goers from seeing and supporting what King does wholeheartedly. Likely it is the fact that these gender dichotomies, and the stories and characterizations they suggest, are so significantly embedded in the cultural landscape it is a challenge for viewers to see that orthodoxy so thoroughly dispensed with on stage.

My primary research goal included an effort to make sense of the marginalization of this company and the subtext behind critical descriptions oftentimes labelling King's work as nebulous and the dancers as everything from diverse or muscular to 'creaturesque' (a term used in conversation with company member Courtney Henry as we spoke about the history of audiences misinterpreting King's aesthetic). This led to what has become a long-time investigation into the historiography of King's work and how his ballets, I argue, continue to mark a point of divergence from the milieu that many in the United States are dubbing 'contemporary ballet'.[6] Seemingly rooted in semantic contradiction, even the name LINES complicates preconceived ideas of form. King surely does not use LINES to obfuscate, nor did he name his company as a nod to ballet's privileging of alignment; instead the term references infinity, mathematical concepts of continuity, and nature's horizon, which appears to anchor the sky to Earth below. The following quote, authored by King, explains these ideas and appears on the AKLB website. When asked about the genesis of the company's name during various talk-backs or pre-performance lectures, he regularly offers some part of the following in response:

> The term LINES alludes to all that is visible in the phenomenal world. There is nothing that is made or formed without a line. Straight and Circle encompass all that we see. Whatever can be seen is formed by a line. In mathematics it is a straight or curved continuous extent of length without breadth. Lines are in our fingerprints, the shapes of our bodies, constellations, geometry. It implies genealogical connection, progeny and spoken word. It marks the starting point and finish. It addresses direction, communication, and design. A line of thought. A boundary or eternity. A melodic line. The equator. From vibration or dot to dot it is the visible organization of what we see.

Taking this 'definition' as source for King's creations, it clarifies his intimate concern to find points of connection. Despite the sense of abstraction in his words, many of King's ballets do have narrative threads – it is simply that the characterizations generally found in the narratives do not rest comfortably with the masculine/feminine divide. In other words, King does not look for a woman to be the soft counterpart to a sturdy male; instead he seeks out dancers with the facility to extend their reach past personalities and styles in order to dance in ways that might be unfamiliar – especially after years of disciplined training in a system resolutely based in adhering to the bifurcation of gender. Hence, the AKLB dancers are tasked with disavowing such sensibilities that to King's chagrin many be deemed part of ballet.

The lines metaphor works for King on many levels; the usage affords the opportunity to pay homage to what has come before, all the while suggesting endless forward movement. His observation that a line can be a circle illustrates the perceptual shifts the choreography urges us to make while watching his ballets. Is it really a drag if a dancer is being pulled across the floor with legs separated as if he or she were on the way down to the splits, or might it be that the dancer is being lifted in another plane? How can a movement during which one dancer is pushing another down to the ground actually convey strength for the dancer on the floor? Is a solo ever really an independent act, or might it more appropriately be understood as a *pas de deux* between the dancer and another part of his or her self, the interaction with the audience, or a higher presence? Such lines of inquiry highlight how King's interest in reconfiguration have proved seminal in the process of developing work and harnessing the specificity he feels ballet needs in order to convey ideas. Lines, although subject to reorientation, are defined, meticulous, careful, and ordered. King's ballets correspond to this philosophy, as he takes such qualities (key components of the ballet vocabulary) and finds within them emotion, fluidity, fragility, and uninhibitedness. Speaking to this process, he shared in a science-based publication, 'Everything that exists is governed by laws. Too often people think art is the realm of whim and self-expression. While in actuality, art makers are fanatically obsessed with accuracy in form, idea, statement, and feeling' (Ferguson 2015: 40). Subsequently, the choreographies do not follow a singular linear narrative, but they do rely on perceptions of what lines aspire to as the momentum to navigate a less structured course.

If one were to trace the history of AKLB traditionally there are clear markers where King's interest in various dynamisms seemed heightened and was noticeable from a choreographic standpoint. From the company's inception, he has consistently dealt with issues that can be theorized in relation to gender, and over time the repertoire has spoken to that in various ways. King began his company in 1982 in San Francisco – a US city in which many choreographers find themselves able to sustain a livelihood in the arts. At first it was an all-female contingent; shifts have led to a near even split among female and male dancers in the ensemble nowadays. They have two regular seasons in San Francisco, but find the majority of their tours booked abroad in France and other Western European countries. In the course of its now thirty-plus-year existence, King has produced a body of work that highlights collaboration as he remains the sole choreographic voice (with a handful of exceptions over the years, and of those few the choreographers mostly had some current or past affiliation with the company). He has created ballets that pair his dancers with Shaolin monks, Kyoto players, the Bayaka from the Central African Republic, tabla masters, such as frequent collaborator Zakir Hussain, jazz greats, such as Jason Moran, well-known vocalists, like Lisa Fischer, and Bach concertos. In each of these ballets King did not just make steps, but tasked the dancers with delivering thoughts through the medium of dance. For this reason, gender as commonly understood had to be disregarded for a more nuanced consideration. From the very beginning discussions surrounding this company have time and again referenced diversity. This is often meant in connection to King's non-Western musical selections (the 'othering' of identity previously mentioned); however, it is made visible through his philosophical comprehension of ballet as a practice with the capacity to show and elicit innovative methodologies about gender.

In previous essays I have considered how King mined 'masculine' or 'feminine' energies, regardless of the biological sexes of the dancers, as certain bodies yielded such investigations (Nunes Jensen 2009). Over time there has been a shift in how King's ballets might be read, with greater emphasis on equanimity – thereby prompting the re-articulation of gender models herein. King and his dancers have been working past the masculine/feminine dyad for decades, as seen in early ballets like *Stealing Light* (1986), during which man and woman dance together seeking spiritual rather than romantic connection, and *Lila* (1989), wherein the ballerinas walk in a crab-like crouch *en pointe*, demonstrating strength. Later came ballets like *Migration* (2006) and *Dust and Light* (2009), in which the dancers, regardless of gender, play to qualities of both power and grace. These examples show how what years ago might have been understood as taking on the characteristics of the opposite sex is now rearticulated through a contemporary lens that recognizes the artificiality of such logic.

With a cue from theorists who seek to engage worn-out categories of masculinity and femininity in pioneering ways, here I analogously ask what a more nuanced approach to gender and dancing bodies might offer towards understanding the choreographic methodologies behind this ballet company. Is it possible for ballet bodies not to mimic sociological presumptions of difference and still keep the form largely intact? How might elements such as the *pas de deux* be reimagined to suit themes outside of the storybooks? How do King's dances rework ballet technique to circumvent gender archetypes and where does that locate AKLB in dance history?

Because King does not use narratives, casting, costuming, or choreography in accordance with masculine/feminine oppositional categories, I first began to see how he originated roles for dancers as they related to internalized understandings of self. So it was never about masculinity and femininity proper in as much as it was about what energy he sought to mine and through which body he might nurture that idea. Company alumna Katherine Warner shared with me, 'When working with Alonzo, as work was being developed, I felt as if I was doing my own work – rather than putting on movement given by choreographers. I was so inspired by the concepts we were working with, that it felt as if the work was just me' (Nunes Jensen 2009: 136). Warner's sentiments are a hallmark of dancers who have worked for King as she conveys how his process has centralized concepts and ideas over gendered roles. King's is a world wherein ballet vocabulary is celebrated while its gender mores are undone. As Warner's quote attests, he seeks to cultivate movement through the dancers instead of asking them to play certain parts. This process yields ballets within which each dancer feels his or her individual sense of self can more fully develop sans the pressure to enact male or femaleness.

Along these lines, current company member Courtney Henry shared with me, 'Ballerina is not who I am anymore' during a phone conversation in 2016. Henry did not have to elaborate upon the statement or intention behind it; it is something I have heard a number of times from the ranks of King's company as the organization has for years enticed ballerinas and danseurs with gorgeous lines only to push them miles beyond neoclassicism and into King's philosophically minded dance of why and how movement can mean. Those who do ballet for King might initially be drawn to the way his dancers move irrespective of gendered norms, but quickly realize he sees the form as a way to create an open space for thought over any codified vocabulary or rigid personifications of man or woman. For this reason, they often avoid the ballet classifications 'ballerina' and 'danseur' that evoke both gender and status, in favour of the broader term 'artist'.

King's treatment of gender fosters engagement with contemporary scholars, like Judith Kegan Gardiner, who contends most theorists today 'question older binaries that now seem simplistic and potentially distorting and exclusionary – for example, the binaries that divide men and women, masculine and feminine, heterosexual and homosexual, white and black, individual and society, structure and agency' (2002: 12). Gardiner posits that other categorizations, such as age, have fecund potentiality when it comes to reassessing how gender is conceived. Citing a paragraph from bell hooks's *Killing Rage* as an epigram to her chapter, in which hooks suggests that parenting is about teaching 'both females and males the capacity to be wholistic [sic], to be capable of being both strong and weak, active and passive', Gardiner puts forth the idea that age relates to gender (hooks in Gardiner 2002: 90). Maintaining that her position is markedly different from hooks's in that the latter contends there is a relationship between 'biology' and the 'inevitable' aging of a boy into a man and a girl into a woman that she feels is problematic in its attempt to reduce complexity for a broader unification, Gardiner agrees that feminist theory can be served from studies of 'age categories' as 'analogies for non-polarized ways of conceptualizing gender' so that gender might be 'understood developmentally in terms of change over the life course and in history rather than in terms of a static and binary opposition between masculine and feminine' (91).

Following Gardiner and hooks, who seek substitute means by which to view gender, such as age or maturation, I put forth the notion that an acute awareness of movement can also lead to a more nuanced perspective if ballet choreographers are willing to accept the responsibility of working in a different manner. The AKLB dancers have the leeway to reconceive masculinity and femininity as beyond notions of either – ideas that are entrenched sociologically and within the context of ballet writ large – because the choreography they dance does not fit neatly within the form's limits. This postulation progresses earlier research in which I discussed the very clear relationship between masculinity and femininity in King's work as being evident even if altered (Nunes Jensen 2009).

King's philosophy of ballet eschews gendered typecasting. This does not indicate an extreme point of departure from other ballet choreographers in the twenty-first century (or even some working in the late twentieth century). Nor does the fact that aesthetically his company presents tall dancers with an unmistakable dexterity, allowing them to move freely between parallel and turned-out positions, fixed and fluid arms, *demi-pointe* and deliberate flexed feet, and to execute lifts interspersed with drags, tows, and slides. What does set his work apart is that the dancers accept the charge to be vulnerable to new circumstances, to absorb the beauty in a very different conveyance of virtuosity, and to identify themselves as part of a larger entity that is simultaneously marked by gender and capable of rejecting the inadequacies inherent in stereotypical classifications of humankind.

In April 2015 LINES premiered *Biophony*, a piece that would illuminate these ideas of moving irrespective of traditional gender constructions. Although the treatment of gender in this ballet is not radically altered from King's other choreographies, I focus on this piece here as it provides a chance to re-channel previous ideas about masculinity and femininity into a collective voice. When one watches *Biophony* (and the piece toured widely) the score and patterns of danced movement create an undistinguishable world. There are sounds that certainly emanate from animals, but which? Likewise, the dancers move in ways that could be read as citing an awkward bird wing or strut and yet they balance carefully so as never to be in danger of falling into cliché, imitation, or rendering themselves as objectifications. King spoke to this point in a 2015 interview with *SciArt in America*, explaining, 'Your aim is not to "imitate" the look of nature or mimic its appearance, but to locate its essence and manner of operation. To mimic it would be the failed portrait' (Ferguson 2015: 40).

The ballet stemmed quite uniquely from field recordings collected by bio-acoustician Bernie Krause, and with score by Richard Blackford. Dancer Courtney Henry remembers how Krause initially explained to the dancers that there was 'this incredible orchestra that is already there' and 'how each layer of the food chain of evolution has a clear channel they have to get through to be heard, to communicate' so 'each animal has their own frequency' (interview with author). This revelation, as it felt to Henry, not only was a way to understand how animals might retain audibility within the soundscape of nature, but also directly speaks to how the AKLB dancing bodies move to varying frequencies.[7] Writes Krause in his book, *The Great Animal Orchestra*,

> The planet itself teems with a vigorous resonance that is as complete and expansive as it is delicately balanced. Every place, with its vast populations of plants and animals, becomes a concert hall, and everywhere a unique orchestra performs an unmatched symphony, with each species' sound fitting into a specific part of the score. It is a highly evolved, naturally wrought masterpiece.
>
> (2012: 9–10)

In *Biophony* the dancers corporealize King's aesthetic. There is continual unsynchronized movement that ironically highlights a camaraderie among dancers. Here this is read as a metaphor for his philosophy that ballet, too, is composed of a collectivity.

For years King has placed prominence on relationship, and for just as long, he has been labelled as a choreographer whose work celebrates diversity. Difference, though, has never been the heart of the work for King; on the contrary it has always been about cultivating a unified harmony. What *Biophony* does expertly is use sound to materialize King's understanding of dance and nature in constant conversation. The dancers move as we would expect animals to – independent of one another but aware. As we rarely look to the natural world to demonstrate 'gender' in movement, King's dancers enable this possibility. We watch a man do multiple front attitude turns with soft undulating arms, *plié retiré*, and sixth position *sauté*, just as we see women with strong straight arms showing crisp *tendu* and deep lunges. The ambiguity heard in the score is seen in the dancers, who are not signifiers of masculinity or femininity but members of a species.

Absent a linear narrative in the soundscape, King's choreography avoids proverbial sequencing and categorizations. This is achieved in part because the dancers are constantly moving – thereby eliminating any time for poses that customarily reinforce gender stereotypes in ballet. In addition, the dancers in *Biophony* frequently execute the same phrases concurrently or dance them in a canon, which further diminishes the audience's need to view any one dancer as different from another. King's dancers show, through their perpetual motion, that the frequencies Krause described are always present. As the company members move independently and then connect to the group, Krause's soundscape fosters a new relationship between music, gender, and ballet. Current cultural discourse embraces a multiplicity of voices about contemporary ballet, its resonance(s), and how the genre (if it should be so termed) is evolving.[8] Within *Biophony* community is witnessed as the dancers have the ability to sound at varying levels while in concert. It is a way of thinking about the aesthetic that heretofore has eluded discussion but provides an important through-line to the work. In recent years King has begun to refer to his dances as 'thought structures'; I maintain that *Biophony* shows how the ballets are also sound structures.[9]

In the year 2000 it seemed imperative to make a case for the ways by which King's ballets diverged from the known codifications of ballet. There was not a great need to individualize AKLB from other companies at that point; rather the responsibility was to insert King into a canon that seemed to have little regard for work that did not replicate ballet's norms. Sixteen years hence new questions are emergent about why King's dances consistently operate on another frequency when compared to a host of others who use a similar movement aesthetic. Taking *Biophony* as a manifestation of the idea that a shared humanity can respond to various resonances, the piece does much more than present itself in performance; it summarizes an ideological perspective that has for years been both foundational and a point of extension for ballet's LINES.

As much of the company repertoire has shown, the work materializes opportunities to push past ballet's tropes, thereby illustrating non-dyadic gender relationships. The historical significance of this company, as delineated herein, is greatly due to the fluid treatment of gender in spite of ballet's unfailing adherence to Western European traditions. Methodologies that embrace gender non-conformity are not only worthy of note from a choreographic standpoint but also vital for the perpetuation of the form we know as ballet. As King's dancers move in ways that signify neither masculinity nor femininity, his ballets are a testament to a long-standing choreographic philosophy – one that has proven foundational for the new genre of contemporary ballet. Two decades into the twenty-first century finds the state of ballet to be somewhat in flux. Time-honored classical companies, alongside small pick-up groups and everyone in between, seem to present ballets that follow another template. Is it Balanchine extended beyond? Is it the influence of Forsythe's innovations? Or might it be other choreographers like Alonzo King who stand to write the historiography of contemporary ballet through their approaches to the form? King would be the first to disavow himself as the leader of such a movement; still it is clear that his dancers are unquestionably presenting works with the ability to transform and impact how ballet is studied for years to come.

Notes

1   More often than not when the word 'diversity' is used in an American ballet context it is meant to point out that the company is composed of non-White dancers. Classifications like muscularity or athleticism are also employed with a racial subtext.

2   Although spirituality might be interpreted in a myriad of ways, I have maintained King's ballets centralize elements that are viscerally and philosophically linked to sociological understandings of what it means to be spiritual. This conclusion is based on both choreographic observation and the dancers' acknowledgements and is reaffirmed in critical reviews. Roslyn Sulcas, writing for *The New York Times*, titled her 2009 review of the company at the Joyce 'When Somber Sounds Are Heard, Something Spiritual Arises'.

3   In 'OutLINES for a Global Ballet Aesthetic' I apply the concept of syncretism to King's works and make a point of distinguishing this from critics who have asserted his ballets are fusions. The connection and conveyance of spirituality, coupled with the fact that of the postcolonial constructions syncretism (as opposed to hybridity or creolization) relates to ideas and not biology, substantiate this enquiry (2008: 373). Also see 'Transcending Gender' for more on King's use of spirituality (Nunes Jensen 2009: 131).

4   In order to point out some dissimilarities I have previously turned to both scholars and dancers. See 'Transcending Gender' (Nunes Jensen 2009), wherein former dancer turned choreographer Christian Burns candidly asserts that in working with both King and Forsythe,

> I have heard people say that they [King and Forsythe's dances] look so similar and wonder who was influenced by whom. I am not so sure if they were necessarily influenced directly by one another . . . They came to the same place from very different places.

5   He concludes with calling Forsythe an 'intellectual' and King 'very spiritual' so that 'the two couldn't get more different actually' (Nunes Jensen 2009: 137). Others, such as Senta Driver and Heidi Gilpin, offer more theoretical analyses of Forsythe's process.
5   King's ballets neither make exclusive use of pointe work nor denounce it. Importantly, he does not use the shoes interchangeably between men and women, which supports the analysis herein that he does abide by familiar ballet practices all the while moving in non-traditional directions.
6   The categorization of 'contemporary ballet' as separate from ballet is something many dancers and scholars would take issue with and is heard more and more in the US dance scene. It is also crucial to note that the term 'contemporary' as applied in a European and/or broader global context has decidedly different connotations.
7   King is not the first to use soundscapes or to create a work wherein the essence of animal life is portrayed. In fact, this discussion might remind many of American modern dance choreographer Merce Cunningham's *Beach Birds* (1991) and the subsequent *Beach Birds for Camera* (1993). The obvious differences between King's ballet and Cunningham's piece have to do with the treatment of musicality (so that the former was reliant on sound for inspiration while the latter choreographed independently), the timing of the piece (as Cunningham's work did not adhere to count structures and therefore the performance of the work was different in length each time), and the fact that King did not rely on birds alone but utilized a multiplicity of animal voices.
8   The 2016 Society of Dance History Scholars special topics conference 'Contemporary Ballet: Exchanges, Connections and Directions' brought together over 100 scholars, practitioners, and choreographers in New York City to discuss issues relevant to the state of ballet globally. Questions surrounding the historicity of contemporary ballet, how dancers are trained to perform this type of repertory, and the ways through which contemporary ballet is (re)presented to audiences circulated. The impetus behind the event was to locate this moment in ballet history and reinvigorate ballet studies in the academy.
9   As per the company website, 'King calls his works "thought structures" created by the manipulation of energies that exist in matter through laws, which govern the shapes and movement directions of everything that exists'. www.linesballet.org/company/alonzo-king/

Bibliography

Alonzo King LINES Ballet, 'Alonzo King', www.linesballet.org [accessed 28 May 2016].

Ferguson, Joe (2015) 'Collaboration: Biophony an Evolutionary Collaboration', *SciArt in America*, June, 36–42.

Gardiner, Judith Kegan (2002) *Masculinity Studies Feminist Theory: New Directions*, New York: Columbia University Press.
Henry, Courtney (2016) Phone interview with author, April 12.
Krause, Bernie (2012) *The Great Animal Orchestra: Finding the Origins of Music in the World's Wild Places*, New York: Little, Brown.
Nunes Jensen, Jill (2005) *Re-Forming the Lines: A Critical Analysis of Alonzo King's LINES Ballet*, PhD dissertation, University of California, Riverside.
Nunes Jensen, Jill (2008) 'OutLINES for a Global Ballet Aesthetic', *Dance Chronicle*, 31:3, 370–411.
Nunes Jensen, Jill (2009) 'Transcending Gender in Ballet's LINES.' In Jennifer Fisher and Anthony Shay, eds. *When Men Dance: Choreographing Masculinities across Borders*, New York: Oxford University Press, 118–145.
Sulcas, Roslyn (2009) 'When Somber Sounds Are Heard, Something Spiritual Arises,' *New York Times*, May 7, www.nytimes.com/2009/05/08/arts/dance/08line.html [accessed 10 November 2016].

Chapter 19

Giselle and the Gothic
Contesting the Romantic idealisation of the woman

GERALDINE MORRIS

FIRST PRESENTED IN PARIS in June 1841, *Giselle* caused a sensation (Moncrieff 1842). When it arrived in London nine months later, the reception was no less enthusiastic. Within the year, it spawned a melodrama and, later, embodiments in literature and opera. What was it about this work that so fascinated the audience of the time?

The conventional answer is that this was a Romantic ballet idealising the notion of love and portraying the struggle of the male protagonist for the unattainable feminine ideal.[1] But this explanation obscures the darker, more Gothic tropes inherent in the ballet. Drawing on those aspects not only brings it closer to Théophile Gautier's conception of a *danse fantastique* but also emphasises other features that a Romantic interpretation masks – for example the plight of the jilted woman, manifest in the wilis, and the eroticism inherent in the Gothic genre. If the roles of women are foregrounded, we are made more aware of the patriarchal agenda prevalent in nineteenth-century culture and of the perception that the unmarried female was threatening. In one sense the broad and more general label of Romantic can be applied, but emphasising the Gothic allows for a serious reconceptualisation of the role of women in *Giselle*, one that is not compatible with or (at least) departs seriously from the more mainstream, traditional, idealised Romantic take and, crucially, the macabre presence of the wilis becomes more dominant.

Unlike the late nineteenth-century children's fairy books, the wili is a threatening, erotic and potentially evil creature that has more in common with the ghosts of Gothic fiction than with the harmless creatures of the later tales.[2] I want to return to the culture of the time, so that we can understand the ballet differently. Centring on its Gothic roots gives an alternative reading and one that I suggest accounts for its reception at the time. According to Carole Silver the nineteenth century was fascinated by the occult. It was a way of externalising evil by focusing on the more terrifying spirits (2000: 149). Looking at *Giselle* from a Gothic perspective divests it of the baggage acquired over the centuries and encourages us to read it as a darker work.

I begin by discussing the contested issue of the Gothic and its relationship with the Romantic and then consider the presence of Gothic themes in some nineteenth-century ballets. This highlights Théophile Gautier's role in forming the libretto, drawing attention to his short stories and their uncanny and *fantastique* content. The extent to which the ballet is steeped in those traditions of the nineteenth century that were cruel and adverse to women is then evident. I move on to discuss embodiments of the work in other media. Exploring those works puts *Giselle* in its contemporary context and, because Gothic features are central to them, the case for the ballet as a Gothic work is strengthened. In other words, in literature, theatre and opera *Giselle* was interpreted as Gothic. By adopting a less orthodox approach, the love aspects in the ballet diminish, indicating not only how women were perceived but also the importance of the supernatural to the contemporary culture.

According to David Punter the question 'what is Gothic?' is complex and cannot be answered definitively (2012: 2). It can blend with the Romantic, and Gothic novels are sometimes described as Romantic. But Emma McEvoy argues that, while Gothic texts can be studied as Romantic texts without losing their Gothic roots, the supernatural and uncanny originate in the Gothic (2007). Gothic literature involves phantoms; it occurs in medieval buildings or dark woods; it has to do with the uncanny and bodily harm, with death and insanity (Punter 2012). The erotic is foregrounded and the fictitious ghostly women frequently become central.

Across Europe, Gothic arts tended to adopt similar themes, but these varied in emphasis and influence. As Neil Cornwall argues, much of what can be called Gothic fiction in France stems from English Gothic writing and that of the German Romantic writers (2012).[3] Cornwall considers *Le diable amoureux* (1772) by Joseph Cazotte to be the earliest French Gothic novel. It emphasised erotic temptation and the supernatural, becoming a ballet in 1840. An essay by Walter Scott on E.T.A. Hoffmann (1829) led to the revival of interest in the Gothic that came to be known in France as *le fantastique* and *l'école frénétique*. Cornwall identifies Gautier and Charles Nodier as writers of Gothic fiction. Nodier's *Trilby ou le lutin d'Argail* (1822) was the basis for *La Sylphide* (1832), another ballet dealing with death and the occult. *Giselle* is part of this genre of the *fantastique*, but over time its Romantic aspects have been more fully highlighted.

Difficulties arise when attempting to distinguish between the Romantic and the Gothic since tropes are often shared. Few scholars agree on what constitutes the Romantic and how it differs from the Gothic. It is highly debated and extensively written about, so much so that I cannot address it in any detail here. Yet, as Michael Gamer observes, the Gothic was central to British culture from 1790 to the early decades of the nineteenth century and, until the 1970s, was considered 'as at best a novel sideshow of romanticism, and at worst an embarrassing and pervasive disease destructive to national culture and social fabric' (2000: 8). According to Gamer, William Wordsworth located Romanticism exclusively in Edmund Burke's sublime (1757) while he declared Gothic to be part of popular culture and evidence of 'false taste' (15). In particular, he was irritated by its unprecedented popularity. It was vilified by the critics, leading to 'romantic ideology's privileging of alternative aesthetics like the sublime and "elegiac"' (Gamer 2000: 24). They identified the Gothic as having traits of 'sentimentality, femininity and pulp popularity . . . rendering it trivial and ephemeral' (Gamer 2000: 8). Wordsworth after all encouraged his readers to distinguish between popular supernaturalism and poetic naturalism, the latter being superior to the former. This association of the Gothic with popular culture could be the reason why British critics, writing in the 1940s and 1950s, promoted *Giselle* and other mid-nineteenth-century ballets as Romantic. Their aim was to situate ballet in high art and associating it with the Gothic might have rendered it melodramatic, locating it in popular culture.

After the rationality of the eighteenth century, what was it that led art away from this to focus on the supernatural? Anxieties associated with industrialisation and an economy rooted more in industry than the countryside are generally thought to have created an interest in the paranormal. Silver points out that the fascination with ghostly creatures is seen in the literature and drama (and dance) of the nineteenth century (2000: 3). She argues that it was an attempt to 'reconnect the actual and the occult' (2000: 3).[4] Fred Botting claims that the introduction of Gothic themes can be seen as part of a

> wider process of political, economic and social upheaval: emerging at a time of bourgeois and industrial revolution, a time of Enlightenment philosophy and increasingly secular views, the eighteenth century Gothic fascination with a past of chivalry, violence and magical beings, and malevolent aristocrats is bound up with the shifts from feudal to commercial practices in which notions of property, government and society were undergoing massive transformations.
> (Quoted in Punter 2012: 13–14)

The theatre arts in France were particularly affected by economic changes introduced by the July Monarchy (1830–1848). These touched the Paris Opéra (Théâtre de l'Académie de musique royale) by withdrawing most of the royal funding. In 1831, wishing to off-load costs, the state commercialised the opera, appointing Dr Louis Véron as the new director (Guest 2006). Overturning the taste for neoclassical subject matter in opera and ballet, Véron encouraged the growing bourgeoisie delight in both Gothic and Romantic tales. But, as Silver argues, it was the spirits who were 'perceived as cruel participants in antisocial acts' that most fascinated writers and audiences (2000: 149).

Véron's first acclaimed production, *Robert le Diable* (1831), was particularly relished for its dance scene in which the ghostly spirits of fallen nuns, newly risen from their tombs, dance a bacchanal. These are carnal women, who seduce and entice the men whom they encounter. Gautier describes the nuns as uncanny beings with

> frozen veins [who] deserted the pure joy of Heaven for the profane sensuality of world. The slabs of the tombs open, and the phantoms rise and form vague shapes in the shadows . . . female forms moving beneath the white pallor of their shrouds with deathly sensuality.
> (Quoted in Guest 1986: 330)

The dancers were clothed in diaphanous dresses, which, combined with the greenish tinge of the gas lighting, gave them their ghostly, ethereal qualities. Set in a medieval world, the hero, Robert, is said to be the devil's son. These scandalous creatures caused something of a sensation and attracted the attention of poets and writers, while the Gothic narrative and erotic presence of the ghostly, white-clad nuns also captivated the audience. This opera launched not only ballet as a popular cult but also the commercialisation of the Académie, making a celebrity of its principal dancer, Marie Taglioni. Over the following two decades, other ballerinas would be similarly venerated. One of these, Carlotta Grisi, had in 1840 made a strong impression on the public and it was for her that Gautier conceived *Giselle*.

Its libretto has roots in Germanic culture, but comes from heterogeneous sources. It was largely the brainchild of Gautier. Applauding a passage in Heinrich Heine's *De l'Allemagne* (1835), Gautier focused on the description of the 'elves in white dresses, whose hems are always damp . . . of snow-coloured wilis who waltz pitilessly' (quoted in Smith 2000: 67). Heine hints at meeting these wilis, the spirits of jilted women, in the misty moonlight of a German wood. Their passion for dancing and their unfulfilled lives lead them to rise at midnight. Describing them as alluring and seductive, Heine writes that

> dressed in their marriage garments, and sporting like elves in the bright Moonlight these Brides of Death have an air so winning, a grace so seductive, smiles so perfidious that they are irresistible. It is in vain their unhappy victims would fly; they follow and own in death their fatal fascination 'from De L'Allemagne par H Heine.'
> (Quoted in Moncrieff 1842: n.p.)

Unmarried and uncontrolled, these women find fulfilment in dancing, and vengeance in luring men to death. Unable to create a two-act libretto from this, Gautier took his inspiration for the first act from Victor Hugo's (1802–1885) poem *Fantômes* in *Les orientales* (1884 [1829]). The final version was a further collaboration between Gautier and Jules-Henri Vernoy de Saint-Georges (1799–1875).

But it was the eroticism and darkness of the wilis and their music in which Gautier revelled most. The music, he wrote in 1841, conveys 'the fantastic in a way that is graceful and full of melody' (quoted in Guest 1986: 330). The word 'fantastic' reflects the ballet's macabre tones and Gautier's writing constitutes a supreme example of the genre of '*fantastique*' literature (Meglin 2005). He wrote a number of Gothic short stories between 1831 and 1841, most of which relate to female spirits. In those tales, the females tend to be a succubus or a vampire; they are alluring and dangerous, irresistible and wanton but motivated by hate for the living. These female ghosts were thought to be the spirits of those who had led wrongful lives, like the erotic nuns in *Robert le Diable*. We do not know about the earthly lives of the wilis, but the fact of their having been jilted and their similarity with the ghostly nuns hint at carnal knowledge.[5] Gautier's wilis perform 'the most graceful and alluring poses' but it was the waltzing in both his stories and the ballet that was further proof of the degenerate nature of the spectres (Gautier quoted in Guest 2006: 101).

His 'La cafetière' (1836) is a Gothic nightmare story in which the objects in the protagonist's room come alive at night and swirl about the room, performing mad, frenzied, waltzes. Waltzes dominate the ballet and according to Joellen Meglin,

> [t]he waltz carried currency in the *ballet fantastique* precisely because it was part of a larger discourse on the fantastic. Act II of the libretto of *Giselle* refers to a 'fantastic music', 'the fantastic ball', the 'fantastic and tumultuous round of the Wilis' and also to a 'rapid waltz'.
> (2005: 91)

Contemporary articles on the social waltz discuss at length female sexuality and the effect of waltzing on the 'frail' female body (Wilson 2009). Performing the waltz created a 'sense of vertigo and euphoria . . . mak[ing] the dance inappropriately "exciting" for women' (Wilson 2009: 132). The sight of furiously waltzing wilis betrayed their sexuality and decadence and according to Arkin and Smith identified them as Germanic (1997).

The wili is actually a species of vampire or succubus, and although these vampire qualities are less evidently the focus of today's performances, they were central to those in the nineteenth century (Beaumont 1948: 19). Throughout most of that century, vampires were frequently perceived as female. For instance, in Sheridan Le Fanu's *Carmilla* (1871) and Samuel Taylor Coleridge's 'psychosexual' poem *Christabel* (1816), the vampires are women, erotic and tempting, like the wilis (Thomson 2012: 88). Myrthe, the coldly beautiful wili queen, is a particularly malevolent and hostile ghost, who commands her acolytes to attack the men with whom they come into contact.

Giselle's themes embody many concerns of the Gothic – duplicity, madness, suicide, wealth, class, and the supernatural – and this is mirrored in the music (Warwick

2007). The events of the ballet take place in medieval Silesia, then in Prussia, its Germanic location perceived as a suitably Gothic setting. It is the music by Adolphe Adam, though, that first introduces a deathly chill, invoking the ghostly wilis in Act I. In the early scene between Giselle and her mother, Berthe, the music conveys both Berthe's premonitions and her daughter's disobedience. Giselle continues to dance, despite Berthe's warning that it will cause her death and turn her into one of those ghosts 'who rise from their graves in shrouds, forc[ing] men to dance with them' (Smith 2000: 180). Marian Smith notes that as with recitative in the operas of the time, the music was composed *parlante* to indicate the words that were mimed by the characters. Twenty-two measures of Berthe's mime are devoted to the wilis, and audiences, familiar with this practice, would have recognised the ominous tones in the music, alerting them to the uncanny. Punter argues that the uncanny contains the link between 'premonition and the fulfilment of that premonition' (2007: 129–136). So the music forewarns of death and the wilis, both of which dominate Act II.

Act II takes place in an eerie forest, lit by strong moonlight and described by Gautier as

> [r]epresent[ing] a forest by the edge of a lake, overhung by tall pale trees with their roots steeped in the grass and the bulrushes, and with water lilies spreading their broad leaves on the placid surface of the water silvered here and there by the moon.
>
> (Gautier quoted in Guest 2006: 98)

As midnight strikes, some villagers enter and on hearing the bells rush away; bells tolling herald the occult in Gothic fiction and on stage. The reeds part and Myrtha, the wili queen, emerges. Gliding across the stage, she appears illusory and her extensive jumps, so light, soundless and airborne, convey her spectral identity. The shrouded wilis emerge from the undergrowth and perform 'voluptuous dances' around their queen (*The Times* 1841: 5). Myrtha returns to summon Giselle, who arises, shrouded, from her grave. Commanding her to perform a wild, spinning dance, Myrtha initiates her into the group.

Albrecht arrives to mourn Giselle,[6] but not before Hilarion is discovered, forced to dance and drowned in the lake. Smith notes that the fear and terror are reflected in the music when a satanic laugh is heard just as the wilis force Albrecht to dance (2000: 196). Despite being compelled to dance, he is saved by the chiming clock bells, heralding the dawn.

While we cannot be sure of the original choreography, since performances today depend on a re-choreographed version by Marius Petipa (1884), Doug Fullington believes that Petipa made few changes and that what we see today is close to the 1841 production.[7] As well as vertiginous waltzes and airborne jumps, a recurring motif in Act II is the arabesque. And because the long filmy skirts worn by the wilis help to dissolve the body, flight is suggested. Arabesques are also found in Act I but these are short, abrupt and lively, as befits the living. The dancing of Act II alternates between luscious backbends, smooth and continuous arabesques, sustained and gliding *bourrée couru*, waltzes and soaring leaps. The movement is appropriately fantastic, enriching the ghostly atmosphere of the scene. Reviewers praised the dancers for the clarity of their mime, through which the audience interpreted the story, and yet the choreography is such that audiences could have imbibed the supernatural and the erotic through the dancing alone.

Can we learn more about the work's Gothic credentials from examining its transferal into other media? The earliest of these was a melodrama produced at Sadler's Wells, entitled *Giselle or the Phantom Night Dancers*. In 1841, the Wells was on the outskirts of London and mainly spoke to popular culture, so the emphasis on the Gothic traits served to remove the play from high art and, as Edward Dent argues, it was still a theatre which entertained the riff-raff (Dent 1945: 16–17). Written by William Moncrieff, it appeared at the Sadler's Wells Theatre on 23 August 1841. Advertised as 'A Dramatic, Melo-dramatic, Choreographic, Fantastique, Traditionary Tale of Superstition', its setting was suffused with Gothic characteristics and the presence of vengeful wilis added to its macabre presentation (Moncrieff 1842: 63).[8] Despite using dance and Adam's original ballet score, it was deemed a play.

The wilis' scenes emphasise the occult: they reside in a lake 'among the mountains, near the High Road'. Close by are the 'Castle of Thuringia' and the 'Witch Wood with the ruins of Saint Walberg's nunnery and Chapel' (Moncrieff 1842: n.p.).[9] Giselle is welcomed as a Bride of Death into the wili sisterhood and clothed by Myrtha in the wili robes. This seems like a collection of Gothic clichés, with its haunted woods, medieval castle and ruined abbey.

Moncrieff alters the denouement and adds new characters. Giselle has a godfather, who saves her from the wilis and reunites her with Hilarion. And her passion for dancing is stressed: 'I'm incorrigible; dancing is my sole pleasure, as Aloise [Albrecht/Loys] is my sole happiness; and dead or alive I will dance' (Moncrieff 1842: 5). But Moncrieff protects himself from accusations of impropriety, since a desire to dance uncontrollably could be regarded as immoral. In the introduction to the published text, he writes that his tale is 'beautifully moral':

> It shows from the penalty it attaches to the inordinate indulgence of the dance, that the pleasures of this life should only be enjoyed in moderation, and that uncontrolled passion inevitably ends in the destruction of those by whom it is encouraged.
>
> (1842: 3)

Aided by Sadler's Wells's exceptional aquatic facilities, real water was used on stage; Myrtha, the wili queen, entered in a 'Translucent Palace of 100 Fountains beneath the Bosom of the Witch's Lake!' (Moncrieff 1842: n.p.). Spectacle was thus central but the ambience and the ghostly atmosphere come from the Gothic. The story having been adapted from the reviews, it appeared in London before the ballet, locating both firmly in the Gothic.

With music by Edward Loder, *Giselle* mutated into an opera, *The Night Dancers*, first performed in 1846. Using a similar narrative to that of the ballet, but presented as a dream, it eliminated the ballet's tragic ending. As its title indicates, the focus was on the supernatural. The opera was hugely successful, with performances abroad and a revival at Covent Garden in 1860.

The following year, in 1861, Charles Dickens published *Great Expectations* and the parallels between the female characters in the ballet and the novel are palpable. As a music lover, he would undoubtedly have attended the opera. Lyrical theatre and music were an important part of his life, since music features frequently in his books as, of course, do ballet dancers (Lightwood 2006; Engelhardt 2009). It is unlikely that he missed seeing *Giselle*, since between 1842 and 1850, it had twenty-five performances, with a further eleven of Act II only. So can we assume that the ballet might have influenced him?

Dickens is not usually conceived of as a Gothic writer, but Punter argues that in his works, the 'grotesque exaggeration of character and location are recognisably "gothic" features' (2012: 1). In the ballet, the wilis destroy the men with whom they come into contact, prompted by their need for revenge. In the same way, the women central to the narrative in *Great Expectations* are set up deliberately to damage the men they encounter. Unlike the wilis, these are not dead women and yet, neither Miss Havisham nor Estella is fully human. Miss Havisham, garbed in her yellowing bridal gown, resembling a shroud, is barely alive and Estella is uncannily spectral; we have no idea what she looks like. She is not physically described and, like a wraith, moves silently around Satis House. Like her adopted mother, she is cold and emotionless, as cruel and spectral as the wilis. Miss Havisham too is merciless and metaphorically sucks the life from those who surround her; through Estella, she attempts to break Pip's heart. Miss Havisham is macabre and distinct from other women in Dickens's fiction, so it is interesting to consider what Dickens's scholars have written on the inspiration for the character.

Speculating on Dickens's source, Harry Stone argues that Miss Havisham's characteristics take her out of the normal: 'her external[:] bridal dress, all white accoutrements and ever-present staff . . . her personality: cold, formal, conceited, eccentric and man-hating; and her history – jilted and thereby frozen forever . . . in the ghostly garments of her dead love' (1979: 281). Stone could be describing the wilis, though he believes she was constructed out of everyday events, one of which is recalled in Dickens's magazine *Household Words* (1853). As a youngster, Dickens used to pass a woman who walked up and down Berners Street:

> The White Woman is her name. She is dressed entirely in white, with a ghastly white plaiting round her head and face, inside her white

bonnet. She even carries . . . a white umbrella. With white boots, we know she picks her way through the winter dirt. She is a conceited old creature, cold and formal in manner.

(Quoted in Stone 1979: 281)

Dickens alleged she had been jilted but Stone maintains this was imagination.[10] In an earlier piece in *Household Narratives* (1850), another reclusive woman is described. Dressed in white, she went mad because a rejected suitor had blown his brains out while sitting next to her (Stone 1979). So madness characterises the women.

Both these women could indeed have been triggers for Miss Havisham but neither has the fatalistic and vengeful desire to seduce men and lure them to their deaths. Myrtha and the wilis aim to kill. Dickens's scholars, apart from Molly Engelhardt, have not examined *Giselle*; the general trend is to accept Stone's sources, though Englehardt considers Miss Havisham to be a Gothic version of the wili (2009: 98).[11] Like it, Miss Havisham is a jilted woman, similarly garbed in her wedding dress, who baits men. Dickens, we know, was fascinated by the occult, so it is quite possible that the ballet remained in his consciousness, describing Miss Havisham as 'the witch of the place'. And her age coupled with her spinster status would have led contemporary readers to interpret her as a witch (Raphael 1989: 401). The wilis, however, remain young; their white faces, still beautiful, are unaffected by decay: 'Embodying the mythic horrors of countless cruel mothers, stepmothers and witch-like figures, Miss Havisham has often been described as an irrational and vindictive female figure' (Raphael 1989: 401). At the time, unmarried women were regarded with suspicion and those who were jilted often incurred the contempt of the community. Grotesque and redundant, for whom even the devil found no use, the Victorian old maid was thought of as some sort of omen, a witch in disguise and frequently allied with the fallen woman (Auerbach 1982).

It was generally accepted that there was an association between the stage performer and Victorian pornography (Engelhardt 2009). The jump to the jilted bride as a fallen woman is not a great step to make particularly because there was 'a long-held belief that sex with a fiancé was acceptable, since the couple were to be married anyway' (Frost 1995: 99). While intercourse outside marriage was shunned, it frequently occurred among engaged couples. John Mueller (1981) raised the issue of Giselle's virginity. He questions Cyril Beaumont's assumption that Giselle's descent into fatal madness is caused by neurosis, arguing that although Giselle may be overly trusting, she does not appear to have neuroses. Mueller makes a powerful case, arguing that Giselle's madness makes more sense if she and Albrecht had already become lovers. Like Ginger Frost (1995), he claims that in many societies once a couple was engaged, it was acceptable and even the norm to consummate the relationship. This approach is consistent with the original libretto that makes it clear that in the opening scene, Giselle is already awaiting Albrecht and runs into his arms (Beaumont 1948: 40). Her madness makes more sense if the relationship had been consummated and would have led to her becoming an outcast in the village.

Female sexuality was subject to a range of extreme interpretations, moral panics and sexual misunderstandings and, in some Gothic novels, the depictions of 'extremes of femininity for which they stand – the virginal Emily and the lascivious Matilda, serve as troubled reminders of culture's struggle to represent and understand women's sexual responses and desires' (Johnson 2002: 44).[12] And the bands of 'extremely feminine', uncontrolled women in the ballet have parallels with these Gothic creations. If betrothed couples had consummated their relationship, it would have had repercussions for the women, particularly if the marriage did not happen.

Conclusion

My argument centred on the Gothic or *fantastique* aspects of *Giselle*. As a result, precedence was given to the supernatural and more malevolent aspects of the work, linking it more obviously with the contemporary zeitgeist; in other words with the fascination, both in France and England, for the occult, the ghostly and the malevolent spirit. By concentrating on these more macabre aspects, the issue of the jilted woman came more to the fore. A society that incarcerates its jilted women in a dark and creepy house or makes spiteful, erotic ghosts of them is one that appears to have deep anxieties about women. Drawing attention to the parallels between the characters in both *Great Expectations* and *Giselle* brings this issue into focus and also demonstrates how two seemingly opposing genres, the 'realist' (Dickens's novels are frequently described as realist) novel and the ballet *fantastique*, can be linked. Both deal with issues such as madness, the unmarried woman and the erotic feelings provoked by the spirit being, even though Estella is not a ghost. I have drawn attention to the connections with Dickens to give an additional avenue for inspiration for those staging *Giselle*; it also casts a bleaker light on the work.

What seems to have appealed to Gautier was the anarchic nature of the vampire or ghostly woman. His writing in both his short stories and his theatre reviews is frequently concerned with sensuality and with desire and this appears to have resonated with audiences and readers of his work. While the notion of an idealised woman is the conventional interpretation of the ballet, this does not encourage us to understand the more complex attitudes of the contemporary society and also limits performances of the work. Shifting the perspective gives us an alternative interpretation of the ballet, one that may be closer to that experienced by nineteenth-century audiences, and also encourages us to engage with the effects of a patriarchal culture on women.

Notes

1 Most of today's productions make this claim in their programme notes, though that of Pacific Northwest Ballet does raise the issue of the occult on its website; see www.pnb.org/repertorylist/Giselle.
2 For instance, Andrew Lang's *The Blue Fairy Book* (1889).
3 This point is more fully developed by Cornwall in his chapter (2012).
4 See too Arkin and Smith, who attribute the interest in nationalism and folk culture to Herder (1997: 11).
5 This is dealt with later.
6 The character was named Albert in the early productions but his name now has the more Germanic Albrecht.
7 Doug Fullington writes about this online at www.pnb.org/repertorylist/giselle.
8 Mrs R. Honner and Mrs Richard Barnett performed Giselle and Myrtha respectively, while Mr Frampton provided the dancers and also choreographed.
9 No page numbers available. The introductory sections of Moncrieff's book are not paginated. Page numbers commence for the play text.
10 Stone also connects Miss Havisham with Wilkie Collins's novel *The Woman in White*, published initially in serial form in Dickens's weekly magazine *All the Year Round* between 1859 and 1860.
11 See Slater (2009/2011: 273–4) for evidence of the use of Stone. To describe Miss Havisham as a Gothic wili seems to be a tautology, since I claim the wilis are Gothic.
12 Emily in *The Mysteries of Udolpho* (Ann Radcliffe, 1794) and Matilda in *The Monk* (Matthew Gregory Lewis, 1796).

Bibliography

Anon, *The Times* [London] (1841) 'Giselle, Ou Les Wilis', 3 Aug: 5, The Times Digital Archive.
Arkin, Lisa and Marian Smith (1997) 'National Dance in the Romantic Ballet', in Lynn Garafola, ed. *Rethinking the Romantic Ballet: New Perspectives on the Romantic Ballet*, London: Wesleyan University Press, 11–68.
Auerbach, Nina (1982) *Women and the Demon: The Life of a Victorian Myth*, Cambridge, MA: Harvard University Press, 150.
Beaumont, Cyril (1948) *The Ballet Called Giselle*, London: C.W. Beaumont.
Botting, Fred (2012) '"Gothic Darkly" Heterotopia, History, Culture', in David Punter, ed. *A Companion to the Gothic*, Oxford: Blackwell, 3–14.
Cornwell, Neil (2012) 'European Gothic', in David Punter, ed. *A New Companion to the Gothic*, Oxford: Blackwell, 64–76.

Davis, Jim and Victoria Emeljanow (2001) *Reflecting the Audience: London Theatre Going 1840–1880*, Hertfordshire: University of Hertfordshire Press.
Dent, Edward J. (1945) *A Theatre for Everybody: The Story of the Old Vic and Sadler's Wells*, London: T.V. Boardman.
Dickens, Charles (1860, this edition 1894) *Great Expectations*, Boston: Houghton, Mifflin, The Riverside Press, Cambridge.
Engelhardt, Molly (2009) *Dancing Out of Line: Ballrooms, Ballets and Mobility in Victorian Fiction and Culture*, Athens, OH: Ohio University Press.
Frost, Ginger S. (1995) *Promises Broken: Courtship, Class and Gender in Victorian England*, Charlottesville: University Press of Virginia.
Gamer, Michael (2000) *Romanticism and the Gothic: Genre, Reception and Canon Formation*, Cambridge Studies in Romanticism, No. 40, Cambridge: Cambridge University Press.
Gautier, Théophile (15 March 1870) 'Opéra Revival of *Robert le diable*', in *Journal Officiel de L'Emprie Français*, in Ivor Guest, trans. and ed., (1986) *Gautier on Dance*, London: Dance Books, 330.
Gautier, Théophile (1976) *My Fantoms*, translated and collected by Richard Holmes, London: Quartet Books.
Guest, Ivor, trans. and ed. (1986) *Gautier on Dance*, London: Dance Books.
Guest, Ivor (2006) *The Paris Opéra Ballet*, Alton: Dance Books.
Hugo, Victor (1829/1884) *Les orientales*, Paris: Hachette et cie.
Johnson, Tracy (2002) 'The Fear Industry: Women, Gothic and Contemporary Crime Narrative', *Gothic Studies*, 4:1, 44–62.
Kontou, Tatiana and Sarah Willburn (2012) *Occult*, Aldershot: Ashgate.
Lightwood, James, T. (2006) *Charles Dickens and Music*, Middlesex: The Echo Library.
Lumley, Benjamin (1864) *Reminiscences of the Opera*, London: Hurst and Blackett.
Meglin, Joellen (2005) 'Behind the Veil of Translucence: An Intertextual Reading of the Ballet Fantastique in France 1831–1841: Part Three: Resurrection, Sensuality, and the Palpable Presence of the Past in Théophile Gautier's Fantastic', *Dance Chronicle*, 28:1, 67–142.
Moncrieff, William (1842) *Giselle or the Phantom Night Dancers*, London: J. Limbard.
Mueller, John (1981) 'Is Giselle a Virgin?', *Dance Chronicle*, 4:2, 151–154.
Punter, David (2007) 'The Uncanny', in Catherine Spooner and Emma McEvoy, eds. *The Routledge Companion to Gothic*, London: Routledge, 129–136.
Punter, David ed. (2012) *A New Companion to the Gothic*, Oxford: Blackwell.
Raphael, Linda (1989) 'A Re-Vision of Miss Havisham: Her Expectations and Our Responses', *Studies in the Novel*, 21:4, 405.
Showalter, Elaine (1979) 'The Rise of the Victorian Mad Woman', in Sandra Gilbert and Susan Gubar, eds. *Madwoman in the Attic: The Woman Writer and the Nineteenth Century Literary Imagination*, New Haven: Yale University Press, 73.

Silver, Carole (2000) *Strange and Secret Peoples: Fairies and Victorian Consciousness*, New York: Oxford University Press.

Slater, Michael (2009/2011) *Charles Dickens*, New Haven: Yale University Press.

Smith, Marian (2000) *Ballet and Opera in the Age of Giselle*, Princeton: Princeton University Press.

Smith, Marian (2016) 'A Quintessential Romantic Ballet', Programme article, The Royal Ballet, Royal Opera House Covent Garden, 22 March.

Sorley Walker, Kathrine (1946) '"Giselle" as a Play', *Ballet*, 2:5, 21–24.

Stone, Harry (1979) *Dickens and the Invisible World: Fairy Tales, Fantasy and Novel Making*, Bloomington, IN: Indiana University Press.

Thomson, Douglas, H. (2012) 'The Gothic Ballad', in David Punter, ed. *A New Companion to the Gothic*, Oxford: Blackwell, 77–90.

Townshend, Gale (2014) 'Introduction', in Gale Townsend, ed. *Terror and Wonder: The Gothic Imagination*, London: The British Library, 10–37.

Walpole, Horace (1764/2008) *The Castle of Otranto: A Gothic Story*, Oxford: Oxford World's Classics.

Warwick, Alexandra (2007) 'Victorian Gothic', in Catherine Spooner and Emma McEvoy, eds. *The Routledge Companion to Gothic*, London: Routledge, 29–37.

Warwick, Alexandra (2014) 'Gothic, 1820–1880', in Gale Townsend, ed. *Terror and Wonder: The Gothic Imagination*, London: The British Library, 94–123.

Wilson, Cheryl A. (2009) *Literature and Dance in Nineteenth Century Britain*, Cambridge: Cambridge University Press, 132–171.

Index

3rd Floor Dance Library and Dance Archive (Gothenburg) 154–6

Adam, Adolphe 240, 241
African American dance 4, 45; choreographing Black themes 50–2; concert dance 50, 52, 71; and dance history 46–7; and slavery 47, 174; sources for 52–4; vernacular and social dance forms 48–9, 187, 193, 217; *see also* civil rights movements; hip hop; jazz dance
African American dancers 71, 72, 187, 195; *see also under* names of individual dancers
African American history 16; Jim Crow laws 48, 49, 51; lynchings 48, 50; racial segregation 51; *see also* civil rights movements; Harlem Renaissance
African American musical forms 46, 48, 218
Africanist aesthetics 45
African traditions 46, 72
Ailey, Alvin 51, 82; *Cry* 52
Alhambra Theatre (London) 27, 29
Allan, Maud 137, 144

Allen, Woody 193
Americana in dance 218–19
American Ballet Theatre (ABT) 210
American in Paris, An 193, 194; '''S Wonderful', musical number in 188–90
Amin, Takiyah Nur 4
appropriation and counter-appropriation, cultural and historical 125–30; *see also* orientalism
Après Midi d'un Faune, L' (Vaslav Nijinsky) 73, 75
Archer, Kenneth 74–5, 140
Archive and the Repertoire, The see Taylor, Diana
archives 110, 138–9, 153; dancers as embodied (living) archives 6, 38–9, 95, 99–104, 154–6; digital archives 110, 148, 149, 154; interaction with 153–4; plural nature of 149; political activism with 154–7; *see also* Scenarkivet.se; source material; West Swedish Dance Archive
Arkin, Lisa 64, 239, 245n
Arnold, Richard (role in *Enigma Variations*) 96

Arundale, Rukmini Devi 126
Ashton, Frederick 95–7
Astaire, Fred 186–8, 190, 191, 193–5, 212

Badham, John (film director) 193
Balanchine, George 82, 190, 210, 212, 213; *Mozartiana* 72
ballet: as codified technique 33–4, 37–8; contemporary ballet 225, 228, 231–2, 233n; history of 56–9
Ballet Comique de la Reine, Le 57, 59, 60, 61–3, 67n
ballet d'action 64, 65
ballet de cour 59, 62, 116
Ballet des Polonais 56
Ballet Russe de Monte Carlo 72, 76, 217, 218
Ballets des Champs Élysées, Les 217
Ballets Russes de Serge Diaghilev, Les 73, 74, 117, 119
Banbury, Emily (Empire Theatre dancer) 24
Banes, Sally 198
Bannerman, Henrietta 6
Baronova, Irina 76–7
Barr, Margaret 11
Barreca, Regina 214
Battle, Robert 82
Bausch, Pina 36, 41, 203
Beatty, Talley 50
Beaujoyeulx, Balthazar de 59–61, 63, 67n
Beaumont, Cyril 243
Beauvoir, Simone de 216–19
Bel, Jérôme 62, 63, 198
Bertha or Berthe (role in *Giselle*) 64, 240
Bettis, Valerie 218
bharatanatyam 36, 41, 126
Bie, Oskar 137
Big Dance Pledge, The 42n
Black dance, definition 45; see also African American dance

Blue Fairy Book, The (Andrew Lang) 245n
Blunden, Jeraldyne 51
boom shots (in film) 188–9
Booth, John Bennion 29
Botting, Fred 237
Bourne, Colin 105n
Bremer, Lucille 188
British Empire, and India 125–7, 131
Brooks, Bonnie 83
Brown, Carolyn 87, 88, 91
Brown, Trisha 51, 83, 87, 100, 104, 199, 202, 218
Bubbles, John 191
Burke, Edmund 237
Burt, Ramsay 119
Butler, Judith 174

Cage, John 85
Calloway, Cab 195
Camryn, Walter 214
CandoCo 206
Carefree, 'The Yam', dance number in 188
Carr, Jane 95
Carter, Alexandra xiii, 4, 109–10, 160
Catterson, Pat 86
causation (and agency) 112–13, 140, 173, 175, 182–3
Cavallazzi, Malvina 25
Cazotte, Joseph 236
Certeau, Michel de 145
Chakrabarty, Dipesh 163, 164–6
Chakravorty, Pallabi 124, 127
Chan, Iris 100, 101, 192, 103, 104, 105n
Chandralekha 39
Chant, Laura Ormiston 23
Chapman, John 59, 61, 116
Charisse, Cyd 195
Chase, Lucia 210
Chatterjea, Ananya 163, 164, 166, 168

Chaudhry, Farooq 35, 42n
Cherkaoui, Larbi Sidi 39, 42n
Chevalier, Maurice 186, 193
Chicago Opera Ballet 217
Childs, Lucinda 51, 199, 202, 218
China, dance in 109, 160, 162, 163, 166, 167, 168, 170n; and diaspora 161; and US hegemony 111, 161–3, 166, 169
Christiansen, Lew 190, 210, 212
City Contemporary Dance Company of Hong Kong 161
civil rights movements (USA) 48, 51, 224
Clair, René 186
Clark Center for the Performing Arts 51
Clarke, Gil 101
Clavé, Antoni 219
Cloud Gate Dance Theatre of Taiwan 161
Cohan, Robert 95, 98, 99; *Stabat Mater* 98, 99, 105n
Cohen, Selma Jeanne 59, 60, 61, 73
Coleridge, Samuel Taylor: and poem *Christabel* 239
collective memory 5, 12, 16
colonialism 54n, 111, 127, 164, 165, 167; *see also* postcolonialism
conditions of possibility 112–13, 173–5, 182–3
Conroy, Renee 57
continuity and change through time 3, 5, 14, 56, 57, 59, 87, 91, 112–13, 116–17, 144–5
Copland, Aaron 79n, 219
Coppélia 115
copyright 78, 152
Cornalba, Elena 25, 30
corps de ballet 4, 13, 28, 29, 211
Cover Girl (musical film, 1944), Gene Kelly in 187, 189, 190, 192; Ira Gershwin/Jerome Kern song 'Make Way for Tomorrow' in 187
Craine, Debra 78

Crisp, Clement 76, 77
Croce, Arlene 188
cultural studies 114–15, 120, 143, 174, 217
cummings, e.e. 214
Cunningham, Merce 6, 39, 50, 51, 67n, 69–90, 91, 92n; dance works: *Events* 82, 88; legacy and 'Legacy Tour' 82, 83, 84, 86, 90, 91; *Summerspace* 87, 88; *Totem Ancestor* 90, 92n; *Winterbranch* 89; *see also* Dance Capsules

Dafora, Asadata 49–50
Daly, Augustin 128, 181
Damasio, Antonio 10, 15, 18n
Damsel in Distress (musical film, 1937) Fred Astaire in 186–7, 188
Dance Capsules 6, 83–4, 87, 92n
dance heritage 5, 38, 40, 72–3, 100, 104; of Cunningham work 91; 'dance heritage' *versus* 'dancing heritage' (Akram Khan) 34, 35, 41; as identity 12, 40; in India 123–34
Dance Heritage Coalition 148
dance history, curriculum of 44–7, 52–3, 114–16; *see also* history
Dance Museum, Stockholm 138
dance preservation 6–7, 69, 71–3; of Cunningham legacy 83, 85–6; *see also* reconstruction
dance studies, field of 3, 53, 114, 173
dance work, concept of 57–9, 62, 66
Dancing Women: Female Bodies on Stage (Sally Banes) 117–18
danse d'école 210, 219
Davies, Siobhan (and Company) 95, 100; dance work: *Bank* 100–4, 105n; *see also* Siobhan Davies Replay
Daye, Anne 62
De Angelo, Dawn 74–5

DeFrantz, Thomas 53
De Keersmaeker, Anne Teresa 113, 202–6; dance works: *Fase* 202; *My Walking Is My Dancing* 206; *Rosas Danst Rosas* 202–4; see also Rosas Remix Project
De l'Allemagne (Heinrich Heine) 238
Democracy in America (de Tocqueville) 176
Denby, Edwin 219
Denishawn school and company 48, 49, 74, 180
Dent, Edward 241
devadasis 126–7, 131
diable amoureux, Le 236
Dickens, Charles 242, 243, 244; *Household Narratives* 243
Dils, Ann 74–5
Dilthey, Wilhelm 17
Director, The 181
Dirlik, Arif 168
Dolan, Jill 211–12
Donen, Stanley 186, 188, 189, 191
Donnelly, Anne 99, 101
Duchamp, Marcel 84
Duncan, Isadora 48, 112, 137–8, 141–2, 144, 145, 175, 177, 181–2; *Rubaiyat of Omar Khayyam* 181–2
Dunham, Katherine 49, 50, 217
Dying Swan, The (Michel Fokine) 6, 75–8

Eliot, Karen 6, 7
embodiment 95–7; of canonic dances 3, 94, 96–7, 99–100; of heritage 33–4, 124, 126; of imperialist values 162
Empire Palace of Varieties (audience 28; ballerinas 25; closure threats 23–4; *corps de ballet* 4, 25–6; working conditions 23–5)
Engelhardt, Mollie 243
English National Ballet 16, 33, 38

Enigma Variations (Frederick Ashton) 56, 95, 96, 97
Erll, Astrid 12, 14
Ermarth, Elizabeth Deeds 145–6
eroticism 236, 239, 244
Eurocentrism 133, 163
Europe, provincialization of 164–5

facts, status of 6, 10, 11, 30, 114–17, 119, 131, 149, 153
Fagan, Garth 52
Faison, George 52
fantastique, le 235, 236, 239, 244; see also gothic, the; romanticism
Farber, Viola 86
Faust (Empire ballet) 25–6, 27, 28
Feidelson, Lizzie 90–1
feminism 114, 115, 175, 212, 214, 215, 216–17, 229; materialist feminism 112, 211, 220n; and patriarchy 235, 236; see also gender issues
Fifteen Years of a Dancer's Life (Loie Fuller) 178
Fitton, Isabel 96
Flaubert, Gustave 216
Fokina, Vera 77, 78
Fokine, Isabelle 6, 76, 77, 78
Fokine, Mikhail (Michel) 6, 58, 65, 76–7, 78
Fontaine, Joan 188
Ford Foundation 213
Fordism 212
Fosse, Bob 193
Foster, Susan 6–7, 14, 86, 87
Foucault, Michel 112, 116, 173–4, 182–3
Frank, Edgar 138–9
Franko, Mark 174
Frederick Ashton and his Ballets (David Vaughan) 118
French new wave (cinema) 191; *Les Demoiselles de Rochefort* 193
Frolique, La (Empire ballet) 23
Frost, Ginger 243

Fuller, Loie 48, 112, 141–2, 145, 175, 177–8, 184n
Fullington, Doug 240, 245n

Garafola, Lynn 119, 210, 211, 217
Gamer, Michael 236, 237
Gautier, Théophile 235, 236, 238–40, 244; *La Cafetière* 239
gender issues 111–12, 119, 126–7, 143, 174, 175–81, 213–17; as a fluid representation 223–31; *see also* feminism; self and subjectivity
Genné, Beth 113, 195n
Gershwin, George, music for *Shall We Dance* 186, 193
Gershwin, Ira 187
Girl I Left Behind Me, The (Empire ballet) 23
Giselle (Akram Khan) 33
Giselle (Coralli, Perrot) 57, 63–5, 114, 119, 235–7, 239, 242, 244, 245n; in London 235, 241, 242; in Paris 235
Giselle or the Phantom Night Dancers (Montcrieff, William) 241–2
globalisation 32, 35, 46, 50–1, 111, 123, 161–4, 166, 168, 169, 170n
Goehr, Lydia 58
Goggans, Jennifer 87–91, 92n
Gordon, David 198, 199
Gormley, Anthony 42n
Gothenburg (Sweden) 149, 150, 152, 154, 155, 157n
gothic, the 235, 236–7, 239, 240–4
Graham, Martha 9, 49, 50, 58, 83, 86, 92n, 95, 98, 190, 199, 218; dance works: *Cave of the Heart* 95; *Clytemnestra* 98, 104n; *Diversion of Angels* 98; *Night Journey* 98
Gramsci, Antonio 130
Great Expectations (Charles Dickens) 242, 244
Grisi, Carlotta 238
Guangdong Modern Dance Company 162

Guest, Ivor 119, 183n
Guha, Ranajit 125–6
Guillem, Sylvie 39, 42n
Guo, Mingda 166, 167, 168
Guy, Edna 49

Haigood, Joanna 16
Halbwachs, Maurice 12, 13
Hammergren, Lena 5, 15, 110
Hardy, Thomas 22
Harlem Renaissance 49
Harris, Andrea 212
Harris, Henry B. 179, 180
Hartley, L.P. 94
Haskell, Arnold 59
Hay, Deborah 199
Heine, Heinrich 238
Henri III, King of France 60
heritage *see* dance heritage
Hilarion (role in *Giselle*) 64, 240, 241
hip hop 46, 53, 54n, 193; in films: *Beat Street* 193; *Flashdance* 193; *Wild Style* 193
historian, role of the 4, 13–14, 17, 44, 66, 109–10, 114, 117–18, 120, 130, 131, 133; and historical imagination 16
history: from below 156; bias in 4, 110, 117, 118; and the canon 58, 63, 94, 104, 119, 212, 231; dominant narratives in 44, 49; interdisciplinarity in 53; narrative structure in 112–15, 141–6, 123; totalising nature of 115–17; for a usable past 6, 17, 70–2, 79n; *see also* causation (and agency); continuity and change through time; facts, status of; ideology; memory and dance history; oral history; source material; time and dance history
HIV/AIDS 72
Hodson, Millicent 74, 75, 140
Hollywood 77, 187
Houston Ballet 211

Howard, Andrée 210
Hugo, Victor *Fantômes* 238
Humphrey, Doris 49, 50, 74, 190; *The Banshee* 74–5
Husbands, Chris 115, 118
Hutcheon, Linda 115, 116, 117, 119
Hutchinson Guest, Ann 73–4, 75

identities 3, 5, 16–17, 32, 40, 142, 174–5; colonial and postcolonial 124–5; *see also* gender issues; race, issues of; self and subjectivity
ideology 111–12, 124, 162, 164, 166–9, 174–6; romantic ideology 237
imperialism 54n, 162, 165, 167; *see also* colonialism
independent dance companies 148–50, 151, 154–5, 156
India, cultural nationalism in 111, 124, 128, 129; and the British Empire 125–7, 131; historiography 124–6; Indian modern dance 131–3; scholarship on 123–4, 126–7; subaltern histories 127–31
Indian classical dances *see bharatanatyam*; *kathak*; *odissi*
Indian People's Theatre Association 131–3
intertextuality 141–2, 143, 216
It's Always Fair Weather (musical film, 1955), Gene Kelly in 191–2

Jackson, Janet 186, 195; *It's Alright* 195
Jackson, Michael 186, 194, 195; in: *Bad* 194; *Beat It* 194; *Billie Jean* 194; *Black or White* 194; *Thriller* 194; *The Way You Make Me Feel* 194
Jamison, Judith 82
Jaques-Dalcroze, Émile 168
Järvinen, Hanna 94
jazz dance 8, 48, 53, 187, 191, 193, 218

Jenkins, Keith 117, 120, 136, 145
Jeschke, Claudia 74
Jeux (Vaslav Nijinsky) 74, 75
Joffrey, Robert 74
Jones, Bill T 52
Jones, Susan 214, 220n
Jooss, Kurt 69, 139
Jordan, Stephanie 57
Jowitt, Deborah 120, 145
Judson Dance Theater 51–2, 94, 109, 113, 197–9, 201–2
Julliard School 89, 92n

Kansas City Ballet 90
Kapoor, Anish 39, 43n
Karsavina, Tamara 117
kathak 5, 33, 35–9, 42n, 127; *abhinaya* in 33; 'contemporary *kathak*' 32, 33, 35, 42n; *palta* in 33
Kavanagh, Julie 118, 119
Kelly, Gene 186–95
Khan, Akram 32, 33, 34, 40, 41, 42n; dance works: *Kaash* 39, 43n; *Loose in Flight* 42n; *Sacred Monsters* 38, 42n; *Zero Degrees* 37, 42n; *see also Giselle* (Akram Khan)
Kimball, R. 187
King, Alonzo 112, 223–9; Alonzo King LINES Ballet 223, 226–7, 228, 231; dance works: *Biophony* 230–1; *Dust and Light* 228; *Lila* 228; *Migration* 228; *Stealing Light* 228
King, Eleanor 74–5
Kirkland, Gelsey 142
Kirov Ballet 76, 77, 78
Kirstein, Lincoln 56–60, 62–4, 66, 212
knowledge, privileging of 110, 114–15, 119–20
Koritz, Amy 137–8
Kourlas, Gia 211
Kraus, Richard 59
Krause, Bernie 230–1
Kreutzberg, Harald 217, 219

Kriegsman, Sally 72–3
Kumudini *see* Lakhia, Sreemati Kumudini

Laakkonen, Johanna 119, 121n
Laban, Rudolf von 68, 70, 168
Labanotation *see* notation, dance
Lakhia, Sreemati Kumudini 35, 36, 42n
Landis, Michael 194
Lanner, Katti 25, 27
Le Fanu, Sheridan 239
Lent, Patricia 87, 88, 91, 92
Levinson, André 64, 65
Lewis, Sinclair 216
lieux de mémoire 14, 18n
Lindqvist, Sven 156
Lion, Katarina 140
Living in a Big Way (musical film 1945), Gene Kelly in 191
Lloyd Dilley, Barbara 86
Loder, Edward 242
London Contemporary Dance Theatre and School 95, 99, 114; postgraduate company, EDge 95, 100, 101, 102, 103, 104, 105n
London Festival Ballet 217
Loring, Eugene 190, 218; *Billy the Kid* 218
Love Me Tonight (musical film, 1932) 186, 193
Lubitsch, Ernst 186
Luhrman, Baz (dir.), *Strictly Ballroom* 193
Lund, Gun 151, 154–6
Lyons Opera Ballet 89

Macaulay, Alastair 82–3, 92n
McEvoy, Emma 236
McGehee, Helen 95
McGowan, Margaret 61
Machinal (Sophie Treadwell) 216
McIntyre, Dianne 52
McKayle, Donald 50
Mackrell, Judith 76–7
McNamara, Joan 94

Maharaja, Pandit Birju 35, 36, 42n
Main Street (Sinclair Lewis) 216
Makkonen, Anne 94
Male Dancer, The (Ramsay Burt) 117
Mamoulian, Rouben 186
Mangaldas, Aditi 36
Markova, Alicia 72, 77
Marks, Victoria 113, 200, 206; dance works: *Dancing to Music* 200–1; *Outside In* 206
Martin, John 214, 218, 219
Marwick, Arthur 119
Meglin, Joellen 112, 220n, 239
memory: Akram Khan on 37; autobiographical (personal) memory 8–9; body memory 10, 11; construction of 10–12; distortions of 8; memory-based dance staging 75, 78; sensory experience of 8, 14–15, 16; as time travel 15–16, 17; *see also* collective memory; *lieux de mémoire*; oral history
memory and dance history 4–5, 9, 11–14
memory studies 9–10
Mercer, Kobena 174
Mérode, Cléo de 144
MGM 188
Milhaud, Darius 219
Mille, Agnes de 210, 212; *Rodeo* 219
Miller, Bebe 52
Miller, Joan 51
minimalism 197, 201, 205, 206
Minnelli, Vincente (director), and choreographed camera 186, 188, 189; *see also* boom shots (in film)
minstrel shows 47–8; *and* 'metaphorical minstrelsy' 174
Mitra, Royona 4, 134
modern dance 5, 58, 72, 83, 101, 112; in Britain 102–3, 115; in China 111, 162–3, 165–9; in Europe 137; in India 131–3; in USA 48–51, 69, 76, 112, 128–9, 197, 198, 200, 217–18, 224

modernism 212, 213, 214
Moncrieff, William 241
Moross, Jerome 214, 218, 219
Morris, Geraldine 96, 111
Mueller, John 243
musicals, on Broadway 49, 50, 190
My Life (Isadora Duncan) 181

nachnis 129–31
nautch dancers 126, 128, 131
Neels, Sandra 86
Nevin, Ethelbert 181
New Dance Group 49, 50
New Negro movement, The 49
New York, New York 193
New York City Ballet (NYCB) 210, 213
New York Times 182, 192, 210, 214, 218
Nicholas, Larraine 4
Nicholas, Mino 74–5
Nicholas Brothers 191, 195
Night Dancers, The 242
Nijinska, Bronislava 210, 214, 217
Nijinsky, Vaslav 58, 73–4, 75, 117, 118, 207
Nikolais, Alwin 167
Noces, Les (Bronislava Nijinska) 214
Nodier, Charles 236
Noguchi, Isamu 219
Noland, Carrie 84
Norman, Marsha 211
notation, of dance 6, 70, 72; Beauchamps-Feuillet 62; Benesh 70; Kinetography Laban 70; Labanotation 62, 70, 74; of music 70
Nunes Jensen, Jill 112
Nye, David E. 138–41, 143, 145

Odette (role in *Swan Lake*) 77, 78
odissi 127
Ohno, Kazuo 174; *Suiren* 174
Oliver, Cynthia 52
On Brighton Pier (Empire ballet) 27
On the Town 191–3

oral history 4, 6, 10, 13, 16–17, 96
Order of Things, The (Foucault) 173, 182
Orientales, Les (Victor Hugo) 238
orientalism 48, 74, 111, 127–9, 174, 178–80

Pacific Northwest Ballet 245n
Page, Ruth 112, 190, 210, 212–14, 216–20n; dance works: *Alice in the Garden* 219; *American Pattern, An* (with Bentley Stone) 213–17; *Americans in Paris* 217; *The Flapper and the Quarterback* 217; *Frankie and Johnny* (with Stone) 213, 218, 221n; *Lament for Ignacio Sánchez Mejías* 213–14
Pal Joey (Rodgers and Hart) 190
Pan, Hermes 60, 186
Paris Opéra (Théâtre de l'Académie de musique royale) 237, 238; and July Monarchy 237
Parker, Dorothy 214; poems: 'A Fairly Sad Tale', 'Inventory', 'Unfortunate Coincidence' 214
Pavlova, Anna 76–7, 78
Paxton, Steve 51, 198, 199
Pennsylvania Ballet 187, 210, 213
People's Republic of China (PRC) 167
Perpener, John 71
Perron, Wendy 82, 85, 91
Persson, Lars 154–6
Perugini, Mark E. 28
Peters, Michael 194
Petipa, Marius 119, 240
phenomenology 16, 216
placism 5, 161, 163, 168
politics *see* appropriation and counter-appropriation; colonialism; identities; imperialism; postcolonialism; race, issues of; social class
Polovtsian Dances (Michel Fokine) 78

Pomare, Eleo 51, 52
postcolonialism 40, 111, 124–7, 130–1, 149, 164–6, 167, 232n
Postlewait, Thomas 141, 142
postmodern dance 4, 52, 111, 120, 161–6, 169, 198, 202, 206
postmodernism 71, 114, 116, 117, 119, 120, 146
poststructuralism 114, 173–4, 175
Preger-Simon, Marianne 90
Preston-Dunlop, Valerie 97
Primus, Pearl 50, 51
Prins, Gwyn 96
Protas, Ron 83
provincialization 164, 165, 166, 169
Prussia, as Gothic setting 240
Punter, David 236, 240, 242
Purkayastha, Prarthana 4, 41, 111

race, issues of 4, 40–1, 124–9, 192, 194; *see also* African American history
Rainer, Yvonne 113, 198–9, 201, 207; *RoS Indexical* 113, 207; *see also* Trio A (Yvonne Rainer)
Rambert, Marie 217
reconstruction (of dances) 6, 69–75, 78–9; of *ballets de cour* 116; of *The Dying Swan* 75–8; of *Le Sacre du printemps* 140; of *Summerspace* 87
re-creation, reinvention, revival 73–5; *see also* Rainer, Yvonne, *RoS Indexical*; *see also* restaging
Reich, Steve 201, 202
Reid, Albert 86
Reinhardt, Max 139
Remisoff, Nicolai 214
restaging 87, 88, 89, 90
Reynolds, Nancy 72
Ricoeur, Paul 13, 15
Robbins, Jerome 192, 193, 194, 210, 212, 219; *Fancy Free* 219
Robert le diable 238, 239
Roberts, Daniel 89, 90, 91, 92n

Rogers, Ginger 193, 212
romantic ballet 64, 65, 111, 145, 235
romanticism 237
Rosas Remix Project 113, 204–6
Rosen, Astrid von 110
Roubicek, Sasha 101
Roy Chowdhury, Reba 131–3
Rubidge, Sarah 96, 100
Russian Imperial Ballet 115

Sacre du Printemps, Le (Vaslav Nijinsky) 74, 113, 140, 207
Said, Edward 127, 182
St. Denis, Ruth 48, 111, 112, 128–9, 138, 175, 177, 178–81; dance works: *Egypta* 180; *Incense* 179; *Radha* 174, 179
Sarkar Munsi, Urmimala 129–31
Saroyan, William, *The Time of Your Life* 190
Sarukkai, Malavika 36, 41
Saturday Night Fever (musical film 1977) 193
Sawhney, Nitin 39, 42n, 43n
Saxon, Deborah 101, 102, 103, 105n
Scenarkivet.se (Stage Archive.se) 151–3, 155
Schama, Simon 119, 121
Scorsese, Martin 193, 194
Scott, Walter 236
Second Sex, The (Simone de Beauvoir) 216
Secret Muses (Julie Kavanagh) 118, 119
Sednova, Sophie 100, 102
self and subjectivity 174; feminine subjectivity 112, 213–19
Semenova, Tatiana 210–11
Seth, Sanjay 111, 133, 134
Shall We Dance (musical film 1937), Fred Astaire in 'walking the dog' 193
Shawn, Ted 48, 180
Sheets-Johnstone, Maxine 11, 96, 97

Sibley, Antoinette 96
Siegel, Marcia 7, 70, 113
Silver, Carole 235, 237
Singin' in the Rain (musical film 1953) 187, 189, 191, 192, 194, 195
Siobhan Davies Replay 101, 153
skirt dancing 178
Sleeping Beauty, The 115
Smith, Marian 64, 65, 239, 240, 245n
social class 4, 23, 111, 124, 127, 129–31, 174–83, 190–4, 215–16, 239; and female patronage 180–2; and royal patronage 129; *see also* structure and agency
Sokolow, Anna 50, 51
Somes, Michael 96, 97
Sommer, Sally 177–8
Sorel, Felicia 50
Sorrell, Walter 59
Sound of Music, The (musical film 1965) 193
source material 6, 13, 15, 110–11; for African American dance history 52–4; attitudes towards 118–19; evaluation of 136–44; individual life stories 141–6; *see also* archives; Dance Capsules; oral history
Sparti, Barbara 59, 61
spectacle 22, 59, 60, 61, 207, 215, 242
Spivak, Gayatri Chakravorty 130
Srinavasan, Priya 128
Still, William Grant 219
Stone, Bentley 213, 214, 218, 219
Stone, Harry 242, 243, 245n
Stone Camryn School of Ballet 214
Strohm, Walter 188, 189
structure and agency 143–4
subalternity 4, 127–31
sublime, the 237
Sufism 34
Summers, Elaine 197

Sweating Saris: Indian Dance as Transnational Labor (Priya Srinivasan) 128
Sweet Charity (musical film 1968) 193
Swift, Graham 21, 30
Swinston, Robert 87
Sylphide, La 63, 64, 236
Symons, Arthur 27, 28

Taglioni, Marie 64, 238
Tamiris, Helen 49, 50
tap dancing 187, 191, 217, 218
Taylor, Diana 16, 156
Taylor, Paul 51, 69, 83
Tchelitchew, Pavel 219
technology, influence of: on digital archiving 151, 157; on electronic reproduction of dance 73, 202; on globalisation 35, 174, 202
temperance movement, America 176, 177–8
Terpsichore in Sneakers: Postmodern Dance (Sally Banes) 120
Tharp, Twyla 218
Thomas, Helen 5, 6
time and dance history 4–5, 9, 14–17, 36, 41; anachronism and bias in 58–9, 160; diachronic and synchronic perspectives 144–5; ephemerality of 7, 70, 72, 118, 197; periodisation 115–16; porous nature of 113, 201; *see also* continuity and change through time
Time of Your Life, The, Gene Kelly in 190
Tocqueville, Alexis de 176
Tomko, Linda J. 112–13, 116
Toumanova, Tamara 72
Travolta, John 193
Treadwell, Sophie 216
Trilby ou le lutin d'Argail 236
Trinity Laban 92, 95, 97, 98, 101, 103, 104n, 105n

Trio A (Yvonne Rainer) 198–9, 202, 207; in *Rainer Variations* (film, Charles Atlas) 199
Tulving, Endel 9

Valois, Ninette de 210, 217
vaudeville 48, 143, 179, 180
Vaughan, David 82, 83, 85, 118
Vernoy de Saint-Georges, Jules-Henri 238
Véron, Louis Dr. 237, 238
Véronique Doisneau (Jérôme Bel) 62, 63, 198
videos, pop 186, 193–5

Walton, Kendall 62, 63, 66
waltz 239, 241
Weidman, Charles 190
Weisberger, Barbara 210
Werktreue 58
West Side Story (musical film 1961) 186, 192, 193, 194
West Swedish Dance Archive 150–1
White, Hayden 140

Whitman Sisters 143
Wigman, Mary 69
Wilcox, Emily 5, 111
Wilhelm (William Pitcher) 26, 28
wilis 235, 238–43
Williams, Wilson 50
Winfield, Hemsley 49
Wise, Robert 193
women's voluntary groups 175–8
Woolf, Virginia 214
Wordsworth, William 237
World War II 50, 192, 213
Wright, Peter 96, 101
Wudao (Beijing dance journal) 166

Xia, Yu 166, 167, 168

YouTube, influence of 35; *see also* Rosas Remix Project

Zanfretta, Francesca 25
Zanina (1881) 128
Zollar, Jawole Willa Jo 52